THE NEW DEAL IN THE URBAN SOUTH

THE NEW DEAL IN THE
URBAN SOUTH

DOUGLAS L. SMITH

Louisiana State University Press
Baton Rouge and London

97   96   95   94   93   92   91   90   89   88   5   4   3   2   1

Designer: Laura Roubique Gleason
Typeface: Melior
Typesetter: Focus Graphics
Printer: Thomson-Shore, Inc.
Binder: John H. Dekker & Sons, Inc.

Library of Congress Cataloging-in-Publication Data
Smith, Douglas L. (Douglas Lloyd), 1947–
    The New Deal in the Urban South / Douglas L. Smith.
        p. cm.
    Bibliography: p.
    Includes index.
    ISBN 0-8071-1394-8 (alk. paper)
    1. New Deal, 1933–1939—Southern States. 2. Southern States—
History—1865–1951. 3. Southern States—Economic conditions—1918–
4. Cities and towns—Southern States—History—20th century.
5. Southern States—Public works—History—20th century. I. Title.
F215.S63 1988
975'.042—dc19   87-29645
                                                                    CIP

With love
to Peggy, Caroline, and family

CONTENTS

PREFACE

In the first volume of the *Southern Economic Journal*, published in 1935, sociologist Walter Matherly noted that "the cities of the Old South were exclusively commercial; they were centers of surrounding agricultural territories; they were largely the products of agrarianism. But with the rise of industrialism, new types of cities appeared. These cities have little or no connection with the agrarian South; they are manufacturing centers—industrial cities similar to scores of industrial cities in the Northeast and in the Middle States." This alleged similarity is an overstatement to be sure, particularly in view of recent historical scholarship emphasizing the "southernness" of the region's cities in the twentieth century. Blaine Brownell has found, for example, that while southern cities as early as the "booster-mania" 1920s "appeared to be developing . . . a consciousness of [urban] complexities and interdependencies," a conservative leadership group dominated municipal affairs throughout the region, perpetuating an urban ethos of expansion, order, unity, and tradition. Similar in tone is David Goldfield's *Cotton Fields and Skyscrapers*, which argues persuasively that the South through the years has effectively "retained its traditions among the cities and factories and molded both to its own distinct image." Focusing on three omnipresent features of southern cities—a dependency on staple agriculture, the biracial society, and the colonial economy—Goldfield writes that "the world of the cotton field and the skyscraper are essentially the same."[1]

1. Walter J. Matherly, "The Urban Development of the South," *Southern Economic Journal*, I (February, 1935), 21; Blaine A. Brownell, "The Urban Mind in the South: The Growth of Urban Consciousness in Southern Cities, 1920–1927" (Ph.D. dissertation, University of North Carolina, 1969), 215, and *The Urban Ethos in the South, 1920–1930*

It is difficult to imagine, however, that the social and economic upheavals of the depression, and the unparalleled federal activity that resulted, could have come and gone without effecting changes in the southern cities, changes beyond the "bricks and mortar" of the various public works projects. Yet while modern scholarship has produced countless works on the Great Depression and the New Deal, most have emphasized themes with national implications—the emergence of federal authority and the beginnings of the "welfare state," the rise of the institutional presidency, the experimentation with central economic planning (what Otis Graham, among others, has termed the rise of "broker statism"), the formation of big labor, and the realignment of political party constituencies. In addition are monographs focusing on the nationwide impact of one or two New Deal programs or policies and numerous administrative and political histories isolating particular regions or individual states.[2]

In contrast, the purpose herein is to focus on the grass-roots implementation, operation, and effects of the major federal programs of the depression period. Of concern is the impact of the economic downturn and subsequently the New Deal on the lives of southern city residents and on the course of southern urban development, including political trends, the advancement of an urban consciousness in the cities, and the fate of the prevailing regional urban ethos as Brownell, Goldfield, and others have defined it. The work will also demonstrate, it is hoped, that local history—community-level experiences and reactions—can enhance our understanding of a subject generally viewed from a national perspective.

The similarities among the four cities included in this study— Atlanta, Birmingham, Memphis, and New Orleans—in part determined their selection. They all lie in the geographic region defined as the Deep South, with roots dating well back into the nineteenth century or earlier. The project was purposely limited to the southeastern area because of the many cultural and economic differences between the border and Deep South states and between the older and the more recently populated Sun Belt cities. Indeed, the four urban areas in

(Baton Rouge, 1975), 188; David R. Goldfield, *Cotton Fields and Skyscrapers: Southern City and Region, 1607–1980* (Baton Rouge, 1982), 3–11.

2. Included among the most valuable state and local studies are Michael S. Holmes, *The New Deal in Georgia* (Westport, 1975); John Dean Minton, "The New Deal in Tennessee" (Ph.D. dissertation, Vanderbilt University, 1959); Robert Cotner *et al.*, *Texas Cities and the Great Depression* (Austin, 1973); John Braeman, Robert Bremner, and David Brody (eds.), *The New Deal*, Twentieth Century America Series, II: *The State and Local Levels* (Columbus, 1975).

question were by far the region's largest cities during the depression era. The populations of Birmingham, Atlanta, and Memphis numbered nearly 260,000 each, and the population of New Orleans was about 450,000. Furthermore, each municipality had a sizable black population, ranging from 28 percent of the total number of residents in New Orleans to 38 percent in Birmingham; and more than 90 percent of all whites were of American ancestry, most from southern families. Black residents tended to remain the "separate one-third" throughout the period, although their inclusion in the federal programs, even if marginal, had a clear effect.

Key population differences among the four cities was an equally important consideration in their selection. Atlanta, Birmingham, and Memphis were part of the New South phenomenon of post–Civil War economic development. In particular, industrial advancements and resultant population growth were of recent origin, with dramatic gains in each having occurred in the early years of the twentieth century. During the 1920s, for example, Atlanta's population increased by 35 percent, while that of Birmingham grew by 45 percent and that of Memphis by 56 percent.[3] Thus, many urban residents were first- or second-generation city dwellers, not far removed from the rural or small-town South, where regional life-styles and values had changed little in the past several generations.

In contrast, New Orleans was a far older city, and its population had not grown as rapidly during the new century. Likewise, Crescent City manufacturing, port activity, and other economic forces had not experienced rapid expansion during the immediate predepression period. While the city in 1930 remained the largest in the region, it had been steadily losing ground to the New South urban areas, particularly Atlanta, as the dominant business and financial center. Because most New Deal programs would be regionally directed out of Atlanta, it seems likely that the Georgia city would surpass New Orleans in the 1930s as the "capital of the South."

By 1930, the economies of the four southeastern cities all depended on manufacturing and on a growing retail and wholesale trade. Indeed, a key objective of municipal leaders was to attract new industry. Yet there was no sprawling metropolitan-suburban pattern in the depression South, and each city continued to handle seasonal farm produce as a market center for adjacent agricultural counties. Clearly a small-town atmosphere had not been entirely lost, and Matherly's analysis in the *Southern Economic Journal* notwithstanding, the cities could not be considered modern urban-industrial enclaves without connections to

3. *Abstract of the Fifteenth Census of the United States* (1933), 27–32.

their agrarian regional surroundings. There was a small but growing professional class in each of them, perhaps most evident in the New South cities, especially Atlanta. Still, traditional regional values — kinship, paternalism, racial separation, suspicion, xenophobia — as so well outlined in Wilbur Cash's *The Mind of the South*, remained very much alive.[4]

Key economic dissimilarities among the selected cities were also evident. The ports of New Orleans and Memphis, for example, operated as regional trade centers, and thousands of longshoremen and seamen relied on dock activity for their livelihoods. It is not surprising that when the downturn began in 1930 and 1931, the many small manufacturers in the Louisiana and Tennessee cities successfully withstood the crisis longer than did dock employers. The arrival of fewer cargoes from depressed industrial areas of the country and the rapid decline in the flow of agricultural products after 1930 took a sudden toll on the river and Gulf Coast trades. The farming sector, of course, had enjoyed little of the "prosperity" of the previous decade.

Atlanta was fast becoming the regional retail and wholesale center, and many industries recently relocated in the South had opened central offices in the Georgia capital. The depression would assuredly leave the streets dotted with scores of vacant stores and warehouses. And while Atlanta's manufacturing plants were generally small and diverse, as were those in Memphis and New Orleans, industrial well-being in Birmingham depended almost entirely on coal and steel production. Because the city's firms monopolized a regional market, their output may not have declined as suddenly as in Ohio and Pennsylvania, where competition was far greater. Still, the Birmingham companies were affiliated with United States Steel and other national concerns, and the depression had severe effects in the one-industry city.

A number of political similarities among the four cities were important as well in determining their selection. Throughout the predepression years, a commercial-business elite had captured political control in all of them — men who had amassed wealth and influence during the early twentieth-century boom years. This municipal leadership group — James Key and William Hartsfield in Atlanta, James Jones in Birmingham, T. Semmes Walmsley and Robert Maestri in New Orleans, Boss Edward Crump and Watkins Overton in Memphis — advanced the interests of local industrialists, real estate and commercial businesses, and the banking community. They were committed to

4. U.S. Bureau of Foreign and Domestic Commerce, *Statistical Abstract of the United States* (1935), 77; Wilbur J. Cash, *The Mind of the South* (New York, 1941).

low taxes, limited governmental expenditures, administrative efficiency, and a balanced budget. Above all, an orderly environment was essential, one based on traditional racial and socioeconomic patterns that would continue to be attractive to outside businesses. A conservative, New South creed in the tradition of Henry Grady and boosterism was truly in evidence.

There was one factor differentiating the four cities politically—two were machine run while two were not. In Memphis, the Edward Crump organization remained in power throughout the 1930s; in New Orleans the Choctaw Club, or Old Regulars, led by T. Semmes Walmsley, controlled municipal affairs until replaced by the Huey Long organization in mid-decade. The power struggle in the Crescent City surely became entangled with the operation of the federal relief and recovery programs. The Old Regulars had traditionally gained business support, but after the Kingfish's death in 1935, that backing moved steadily into the Long camp with the ascension of a conservative leadership faction led by Robert Maestri, Richard Leche, and Earl Long.

An important determination herein is the political effects of the New Deal on both the machine and nonmachine cities as their dependency on federal aid grew. The New Deal did not challenge the prevailing New South creed, at least not directly; thus municipal elites were able to sponsor projects designed to make their cities more attractive in the true booster spirit and at the same time maintain efficiency in city hall and social order and political control on their own terms. This did not necessarily mean that there was direct manipulation of voters receiving either work relief or direct assistance. Blacks, for example, who generally could not vote, composed 50 or more percent of the southern urban relief rolls. Yet the decentralized operation of many federal programs and the generosity that New Dealers often showed to their friends allowed city officials to award public works contracts and administrative relief positions to their supporters. In viewing federal operations from the bottom up, it's clear that there could have been few "last hurrahs" in the southern cities, or anywhere in the country for that matter, during the depression decade.

The analysis herein also reveals that in the southern cities, even if more muted than in urban areas elsewhere in the United States, attitudes toward Washington, D.C.'s role in municipal affairs were beginning to change as new relationships between the federal government and urban areas emerged from the depression experience. In *A Nation of Cities*, Mark Gelfand argues that the depression crisis demonstrated that municipal resources were insufficient and that city mayors had little choice but to look to Washington, D.C., for assistance, particularly because hostile rural and small-town interests often controlled state legislatures. Even more important, Gelfand writes, was a "change of heart about the virtues of laissez-faire and municipal self suffi- ciency" expressed by conservative urban business and commercial leaders, who became increasingly fearful for the safety of their real- estate investments amid depression-era blight and decay. The result was that many "dropped their hitherto opposition to federal grants-in- aid." Thus, New Deal housing and other endeavors that linked Wash- ington, D.C., directly with the cities often enjoyed, somewhat iron- ically, "the benevolent protection of private entrepreneurs" and became, although without much forethought, the foundation of future federal policies on urban affairs.[5]

In addition to political considerations, both local and national, this study addresses several questions. How did the economic downturn in the early 1930s affect the southern cities? Were there varying degrees of severity? Who suffered the most from unemployment, production cutbacks, and financial reverses? Did the recent population growth in the New South cities, to which they had not adjusted, complicate depression problems and affect the local reaction to the crisis? What role did municipal authorities play in relief efforts, especially prior to the New Deal? Did the expansion of private and municipal resources, and their institutionalization, suggest a growing acceptance of public responsibility for community needs? Who did and who did not benefit from the release of local, state, and federal relief dollars and from the various emergency public works projects?

More difficult to measure, especially because of the static political climate, is the impact of the socioeconomic upheaval of the depression and the New Deal on one particular aspect of southern urban develop- ment. Was the so-called rural lag in the growth of Dixie cities, defined as the persistence of agrarian, regional values, overcome at least in part? In the 1920s, writes Blaine Brownell, Birmingham seemed to be standing "between the old South and the new, between the rural and the urban, between the past and the future, but the city clearly had one foot solidly forward and did not seem unduly hesitant to advance the other." In his monumental *Emergence of the New South*, George Tindall concludes that the entire South in the early twentieth century, chiefly because of its urban development, "stood between two worlds, one dying and the other struggling to be born."[6]

5. Mark Gelfand, *A Nation of Cities: The Federal Government and Urban America, 1933–1965* (New York, 1975), 65–69, 380–86.

6. Blaine A. Brownell, "Birmingham, Alabama: New South City in the 1920's," *Journal of Southern History*, XXXVIII (February, 1972), 48; George B. Tindall, *The Emergence of the New South* (Baton Rouge, 1967), 787; Martha C. Mitchell [Bigelow], "Birmingham: Biography of a City of the New South" (Ph.D. dissertation, University of

Still, the four cities in question as of 1930 had developed few public service and other community institutions responsive to their fast-growing urban environments. Most residents were "small town" at heart, and surely conservative municipal leaders sought to head off or at least temper new social trends, just as they did during the more recent civil rights struggle. Whenever possible, direct resistance was avoided in favor of the accommodation, mainly for appearances, of just those new ideas that could be manipulated, perhaps integrated, into existing notions of an efficient and orderly community.[7] But even this limited concession, made however grudgingly and from necessity, meant that new social commitments began to take root, and once made, their later undoing would be unlikely as community attitudes and expectations shifted over time. As well, southern city populations in future years would only become increasingly pluralistic, and outside pressures would continue, led by an ever-stronger federal presence. Certainly the urban South in the 1930s was not fully in sync with depression-era cities elsewhere, which George Mowry has said "were in the process of developing a social conscience instead of the individual conscience." Yet the region's cities were continuing to emerge, as suggested by Brownell and Goldfield in *The City in Southern History*, as "links between the traditional South and the contrary influences of northern capitalism and the American mainstream."[8]

Of special concern, then, is the local implementation of the federal relief and recovery machinery that required state and local financial and administrative responsibility. The effects of the social security network, slum clearance and public housing programs, federal planning agencies, and the numerous white-collar service projects were all-

Chicago, 1946), 284; Katherine D. Lumpkin, *The South in Progress* (New York, 1940), 234. The rural lag concept has created some controversy; see Gerald M. Capers, "The Rural Lag in Southern Cities," *Mississippi Quarterly*, XXI (Fall, 1968), 253–62, and Blaine A. Brownell, "Urbanization in the South: A Unique Experience?" *Mississippi Quarterly*, XXVI (Spring, 1973), 106–20.

7. Studies on the major southeastern cities since World War II include Goldfield, *Cotton Fields and Skyscrapers*, 139–73; Edward F. Haas, "The Southern Metropolis," in Blaine A. Brownell and David R. Goldfield (eds.), *The City in Southern History: The Growth of Urban Civilization in the South* (Port Washington, 1977), 159–91; Haas, *DeLesseps S. Morrison and the Image of Reform: New Orleans Politics, 1946–1961* (Baton Rouge, 1974); Harold Martin, *William Berry Hartsfield: Mayor of Atlanta* (Athens, Ga., 1978); David M. Tucker, *Memphis Since Crump: Bossism, Blacks and Civic Reform* (Knoxville, 1980); and Bradley R. Rice, "Atlanta: If Dixie Were Atlanta," and Arnold Hirsch, "New Orleans: Sunbelt in the Swamp," in Richard Bernard and Bradley R. Rice (eds.), *Sunbelt Cities Since World War II* (Austin, 1983), 34–45 and 120–30, respectively.

8. George E. Mowry, *The Urban Nation, 1920–1960* (New York, 1965), 128; Brownell and Goldfield, "Southern Urban History," in Brownell and Goldfield (eds.), *The City in Southern History*, 8.

important in determining the establishment or expansion of municipal institutions responsive to urban residential needs. Such programs included indigent care and public welfare, municipal recreational services, adult and special child education, community job training, public health programs, and local planning and housing endeavors. Most important is whether such commitments—new or expanded—proved permanent, even if only little advanced while in the hands of the existing, New South leadership group. If so, it would seem to suggest the development of a sense of community welfare and the advancement of an urban consciousness as the complexities of urban, industrial life were increasingly recognized. Similarly, the impact of the federal arts projects is an important consideration, as southern cities during the period inched toward maturity as regional cultural centers. Ever so slowly but steadily, they were beginning to resemble modern urban centers of later years.

This study also examines the labor movement in the urban areas during the New Deal period, as the cities shed an identity of being simply overgrown regional towns. The growth of legitimate labor organizations, whether industrial or craft unions, supports the idea of the dilution of traditional regional values, as rank-in-file workers through collective efforts began to confront the uncertainties of urbanization and industrialization. The participation of black workers in the movement is of special concern because, federal guarantees notwithstanding, the viability of unionism depended on the organization of all labor, black and white. Equally important are the reactions of the municipal leadership, the public in general, and the city press, which usually echoed conservative-business political sentiments.

Finally, there is a consideration of the impact of economic dislocation and the federal programs in the urban black communities. Regional racial patterns were not shattered—municipal elites were too devoted to the traditional order—and public service facilities for years after the New Deal period remained separate and unequal. Still, a survey of black leaders and organizations suggests that change was beginning to take root amid the continuity of the period. The inclusion of blacks in New Deal programs, however separately, as well as their displacement by whites in numerous employment categories, caused the revival or establishment of organizations that would become more active on behalf of black residents and neighborhoods. Traditional accommodationist and self-help approaches were not laid aside altogether; yet by the end of the decade, blacks were beginning to demand an equal share, not just a separate one in lieu of exclusion. They were mobilizing through political-awareness campaigns among the young, and as white liberals became true allies rather than just patrons, blacks were beginning to understand the necessity of leading those groups that were in the front lines of the struggle. A new sense of racial consciousness and pride was generated, laying a foundation for the next challenge to the social and political order.[9]

It is hoped that through this study the reader will come to understand the value of local history and how it contributes to our understanding of events usually viewed from a wider, nationwide perspective. It is also hoped that the work will generate a greater understanding of the economic and other hardships of the Great Depression, a catastrophe that still affects the actions of many Americans. The work is also intended to help the reader better understand the magnitude of the federal effort in the New Deal, as well as some of its successes and failures, and how it directly touched the lives of millions of Americans. This important factor sometimes gets shortchanged in broader historical analyses. Finally, this study promises to make a contribution to the existing scholarship on the growth and modernization of the South's cities in the twentieth century, as they developed into metropolitan areas while retaining their southern character.

9. Three recent analyses, arriving at slightly different conclusions, of the overall impact of the New Deal on blacks are Harvard Sitkoff, *A New Deal for Blacks: The Emergence of Civil Rights as a National Issue* (New York, 1978); Nancy J. Weiss, *Farewell to the Party of Lincoln: Black Politics in the Age of FDR* (Princeton, 1983); John Kirby, *Black Americans in the Roosevelt Era: Liberalism and Race* (Knoxville, 1980).

 1

GROWTH AND COLLAPSE: SOUTHERN CITIES AND THE DEPRESSION

It was overcast and humid in New Orleans, January 8, 1930, when late in the afternoon Alexander J. Heinemann stepped from a vacant storeroom at the baseball park bearing his name. A recent $300,000 loser in the stock market, and in poor health, the president of the New Orleans Pelicans had waited alone, preparing to follow a course of action he had rehearsed five days before. Someone must have suspected that all was not right. Earlier in the day, club officials later reported, they had seen the admired sports figure gazing from the grandstand at the home field of one of the South's most successful minor league franchises "as if watching the ghost teams of his memory." At 4:45 P.M., a despondent Heinemann inserted the barrel of a pistol into his mouth and pulled the trigger. Two hours later, the groundskeeper discovered his body lying in a deserted hallway under a sign that read: "A full stomach and a bankroll make a man tempermental [sic]; my daily prayer is to teach me to keep my nose out of other people's business." Apparently Heinemann's associates had respected the latter aphorism, and now their friend was dead.[1]

Fortunately for most victims of the Wall Street crash, and for the millions of others also affected by the Great Depression, their situations never became so desperate. Yet between 1929 and 1933, what had seemed to be a flourishing economy plunged to unknown depths. And in few areas was economic collapse more catastrophic than in the South, including its major cities, where the upheaval adversely affected all residents and almost every facet of urban life. Unemployment soared, while agricultural and industrial production declined

1. New Orleans *Times-Picayune*, January 9, 1930.

sharply. Local relief rolls were taxed to a maximum, and like elsewhere in the country, the suffering of the jobless was most acute in the years prior to the New Deal and federal intervention because public relief stipends proved woefully inadequate.[2] Perhaps worse, the unparalleled growth experienced by the southern cities during the 1920s had the effect of blinding most residents in the early depression months to the reality of an economic downturn.

Although northern cities had recorded greater economic gains in the immediate predepression years, the largest southern municipalities had expanded overall and had reached significant plateaus. The population of Memphis more than doubled during the Roaring Twenties, for example, while during the same period the state reported a population growth rate of only 1 percent. Similarly, while Atlanta was expanding by nearly 50 percent, Georgia on the whole was growing by only 4 percent—the highest growth rate among the Deep South states. Throughout the Southeast, moreover, the urban areas expanded at a far greater rate than did the region as a whole. Thousands moved from small towns to large cities seeking work promised by new manufacturing.[3]

Birmingham offers an excellent example of urban industrial expansion in the South during the 1920s. The city's iron and steel industry, its principal economic force, had never before operated at such high levels of output. By the late 1920s, experts in New York were calling the city the "Pittsburgh of the South." Because steel, iron, and coke production increased steadily throughout the decade, United States Steel in 1930 invested twenty-five million dollars and overhauled several mills owned by its subsidiary, the Tennessee Coal and Iron Company (TCI), which received all of the parent company's southern business. Expansion created jobs, and even during the first depression year, TCI maintained production and employment levels for a time because of advance orders to be filled. Clearly the enlargement of the steelworks supported community expectations of a bright future.[4]

Birmingham's banking resources fared similarly in the 1920s. Late in the decade, the city's financial institutions held total assets up to

2. Howard Odum, *Southern Regions in the United States* (Chapel Hill, 1936), 208; Benjamin V. Ratchford, *Economic Resources and Policies of the South* (New York, 1951), 48–55; Atlanta *Journal of Labor*, January 31, 1936.

3. *Abstract of the Fifteenth Census of the United States* (1933), 27–32.

4. *Polk's Birmingham City Directory, 1941*, 15–16; New York *Times*, February 20, 1930; Tennessee Coal and Iron Division of U.S. Steel, *Biography of a Business* (n.p., 1930), 58; interview with Maurice Allen, southeastern regional labor organizer, May 1, 1975.

three times greater than their holdings in 1915. Construction generally remained healthy throughout the twenties, and building contracts in all southern cities reached their highest levels ever in 1928 and 1929. The value of building permits in Birmingham averaged nearly twenty million dollars each year between 1924 and 1928—a figure five times larger than the corresponding figure for 1920. In 1930, the Alabama community could point to several ongoing building ventures, and residents approved an eight-million-dollar bond issue for additional construction. The activity indeed looked impressive; unfortunately, the handful of large projects gave appearances of a viable construction business. In truth, hundreds of small jobs were disappearing, and building tradesmen were among the first to feel the depression's full effects.[5]

Atlanta in the 1920s also experienced economic development. Threatened by a depression in 1925 because of a panic triggered by the Florida land bust, the city's prominent businessmen initiated the "Forward Atlanta Movement," part of the predepression southern "booster-mania." Supported by the chamber of commerce, the campaign raised $750,000, which during the ensuing five years advertised the city a total of 125 million times in nationwide business publications and major newspapers. The effort successfully lured several hundred new manufacturing and other business establishments to the Fulton County area, offering employment to more than 15,000 and an annual payroll of more than $30 million. According to one student of Atlanta history, the scope and results of the campaign marked "the Forward Atlanta Movement as one of the more successful civic efforts of its kind sponsored during the decade."[6]

Atlanta's financial institutions also prospered in the 1920s. As well, a thriving construction business continued for a time into 1930, with municipal officials believing that contract work would remain healthy for years to come. Throughout the 1920s, the federal government opened several offices in Atlanta, bringing white-collar employment while contributing to building activity and the emergence of the city as the South's air travel center. The city's major steel producer, Atlantic Steel Company, showed a trend much like its rival in Bir-

5. *Polk's Birmingham City Directory, 1941*, 23–24; Birmingham *Age-Herald*, February 12, 1930; Birmingham *News*, December 27, 1931; James Jones, Jr., to W. A. Hardenberg, December 22, 1930, in James M. Jones, Jr., Collection, Drawer 2, Alabama Archives and History, Montgomery.

6. George W. West, "How the 'Forward Atlanta' Fund Has Helped Atlanta," *American City* (October, 1930), 139; Atlanta *Journal*, January 12, 1930; James Robert Thompson, "The Forward Atlanta Movement" (M.A. thesis, Emory University, 1948), 121–27.

mingham, actually increasing its share of the southern steel trade between 1929 and 1932.[7]

Perhaps more subtly, similar economic growth occurred in Memphis during the predepression period. The number of manufacturers located in the area increased throughout the 1920s, and by mid-1930, the city housed more firms than in any other period of its history. An active construction trade further signified economic well-being. Home and industrial building even during 1930 remained active, exceeding levels of 1929. Unemployment in Memphis, as reported by the federal census in mid-1930, stood at less than 4 percent of the city's work force. In Atlanta and Birmingham, unemployment rates were a bit higher but still below 6 percent. Even in New Orleans, the exception to the regional urban boom, unemployment as of mid-1930 had yet to affect the bulk of the labor force.[8]

While economic forces in at least three southern cities appeared healthy on the eve of the depression, the same was not evident in New Orleans. That city did not enjoy significant expansion during the 1920s, falling into second place behind Atlanta as the principal city and financial center of the lower South. Income from manufacturing and per capita output in New Orleans lagged far behind that in the other cities, while the city's overall standard of living was significantly lower. Despite the alluring French Quarter and an abundance of famous restaurants, the city was unable to attract conventions, perhaps best demonstrating its comparative lag. Atlanta, Memphis, and even industrial Birmingham attracted many more such gatherings, with the Tennessee and Georgia municipalities ranking among the ten American cities hosting at least ten thousand conventioneers each year.[9]

Despite the economic differences, each of the cities in question faced the new decade with high hopes. Boosters in Atlanta, Birmingham, and Memphis, for example, proudly pointed to their cities'

7. First National Bank of Atlanta, *Atlanta Resurgens: The First Hundred Years of a City's Progress, Promise and Philosophy* (Atlanta, 1971), 66–68; Benjamin S. Baker to F. Stuart Fitzpatrick, December 5, 1930, and Atlanta: The Employment Situation, n.d., both in Record Group 73, Records of the President's Organization for Unemployment Relief, Central File, National Archives, hereinafter cited as POUR; Harry R. Kuniansky, "A Business History of Atlantic Steel Company, 1901–1968" (Ph.D. dissertation, Georgia State University, 1970), 119–20.

8. *Polk's Memphis City Directory, 1929*; *Polk's Memphis City Directory, 1930*; Memphis *Commercial Appeal*, January 1, 1931; U.S. Bureau of Foreign and Domestic Commerce, *Statistical Abstract of the United States* (1931), 365, 376.

9. Glenn M. Runyan, "Economic Trends in New Orleans, 1928–1940" (M.A. thesis, Tulane University, 1967), 2–7; New Orleans *Times-Picayune*, March 11, 1930, March 5, 1933; Birmingham Chamber of Commerce, *Ledger of Activities for the Year, 1931* (Birmingham, 1932), 14.

unparalleled growth, confident in their faith that expansion was irreversible. Yet in New Orleans—precisely because it had not shared in the boom of the twenties—residents also confronted the uncertainties of the 1930s with confidence. Crescent City civic leaders, as well as the local press, countered the first news of widespread misery in Chicago by suggesting that the stability of the New Orleans economy was its buffer against the downturn that was bringing adversity to areas that had earlier experienced rapid but unstable expansion.[10]

The southern urban press in part forged the general optimism of the cities. Newspapers minimized adverse economic news, concentrating instead on positive signs wherever they could be found. Headlines such as "Depression Fails to Hurt City Seriously" were commonplace, with residents especially taking comfort in escaping the direct effects of the Great Crash. One New Orleans paper surmised, "The stockmarket collapse that shattered so many dreams elsewhere . . . finds our city less affected . . . and in better position perhaps than almost all the rest to carry on through the year without distress." The Atlanta *Journal* went so far as to admonish those who thought pessimistically, inferring that reports of improving conditions "strike us as being nearer the probability and reality of the case than is the dirge of those who stick to the Wailing Wall." The Atlanta *Constitution* likewise urged local residents and all Americans "to quit the low grounds of grief and climb the hills to the heights of a new prosperity." Even in early 1931, the Birmingham chamber of commerce was still predicting that the city "will be decidedly on the upward trend from now on."[11] It cannot be determined, of course, how many civic elites were just voicing high hopes and were never convinced that their cities would be spared.

An attitude best described as the "sunshine syndrome" was the key ingredient in the urban South's initial optimism. Southern newspapers steadfastly maintained that layoffs would be temporary in the winter and that normal employment would return with the arrival of warm weather. Welcoming March, 1931, for example, the Atlanta *Journal* indicated that until then conditions had shown "a bright omen here and there against a gray sky" but the spring would bring a "getting down to business" and a "quickening at the roots as well as in the branches of

10. Newspaper reports indicated that Chicago was bankrupt, that private citizens were volunteering in police, fire, and health departments, and that conditions were forcing the curtailment of many municipal services. See Memphis *Commercial Appeal*, April 26, 1930.

11. *Ibid.*, August 22, 1930; New Orleans *Times-Picayune*, January 1, 1930; Atlanta *Journal*, July 9, 1930; Atlanta *Constitution*, July 30, 1930; Editorial, *Birmingham: Official Organ of the Birmingham Chamber of Commerce*, VII (February, 1931), 10.

economic life." The Atlanta chamber of commerce in 1930 initiated a "reawakening campaign," complete with parades and a civic pageant, to usher in warm weather. According to the Atlanta *Constitution*, the ceremonies demonstrated that with spring "business is coming back to normal and jobs for the unemployed are becoming available once more." The notion that sunshine would somehow cure economic ills was so entrenched that many of the first municipal relief agencies were active only during the winter. The "sunshine syndrome" suggests too that the urban South maintained much of its regional identity, feeling itself somehow isolated from national and international events.[12]

Despite wishful rhetoric about the curing powers of sunshine, a serious economic downturn was evident even to the most hopeful by mid-1931. While many were shocked, believing that the collapse had somehow happened overnight, the subtle but steady erosion of local economies had been ongoing for many months, with conditions reaching their lowest ebb by late 1932. Among the first to recognize the reality was Congressman Robert Ramspeck of Atlanta. Speaking in late August, 1930, he emphatically proclaimed that "our boasted prosperity is a hollow mockery when men and women, able and willing, are denied the right to earn an adequate income."[13]

Late in 1930, urban manufacturers began experiencing the worst effects of the depression. Production cutbacks became routine, workers were released or their wages reduced, and many mills closed their doors. Some shutdowns were temporary, with industries functioning on a piecemeal basis, although too many proved permanent, as hard times and reduced work orders caused even established firms to remain idle for months at a time. Federal surveys showed that in New Orleans, by late 1931, all major industries had reduced work forces and that all were operating only a few days each week at best. In Memphis, by the middle of the same year, the total number of manufacturers had declined by more than fifty, and by 1933, Atlanta had lost nearly one hundred.[14]

In cities throughout the United States, the industrial decline was severe. Between 1929 and 1933, the total number of manufacturing establishments in the nation decreased by one-third, while each of the

12. Atlanta *Journal*, March 27, 1931; Atlanta *Constitution*, May 4, 1930.

13. New York *Times*, April 3, 1932; Atlanta *Journal*, August 28, 1930; interview with Allen, May 1, 1975.

14. Stanley Folmsbee, Robert E. Corlen, and Enoch L. Mitchell, *History of Tennessee* (4 vols.; New York, 1960), II, 300; Minton, "The New Deal in Tennessee," 36; Alice E. Stenholm, Louisiana: Report of a Field Trip, December 5–12, 1931, in POUR, Louisiana File; Atlanta Chamber of Commerce, *Facts and Figures About Atlanta, 1935* (Atlanta, 1936), 22; Atlanta *Journal of Labor*, October 1, 1931.

southern cities lost factories in higher proportions. At the same time, the value of manufacturing output fell, with declines ranging from more than 50 percent in Atlanta and New Orleans to more than 70 percent in Birmingham. The unhealthy state of agricultural production throughout the South, which had been ongoing for some years before 1930, only contributed to the manufacturing crisis. The large farm-related plants in the cities were sometimes able to continue full operations longer than their small-town counterparts, and during the spring and summer months, seasonal employment in agricultural operations did increase at least temporarily. No doubt this enhanced hopes that sunshine would bring economic betterment. Still, the depressed farming sector in time made things difficult for all, regardless of plant size and location. A survey in Memphis by the New York Bureau of Business found in mid-1931 that business was so poor that "there are no positive indications of a turn in any industry."[15]

Declining fortunes in agriculture and related industries in turn meant the curtailment of commercial activity. Between 1928 and 1933 in New Orleans, the volume of foreign trade decreased by more than 50 percent. The total value of tonnage handled by the Crescent City port also fell sharply, declining by 1932 to the levels of 1918 through 1920. Limited activity on the waterfront meant fewer jobs for dock workers and caused a sharp increase in the number of nonresident sailors dry-docked in New Orleans. The situation created a serious transient problem for the Gulf Coast city.[16]

Of all the southern businesses, none suffered more than the large steelworks in one-industry Birmingham. Producers had entered the 1930s optimistically, but by 1931 and thereafter, steel mills were all operating on part-time schedules. In addition to TCI plants, Sloss-Sheffield Steel and Iron and the Woodward Iron Company at first functioned on three-day schedules, but all too soon workers were fortunate to realize a full shift's work every two weeks. From a peak of more than one and one-half million tons in 1929, production in the Birmingham mills declined by one-half in 1931 and by one-half again in 1932. In the coal fields as well, reverses were sharp, with area mines in mid-decade yielding less than nine million tons annually, the same amount produced in 1900 and two to three times less than the output in

15. Memphis *Commercial Appeal*, July 21, 1931. Also see Ralph C. Hon, *Memphis, Its Economic Position* (Memphis, 1935), 22; "Statistical Report," *City Builder* (Atlanta), (July, 1935), 22; Runyan, "Economic Trends in New Orleans," 34; New Orleans *Times-Picayune*, June 30, 1930, February 4, 1931.

16. Louisiana State Board of Commissioners of the Port of New Orleans, *Forty-fourth Annual Report of the Board of Commissioners . . . June 30, 1940* (New Orleans, 1940), 12; Runyan, "Economic Trends in New Orleans," 22.

1926. By 1933, business groups in the city were offering little hope, with the chamber of commerce lamenting that "Birmingham has felt her full share of the depression." The severity of conditions forced the Roosevelt administration later to designate Birmingham as the "worst hit" city in the nation.[17]

The retail trade showed a similar downturn beginning in 1931. The number of stores and the value of sales declined significantly between 1929 and 1933, with reverses in the southern cities being more severe than the national average. In New Orleans, the retail volume by 1933 stood at only 60 percent of the level in 1928, reflecting a community with less buying power than before. Discouraged by the increasing number of unoccupied stores, the Atlanta chamber of commerce in 1932 urged remaining businesses to rent vacant windows for display to maintain the city's façade.[18]

The depressed retail trade sometimes led to price reductions, but any price was often too high for part-time labor or for those with no job at all. Price wars were common, with some taking a violent turn. During a brief milk war in Birmingham, for example, a number of producers brought in vigilantes to pressure Pure Milk Company and other low-price dealers to raise prices. When Pure Milk refused, a series of dynamite bombings resulted, destroying part of one plant and killing two people. For a time thereafter, police accompanied milk trucks as special guards.[19]

Ultimately, manufacturing and retail cutbacks caused a sharp increase in unemployment. The official 1930 census showed minimal joblessness in the southern urban areas; however, little time elapsed between the federal count and the initial depression layoffs. By the end of that year, there was at least one jobless man or woman for every ten normally in the labor force, and thereafter the number rose. By late 1931, unemployment had doubled, with a like percentage working only part time. Industrial employment in Birmingham decreased by 52

17. "Industrial Information," *Birmingham Bulletin*, December 19, 1932, p. 8; interview with Allen, May 1, 1975; interview with Reuben Farr, Birmingham area labor leader, May 2, 1975; Birmingham *Southern Labor Review*, April 13, 1932, May 24, 1933; Birmingham *Labor Advocate*, December 19, 1931; *Birmingham City Directory, 1941*, p. 16; J. Allen Tower, "The Industrial Development of the Birmingham Region," *Bulletin of Birmingham Southern College*, XLVI (December, 1953), 13; Alabama Mining Institute, "History of Coal" (Typescript in James M. Jones, Jr., Collection, Drawer 3, n.d.); Brownell, "Birmingham, Alabama: New South City," 24.

18. Bureau of Foreign and Domestic Commerce, *Statistical Abstract* (1931), 327; *ibid.* (1935), 77, 781–82; Hon, *Memphis, Its Economic Position*, 20; Runyan, "Economic Trends in New Orleans," 27; Federal Writers Project, *Atlanta: A City of the Modern South* (1942; rpr. St. Clair Shores, 1973), 61–62.

19. Birmingham *News*, July 17–18, 1931; Atlanta *Journal*, July 11, 1931.

percent between 1930 and 1933, while the number of retail jobholders fell by one-third. The nadir came in early 1933, when all communities reported at least 30 percent of their labor forces unemployed, which directly affected between 100,000 and 150,000 individuals in each city. Throughout the early depression years, all of the southern cities reported higher rates of joblessness than the national average of 25 percent.[20]

Those who managed to keep their jobs suffered drastic wage reductions. Spendable income per capita in the cities under examination fell by more than half between 1928 and 1933 — a figure equal to the national decline. In Birmingham, TCI by early 1933 had trimmed weekly pay envelopes between 50 and 75 percent and was threatening workers with dismissal if they questioned the policy. By that year, local sources reported that the average wage of these factory workers had dropped to less than two-thirds of a "minimum maintenance level" ($1,179) established by the federal government. The parent firm, United States Steel, justified the reductions as necessary in order for the corporation to pay stock dividends. Early in 1932, labor sources in the steel city claimed that most industries had effected wage cuts equal to those at TCI and that a ten-hour day was almost universal throughout the area. Some firms reacted to the difficult times a bit differently. In Memphis, several thousand manufacturing jobs held by women in 1929 were lost to men by 1933. Other companies attempted to ease the impact of unemployment by opening soup kitchens or by providing seeds and plots of land for the jobless, displaying a regional sense of paternalism toward their employees.[21]

The rate of unemployment in the southern urban craft unions was generally higher than the overall unemployment rate. In the building trades, for example, sources in Birmingham and Atlanta reported more than 60 percent unemployment as early as 1931, as construction of all types steadily declined. The value of building permits in the Georgia city fell from a $27.5 million high in 1928 to a depression-period low of

20. Unemployment estimates calculated from Frank Miller to Frank Bane, January 12, 1931, W. B. Henderson to [?], November 15, 1930, W. A. Winfrey to J. F. Lucey, February 11, 1931 (Central File), Stenholm, Report of a Field Trip to Tennessee, December 18–22, 1931 (Tennessee File), Louisiana: Report of a Field Trip, December 5–12, 1931 (Louisiana File), all in POUR; Statement on Unemployment in Atlanta, Georgia, November 2, 1932, in National Urban League Records, Box A-35, Library of Congress; "Unemployment Figures," *City Builder* (Atlanta), March, 1934, p. 48; Broadus Mitchell, *Depression Decade: From New Era through New Deal, 1929–1941* (New York, 1947), 45; Runyan, "Economic Trends in New Orleans," 47.

21. Birmingham *Labor Advocate*, November 14, 1931, June 18, 1932; Birmingham *Southern Labor Review*, July 6, 1932, February 3, 1937; *Polk's Memphis City Directory, 1929*; *Polk's Memphis City Directory, 1933*.

just $250,000 by 1933. Decreases were comparable in the other southern cities, causing severe joblessness among construction workers and forcing those at work to accept wages well below scale, weakening an already tenuous union presence.[22] Birmingham reported in 1933 the highest overall trade union unemployment rate of 80 percent. Some labor organizations, such as the Atlanta and Birmingham typographical unions, established emergency funds to aid the jobless temporarily. But as the number of working typographers declined, voluntary and even required contributions to the reserve funds dwindled, forcing union labor, like unorganized industrial workers, to turn to private charities or the community at large for assistance.[23]

Segregated job patterns in most southern businesses at first caused joblessness among whites and blacks to increase equally, especially in the Birmingham steelworks, where "white" and "black" labor were well defined. Yet the trend was short-lived, and despite a handful of contractors who hired unorganized blacks instead of unionized whites, Negroes were soon suffering more than whites from unemployment and wage reductions. Whites began moving into traditionally black positions, becoming bellhops and porters, for example; and among industrial workers, blacks were indeed the first to be let go. By early 1931, the unemployment rate among black males in New Orleans and Birmingham was double that of white males. By 1932, the number of blacks without work in Atlanta and Memphis accounted respectively for 50 percent and 75 percent of the total number of unemployed in the two cities. And between 1931 and 1932, the absolute number of jobless blacks in Atlanta increased by more than 95 percent, while the real number of unemployed whites increased by only 25 percent. Clearly such percentages were disproportionate—as they remain today—with the percentage of blacks to total residents in the southern cities ranging from 28 percent in New Orleans to 38 percent in Birmingham.[24]

22. Bureau of Foreign and Domestic Commerce, *Statistical Abstract* (1935), 789–90; Birmingham *Southern Labor Review*, April 23, 1930.

23. Birmingham *Southern Labor Review*, December 10, 1930; *American Federationist* (December, 1930), 1513, and (March, 1933), 293; Unemployment Report: Atlanta, Georgia, July 1, 1932, in POUR, Georgia File; memorandum, Unemployment Relief Committee to Atlanta Typographical Union No. 48, August 1, 1932, and Walter Grant to Chairman of the Printers Voluntary Relief Fund, November 10, 1931, both in Atlanta Typographical Union No. 48 Papers, Southern Labor Archives, Georgia State University, Atlanta.

24. Interview with Arthur D. Shores, Birmingham civil rights attorney, May 1, 1975; Atlanta *Constitution*, January 6, 1933; Richard Sterner, *The Negro's Share: A Study of Income, Consumption, Housing and Public Assistance* (New York, 1943), 362; Statement on Unemployment in Atlanta, Georgia, November 2, 1932, in National Urban League

As if conditions for blacks were not bad enough, municipal officials in New Orleans created additional problems. In 1931, Mayor T. Semmes Walmsley proposed the enforcement of a twenty-three-year-old ordinance that forbade the hiring of individuals who were not qualified voters by city contractors except when there was excess work and a lack of eligible labor. So during the depression, black employment opportunities were nil. In 1932, city leaders successfully restricted employment on an extensive bridge project only to qualified voters, despite funding from the federal Reconstruction Finance Corporation (RFC). The city required that prospective workers exhibit poll tax receipts for 1931 and 1932 as well as evidence of voter registration. Similar efforts elsewhere by the city apparently succeeded. One survey indicated that between January and August, 1930, all black employees, more than 1,800 in all, lost their jobs in the municipal cotton warehouse.[25]

The adoption of a controversial dock ordinance was Mayor Walmsley's most blatant effort to restrict black employment. In August, 1932, city officials approved a statute reserving employment on publicly owned wharves to eligible electors, thereby threatening the jobs of thousands of black longshoremen. Both daily newspapers, the dock's principal hiring agent (the New Orleans Steamship Association), and the New Orleans Board of Trade condemned the resolution as a misguided policy that might jeopardize traditional social, economic, and political arrangements. One press account concluded that if voting was used to threaten Negro jobs, "thousands will seek to recapture the right in the only way left open . . . by registering and voting in our elections." Only the ineffective white local of the International Longshoreman's Association (ILA) defended the ordinance, with its leader, T. J. Darcy, hoping to secure additional jobs for whites on the waterfront.[26]

Fortunately, the statute never took effect. Upon its approval, the United States Circuit Court of Appeals issued a temporary restraining order when steamship operators in New York and Puerto Rico challenged the city's interference with interstate commerce. Following a subsequent hearing, the federal judiciary permanently enjoined the enforcement of the ordinance, thereby ending the controversy. What

Records, Box A-35; Bureau of Foreign and Domestic Commerce, *Statistical Abstract*, (1935), 23, 31; Harry Hopkins to John H. Bankhead, March 14, 1935, in Record Group 69, Records of the Federal Emergency Relief Administration, Alabama File, National Archives.

25. New Orleans *Times-Picayune*, December 11, 1931; *Louisiana Weekly*, August 9, 1930, August 27, 1932, January 21, 1933; Roy Wilkins to T. Semmes Walmsley, January 26, 1933, in Records of the National Association for the Advancement of Colored People, Box G-82, Library of Congress; James Gayle to Jesse O. Thomas, January 6, 1934, in National Urban League Records, Box A-43.

26. New Orleans *Times-Picayune*, July 30, 1932.

was not settled, however, was the uncertainty of the Negro's plight in New Orleans or, for that matter, elsewhere in the South.[27]

The economic downturn adversely affected local governments and civic institutions in addition to individual wage earners. Employment lost and manufacturing reverses meant a lower tax base and diminished operation revenue for all municipalities. In the face of increasing tax delinquencies, cities reduced public employment, cut services, and eventually turned to local banks for operating capital. The situation in Atlanta was representative. A municipal statute authorized officials there to borrow a maximum of two million dollars a year from financial institutions. As of 1933, the city had relied on loans for so many years that it no longer had total control of its annual expenditures. The Atlanta banking establishments reserved the right to approve the city's annual budget.[28]

Like their counterparts in the private sector, municipal employees experienced difficult times. The workers remaining on Birmingham's payroll by 1933 had accepted four salary cuts of 10 percent each, with similar trends prevailing in Atlanta, Memphis, and New Orleans. In place of cuts, other employees reluctantly "donated" a number of workdays each month to city hall, without pay. Conditions also resulted in the curtailment of police, fire, health, and other municipal services. In Birmingham, the city's public health program, one of the first civic programs to be slashed, practically disappeared during the early 1930s. By 1934, the southern steel center was spending only seventeen cents per capita on health services, compared to a national per capita average of seventy cents. Cities turned to scrip in lieu of salaries as well. While some retailers accepted the substitute dollars, recipients often had to redeem their notes at local banks or with loan sharks, both of whom discounted the notes at least 20 percent.[29]

A political affair made the financial situation in New Orleans unique. The Crescent City faced financial disaster at the decade's outset, laboring under a $3.5 million debt and surviving on bank loans even before experiencing the worst of the depression. Complicating matters, the New Orleans political machine in mid-1930 became

27. *Ibid.*, July 29–31, August 2, 5, 12, 1932.

28. Atlanta *Constitution*, January 16, July 1, October 9, November 20, 1932, January 1, February 4, 1933; Franklin M. Garrett, *Atlanta and Environs: A Chronicle of Its People and Events* (3 vols.; New York, 1954), II, 904.

29. Atlanta *Constitution*, February 3, March 5, 1932; Atlanta City Council Minutes, XXXIV, August 17, 1931, City Hall, Atlanta; New York *Times*, July 25, 1932; Memphis *Labor Review*, January 22, 1932; Birmingham *Post*, April 1, 1930, April 28, 1932, March 8, 1933; Birmingham *News*, September 16, 1932; "Civic Candor," *Survey* (April, 1934), 132; "The Depression and Public Health Expenditures," *American Journal of Public Health*, XXIV (July, 1934), 755.

involved in the first of many confrontations with Governor Huey Long. The city's Old Regulars made it clear that they would not support the Kingfish's candidacy for the United States Senate, while simultaneously leading the opposition against several of the governor's plans in the state legislature. Determined to make the affair a test of political strengths, Long maneuvered to destroy his rivals by undermining city revenues. He first pressured state banks into curtailing loans to the city and then ordered the state tax commission to seize the city's tax rolls. For a time, New Orleans could not collect taxes even as they came due, forcing officials to secure substantial loans from a New York bank. Walmsley countered through the courts, and ultimately the Louisiana Supreme Court ordered the release of the city's books.

The court order was a political truce that settled matters for a while, postponing the final showdown for a couple of years. Municipal officials could not afford an extended confrontation; besides, Long proved his strength by winning the Democratic senatorial primary, notwithstanding Old Regular opposition. As part of the settlement, Walmsley pledged support for the governor's legislative proposals and for a number of Long's candidates in the forthcoming 1932 elections. The Kingfish in turn promised sufficient state aid to the city, which allowed it to reduce its deficit and initiate a major works program. All too soon, conditions would again force New Orleans to turn to banks for assistance, but the truce had at least opened the door for such loans, which assured the maintenance of full municipal services for a longer period than in many other regional cities. The confrontation of 1930 and 1931, however, also foreshadowed a later clash, with city finances again as the battleground.[30]

School systems fared no better than other public institutions. The city budgets in Birmingham, Atlanta, and Memphis allocated fewer dollars each year for education, and in New Orleans, the school board itself became indebted to local financial establishments. Teachers were the first to suffer. They saw their meager salaries reduced, while their classrooms became grossly overcrowded. Educators in Memphis, even more so than other municipal employees, received several payments in scrip, and when salary reductions failed to save sufficient funds, a more general austerity program resulted. By the 1932–1933 academic year, special programs had disappeared from the city schools, including adult night classes, guidance services, vision correction and testing programs, and hygienic and psychiatric counseling, as well as voca-

30. New Orleans *Times-Picayune*, June 14–15, 19, 25, July 16, August 9, September 17, 25, November 5, 22, 29, 1930, March 8, 11, October 2, November 5, 1931. For an analysis of the settlement, see T. Harry Williams, *Huey Long* (New York, 1969), 504–13.

tional training financed in part under the federal Smith-Hughes Act.[31]

Retrenchment in education took its most serious twist in Atlanta, where school authorities vehemently opposed city council demands to cut programs. Rather, the Atlanta Board of Education demanded additional funding—it received not a cent from county coffers even though taxes paid by city residents accounted for 85 percent of the county treasury. The conflict became so heated that councilmen at one point began talking about replacing the board with a new group of trustees. Because state legislative concurrence was needed, the threat remained just a threat, although city administrators brought it up on several occasions thereafter. Even when Georgia lawmakers ordered that the city schools receive an increased percentage of Atlanta's budget, a decision that only aggravated hostilities during difficult times that called instead for cooperation, most school service programs were curtailed anyway.[32]

The many students whose parents were unemployed caused further problems for urban school systems. Full attendance was never assured, even though educators in all cities successfully operated schools for complete terms. According to public welfare officials in New Orleans, as many as ten thousand children lacked "apparel conforming to standards of comfort and decency; the majority are home because torn and ragged garments shame them before their fellows." The crisis in education, moreover, lasted throughout the decade. As late as 1937 and 1938, full teacher salaries in Birmingham and New Orleans remained unrestored, and officials still could not guarantee full terms without the aid of emergency funds.[33]

Despite urban financial needs, local banks were neither able nor always willing to grant municipal loan requests. Total banking deposits and resources recorded sharp declines early in the 1930s, and like all depressed businesses, banking reached a low point in 1932 and 1933. Banking failures were apparently more frequent in the rural communities than in the southern cities, with the fate of urban finan-

31. Atlanta *Journal*, July 12, 1931, February 23, 25, 1932; Atlanta *Constitution*, March 5, 1932; New Orleans *Times-Picayune*, March 16, April 10, 1930, March 12, June 3, August 7, 1932; Lewis J. Todd, "Development of Public Secondary Education in New Orleans, 1914–1941" (M.A. thesis, Tulane University, 1941), 84; Statement of Budget Expenditures for the Year Ending June 30, 1932, n.d., and E. C. Ball to Watkins Overton, January 21, 1933, both in Mayor's Correspondence File, Drawer G, Memphis and Shelby County Archives, Memphis.

32. Atlanta *Constitution*, August 17–18, 1931, May 12, 1932, February 2–4, 24, 26, 1933.

33. Roman Heleniak, "Local Reaction to the Great Depression in New Orleans, 1929–1933," *Louisiana History*, X (Fall, 1969), 302–303; New Orleans *Times-Picayune*, September 29, 1931, July 23, 1937; Birmingham *Post*, January 21, April 27, 1938.

cial institutions varying from place to place. In Memphis, there were no major closings—a loan from the RFC averted the one near-panic—while in Atlanta, a number of banking consolidations in the 1920s apparently kept financial establishments solvent throughout the depression period. When banks in both cities closed during the federal banking holiday in March, 1933, all reopened within a week, although federal and state banking authorities placed withdrawal restrictions on some for several months thereafter.[34]

Neither the Birmingham nor the New Orleans banking community was so fortunate. As early as January, 1930, banks and their branches began closing in Birmingham, and before the holiday of 1933, the city had lost four major financial institutions. Between 1928 and 1932, total banking resources in Birmingham declined from $131 million to $82 million, while total bank deposits fell from $101 million to less than $60 million. The City Commission Council responded by adopting two ordinances that declared it illegal to publish or circulate damaging innuendos concerning the solvency of Birmingham's banks.[35]

Conditions in New Orleans were even more serious. During a congressional hearing early in 1933, Hamilton Fish of the House Banking Committee charged that New Orleans financier R. S. Hecht, president of both Hibernia Bank and Trust and Continental Bank and Trust, had misused federal funds in covering debts that one bank owed the other. Intensifying concerns was the fact that Hecht was chairman of the regional RFC advisory committee. Disclosure of the charges caused many out-of-state depositors to begin withdrawing funds from Hibernia. Civic leaders next braced for a run on the bank by Crescent City patrons. Substantial RFC loans to the two institutions in the end halted the panic.

The short-lived run in February, 1933, proved only the first in a series of setbacks affecting banks in New Orleans. Within a year, the state banking commission had ordered into liquidation at least six major financial institutions, reporting only three banks operating normally. Although two of the troubled banks later reorganized, with one reopening as part of a merger, thousands of Crescent City residents

34. Bureau of Foreign and Domestic Commerce, *Statistical Abstract* (1941), 321–22; Memphis *Commercial Appeal*, January 23, 26, May 2, 7, 1933; Atlanta *Constitution*, March 15, May 7, 1931; Georgia State Department of Banking, *Thirteenth Annual Report of the Department of Banking* (Atlanta, 1932), xii–xiii; Governor's Proclamation, April 18, 1933, in Hill McAlister Papers, Box 70, Tennessee State Archives and History, Nashville.

35. Alabama State Office of the Superintendent of Banks: *Report of the Condition of State Banks in Alabama . . . December 30, 1931* (Montgomery, 1932), *Report . . . 1932* (Montgomery, 1933), *Report . . . 1933* (Montgomery, 1934); *Birmingham City Directory, 1941*, 23; Birmingham *Age-Herald*, January 29, 1930.

lost all or parts of their savings. Most of the banks that closed never reimbursed their patrons in significant amounts, and even when there was some repayment, only middle- and upper-class residents—the large, steady depositors—managed to recover anything at all.[36]

Clearly the southern cities in the early 1930s were experiencing a period of severe economic upheaval. Based on previous growth, the municipalities had entered the depression decade optimistically, and despite subtle reverses from the outset, communities had failed to perceive a crisis until late in 1931. Yet by the end of 1933, unemployment, wage reductions, and lost savings affected thousands, as did the curtailment of city services. Perhaps the larger industrial cities in the Northeast and Midwest endured greater business reverses and more jobs lost, but the thousands ailing in the southern communities were nonetheless desperate. While times were the harshest, moreover, all localities were left alone to meet the problems as best they could. The attempt to relieve depression miseries would demand a great effort and commitment by individuals and local institutions.

36. Louisiana State Department of Banking, *Twentieth Biennial Report . . . 1932–1933* (Baton Rouge, 1933), xxviii–xl; Runyan, "Economic Trends in New Orleans," 304–306; New Orleans *Times-Picayune*, February 2, 6–7, March 3, May 4, 1933, January 5, December 10, 1936.

 2

URBAN BOOSTERS AND
THE INADEQUACY OF MUNICIPAL SERVICES

In June, 1930, scattered groups of Atlanta extremists joined forces to combat general economic decay and mounting unemployment in perhaps typical southern fashion. Calling themselves the American Fascisti Association, the self-styled fascists enjoyed an initial appeal under the leadership of former Fulton County legislator Joseph O. Wood, local businessman Holt Gweinner, and Georgia agricultural commissioner and future governor Eugene Talmadge. By July, scores of men dressed in black, displaying Nazi armbands, could be seen daily roaming the streets of Atlanta, and a number of clothing stores were even advertising attire as "the kind you have to have to join the Black Shirts." At their peak, the Black Shirts boasted a following of more than 40,000, although investigations later revealed a dues-paying membership of fewer than 1,200 individuals. Nevertheless, the fascist movement exploited economic uncertainty and racial bigotry for three months throughout the Atlanta area.[1]

The Black Shirts had one goal—the replacement of all Negro labor with white workers. Sponsoring frequent public rallies, they pressured employers to release blacks and hire white replacements from among those registered with their own employment bureau. Desperate tactics

---

1. Julius W. Dudley, "A Brief Study of Three Subversive Organizations in Atlanta, Georgia, 1915–1946" (M.A. thesis, Atlanta University, 1969), 60–76; John Hammond Moore, "Communists and Fascists in a Southern City: Atlanta, 1930," *South Atlantic Quarterly*, LXVII (Summer, 1968), 435–54; Benjamin Stolberg, "Buzz Windrip: Governor of Georgia," *Nation*, March 11, 1936, pp. 316–18; press release, October 27, 1930, and clipping, August 2, 1930, both in Records of the National Association for the Advancement of Colored People, Box 3-127, Library of Congress; Atlanta *Constitution*, July 20, 22, 27, 1930.

were common, including the framing of black bellhops in hotel rooms with white prostitutes. The organization was active politically as well, running an extremist candidate against incumbent conservative Robert Ramspeck in the Democratic congressional primary in 1930. Night-riding was also frequent, and perhaps the best measure of Black Shirt popularity was the slow response of local police to the sometimes violent vigilante outbursts. Not until the slaying of Dennis Hubert, a fifteen-year-old black youth, did Atlanta lawmen finally move in with arrests and convictions and thereafter a more active police watch.

Fortunately, the Black Shirts movement was short-lived, as a com-bination of internal and external forces quickly undermined its appeal. First, and no doubt prompted by the Hubert murder, city newspapers in August joined a statewide press campaign calling for justice. Local editorials began echoing the sentiments of the *New Republic*, which referred to the fascist movement as "another of those cracker attempts to capitalize on race prejudice."[2] Second, a leadership crisis caused a bitter split within the ranks when Gweinner and Wood divided over the issue of organizing a separate women's unit. Third, little support from existing extremist groups was to be had. The Ku Klux Klan, for example, was openly critical of the Nazi upstarts, calling the organiza-tion un-American and charging that it took orders from Mussolini.

The most important cause of the Black Shirts' demise was lukewarm public support. In mid-1930, unemployment was affecting few in Atlanta and was not seen as threatening. Local employers thus withstood Black Shirt pressure, with the result that promises to deliver jobs remained unfulfilled. Finally, the Fulton County Superior Court not only refused to charter the organization but enjoined the fascists from operating anywhere in the state of Georgia. By the late fall, 1930, about one hundred days after its rise, the Nazi nightmare in Atlanta had become a bad memory.

Despite the fascist outburst, the southern urban areas generally forsook a search for scapegoats during the depression years. Instead, the municipalities slowly came to realize the inevitability of a crisis and the necessity of cooperative action—the joining together of local resources to bolster failing businesses while offering some aid to the thousands in need. The institutionalization of heretofore fragmented community services—mainly relief for the indigent and unemployed, and scattered private service organizations—was typical of the way cities elsewhere responded to depression miseries and was in line with President Herbert Hoover's calls for voluntarism.[3] Of course coopera-

---

2. Edwin Tibble, "Black Shirts in Georgia," *New Republic*, October 8, 1930, p. 204.
3. For a more general study of urban reactions to the depression, see James J.

tion in the Dixie cities (as elsewhere) had some shortcomings, as business and labor leaders often remained at odds, and businessmen and politicians were cautious about contributing public revenues for relief. Still, the cities demonstrated in the depression period a growing concern for community welfare in the broad sense—a trend that continued with the coming of federal programs and new directions later in the decade.

Southern business leaders made the first moves to combat the depression by revitalizing booster campaigns of a few years earlier. Like the "Forward Atlanta Movement," such efforts involved the purchase of space in the New York *Times, Wall Street Journal, Atlantic Monthly, Time,* and other nationwide publications. Not satisfied merely with advertisements, the Association of Commerce of New Orleans opened a promotional office on New York's East Side "to tell our story to New York in general" and to be "strategically located so as to be convenient to New York executives who are expressing interest in the industrial possibilities of New Orleans." Unfortunately, few manufacturers in 1931 and 1932 found themselves able to relocate or expand.[4]

Commercial interests in the cities also ran promotional campaigns to attract the attention of local buyers. Gimmicks ranged from special "consumer days" in Birmingham and New Orleans to the more elaborate "Anti-Hording" drive in Atlanta or "Break the Buyers Strike" and "Share the Work Week" in Memphis. In the last campaign, employers promised not to hire married women and agreed to establish a thirty-hour work week for all labor. City bus lines and taxi companies cooperated by reducing fares, while parking lots lowered rates for out-of-town visitors and downtown restaurants trimmed menu prices. Buying contests were common, such as the "Good Samaritan Campaign" in Atlanta, which encouraged organizations to save sales receipts for prizes donated by local merchants.

Business organizations, working with fraternal orders, also canvassed employers and homeowners, urging the maintenance of wage scales and the creation of odd jobs for the unemployed. The Birmingham Employment and Improvement Campaign in the spring of 1932 was typical. American Legionnaires and chamber of commerce officials interviewed businessmen and visited homes throughout the city. Also involved was the Women's Economic Council, which served

Hannah, "Urban Reaction to the Great Depression in the United States, 1929–1933" (Ph.D. dissertation, University of California at Berkeley, 1956).

4. New York *Times,* June 22, 1930; Atlanta *Constitution,* March 11, 1930, August 16, 1932; Atlanta *Journal,* March 27, 1932; New Orleans *Times-Picayune,* April 5, 1930; Birmingham *News,* October 1, 1930.

as a coordinating body for the Parent Teacher Association, the Women's Christian Temperance Union, local garden clubs, the Council of Jewish Women, and other professional organizations.[5]

Organized labor groups worked similarly to combat depression effects. Unionism in the 1920s had fared poorly throughout the United States, particularly in the South; consequently, only the building trades and a handful of skilled crafts had any real strength. Men who echoed the "business-union" policies of American Federation of Labor (AFL) president William Green dominated southern urban trades councils, but despite their conservative sentiments, they enjoyed the friendship of few urban employers. The handful of industrial unions that at one time had contracts were simply defunct by 1930. Typical of many southern employers, Birmingham businessmen and industrialists had long exploited racial tensions among steel and mining employees to limit labor's effectiveness. In turn, the business depression in the early 1920s, followed by the nationwide open-shop movement, undermined even the few "lily white" industrial organizations scattered throughout the region. As of 1930 in Atlanta, less than 7.5 percent of nonagricultural workers were unionized, and that small number represented more than one-half of all organized labor in Georgia.[6]

Yet in early 1931, with labor leaders hoping to exploit an increasing awareness of job insecurity, the AFL launched a major organizing campaign throughout the South. The central labor councils in the major cities heeded the call, sponsoring extensive local drives while urging their respective state federations of labor onward. Green designated Birmingham as the central headquarters for the regional effort, although national leaders concentrated their energies in the Danville, Virginia, textile mills, where they hoped to rebound from the colossal failures of 1929.[7]

The new drive lasted about two years but, as was evident early, was doomed to failure. In Atlanta, which was representative, the first year

5. Atlanta *Constitution*, November 20, 1930, March 4, 1932; Memphis *Commercial Appeal*, October 9, 1932; New Orleans *Times-Picayune*, October 4, 1932, February 14, 1933; Birmingham *Age-Herald*, March 17, 1932; "Chamber of Commerce Report," *Birmingham Bulletin*, July 27, 1931, March 28, 1932.

6. Atlanta *Journal of Labor*, March 4, 1932; Mercer G. Evans, "The History of the Organized Labor Movement in Georgia" (Ph.D. dissertation, University of Chicago, 1929); Mitchell, "Birmingham: Biography of a City," 139, 280–81; Freddie Ray Marshall, "History of Labor Organization in the South" (Ph.D. dissertation, University of California at Berkeley, 1955), 200; Horace R. Cayton and George S. Mitchell, *Black Workers and the New Unions* (Chapel Hill, 1939), 321.

7. Birmingham *Age-Herald*, January 11, 1930; Marshall, "History of Labor Organization," 281–91; *Federationist* (New Orleans), April 25, 1930; Memphis *Labor Review*, April 15, 1932; Atlanta *Journal of Labor*, January 24, 26, 1930; New York *Times*, April 1, 1937; Birmingham *Labor Advocate*, November 11, 1930.

brought only six new affiliates into the local federation. By the end of 1931, the ever-increasing number of unemployed forced most unions to switch to defensive from offensive tactics. Thereafter, unionists did well just to maintain the membership they already had. According to Birmingham labor leaders in mid-1932, joblessness was deterring new organization and "efforts have been directed to the task of helping to maintain the morale of the membership and to keep up the fight to hold our forces intact so that we may be in a position to present a solid front when and if the terrible economic depression comes to an end."[8]

A specific incident in Atlanta clearly exemplified labor's dilemma. In March, 1931, members of the International Brotherhood of Electrical Workers walked out of Georgia Power Company plants in a contract dispute. The firm immediately ordered a lockout and began importing, hiring, and housing guards to protect strikebreakers. The matter remained unsettled throughout the spring and summer months, and even city hall's backing of labor seemed to mean little. Atlanta councilmen attempted to pressure Georgia Power by supporting a public utilities movement, but when state lawmakers adjourned in September without acting on the municipal ownership issue, it was clear that union efforts were hopeless. A handful of employees later recovered their jobs without the benefit of a union contract. Not until 1934, under section 7(a) of the National Industrial Recovery Act, did the brotherhood win recognition and bargaining status.[9]

A second example of labor's failure in the early 1930s involved a struggle on the New Orleans waterfront. In March, 1931, the segregated locals of the ILA called a strike, seeking to recover bargaining rights lost during the preceding decade. The city trades council and the Louisiana Federation of Labor endorsed the walkout, in which both black and white unionists cooperated. Most of the violence that followed was targeted at the former group. Strikers and strikebreakers clashed daily, as city and law enforcement officials sided with employers. Dock foremen who distributed work assignments were anti-union as well, and memories of a violent streetcar strike in 1929 did little to help the union gain public sympathy. The affair remained volatile throughout April and May, and even efforts by the secretary of labor and federal mediators accomplished nothing. Finally, in mid-June, when a federal judge issued an injunction against strike leaders,

8. Official Report of the Thirtieth Annual Convention, May, 1932, in Records of the Alabama Federation of Labor Files, Alabama AFL-CIO Office, Birmingham; Hannah, "Urban Reaction," 173–74.

9. Atlanta *Journal of Labor*, March 27, April 9, May 7, 28, June 18, 25, September 17, October 1, 1931, January 12, 1934.

the confrontation ended and union members returned to work. Without federal guarantees, hiring agents on the New Orleans docks, like employers throughout the country, continued to hold the upper hand.[10]

With buying contests and other efforts failing to stimulate local economies, hundreds of individuals began turning to charitable agencies for assistance. Unfortunately, during the early depression period, needs remained unfulfilled, as private philanthropies and relief societies dependent on voluntary subscriptions were the only relief-giving bureaus available. Only Birmingham had previous experience with public assistance. That city had opened a central agency in 1916, but civic officials in 1924 had abandoned the experiment and turned over the commission's duties to a division of the Red Cross. Although Atlanta, as well as the other cities under examination, in 1930 had official departments to channel municipal contributions to hospitals and charities, the appropriations involved represented a small percentage of total urban expenditures, and such bureaus usually confined their work to overseeing the administration of public hospitals.[11]

In part, this seeming lack of preparedness was the result of decades of unparalleled and unplanned expansion. As well, most residents were still "small town" at heart, and the municipal leadership, identified as a "commercial-civic" elite by southern historian Blaine Brownell, remained committed to a New South creed that contained few progressive inclinations. Their booster rhetoric notwithstanding, according to David Goldfield's perceptive *Cotton Fields and Skyscrapers*, southern urban officials were forever interested in protecting their own political and economic interests while maintaining those southern institutions (a uniform low-wage system and the dual society) that enhanced those interests. Thus, the development of urban programs and services responsive to general community welfare had not kept pace with population growth. When thousands were suddenly jobless and homeless, adequate provisions for their well-being simply did not exist. Complicating matters was an ongoing rural migration to

10. Freddie Ray Marshall, *Labor in the South* (Cambridge, 1967), 202–203; New Orleans *Times-Picayune*, September 20, 1930, March 3, 5, 21, 27, April 8, May 1–3, 13, June 8, 15, 1931; Marshall, "History of Labor Organization," 291–94; Arthur R. Pearce, "The Rise and Decline of Labor in New Orleans" (M.A. thesis, Tulane University, 1938), 86–104.

11. Lyda Gordon Shivers, "The Social Welfare Movement in the South: A Study in Regional Culture and Social Organization" (Ph.D. dissertation, University of North Carolina, 1935); Robert W. Cooper, *Metropolitan County: A Survey of Government in the Birmingham Area* (Birmingham, 1949), 100; Atlanta City Council Minutes, XXXIV, August 17, 1931, City Hall, Atlanta; H. J. Early to Aubrey Williams, January 4, 1934, in Record Group 69, Records of the Civil Works Administration, Louisiana File, National Archives.

the cities and mounting transient problems, with newcomers seeking either employment or aid from already overburdened charities.

The severity of the depression crisis pointed out all too painfully the inadequacy of public services in the southern cities. The institutionalization of local resources, especially the eventual centralization of relief work as an initial step toward permanent public welfare, suggests an increasing awareness of those shortcomings and a readiness to address them, at least in part. It can thus be argued that a southern urban consciousness, which Brownell has found was unfolding prior to 1930, advanced during the depression, even if within the existing political structure. New social service institutions appeared, and old ones were either revived or expanded. When left to their own limited means, of course, the cities could do little to alleviate the overwhelming adversity, and sometimes would do little given the municipal leadership's hesitancy to alter the status quo. Not until the coming of federal funds and direction in mid-decade would the notion of social responsibility make more than marginal headway.[12]

The earliest relief efforts in all localities found the unemployed selling oranges or the like on street corners, although such gimmicks could hardly be considered a principal means of relief. City administrators also looked to local community chests to ease the crisis. Similar to those in nearly every small town in the country, such organizations coordinated affiliate agencies ranging from the Boy Scouts to family aid societies and solicited funds through annual campaigns. Not surprisingly, community chest financial goals began increasing dramatically in 1930, particularly emergency quotas for affiliates with relief responsibility. The Memphis Community Fund reacted to increased demands first by adopting biannual drives and ultimately, in 1932 and 1933, by suspending the general solicitation, allowing members to seek funds independently. The Tennessee operation simply could not raise sufficient resources on a voluntary basis, despite having the active support of the chamber of commerce, city officials, and the local press. Such subscription agencies, however, would not disappear altogether, and many continued as important service organizations even after the later establishment of permanent departments of public welfare.[13]

As community chests curtailed services, municipal officials could

12. Brownell, "The Urban Mind in the South," 215–16; Goldfield, *Cotton Fields and Skyscrapers*, 160–62; William D. Miller, *Memphis During the Progressive Era, 1900–1917* (Madison, Wis., 1957), 191.

13. Memphis *Commercial Appeal*, May 22, November 28, 1931, March 7, November 18, 27, 1932, January 8, 1933; Atlanta *Constitution*, April 1, 1930, October 25, 1931, November 2, 6, 25, 1932; Atlanta *Journal*, May 27, 1930, February 22, 1931; Birmingham *Post*, March 10, 14, 1932; New Orleans *Times-Picayune*, November 30, 1930, October 18,

not long postpone the sponsorship of city-directed relief bodies. In March, 1930, New Orleans opened the first of what were called "mayor's commissions for unemployment," and by that winter, similar committees were also active in Memphis and Atlanta. Directed by prominent civic leaders, they began as clearinghouses for private agencies and church groups. Although they were initially thought to be temporary—and some at first limited their operations to the winters only—their involvement in relief steadily increased as conditions worsened. By 1932, most were operating their own service centers and sponsoring work relief projects, while still coordinating private and other public endeavors.[14]

The municipal commissions were never adequately financed. The cities periodically sponsored community fund-raising events in their behalf, such as citywide penny collections or designated days at the racetrack, with all proceeds donated to relief. Some schemes successfully raised money, although others, such as "The Soul of a Nation" pageant in New Orleans, lost thousands of dollars despite the joint sponsorship of municipal authorities and the local press. In Atlanta, Mayor James Key risked the ire of religious groups by opening movie theaters on Sundays to raise relief funds. He even urged the repeal of Prohibition laws, suggesting that liquor tax revenue be used for the same purpose. Atlanta ministers reacted by joining a recall movement in early 1932 spearheaded by labor leaders angry over Key's curtailment of wage increases due under city contracts. The mayor barely survived the recall effort, although polls showed that the majority of Atlanta residents favored either the repeal or the modification of the Volstead Act.[15]

Alternative financing had to be found, because continuing monetary problems were forcing local charities to suspend work for weeks at

---

1931, December 23, 1932; New Orleans Community Chest Report, September 3, 1931, Stenholm, Louisiana: Report of a Field Trip, December 5–12, 1931 (Louisiana File), T. G. Woolford to Walter Gifford, October 16, 1931 (Atlanta File), all in Record Group 73, Records of the President's Organization for Unemployment Relief, National Archives, hereinafter cited as POUR.

14. New Orleans Times-Picayune, March 14–15, 1930; W. A. Winfrey to J. F. Lucey, January 8, February 11, 1931, Frank Miller to Frank Bane, January 12, 1931, all in POUR, Central File.

15. Thad Holt, General Status of Relief Funds in Principal Southeastern Cities, September 26, 1931, Stenholm, Report on Georgia Field Trip, October 13–14, 1931 (Georgia File), Stenholm, Louisiana: Report of a Field Trip, December 5–12, 1931 (Louisiana File), Stenholm, Report of a Field Trip to Tennessee, December 18–22, 1931 (Tennessee File), all in POUR; Memphis Commercial Appeal, June 23, 1932; Atlanta Constitution, July 31, 1934; New Orleans Times-Picayune, July 23, 1932; Atlanta Constitution, April 16, 1930, November 21, December 24, 1931, May 30, 1932.

a time. Neither the machine nor the nonmachine city administrations, however, were quick to allocate municipal funds for new social services even for emergency purposes. Their conservative, New South sentiments were unshaken; consequently, they felt obligated, at least initially, to do little more than encourage private agencies, perhaps offering to help coordinate existing relief efforts. Ever increasing tax delinquencies further hindered the prospect of public relief funding. In Memphis, unpaid accounts increased annually from about $1.5 million in 1928 to more than $9 million in 1932. Statistics were comparable elsewhere, despite low tax rates, which in Birmingham were lower than those of any other city in the nation with a population in excess of 180,000.[16]

When the maintenance of even minimum services forced cities to seek bank loans, a number of vocal lobbyist groups swung into action. Led by the urban press, with its own booster sentiments, organizations such as the Atlanta Taxpayers League, the Memphis Property Owners Association, and the Jefferson County Association to Secure Economy in Government all campaigned for reduced spending, balanced budgets, and efficiency in local government. They reminded residents of recently uncovered tax scandals in Atlanta City Hall while publicizing a series of unproved allegations of financial irregularities in Memphis and New Orleans. Opposing the prospect of bank loans, editorials in Atlanta and Birmingham applauded special state statutes that restricted the possibility of borrowing on anticipated local revenues.[17] The major dailies also condemned thoughts of federal involvement in relief—the so-called national dole. The Atlanta *Constitution* in early 1931 was especially alarmed when Democratic congressional leaders

16. George M. Reynolds, *Machine Politics in New Orleans, 1877–1926* (1936; rpr. New York, 1968), 138; Lorin D. Peterson, *The Day of the Mugwhump* (New York, 1961), 204; William D. Miller, *Mr. Crump of Memphis* (Baton Rouge, 1964), 201; Brownell, "Birmingham, Alabama: New South City," 21–48; Brownell, "The Urban South Comes of Age, 1900–1940," in Brownell and Goldfield (eds.), *The City in Southern History*, 150–51; Goldfield, *Cotton Fields and Skyscrapers*, 160–61; Birmingham *Post*, December 25, 1931; *Financial Statistics of Cities Having a Population of over 30,000* (1928), 154, 502–503, and (1932), 56, 201.

17. Atlanta *Journal*, January 18, 25, February 18, 1930, July 6, 1931, April 19, May 26, 1932; New York *Times*, May 5, 1931; Garrett, *Atlanta and Environs*, III, 867–68; Harry C. Ash, "The Story of Atlanta's Own Graft Investigations as Told by Local Newspapers" (Typescript in Robert Woodruff Library, Emory University, 1932), 54; New Orleans *Times-Picayune*, March 2, September 27–30, October 2–3, 11, 1930, February 25, August 8, 1931, July 2, 1932; Memphis *Commercial Appeal*, July 1, 1931, February 4, 1933; Atlanta *Constitution*, July 25, August 19, November 22, December 22, 1931, February 14, December 18, 1932; Jones to Hardenberg, December 22, 1930, in James M. Jones, Jr., Collection, Drawer 2, Alabama Archives and History, Montgomery; Birmingham *News*, July 26, August 5, 1931.

introduced a federal relief bill that, according to one writer, "justly alarm[s] and repel[s] popular confidence" and "show[s] what a straight-shooting prophet President Grant was when he said: 'The democrats can be trusted always to act the fool at the right time to benefit the republican party.'"[18]

Not until the winter of 1931–1932 were the first municipal funds reluctantly made available to urban relief agencies. The Central Relief Committee in Atlanta, for example, received initial public appropriations that winter, and by mid-1932, the agency was sponsoring a modest work relief program while operating shelters for homeless Atlantans and transients and providing seeds and garden plants to the jobless. In cooperation with the Atlanta Restaurant Association, the civic group also supported a community kitchen that served thousands of hot meals daily.[19]

Birmingham was the first of the southern cities in question to issue special bonds—another means of funding emergency relief. In early 1931, voters approved the issuance of $500,000 in bonds, while City Commission Council president James Jones vetoed in the same year the proposed release of a municipal surplus for relief purposes. An employment service within the city's department of public works cooperated with the Family Service Society of the Red Cross, staffed by social workers previously active in the old Jefferson County welfare department, to oversee the effort. The money primarily funded work relief but was also channeled into direct aid, emergency gardening, transient care, and a hot meal program. Unfortunately, the half-million dollars barely lasted a year, with the result that authorities in Birmingham, like their counterparts in Atlanta in 1932, reluctantly began allocating funds directly for relief, but only after the city found no buyers for its special bonds on the open market. Simultaneously, and despite depression conditions, Birmingham commissioners raised the local gasoline tax by a penny per gallon.[20]

18. Atlanta *Constitution*, February 3, 1931. For similar sentiments, see *ibid.*, December 29, 1931, February 2, 1932; New Orleans *Times-Picayune*, July 29, 1932; Birmingham *Post*, February 2–3, 1932; Memphis *Commercial Appeal*, December 31, 1931, February 18, July 10, 1932.

19. Atlanta *Constitution*, June 25, 1932.

20. Birmingham *Post*, December 12, 1930, February 23, June 23, December 1, 1931, February 11, 16, April 2, 20, May 11, 1932; Robert E. Bondy to Parker R. Lee, December 20, 1930, A. J. Hawkins to N. K. Plunket, June 11, 1931 (Central File: Alabama), J. M. Jones to Harry L. Kinnear, November 20, 1931 (Birmingham File), all in POUR; Jones to Hugo Black, February 3, 1932, in James M. Jones, Jr., Collection, Drawer 2; Bessie A. Brooks, *A Half Century of Progress in Family Welfare Work in Jefferson County* (Birmingham, 1936), 35–39; George H. Watson, "Birmingham Park System Gains Through Unemployment," *American City* (August, 1931), 112–13.

New Orleans also turned to issuing bonds for relief purposes when voters in 1932 approved a special $750,000 issue for the welfare commission. Used at the rate of $60,000 each month, the money replaced funds that up to then had been raised by mandatory 5 percent monthly "donations" from the paychecks of city employees. The bond funds provided one or two days labor each week in city parks for unemployed heads of families. Still, only a small percentage of the total number of jobless people received work relief; in fact, throughout the early 1930s, New Orleans contributed nothing from general revenues for emergency relief purposes. A $2,000 appropriation to the Family Service Society of the community chest represented the Crescent City's annual expenditure for indigent care.[21]

A reliance on voluntary generosity and limited public funding doomed even the best-intentioned relief efforts to inadequacy. In 1932, a federal survey found that the amount of relief per family nationwide averaged only $19.00 per month, about half of a minimum standard prescribed by the United States Department of Agriculture. No southern city provided relief equal to the department's guideline, and only New Orleans, where work relief paid $2.50 per day and direct food assistance averaged about $4.69 weekly per family, approached the national average. In Atlanta, where nearly 100,000 individuals depended on public or private aid as of mid-1932, the overwhelming burden forced the Central Relief Committee to close all work relief projects and put remaining funds into direct assistance allocations of $1.30 per week for each family. In Memphis, the Mayor's Emergency Commission ceased operations altogether in late 1932 rather than seek bank loans to fund its work, and at the same time, the privately operated Family Welfare Society closed its doors. Likewise, in Birmingham limited resources kept all Red Cross aid at pitifully low levels. Not surprisingly, numerous Hoovervilles surrounded each of the major southern cities—cardboard and newspaper homes that the New Orleans *Times-Picayune* sarcastically described as "cheerful looking and rather trim."[22]

21. New Orleans *Times-Picayune*, February 2, 6, 11, June 2, July 7, 1931, May 4, 1932; New York *Times*, April 3, 1932; Thomas B. Becnel, "Unemployed Build Two Roadways in New Orleans City Park," *American City* (June, 1933), 70; Evelyn C. Beven, *City Subsidies to Private Charitable Agencies in New Orleans* (New Orleans, 1934), 27, 43.

22. Atlanta *Journal of Labor*, December 2, 1932; New Orleans *Times-Picayune*, June 19, 1932, January 8, August 29, 1933; Atlanta *Constitution*, September 4, 23, 28, 1932; Compilation of Relief Expenditures, n.d., in POUR, Central File: Tennessee; Memphis *Commercial Appeal*, March 1, 1933; "Conditions Showing Possible Need for Federal Aid," *Survey* (February, 1932), 465; Birmingham *Post*, October 26, 1931, January 5–6, 1932; Brooks, *A Half Century of Progress*, 44–45.

Although never denied relief outright—that could jeopardize social order—urban blacks obtained mainly the meager direct handouts from community sources following the collapse of their own neighborhood relief efforts. Advisory groups of black ministers and educators often coordinated city relief activities within their communities. Whites received the majority of work relief positions, with the needs of whites on direct assistance always being cared for before those of blacks. The Central Relief Committee in Atlanta in late 1932, for example, distributed a maximum of $0.75 in grocery orders per week to black families and up to $2.50 per week to white families. National Urban League officials there feared that a "relief mentality" would result among the blacks, indicating that "the dole is rapidly becoming the accepted policy of relieving distress among Negroes and just as rapidly being accepted by them without protest." The conservative southern black newspapers, reflecting the prevailing accommodationist attitude, generally endorsed municipal relief policies, inequities notwithstanding. One exception was the *Louisiana Weekly*, which suggested that perhaps the general awareness of suffering would increase if black groups showed some support for "communist" ideas. Blacks in New Orleans received no public relief until the advent of federal programs, relying solely on private charities and on a handful of work positions created by the 1932 bond issue.[23]

If cities were unable or unwilling to allocate sufficient unemployment assistance, little support was forthcoming from their state governments. Legislatures provided minimum administrative funding for state welfare departments, and these agencies did little more than assist in the local planning of jails, child-care centers, and county programs for dependents, delinquents, and the like. The Georgia Board of Public Welfare, for example, received annually no more than forty thousand dollars in the early 1930s, prompting one historian to conclude that no legislature in history could "compare in stupidity, selfishness, and lack of purpose with the body that twiddled its thumbs while the fires of hope died to ashes in the hearts of citizens."[24] Even the eventual creation of emergency relief councils by southern governors had few

23. Minutes of the Board of Directors of the Atlanta Urban League, January 6, 1933, Atlanta Urban League Office; Atlanta Community Chest, *Community Life in Atlanta* (Atlanta, 1931), 1; Atlanta *Daily World*, December 15, 1931; Memphis Community Fund, *Annual Report, 1931* (Memphis, 1931), 12; Memphis *World*, September 18, 1931; Atlanta *World*, January 22, 1932; *Louisiana Weekly*, August 2, 1930, March 12, 1932; New Orleans *Times-Picayune*, February 2, 1933; Robert Morgan, Sr., "Public Relief in Louisiana from 1928–1960," *Louisiana History*, IV (Fall, 1973), 369; John L. Williams, "Struggles in the Thirties in the South," in Bernard Sternsher (ed.), *The Negro in Depression and War: Prelude to Revolution* (Chicago, 1969), 173.

24. James T. Patterson, *The New Deal and the States: Federalism in Transition*

positive effects. The special agencies distributed no funds, functioning mainly in an advisory capacity to lawmakers, who occasionally released funds early for highway and other previously approved state construction projects.

The southern state most involved in urban relief was Louisiana. The reason was clearly political and entangled with the conflict between the Longs and the Old Regulars. In mid-1931, when officials in New Orleans announced the suspension of their second emergency relief commission, Governor Long seized the opportunity to extend his influence in the city. The governor offered state financial aid to destitute families (which never amounted to more than the early release of previously allocated monies), provided he be allowed to dispatch a number of his lieutenants, including future mayor Robert Maestri, to insure the continuation of local relief work. It was the Long group, working with Mayor Walmsley's office, that structured the 5 percent donation scheme that funded municipal relief until the $750,000 bond election in the spring of 1932. Long's cooperation with the Old Regulars generated allegations of political influence in the relief process. Few specific charges were revealed in the early depression years, for when Alice Stenholm of the President's Organization for Unemployment Relief (POUR) visited the Crescent City in late 1931, neither the mayor nor Governor Long nor members of the local relief commission would grant her an interview.[25]

Federal aid to the cities during the early depression period was likewise minimal. President Hoover's image as a do-nothing has been challenged, and rightly so, yet most federal endeavors prior to 1933 had little direct effect on the lives of the most needy. RFC loans to large banks and businesses reached few individuals, and even special appropriations for highway work and similar construction projects channeled few funds into the hands of the indigent. Furthermore, the twelve regional branches of the Federal Home Loan Bank could not even assist all of the white, middle-class homeowners in need of help, much less any others who were needy.[26]

(Princeton, 1969), 48; Atlanta Social Planning Council Pamphlet, in Rhoda Kaufman Papers, Georgia State Department of Archives and History, Atlanta; Georgia State Department of Public Welfare, *Directory of Georgia Agencies and Institutions* (Atlanta, 1932), 10–12; Organization of the Alabama Emergency Employment Commission, n.d. (Central File: Alabama), and Watkins Overton to Charles C. Gilbert, January 23, 1932 (Tennessee File), both in POUR.

25. New Orleans *Times-Picayune*, July 17, 21, October 16, 1931, January 22, 1932; Stenholm, Louisiana: Report of a Field Trip, December 5–12, 1931, in POUR, Louisiana File; Williams, *Huey Long*, 643–44.

26. New Orleans *Times-Picayune*, June 7, 1930, February 17, September 28, 1932,

Directed by Owen D. Young and Walter Gifford, POUR was an early Republican party effort to involve Washington, D.C., in the relief process. Established to assist local charitable groups, the commission worked quietly in all southern cities except New Orleans, where municipal authorities refused its services. In Birmingham and Memphis, POUR assisted the League of Women Voters and similar organizations in sponsoring employment bureaus and indigent care. It also promoted back-to-school programs, garden projects, and works projects, while helping wholesalers, retailers, and relief committees in the administration of food surpluses. But POUR was never more than advisory; businessmen, not social workers, controlled the national staff and, like Robert Woodruff of Coca-Cola in Georgia, also directed state and local cooperating groups. POUR's limited activities prompted one disgruntled Atlantan to conclude that "the President of the United States . . . is a menace to the working people of America" and is leading the Washington, D.C., "sapheads . . . in producing a revolution in this country."[27]

When President Hoover in July, 1932, signed the Emergency Relief and Construction Act, authorizing emergency RFC loans to states and localities, applications were quickly forthcoming from executive commissions in nearly all southern states. When Alabama governor B. A. Miller hesitated to apply, Birmingham city commissioners moved on their own, despite the rhetoric of their president a few months before that "we do not favor a Federal appropriation to assist local governments in meeting emergency burdens." In August, 1932, the steel city became the first major southern municipality to receive RFC monies, with New Orleans and Atlanta following shortly thereafter. A feud between Memphis boss Edward Crump and lame-duck governor Henry Horton over in-state allocations delayed RFC loans for all of Tennessee. The Memphis despot persuaded the federal government to hold the state's funding until the inauguration in January, 1933, of his recently elected machine candidate.[28]

January 8, 27, 1933; Atlanta *Constitution*, March 27, 1931; Memphis *Commercial Appeal*, February 20, October 6, 1932.

27. Ira Harrelson to Owen Young and Gifford, November 3, 1931, in POUR, Central File: Georgia. Also see Walmsley to Kinnear, November 23, 1931 (New Orleans File), Mrs. Clifford Adams to Lilian Gilbreth, November 4, 1930 (Alabama Women's File), Alice Dickson to Adams, February 17, 1931, Dickson to Mr. Eldren Rogers, February 18, 1931 (Tennessee Women's File), Gilbert to P. D. Huston, October 6, 1932 (Tennessee File), Robert Woodruff to Gifford, November 17, 1931 (Georgia File), all in POUR.

28. Jones to Robert M. LaFollette, Jr., December 24, 1931, in James M. Jones, Jr., Collection, Drawer 2; Morgan, "Public Relief in Louisiana," 370–71; Alabama Relief Administration, *Two Years of Federal Relief in Alabama* (Wetumpka, Ala., 1935), 21; Memphis *Commercial Appeal*, July 20, 28, October 14, 1932, January 23, 1933; New

Private and public relief groups in all cities made use of RFC loans to fill grocery orders for those on direct assistance and to create a limited number of public works projects, paying a daily wage of between $1.25 and $2.40. Few localities received sufficient aid even to meet minimum needs, and requests were far greater than the RFC's initial $300 million budget. Between August, 1932, and late 1933, Birmingham and surrounding Jefferson County received nearly $1.7 million—as much as any other metropolitan area in Dixie—with appropriations to the southern states ranging from a low of $500,000 to Georgia to a high of $8.4 million to Louisiana. Somewhat puzzling is that Mississippi during the same period, with its few urban areas, received more assistance than did Georgia, Alabama, or Tennessee.[29]

It seems that with assistance from all sources so inadequate, the urban jobless would have demanded greater benefits. But they formed no cohesive unit; consequently, only in New Orleans did an organization of the unemployed successfully influence municipal policy. Led by Rene C. Poursine, the Crescent City group in mid-1931 led a series of demonstrations and strikes among emergency jobholders that in part prompted local authorities to accept state assistance in relief administration rather than cease operations. Elsewhere, efforts to mobilize the jobless never gained momentum, in part owing to the steadfast opposition of city authorities. The Unemployed Citizens League and the Trade Union Unity League were active for a time in Memphis and Birmingham respectively, but neither gained a following. In most cases, would-be organizers mistakenly announced their leftist sympathies, which turned most southerners against even the most benign organizational endeavors.[30] Racial prejudice also contributed to the determined opposition, as exemplified in two cases.

In the spring of 1930, Atlanta police arrested a group of blacks and whites for working among the unemployed. Charged with the violation of a one-hundred-year-old slave insurrection law (modified in 1868 to

Orleans *Times-Picayune*, August 17, 1932; Atlanta *Constitution*, September 28, 1932, January 19, 1933.

29. E. M. Henderson, Sr., "Public Relief in Jefferson County: A Brief History" (Typescript in Birmingham Public Library), 62; Atlanta *Constitution*, July 30, 1932, January 9, February 23, 1933; Memphis *Commercial Appeal*, February 18, 21, 1933; New Orleans *Times-Picayune*, November 27, 1932; Birmingham *News*, July 27, 1932, April 3, 1933; Memphis *Press Scimitar*, July 6, 1933.

30. Stenholm, Louisiana: Report of a Field Trip, December 5–12, 1931, in POUR, Louisiana File; New Orleans *Times-Picayune*, July 12, 14, 1931, October 17–20, 1932, February 2, 1933; Memphis *Press Scimitar*, December 8, 1932; Memphis *Commercial Appeal*, January 11, March 1, 1933; "Cooperative Self Help Among the Unemployed: The Barter Movement in Memphis," *Monthly Labor Review*, XXXVI (April, 1933), 717–20; Cayton and Mitchell, *Black Workers*, 337–40.

include the organization of freedmen), the Atlanta Six faced prison terms or even the death sentence if convicted. During ensuing legal battles, the Fulton County solicitor general announced that he would "demand the death penalty for every communist who comes into the state," and local grand juries twice indicted the six under the Georgia statute. Ultimately, the county dropped charges as a result of the United States Supreme Court decision in the Angelo Herndon affair.[31]

In July, 1932, Atlanta authorities arrested Herndon, a young black relief organizer, and charged him with "inciting a group of Georgia's population to armed insurrection and the seizure of a major portion of five Southern states for the establishment of a Soviet republic independent of the United States."[32] A county court found young Herndon guilty under the Georgia insurrection statute in January, 1933, and sentenced him to twenty years on a chain gang.

For the next fifty-two months, the Herndon case captured its share of national headlines. Even, or perhaps especially, when the National Association for the Advancement of Colored People (NAACP), the American Civil Liberties Union (ACLU), the National Bar Association, and the AFL all rallied to the young man's defense, the Georgia Supreme Court twice upheld the state law and the county court's decision. In May, 1935, the United States Supreme Court by a six to three vote upheld Herndon's sentence, and in October, the federal court refused to rehear the case. Not until August, 1937, when the case reached the country's highest tribunal for the third time, did the federal judiciary declare the Georgia law unconstitutional. The decision immediately released Herndon and eighteen others under similar indictments.

Of course few doctrinaire Communists circulated among the South's urban unemployed. Perhaps the suffering of the Atlanta Six and Angelo Herndon deterred would-be organizers, but the major obstacle was simply that urban residents were suspicious of any outside organizers, including legitimate labor leaders, especially those who worked among whites and blacks together. Even Congressman Hamilton Fish, who brought his House of Representatives committee to Birmingham to investigate communism in the region, uncovered few "card carriers." Yet Fish's exaggerated reports of radicalism in the

31. Moore, "Communists and Fascists in a Southern City," 434–43; Walter Wilson, "Atlanta's Communists," *Nation*, June 25, 1930, pp. 730–31; Atlanta *Constitution*, April 5, 1930.

32. Atlanta *Constitution*, November 24, 1935. Also see John Hammond Moore, "The Angelo Herndon Case, 1932–1937," *Phylon*, XXXII (Spring, 1971), 60–71; "The Herndon Case," *Information Service*, October 5, 1935, in Records of the National Association for the Advancement of Colored People, Box D-59, Library of Congress;

South no doubt intensified already existing regional anxieties. It was known, moreover, for city officials to sponsor municipal programs designed to keep so-called unsuspecting blacks from the clutches of radical influences. According to National Urban League investigators, Birmingham designed a plan whereby "hungry, unemployed Negroes are taken out in parks and open spaces and taught to dance, sing and play games in order to prevent them from becoming communists."[33]

Ultimately, it was the political process through which hopes would be channeled and discontent expressed. The popular perception of a "Republican depression" aided Democratic hopefuls in 1932, certainly contributing to Franklin D. Roosevelt's overwhelming victory nationwide. And despite Roosevelt's liberal record as governor of New York, the southern urban press began following him as early as 1930. It endorsed his presidential aspirations from that date forward provided he adopt, according to the Atlanta *Constitution*, "a strong hewed and solid democratic platform, containing fundamental American principles and proposing policies that would meaningfully restore to the people equal rights and equal opportunities." As November approached, the Memphis *Commercial Appeal* concluded that Roosevelt was the candidate of the working people and was "fearless enough to lead the battle for the forgotten man who has never been forgotten by him." On election day, southern urban voters gave Roosevelt between 85 and 94 percent of their votes—a far higher percentage than Democratic presidential candidates had received in any of the past three elections, in which Democrats had lost ground to the Republican party.[34]

Republican political advances throughout the southern cities in the 1920s contrast with the emergence of an urban Democratic base in other sections of the country. In 1920 and 1924, Republicans captured up to 40 percent of the southern urban vote, while four years later, a majority of Birmingham and Atlanta voters marked their ballots for

---

Angelo Herndon, *Let Me Live* (1937; rpr. New York, 1969), 165–409. For a more recent analysis, see Charles H. Martin, *The Angelo Herndon Case and Southern Justice* (Baton Rouge, 1975).

33. Guichard Parris and Lester Brooks, *Blacks in the City: A History of the National Urban League* (Boston, 1971), 226. Also see George Leighton, "Birmingham, Alabama: The City of Perpetual Promise," *Harpers Magazine*, LXXV (August, 1937), 238–39; Birmingham *News*, March 26, July 1, November 15, 1930; Atlanta *Journal*, July 14, November 14, 1930.

34. Atlanta *Constitution*, June 5, 1931; Memphis *Commercial Appeal*, July 3, 1932; Atlanta *Journal*, March 24, 1932; Richard M. Scammon (comp.), *America at the Polls: A Handbook of Presidential Election Statistics, 1920–1964* (Pittsburgh, 1965), 24, 27, 97, 100, 189, 191, 414, 416.

Hoover. In Memphis and New Orleans in the latter year, the Republican party gained more support than ever before. No doubt the nature of Al Smith's candidacy in 1928 drove many city voters only temporarily into the Republican party; whether all would have remained there in 1932 under different circumstances is questionable. But it does seem clear that growing Republican strength in the urban South was cut short by the depression and would not resume until after World War II.[35]

Any notion of a "Roosevelt revolution" in the southern urban centers, or anywhere in the region, demands qualification. Despite Republican advances, the Dixie cities remained fairly "solid," barring extreme circumstances such as in 1928. Furthermore, while Roosevelt's candidacy attracted unprecedented numbers to the polls, the percentage increase in voter turnout in three of the four southern cities was higher between 1924 and 1928 than between 1928 and 1932. In Memphis, the one exception, state and local politics, more than Roosevelt's appeal, accounted for the high voter interest. An independent gubernatorial candidate was offering a serious challenge to Boss Crump's nominee, prompting the Memphis dictator to mobilize all of his forces.[36]

At the very least, Roosevelt's campaign in 1932 generated hope and confidence. Communities throughout America found cause, according to the New Orleans *Times-Picayune*, "to salute the new president and the new congress with an enthusiasm rarely, if ever, matched in its spirit and nationwide sweep." The depression was creating hardships for nearly all Americans, and local resources alone could not bring adequate assistance to the increasing numbers of men and women in need. Anxiously anticipating inauguration day, the same New Orleans newspaper concluded that a great majority of Americans were placing their hopes in the promised New Deal that "they had ordered last November."[37]

35. For analyses of the 1928 election, see Carl Degler, "American Political Parties and the Rise of the Cities: An Interpretation," *Journal of American History*, LI (June, 1969), 50–57; Jerome M. Clubb and Howard W. Allen, "The Cities and the Election of 1928: Political Realignment?" *American Historical Review*, LXXIV (April, 1969), 1205–20.

36. Scammon (comp.), *America at the Polls*, 24, 27, 97, 100, 189, 191, 414, 416; Memphis *Commercial Appeal*, August 18, 1932; Miller, *Mr. Crump of Memphis*, 144–84.

37. New Orleans *Times-Picayune*, March 4, 1933.

3

BLUE EAGLES COME AND GO

It was Thursday evening, one week prior to Thanksgiving in 1933, and thousands of Memphians hurried downtown to enjoy the annual Christmas parade. In addition to the coming of Saint Nicholas, a special treat awaited residents this year. The city had planned a gala festival in support of the new president and his recent brainchild, the National Recovery Administration (NRA). More than 50,000 participated in the march, and more than 125,000 applauded what the Memphis *Commercial Appeal* called the "largest single procession within the memory of the present generation." At least twenty-five colorful floats charmed the crowd as bands played and children waved flags, exhibiting their patriotism without restraint in the cool night air. Of all the performers, the figure in the final float attracted the most attention. Instead of riding in a reindeer-drawn sleigh, Santa Claus in 1933 threw candy to youngsters as he sat atop the statue of a large blue eagle.[1]

Memphis was not the only southern city to organize festivities in support of the NRA. Municipalities throughout the country sponsored blue eagle days, with corps of volunteers soliciting signatures to the President's Reemployment Agreement. Signatories pledged to adhere to the blanket provision of fair competition until the leaders of their particular industries, working with officials in Washington, D.C., structured approved industrial codes. In just a few weeks, 75 percent of the manufacturers and retailers in Memphis subscribed and applied for emblems, while Atlanta enrolled more than fifty-six thousand townsmen in an NRA consumers club. The city's drive, reported the chamber

---

1. Memphis *Commercial Appeal*, November 24–25, 1933.

of commerce, brought together "the largest army of volunteers for civic duty since the World War."[2]

The festival in New Orleans was among the most elaborate anywhere. The city organized a reemployment campaign committee and divided volunteers into regiments. The committee chairman was the general, under whom served lieutenant colonels, majors, and other "commissioned" officers. A men's brigade surveyed local businesses, and a women's division canvassed homes, seeking promises that consumers would patronize only blue eagle establishments. Initial support was so great that some Crescent City retailers recorded losses while they awaited the arrival of their insignias. Local postal authorities, who distributed the emblems, had not received sufficient quantities from Washington, D.C., to satisfy early demands. A majestic parade, terminating in a park where the city had erected a giant pyramid, climaxed the pageant, which lasted several days. More than seven thousand pledge signatories saw their names inscribed on the edifice. On the top of the pyramid stood a nine-foot-tall eagle of blue lights, surrounded by red and white lights that spelled out the slogan We Do Our Part.[3]

Approved by the United States Congress on June 16, 1933, the federal recovery program, including the NRA, created under the broader National Industrial Recovery Act, was launched on August 1 to great expectations throughout the country. Officials in Memphis looked for the creation of at least twenty-five thousand new jobs and a significant increase in the total city payroll within a few months. Business leaders hoped that the effort would promote economic efficiency and eliminate "cut throat competition" without the federal government becoming directly involved in the marketplace. Speaking in Memphis, John E. Edgerton of the conservative Tennessee Manufacturers Association urged that employers and chambers of commerce accept on trial this experimental and rather revolutionary arrangement between government and private enterprise.[4]

Organized labor also had great expectations, hoping that section 7(a) of the National Industrial Recovery Act would mean the abolition of child labor and the sweatshop while stimulating unionism. Labor sources in industrial Birmingham anxiously indicated that "a new era will soon be ushered in, bright with the promise of larger rewards to all

2. *City Builder* (Atlanta), (October, 1933), 2; Memphis *Press Scimitar*, September 1, 1935; Atlanta *Journal*, September 17, 1933.

3. New Orleans *Times-Picayune*, August 3, 16, 19, 22–24, 29, 31, September 2, 1933.

4. Memphis *Commercial Appeal*, June 18, August 1, 1933; Minton, "The New Deal in Tennessee," 125.

those who toil for a living." Ultimately, disillusionment would replace hopes; yet in the early months, few doubted the wisdom of the Memphis *Commercial Appeal's* claim that "our future depends on the National Industrial Recovery Act."[5]

Exaggerated reports of immediate benefits accompanied the urban zeal and were in part responsible for the initial enthusiasm. By October, 1933, sources announced reemployment for thousands, as firms seemingly increased their payrolls overnight. Typical was a report from the Atlanta chamber of commerce that sixty thousand area laborers had found work within fifty days of the recovery act's passage. Other municipalities boasted similar figures, while indicating that in addition to new employment, hundreds of working men and women were reaping benefits as they became covered by the codes.[6]

Such reports were clearly inaccurate. Many of the new employees worked part-time and were therefore exempt from the recovery stat- ute's provisions, although their employers legally displayed blue eagles. Others received work because of slowly improving economic conditions. Southern city economies had reached their nadirs in late 1932, and beginning the following year, the situation slowly began to improve. Still other workers, while counted as new labor, merely replaced employees laid off at the same time. More than a few business- men apparently chose to pay stipulated minimum wages to young whites rather than to older employees or blacks. Federal officials in New Orleans reported in late 1933 that the implementation of NRA codes had resulted in the appearance of additional older men and Negroes on the relief rolls.[7] Exemptions and displacement plagued the NRA and minimized its effectiveness from the start.

Urban newspapers of nearly all political views, including the largest dailies, which generally echoed the conservative, booster senti- ments of municipal authorities, stood ready to give the National Industrial Recovery Act a trial. The Birmingham *News* admitted that government involvement with business "gives rise to some doubts and fears," but agreed with the Atlanta *Constitution* that if half of the president's new acts proved successful, he "will have accomplished

5. Birmingham *Labor Advocate*, June 17, 1933; Memphis *Commercial Appeal*, August 1, 1933.

6. *City Builder* (Atlanta), (September, 1933), 3; Atlanta *Georgian*, September 24, 1933; Atlanta *Constitution*, August 3, 15, 1933. Also see Memphis *Press Scimitar*, October 25, 1933; Birmingham *Age-Herald*, August 4, 30, 1933; New Orleans *Times-Picayune*, September 3, 1933.

7. Aubrey Williams, Field Report: Louisiana, September 13, 1933, in Record Group 69, Records of the Federal Emergency Relief Administration, Louisiana File, National Archives, hereinafter cited as FERA.

more than any president has ever been able to do within so short a time." If any firms refused to fly an eagle, the press remarked, the public would bring them into line because "citizens will cooperate and only patronize Blue Eagle stores." Summarizing the prevailing attitude, the New Orleans *Times-Picayune* concluded that "the National Recovery Act as the president conceives and administers it is, in brief, a law for the public benefit, consistent with American principles and ideals, operating in the American way and depending for its success upon the support of the American public."[8]

The NRA's administrative machinery was quite elaborate. The central Industrial Recovery Board, staffed by the attorney general, the director of the budget, the chairman of the Federal Trade Commission, the secretaries of agriculture, commerce, labor, and interior, and an administrator of industrial recovery (General Hugh Johnson) directed state compliance units through a field division. Below the state offices, which doubled as state National Emergency Council (NEC) bureaus, were local compliance committees, supposedly representing business and labor interests. At first, the President's Reemployment Agreement provided general guidelines, with industries and the government ultimately structuring more than five hundred codes containing provisions of fair competition and prices, maximum hour and minimum wage qualifications, and guarantees of collective bargaining.[9]

Local chambers of commerce handled violation complaints until official state and city compliance units became operative in the early fall of 1933. Typical was the New Orleans council, established in late September, which consisted of seven members representing consumers, industry, retailers, wholesalers, and the legal profession. The community office first heard all complaints, but if the locality and thereafter the state failed to pressure a violator into compliance, investigative results were forwarded to Washington, D.C., for a final decision. If judged guilty by federal administrators, employers could lose their eagles, or if wages were involved, compliance officials could seek restitution in federal court.[10]

8. New Orleans *Times-Picayune*, March 6, 1934; Birmingham *News*, June 11, 1933; Atlanta *Constitution*, June 17, 1933. Only the Atlanta trades council press, which feared the disruption of cordial relations between labor and management, doubted the wisdom of the NRA. See Atlanta *Journal of Labor*, June 2, 1933.

9. NRA Research and Planning Division Report, December 22, 1934, in Record Group 9, Records of the National Recovery Administration, Region IV Records, Samuel Ewing File, Atlanta Regional Archives Branch, hereinafter cited as NRA; Michael S. Holmes, "The New Deal in Georgia: An Administrative History" (Ph.D. dissertation, University of Wisconsin, 1969), 381–96.

10. New Orleans *Times-Picayune*, September 22, 1933; report, n.d., in Hill McAlis-

From the first, the promotion of consumer awareness was one of the NRA's most significant and perhaps lasting benefits in all of the cities in question. Beginning with pledge clubs, municipalities next organized what would become permanent consumer councils to oversee retail outlets. The county units in the Atlanta vicinity were especially active. In the fall of 1934, for example, the Dekalb County Council discovered that some of the milk sold in the metropolitan area was unsanitary and improperly labeled. Further investigation found that much of the imported canned milk contained maggots and other foreign matter. Also, vast quantities of dairy products were arriving from other states, although local dairymen had surpluses on hand. Consumer advocates successfully pressured the Fulton County Milk Commission to tighten its supervision of milk standards.[11]

Consumer groups functioned similarly in Birmingham, Memphis, and New Orleans. In addition to inspecting retail products, the units distributed general economic information, aided in the adjustment of consumer complaints of unreasonable prices, and served as forums for public communication with various administrative agencies. All reported every two weeks to a central bureau in Washington, D.C., and while some local councils curtailed operations when the NRA ended in 1935, the Memphis chapter and others outlived the blue eagle, at first remaining active as part of NEC efforts and then on their own.[12]

Nevertheless, NRA code violations became all too quickly apparent, with many cases surfacing even before the initial enthusiasm had waned. Prior to the creation of the compliance machinery in New Orleans, the Association of Commerce received reports of dozens of cases that it later presented to the various NRA boards for disposition. Postmaster E. K. Lange in Atlanta lamented as early as August, 1933, that while he was issuing hundreds of insignias daily, he suspected that area businesses breached the letter and spirit of the agreements. A mass forfeiture of emblems, however, did not occur immediately. Not until December did the first establishment in Atlanta, the Blue Boar Cafeteria, have its blue eagle withdrawn. Scores of removals followed shortly thereafter, in Atlanta and elsewhere.[13]

ter Papers, Box 77, Tennessee State Archives and History, Nashville; Memphis *Press Scimitar*, September 19, 1933.

11. Dr. Arthur S. Libby and Mrs. P. J. McGovern to Atlanta Civic Organizations, October 14, 1934, and T. L. Byrd to McGovern, December 10, 1934, both in NRA, General Correspondence; Atlanta *Journal*, August 7, 1934.

12. Dillard B. Lasser Job Description Analysis, September 12, 1934, in NRA, Personal Administration; New Orleans *Times-Picayune*, July 13, 1934.

13. New Orleans *Times-Picayune*, August 20, 1933; Atlanta *Constitution*, August 4, December 14, 1933.

The incidence of violations, combined with the inability of the compliance machinery to adjust the increasing volume of complaints, seriously undermined the NRA's goal of harmonizing production and consumption. Despite community pressure, signing the codes was voluntary, with the result that infractions often were the rule and not the exception. As 1934 neared an end, the number of cases reaching Washington, D.C., from state bureaus forced the creation of a new bureaucratic level. In December, a series of regional compliance agencies opened, acting as intermediaries between state and federal units. Federal spokesmen called the change a decentralization of procedures.[14]

Even with a new bureau, an avalanche of cases continued, especially in the Southeast. In March, 1935, the regional office in Atlanta received each week more new cases than five of its eight counterparts and ranked second in the number of unadjusted cases carried over from week to week. Of those complaints that reached the regional level—only 5 percent of all cases reported in the region—many originated in the larger cities. About 25 percent of the southeastern office's first four hundred cases were charges against employers in Atlanta, Birmingham, Memphis, and New Orleans. Clearly the NRA began to falter in the cities as soon as it did anywhere else, despite the presence of administrative offices there.[15]

The complex procedure through which all complaints traveled limited NRA efforts. From the local level, a charge went to the state office, then to the legal adviser, and from there to a field investigator, who handled as many as sixty cases weekly. All recommendations then moved to the state compliance director for approval, and if the matter remained unsettled, the regional board was next in line. If still not resolved, the national council or the courts were the final step. The completion of any case required months, especially as case loads increased. An additional problem was that the majority of cases involved small firms whose owners could not always afford a long trip for either a state or a regional board hearing, even in their own defense. Of the 351 inquests conducted by the southeastern unit through early May, 1935, only 71 defendants were represented, and more than two-thirds of those were from Georgia, 30 from Atlanta.[16]

14. Atlanta *Georgian*, November 23, 1934; *Blue Eagle*, November 19, 1934.
15. W. L. Mitchell to A. Steve Nance, December 7, 1934 (Personal Administration), J. H. Ward to Mitchell, April 3, 1935 (Samuel Ewing File), Lists of Regional Cases to Region IV Compliance Division, n.d. (General Correspondence), all in NRA.
16. Weekly Reports from State Legal Advisers, n.d., Reuben Martin to Phillip E. Buck, May 15, 1935 (Reuben Martin File), Arthur B. Hammond to Mitchell, March 4, 1935, Field Adjuster's Report, Georgia, April 13, 1935, Noel R. Beddow to Mitchell, May

The fundamental weakness of the compliance machinery was its inability or unwillingness to penalize violators. The NRA won a few court battles, but those in noncompliance generally faced only public scorn and the possible forfeiture of their blue eagles. And as the number of violations increased, adjusters became reluctant to recommend the maximum penalty. In the New Orleans and Atlanta hotel trade, for example, officials hesitated to penalize violators because so few hotels statewide were in compliance. Adjusters found it inconsistent to remove one insignia while dozens of other violators continued to display it. The result was that some employees displayed eagles regardless of compliance rulings, while others, such as Adler and Sons' Jewelers in New Orleans, surrendered their emblems voluntarily and asked that new ones not be sent. Still others took the position of the New Orleans Steamship Association and found it unnecessary to sign a code at all.[17]

The textile industry best exemplified noncompliance in the cities and throughout the South. Manufacturers in the scattered company towns rarely adhered to the codes, and even in the larger urban areas, the textile statute was defunct in almost all plants by 1935. Conditions in the Lane Mills in New Orleans were representative. Owned by antilabor zealot Sigmund Odenheimer, the firm began flying the blue eagle in July, 1933. Almost immediately, labor leaders brought charges of noncompliance against the textile boss, who after signing the NRA pledge altered wages of paid apprentices from $0.06 per hour for a 56-hour week to $0.20 to $0.30 an hour for an 18-hour week. At the same time, he raised weekly rents for company houses from $2.00 to $3.00, and as insurance that workers would live in the dilapidated homes, he ordered the automatic subtraction of rents from paychecks. Furthermore, instead of hiring first-year employees at higher wages when their apprenticeships terminated, the plant discharged them to make room for new, cheaper laborers. Eventually, Odenheimer lost his eagle, although his firm continued to obtain and profit from government contracts.[18]

11, 1935 (Administrative Records), Mitchell to State Directors, n.d. (General Correspondence), all in NRA.

17. Ewing to Mitchell, March 7, 1935 (John Grigsby File), Mitchell to Martin, March 8, 1935 (General Correspondence), Hammond to Mitchell, March 28, 1935 (Complaint Records), Southern Master Printers to Frank Healy, May 3, 1935 (Samuel Ewing File), all in NRA; New Orleans *Times-Picayune*, May 9, 1934, February 27, 1935; Birmingham *Labor Advocate*, June 16, 1934.

18. Alexander Kendrick, "Huey Long's Revolution," *Nation*, August 22, 1934, p. 208; New Orleans *Times-Picayune*, July 17, 20, 31, 1933; *Federationist* (New Orleans), January 25, 1935; C. C. Boggs to Bruce Hall, March 5, 1935 (Administrative Records),

Big-business control of code authorities and the compliance machinery further contributed to the NRA's ineffectiveness while demoralizing the hundreds of smaller employers. The largest firms could either afford the established wage guidelines or else maintain sufficient leverage with enforcement personnel to conceal offenses regarding pay scales, bogus company unions, or general working conditions. The system allowed many large employers to pay wages lower than those they were actually able to pay and still appear to be "doing their part." In the Birmingham area, for example, a key figure on the local textile board was Donald Comer, whose family owned Avondale Mills in Jefferson County. Comer helped police the textile industry despite the well-known fact that in his own plant he had "instructed his brothers and foremen to fight to the last ditch any attempt to organize his mills." The large Birmingham industrial interests also influenced the state compliance unit, which according to the state NRA director often caused field adjusters to circumvent the Alabama bureau because of "the inability and uncertainty of our securing their services."[19]

Additional obstacles to NRA efforts were the many code exemptions granted to employers. As of October, 1933, the Memphis office had received more than one hundred applications for exemptions and had rejected only six. Furthermore, codes did not cover professionals, government employees, agricultural workers, domestics, or commission merchants. According to the Alabama NRA office in early 1935, the public was perceiving a "lack of any real prosecution." The state director ultimately concluded that "American business has not advanced to the stage whereby it can and will govern itself fairly and squarely for all concerned."[20]

If the NRA treated employers unequally, very early it also turned a deaf ear to labor. Regional labor officials located in New Orleans and Atlanta, for example, quickly demonstrated that they would be as sterile as the business-dominated compliance machinery was cumber-

telegram, Hammond to Compliance Division, June 6, 1935, memorandum, J. A. Fowler to Mitchell, June 6, 1935 (General Correspondence), all in NRA.

19. W. O. Hare to Thomas McMahon, September 25, 1934, in Alabama Federation of Labor Files, Drawer 30, Alabama AFL-CIO Office, Birmingham; John D. Petree to Ward, August 15, 1935 (Administrative Records), Survey of Cases Brought Before the Regional Compliance Council, n.d. (Reuben Martin File), Lists of Industries with Code Authority Jurisdiction, n.d., Ward to Mitchell, February 18, 1935 (General Correspondence), all in NRA; George B. Tindall, "The 'Colonial Economy' and the Growth Psychology: The South in the 1930's," *South Atlantic Quarterly*, LXIV (Autumn, 1965), 467–78.

20. Petree to Ward, August 15, 1935 (Administrative Records), memorandum, R. S. Beach to Regional Offices, March 13, 1935, John Grigsby to Ewing, April 5, 1935 (Reuben Martin File), all in NRA.

some and unfair. Both parties in either bargaining or wage disputes had to request federal assistance and be amenable to arbitration, and in a conflict wherein the employer had not signed a code, the regional labor units generally refused to offer their services at all. Of course arbitration ensured neither rapid nor impartial action; many labor officials were less than enthusiastic for labor's cause. According to the confidential report of one New Orleans investigator:

> The chairman of the Regional Labor Board is anomaly. Evidently he is committed sincerely to enforcement of codes and to *employed* labor in respect to hours and wages, but declares that 70% of unemployed would not work if it had a chance. Evidently believes that industrialists should be accepted by labor as its protector since organized industry provides its means and livelihood. Says "won't works" might as well be shot but admits he actually doesn't mean that. As to the possibility of employables returning to industry should normal production resume, he has given no thought and doesn't know what could be done.[21]

As for organizational efforts in 1933 and 1934, the small urban craft unions recorded a few victories, while industrial unionism generally lagged behind. In the Fisher body (Chevrolet) plant in Atlanta, for example, the AFL's United Automobile Workers (UAW) successfully promoted its union over a company organization, although the drive included only craftsmen, neglecting the unskilled, who were in the majority. It was significant that local, conservative labor leaders led the campaign—men who, according to the Atlanta *Constitution*, held cooperation between employers and employees in high regard. Craft unions in Memphis were likewise active, and by May, 1934, eighteen new organizations had formed there. A handful of existing unions, moreover, found that section 7(a) of the National Industrial Recovery Act resulted in more favorable contracts. One such case was the settlement in 1934 of the longstanding Georgia Power strike and lockout.[22]

The failure to include blacks regardless of occupational status limited urban craft union gains. Only in jobs wherein Negroes outnumbered whites, such as in the railroad yards or in some coalfield occupations, were blacks more than marginally involved in city trade councils. Under NRA guidelines, the AFL appointed B. C. Baskerville of Atlanta as its organizer among blacks in the Southeast. Yet the urban

21. Elmer Scott, Confidential Report on New Orleans, Louisiana, April 12, 1934, in Marion Alcorn to Williams, April 14, 1934, in FERA, Louisiana File. Also see Atlanta *Constitution*, October 24, 1933, Atlanta *Daily World*, March 2, 1934; Atlanta *Journal of*
22. Atlanta *Constitution*, July 30, 1933; Atlanta *Journal of Labor*, January 25, April 13, July 27, August 17, 1934; Memphis *Labor Review*, May 25, August 3, September 14, 1934; Memphis *Press Scimitar*, September 29, October 6, 1933; Birmingham *News*, September 1, 1933; Birmingham *Labor Advocate*, December 9, 1933.

crafts were disinclined to enforce antidiscrimination clauses previously written into their charters. Taking their cue from AFL president Green, as well as from municipal authorities who favored the current socioeconomic and political order, southern urban locals even supported racial wage differentials in order to keep their organizations "lily white."[23]

The only significant victory for industrial unionism under NRA guidelines occurred in the Alabama coalfields. In mid-1933, William Mitch and William Dalrymple of the United Mine Workers (UMW) launched a drive in Birmingham to attract the more than twenty-five thousand area miners into their organization.[24] A disastrous strike in 1908 had rendered the UMW inactive in the Alabama fields, and revival efforts during and after World War I had met with much resistance. Conditions in 1933 were different. Dissatisfaction among unemployed miners was intense, and Mitch and Dalrymple led an organized, well-financed effort. The two encountered few problems among the miners, as both blacks and whites flocked into the organization. The racial strife that had divided miners for years was in part overcome by the UMW "formula," which stipulated that blacks, who represented 60 percent of all miners, fill a number of administrative offices in each local. When employers proved unreceptive to the union's presence, the UMW called a series of strikes in early 1934 to force the companies to bargain collectively and negotiate an acceptable contract. Violence marked the struggle, during which twenty thousand employees remained off the job.

Most Birmingham area operators reluctantly signed with the UMW in May, including the powerful TCI's captive mines. Wage settlements in the contract did not equal the NRA coal scale in Pennsylvania or in West Virginia, but union recognition was the key demand in this first battle. Taking advantage of their new strength, the mine workers walked out again in the fall, this time winning slight wage increases.

The UMW's success, however, did not establish a trend among

23. Atlanta *Daily World*, November 7, 1933; Marshall, *Labor in the South*, 184; Cayton and Mitchell, *Black Workers*, 323, 328; Raymond Wolters, "Closed Shop and White Shop: The Negro Response to Collective Bargaining, 1933–1935," in Milton Cantor (ed.), *Black Labor in America* (Westport, 1969), 139–52.

24. Information on Birmingham mine workers from Marshall, *Labor in the South*, 143–44; Cayton and Mitchell, *Black Workers*, 322–23; Herbert R. Northrup, *Organized Labor and the Negro* (1944; rpr. New York, 1971), 162–63; Dorothy Siegel, "The Growth of Coal and Steel Unions in Two Companies in Birmingham, Alabama, 1919–1944" (Typescript in Birmingham Public Library, 1969), 26–40; New York *Times*, April 6–7, 17, 19, 1934; Birmingham *Labor Advocate*, January 17, November 25, 1933, March 17, April 7, 21, May 5, 1934; Birmingham *Post*, August 8, 1934.

major southern industries. In Birmingham, efforts by the AFL's Amalgamated Association of Iron, Tin and Steel Workers and the International Union of Mine, Mill and Smelter Workers gained nothing. Mill owners deterred organizational drives by evicting employees from low-rent company houses, by calling commissary accounts due, and by influencing local relief officials to deny aid to strikers. Furthermore, many company unions remained active, such as TCI's Brotherhood of Captive Mine Workers and the segregated locals of the New Orleans Steamship Association, established explicitly to combat section 7(a) of the National Industrial Recovery Act. The latter blocked a legitimate ILA campaign on the Crescent City waterfront in 1935 and, indicative of William Green's conservatism, later gained recognition from national AFL leadership.[25]

Affecting both urban and rural areas, organized labor's greatest disappointment under section 7(a) occurred in the textile industry. The AFL's United Textile Workers (UTW) opened an organizational campaign in 1934 throughout the South. Organizers were active in the Lane plant in New Orleans, in the Avondale Mills in Birmingham, and in the many smaller operations in Atlanta and Memphis. Urban textile employers joined a general strike in August and September, 1934, and like their counterparts in southern mill villages, confronted hostile employers, company goons, and unsympathetic units of the National Guard.[26] Governor Eugene Talmadge declared martial law in Georgia, and many striking Atlanta textile workers found themselves imprisoned in the governor's special concentration camps.

When the UTW abruptly terminated the strike in September, strikers had nothing to show for their efforts. NRA labor officials had been totally ineffective, managing to extract only verbal promises from a few owners to rehire their employees and improve working conditions in their mills. In Atlanta, workers became so disillusioned that many stopped payment of union dues, which hurt the weak labor cause even more.

25. Birmingham *News*, January 17, June 13, 1934; C. L. Pequess to Harry Hopkins, December 1, 1933, Nels Anderson to Thad Holt, August 9, 1934, Albert Jacobs to Hopkins, November 21, 1934, all in FERA, Alabama File; New Orleans *Times-Picayune*, May 19, 1934; Kendrick, "Huey Long's Revolution," 208; Herbert R. Northrup, "The New Orleans Longshoremen," *Political Science Quarterly*, LVII (December, 1942), 533–36.

26. Information on the textile strike from Alexander Kendrick, "Alabama Goes on Strike," *Nation*, August 29, 1934, pp. 233–34; Birmingham *Labor Advocate*, October 20, 1934; James A. Hodges, "The New Deal Labor Policy and the Southern Cotton Textile Industry, 1933–1941" (Ph.D. dissertation, Vanderbilt University, 1963), 261–98; Jackson Trade and Labor Council to McAlister, October 8, 1924, in Hill McAlister Papers, Box 81; Atlanta *Constitution*, September 3, 7–8, 17–25, 1934; Atlanta *Journal of Labor*, December 14, 1934.

The NRA's endorsement of sectional wage differentials further weakened its relationship with organized labor. The matter had special relevance for city wage earners, as urban living costs were higher than regional costs in general and not much below levels reported in similar-size cities located outside of the South. Still, administrators allowed southern employers to amend codes with wage scales below those paid for comparable work in other areas of the country. NRA-approved wages for Birmingham coal operators, as set by General Hugh Johnson, area mine owners, and UMW leadership, were 20 percent below those called for in the Appalachian Agreement, which governed wage scales in the coal industry nationwide. Even the pay increase won as a result of UMW efforts in Birmingham in September, 1934, left sectional differentials intact. And while wage scales in manufacturing employment increased twice as fast in the South as outside of the South between 1933 and 1936—narrowing wage gaps somewhat—more than half of all southern wage earners, including many urban workers, still earned less than one thousand dollars annually.[27]

The NRA codes also left unattended a number of injustices dealt to black wage earners. Some employers, for example, listed blacks as part-time or else elevated them to the title of executive. All codes exempted both categories from coverage. Other firms simply conformed to wage increases on paper only, and when blacks opened their pay envelopes, they discovered few if any additional dollars. Notes such as "this is all we can pay and remain in business," often accompanied paychecks, and in some cases, foremen demanded kickbacks and then intimidated employees in order to keep company chiseling from detection. Throughout the South, moreover, chambers of commerce and elected municipal leaders supported the continuation of both sectional and racial differentials as "regional advantages" in their quest for new manufacturing. Civic elites in Atlanta argued that blacks should prefer differentials to outright displacement.[28]

27. Lumpkin, *The South in Progress*, 169–70; H. M. Douty, "Recovery and the Southern Wage Differential," *Southern Economic Review*, IV (January, 1938), 314–21; Petree to Ward, August 15, 1935, in NRA, Administrative Records; Birmingham *Post*, August 29, 1933; Birmingham *Southern Labor Review*, October 4, 1933; New York *Times*, April 6–7, 23, 1934; Douty, "Recovery and the Southern Wage Differential," 320–21; "Southern Industrial Council Report," *Bulletin of the Southern States Industrial Council* (June, 1936); Donald S. Howard, *The W.P.A. and Federal Relief Policy* (New York, 1943), 768.

28. Edward A. Gaston, Jr., "A History of the Negro Wage Earner in Georgia, 1890–1940" (Ph.D. dissertation, Emory University, 1957), 409–11; *Crisis*, XLI (October, 1934), 300; Atlanta *Daily World*, September 28, 1933; Michael S. Holmes, "The Blue Eagle as 'Jim Crow Bird': The NRA and Georgia's Black Workers," *Journal of Negro History*, LVII (July, 1972), 278–80.

Charges that employers were denying blacks their rights under the codes swamped urban Negro leaders almost before the NRA became operable. The result was the creation of special investigative councils in each of the cities in question, often directed by Urban League offices, seeking redress and restitution from enforcement authorities. Occasionally, blacks won favorable judgments through the compliance machinery or wage restitution through the courts, but most confronted outright prejudice or the unwillingness of officials to enforce decisions. By mid-1934, the black press, which had initially supported the NRA, was interpreting its initials as standing for the "Negro Removal Act." The resignation of Atlantan Forrester B. Washington from the Federal Emergency Relief Administration (FERA) in late 1934 was the direct result of findings that blacks were steadily appearing on relief rolls as displacement in the private sector increased, the NRA codes notwithstanding. Washington returned home and was responsible for rejuvenating the local office of the NAACP.[29]

A number of black workers indeed discovered that blue eagles brought unemployment rather than pay raises and job security. The frequency of the problem varied according to industry and location; in Birmingham, according to Jesse O. Thomas of the Urban League, blacks were "frantic and helpless." Hiring agents in the steel mills there openly preferred white labor to the prospect of increasing the pay of blacks. NAACP investigators confirmed Thomas' assessment, with one national official concluding that "the promise of NRA to bring high wages and increased employment to industrial workers has glimmered" because "from the beginning relatively few Negroes were even theoretically covered by the NRA labor provisions."[30] Reports of whites moving into employment fields that were previously the domain of blacks were also common, even if not always appreciated by tradi-

29. Atlanta *Daily World*, August 27, September 5, November 9, 1933; *Louisiana Weekly*, December 4, 1934; Atlanta Urban League Report, October 6, 1933, in National Urban League Records, Box A-38, Library of Congress; Gaston, "A History of the Negro Wage Earner," 408; Mitchell to L. J. Martin, April 12, 1935, in NRA, Administrative Records; Rolling Chambliss, "What Some Negro Newspapers of Georgia Say About Some Social Problems, 1933" (M.A. thesis, University of Georgia, 1934), 57.

30. John P. Davis, A Brief Note on the Negro and the New Deal, n.d. (Box A-48), Thomas to T. Arnold Hill, September 21, 1933 (Box A-40), both in National Urban League Records. Also see Evan A. Ford to Mitchell, March 24, 1935, and Petree to Ward, August 15, 1935, both in NRA, Administrative Records; Charles A. J. McPherson to Walter White, October 10, 1933, Records of the National Association of Colored People, Box C-2, Library of Congress; Herbert R. Northrup, "The Negro and Unionism in the Birmingham, Ala., Iron and Steel Industry," *Southern Economic Journal*, X (July, 1943), 29. That the NRA benefited blacks in some ways is discussed in Holmes, "The Blue Eagle as 'Jim Crow Bird,'" 280–81; Raymond Wolters, *Negroes and the Great Depression: The Problem of Economic Recovery* (Westport, 1970), 147, 153–55.

tionalists. When white women in Birmingham took jobs as laundresses during a 1934 strike, for example, the Valentine's Day issue of the puritanical *Southern Labor Review* cried out angrily that the notion of the southern woman on the pedestal "has been rudely smashed to smithereens."[31]

Thus, well before the Schechter decision ending the NRA in May, 1935, compliance with the agency's codes had generally collapsed throughout the South. In fact, two federal court cases involving southern firms had put enforcement of the NRA codes on hold three months prior to the final judicial order. The Belcher case in Alabama had resulted in a decision against the NRA, and many interpreted the case's withdrawal from the courts as an admission of defeat. Recovery officials lamented that an "increasing number of complaints remain unadjusted" because the "effect of the withdrawal of the Belcher case has been devastating in this region." Also in March, 1935, *U.S.* v. *Hammond Box Car Company*, involving a New Orleans company, resulted in the federal district court's striking down the entire National Industrial Recovery Act. The case was still on appeal when the Schechter decision was handed down. According to one regional litigation attorney following the decision in the Hammond case, "We are plodding along. . . . looking forward to a Supreme Court decision, or a new law or an extension of the old one."[32]

During the NRA's fading months, its once overwhelming urban support collapsed. Not one major newspaper bemoaned its passing; in fact, the largest dailies celebrated the Schechter ruling. In general, concluded the Atlanta *Constitution*, NRA provisions had "retarded the return of prosperity and blocked business in its efforts to return to normal conditions." The New Orleans *Times-Picayune* indicated as well that the Schechter decision would "promote the nation's march toward progress by keeping its methods and processes sound and on the constitutional path along which we have marched safely and on the whole prosperously for nearly a century and a half."[33] The black press voiced similar sentiments. The Atlanta *Daily World* commented that while the recovery act was a "praiseworthy concept," it proved "little

31. Birmingham *Southern Labor Review*, February 14, 1934.

32. Mitchell to L. J. Martin, April 24, 1935 (Administrative Records), Grigsby to Crocket Owen, March 4, 1935 (John Grigsby File), Fred Koening to Ewing, March 9, April 1, 1935, Ewing to Owen, March 6, April 4, 1935, Grigsby to Ewing, May 18, 1935 (Samuel Ewing File), all in NRA; New Orleans *Times-Picayune*, March 7, 1935.

33. Atlanta *Constitution*, March 1, May 29, 1935; New Orleans *Times-Picayune*, August 27, 1934, February 21, May 29, 1935. The more moderate city newspapers agreed that the NRA had been ineffective but called for a new recovery mechanism to replace the departed "blue eagle." See Memphis *Press Scimitar*, May 7, 11, 1935; Atlanta *Journal*, May 20, 1935; Birmingham *Post*, May 28, 1935.

more than a scrap of paper." Only the labor press, which represented the local crafts, protested the Supreme Court decision. The Birmingham *Labor Advocate* suggested that "on the whole the NRA was of much benefit to the citizens of the United States," despite its being no cure-all. The Memphis Trades Council even went on record in 1935 favoring a two-year extension of the recovery act as written.[34]

By evading codes whenever possible, most employers had long expressed their hostility toward the NRA, and most rejoiced when it was dissolved. By 1935, the Southern States Industrial Council, an organization of manufacturers opposed to the NRA, had become a vocal force throughout the South. Led by urban industrialists such as John Edgerton of Memphis, the council criticized government involvement in industrial affairs and especially condemned section 7(a) of the recovery statute. In early 1935, Edgerton's group distributed more than six hundred questionnaires to southern businesses, and more than 75 percent of those polled declared that the NRA had to go. Even United States Senator Kenneth McKellar of Memphis, a New Deal stronghold, believed the recovery statute to be constitutionally as well as practically unsound. Now or later, said McKellar, the government would have to remove itself from the marketplace.[35]

While the Schechter ruling triggered wage reductions and price wars in some industries, a number of urban businesses initially declared their intentions to continue the codes voluntarily. No doubt the buying public's favor was a strong incentive; so for a short time a few conspicuous provisions, such as those concerning wages, hours, and prices, apparently remained unchanged in a number of urban establishments, with blue eagles remaining on display. But such was not the case for long, for as accurately forecast by the New Orleans *Item*: "This [voluntary adherence] would be fine if it could be accepted as assurance of more or less general operation along the same line for the time being. Unfortunately it can't. For even though nine-tenths of the operators in an industry adopted this course, the few who did not would undercut them in competition that they would have to meet."[36]

In the summer and early fall of 1935, W. P. Robert of the Washing-

34. Atlanta *Daily World*, May 29, 1935; Birmingham *Labor Advocate*, June 1, 1935; copy of a resolution adopted by Atlanta typographers, June 3, 1935, in Atlanta Typographical Union No. 48 Papers, Southern Labor Archives, Georgia State University, Atlanta.

35. McKellar to R. G. Morrow, n.d., Kenneth D. McKellar Papers, Box 329, Memphis Public Library, Downtown Branch; Minton, "The New Deal in Tennessee," 134–36; Lumpkin, *The South in Progress*, 170–71.

36. New Orleans *Item*, June 6, 1935. Also see Beddow to Mitchell, June 25, 1935, Mitchell to Beddow, June 28, 1935, John L. Hynds to Mitchell, June 3, 1935, Ira C. Evans to Mitchell, July 6, 1935, Mitchell to L. J. Martin, June 10, 1935 (General Correspondence),

ton, D.C., NRA office canvassed major urban manufacturers to determine the incidence of adherence to the old codes. Robert discovered that between 75 and 90 percent of all southern urban employers believed that they had benefited somewhat from the NRA. Furthermore, a small number were even amenable to the idea of new codes, providing that labor provisions were excluded. Only Alabama manufacturers had been supportive of new codes in surveys conducted earlier that summer.[37]

But the Robert survey also revealed a strong sense of apathy among most businessmen. According to state offices, voluntary adherence to the codes was dead, and there was little substantial sentiment "for revival of NRA with all of its mistakes, clouded issues and bad administration." Indeed, the Tennessee legislature in late summer defeated a state recovery act that proponents had modeled on the federal statute. Since May, 1935, the economy had shown gradual improvement, thereby minimizing support for a remodeled administration.[38]

The NRA had mixed results for the urban South. Initially, the blue eagle was psychologically significant in all cities. Under President Hoover, cooperation among employers and voluntarism in the private sector had achieved little, while under the NRA, businesses and shopkeepers, as well as consumers, recovered a measure of hope that hard times had devastated some time ago. Unfortunately, a number of circumstances, including code exemptions and wholesale violations, blunted other positive NRA effects. The narrowing of sectional wage gaps in some industries was perhaps the only benefit provided by the NRA in the short run.[39]

Furthermore, the industrial codes seemed to have little to do with the gradual economic recovery that began during their abbreviated existence. By mid-1934, for example, retail sales in the urban South had increased by 25 percent over the previous year. By 1935, construction had improved, bankruptcies were fewer in number, fewer businesses were failing, and new plants were opening while others were

---

Mitchell to Amos A. Fries, June 27, 1937 (John Grigsby File), all in NRA; Memphis *Press Scimitar*, May 29, August 29, 1935; Atlanta *Journal*, May 29, 1935.

37. Beddow to Mitchell, July 3, 1935 (Personal Administration), Ward to Mitchell, August 20, 1935, Joseph Winkers to Lasseter, October 24, 1935, Mitchell to W. M. Gavin, October 31, 1935 (General Correspondence), all in NRA.

38. Beddow to Cornelius Cochran, August 1, 1935 (Personal Administration), Recovery Administration Questionnaire, August 16, 1935, Mitchell to George L. Berry, October 24, 1935 (General Correspondence), all in NRA; National Emergency Report No. 37, n.d., in McKellar Papers, Box 329.

39. H. M. Douty, "Recovery and the Southern Wage Differential," 317.

expanding. TCI, for example, was engaged in a $29 million expansion project in Birmingham.[40] But general recovery would prove slow and erratic, and the number of jobless people remained alarmingly high for years thereafter. Southern urban areas in the mid-1930s were laboring under unmanageable relief burdens, and even the federal government's unprecedented network of relief agencies was not reaching all of the needy. Thus, as the blue eagle fell from its perch, thousands were still in need of employment and other help in the depressed private sector.

40. Hon, *Memphis, Its Economic Position*, 21; Atlanta *Constitution*, December 12, 1935; Atlanta *Journal*, May 17, 1935; Atlanta Chamber of Commerce, *Facts and Figures About Atlanta, 1935* (Atlanta, 1936), 22–24; Birmingham *News*, October 15, 1935; Kuniansky, "A Business History," 131.

 4

THE LAUNCHING OF FEDERAL RELIEF

For the majority of the jobless in the southern cities, the thought of seeking assistance was an unhappy prospect at best. Many were first- or second-generation urban residents who believed that public relief, no matter its source, was necessary only for those unable to work. The predominance of a "rugged individualist" work ethic throughout the region had precluded the establishment of local welfare commissions in both cities and small towns in the past. And because traditional attitudes change slowly, a sense of defeat and frustration characterized more than a few relief applicants in the 1930s, despite their desperate economic situations.

The family provider, or other individual in need in 1933, usually turned for aid to the local office of the FERA, the first of the many New Deal relief agencies. He arrived at relief headquarters only to find scores of once-proud men standing in line in front of him. Once summoned for an interview, he took a seat in a small room, subdivided into individual carrels, where a caseworker listened sympathetically to his story and then added his name to the relief rolls. As he turned to leave, the sight of others about to undergo the same humiliation must have caused pause for thought. Most had never known anything but wage labor. Now as relief applicants, as one student of the New Deal has concluded, they "sat in the waiting rooms, typical 'poor whites,' defeated first by the old plantation system and again by the transplantation system—the slump in the new industry." Their timid appearances formed "painful contrasts to the social workers, bright fresh-colored college girls trooping in at the end of the day's work like beings of a . . . new social order."[1]

1. Holmes, "The New Deal in Georgia," 85.

Organized in May, 1933, one month prior to the NRA, the FERA set a precedent of federal involvement in unemployment assistance that remains part of national policy today. New Dealers designed the relief network to complement recovery and to care temporarily for the needy, at least until former jobholders found new positions in the private sector. Ultimately replaced in 1935, and officially ended in 1937, the FERA for two years directed the nation's relief. Responsibilities included work relief, direct aid, transient care, and a host of special programs.

The failure of local, state, and even early federal efforts to provide adequately for the jobless and other indigents clearly demonstrated a need for a "new deal" in public relief. No doubt the cities were special cases, caring for their own as well as for migrants who arrived daily in search of work, including temporary public employment, or at least assistance from surplus food distribution centers. But by 1933, most municipal relief agencies were relying solely on limited RFC funding, and in Memphis, for example, RFC-sponsored projects accommodated fewer than one-third of those registered for emergency employment, and no one else.[2] This left a majority of the destitute—those persons unable to obtain work assignments or who could not work at all—in desperation. The FERA program thus found increasing numbers of urban southerners willing, however reluctantly, to accept aid; indeed, most of the needy would prove more receptive to federal assistance than they had to local charity, and FERA rolls would climb even higher than previous case loads.

Among the southern cities, the new relief network was most urgently needed in Birmingham and Atlanta. Industrial Birmingham experienced the worst depression effects, and the city had almost 20,000 cases, each representing several individuals, ready for transfer to the FERA in July. In Atlanta, where the economy depended on smaller manufacturing firms in textiles and other products, almost 11,000 cases at midyear were in desperate need. Relief loads steadily increased in both cities and peaked at more than 33,000 in the former and more than 25,000 in the latter. These numbers represented between 25 and 35 percent of the cities' populations—relief percentages well in excess of those in either Detroit (8.5 percent) or New York City (15.5 percent), comparing with the overload in industrial Pittsburgh. Likewise, in New Orleans thousands were jobless and hungry, with the Crescent City relief bureau each month through 1934 recording at least 30,000 cases.[3]

2. Memphis *Press Scimitar,* October 5, 1933.
3. Theodore E. Whiting (comp.), *Final Statistical Report of the Federal Emergency Relief Administration* (1942; rpr. New York, 1972), 177, 179, 235–36; Birmingham *Post,*

Only in Memphis did case loads and relief expenditures remain comparatively low. The peak numbered in excess of 10,000 cases, although between April, 1933, and the same month in 1934, more than 25 percent of the city's 230,000 residents received federal aid at one time or another. Had economic miseries equaled those in Birmingham or Atlanta, Memphis boss Crump, a New Deal supporter, certainly would have used his influence with state and federal authorities for additional funds. But of the major southern cities, Memphis was least affected by the depression, and recovery seemed to begin sooner there. The city did not depend on heavy manufacturing—diverse industry prevailed—and as the river trade increased after 1933, the economy picked up a bit as Memphis served as a market center for a large rural, agricultural region.[4]

Directed by Harry Hopkins, the FERA was a decentralized operation, with Washington, D.C., allocating funds to state bureaus, which in turn channeled them to city and county units. Regional offices supervised the nearly autonomous state emergency relief administrations, established throughout the southern states in the summer of 1933 and generally staffed by those who had handled RFC projects through the now defunct governors' councils. Locally, city and county relief staffs investigated area needs and supervised emergency work projects while distributing direct assistance. The local Emergency Relief Administration (ERA) director in turn represented his subdivision on the executive committee of the state agency.[5]

More importantly, the presence of local ERA personnel in the cities led directly to the organization of municipal boards of public welfare. The first appeared in Birmingham in 1933, followed by one in New Orleans in 1934 and then units in Atlanta and Memphis in 1935. At first, the municipal agencies did little more than direct public funds to private charities; yet one federal investigator concluded that they were

---

May 18, September 13, 1934; Katherine D. Wood and Gladys L. Palmer (comps.), *Urban Workers on Relief: The Occupational Characteristics of Workers on Relief in 79 Cities, May 1934* (2 vols., Washington, D.C., 1934), II, 270; Atlanta Social Welfare Council, *Relief and Service Statistics of Public and Private Agencies in Atlanta and Fulton County, 1934 and 1935* (Atlanta, 1935), 2.

4. Memphis *Press Scimitar*, April 4, 1934; Whiting (comp.), *Final Statistical Report*, 267.

5. Arthur M. Schlesinger, Jr., *The Coming of the New Deal* (Boston, 1959), 267–80, vol. II of Schlesinger, *The Age of Roosevelt*, 3 vols.; Robert Morgan, Sr., "Public Relief in Louisiana from 1928–1960," *Louisiana History*, IV (Fall, 1973), 371; Holmes, "The New Deal in Georgia," 55–62; Tennessee Department of Public Welfare, *First Annual Report . . . June 30, 1939* (Nashville, 1939), 4–5; Minton, "The New Deal in Tennessee," 89; Georgia State Department of Public Welfare, *Report for . . . 1935* (Atlanta, 1936), 81–83.

at least "one indication pointing to [the] assumption of local responsibility."[6] And after 1935, their functions expanded when Washington, D.C., altered its relief strategy and turned over "unemployable cases" to local welfare units. Furthermore, the cities did not dismantle the local agencies when FERA offices closed, nor did they collapse because of a lack of community support, which had forced the termination of Birmingham's first such agency in the previous decade.

In most states, the FERA network remained decentralized throughout its tenure. The same would be true for succeeding federal relief programs, allowing for local discretion in the distribution of public jobs and funds. In Louisiana and in Georgia, however, the threat of political interference in the relief process from anti–New Deal state administrations, led by Huey Long and Eugene Talmadge respectively, made greater federal involvement necessary. The situation in Louisiana had special significance for New Orleans, because in 1933 the showdown between the Kingfish and the city's Old Regulars began anew.

In October, 1933, Hopkins ordered the reorganization of the Louisiana Emergency Relief Administration (LERA), previously established by the Long machine. Regional supervisor Aubrey Williams first fired all of Long's henchmen, including future New Orleans mayor Robert Maestri, and appointed new relief personnel under Birmingham native Harry J. Early. The new arrangement remained until early 1935, when it became evident that the Kingfish had wooed Early into his machine and that relief funds for New Orleans would become entangled in Long's effort to break the Crescent City organization.

Hopkins thus acted a second time. In 1935, he replaced Early with Frank Peterman and federalized the entire Louisiana relief apparatus. Thereafter, Washington, D.C., worked directly with federal personnel, even bypassing a Louisiana legislative statute that required state approval of all federal projects. The result was that throughout 1933 and 1934, the New Orleans ERA unit handled more than one-third of all state relief monies—a figure equal to the proportion of state funds expended by the Birmingham and Atlanta bureaus. New Orleans received more real dollars from the FERA than did any other southern city, and its per-case allocation was higher.[7]

Of course Hopkins never removed local and state politics alto-

6. Elmer Scott, Confidential Report on New Orleans, Louisiana, April 12, 1934, in Marion Alcorn to Williams, April 14, 1934, in Record Group 69, Records of the Federal Emergency Relief Administration, Louisiana File, National Archives, hereinafter cited as FERA.

7. New Orleans *Times-Picayune*, September 19, October 11–12, 1933, April 19, 1935; Patterson, *The New Deal and the States*, 30–31; Whiting (comp.), *Final Statistical Report*, 251, 257; M. J. Miller to Holt, November 13, 1934, in FERA, Alabama File.

gether from the relief process. The New Orleans indigent, for example, applied for assistance through precinct captains (Old Regular patronage), who in turn determined eligibility standards. And when the Kingfish curtailed the flow of state tax revenue to New Orleans in 1935, LERA and local relief officials countered by allowing all unpaid municipal employees to collect public assistance. Politics was responsible as well for the frequent turnover of caseworkers in the Orleans Parish Department of Public Welfare during its formative months. Long and city leaders vied for control of the new agency, with one federal investigator reporting that "any special effort of consequence is the football of politics" because "what seems to be universal in New Orleans" is that "social movements are tested purely on the basis of their political expediency." The same report concluded that many social workers who had given "liberally in time and energy" became so discouraged that they returned to the private sector because the work soon "became drudgery."[8]

Also in Georgia, where Talmadge controlled executive affairs through 1936, political circumstances forced Hopkins to be aware of interference in relief work. The national director, for example, ordered that Georgia Emergency Relief Administration (GERA) director Gay Shepperson supervise federal relief with full decision-making authority in order to circumvent the governor, who led opponents of the New Deal in the Anti-Carpetbagger Association and the Anti-Scalawag League. The stubborn Talmadge naturally opposed the arrangement and seized every opportunity to criticize Shepperson and the entire federal operation. He claimed that the GERA director represented "the importation of yankees into Georgia federal posts" and declared repeatedly that New Dealers "have got it in for the Old South." Evidence showed that 97 percent of GERA personnel lived in Georgia; Shepperson hailed from Virginia. Finally, in May, 1935, Hopkins federalized relief in Georgia as he had in Louisiana. State political interference, therefore, never prevented federal aid from reaching Atlanta's needy— which would have happened had either Talmadge, who harbored no love for cities, or the state legislature, in which rural counties were grossly over represented, gained control.[9]

8. Scott, Confidential Report, in Alcorn to Williams, April 14, 1934, in FERA, Louisiana File. For a more detailed examination of the later WPA period in Louisiana, see Betty M. Field, "The Politics of the New Deal in Louisiana, 1933–1939" (Ph.D. dissertation, Tulane University, 1973).

9. Memorandum, Alana Johnstone to Hopkins, January 19, 1935, in FERA, Georgia File; Holmes, "The New Deal in Georgia," 183–84; Patterson, The New Deal and the States, 137–38; Benjamin Stolberg, "Buzz Windrip—Governor of Georgia," Nation, March 11, 1936, p. 317; New York Times, March 3, 1935; Atlanta Journal, May 19, 21, 1935.

In Atlanta, local relief officials managed relief competently and in a businesslike fashion. The same was true in Birmingham, although perhaps less surprisingly, because that city never faced the threat of outside interference in relief administration. Thad Holt of the Alabama Emergency Relief Administration (AERA) and Shepperson of the GERA were dedicated state directors, which ensured that Jefferson and Fulton county staffs handled funds efficiently for maximum individual and community betterment. The only administrative problem in Birmingham occurred in early 1934, when local business interests attempted to prevent striking miners from obtaining relief. Federal authorities responded by organizing a labor advisory board to prevent discrimination against workers legitimately seeking union recognition. The one general inequity throughout the South was white domination of the early work relief positions. Although blacks accounted for nearly one-third of the population of each of the cities in question and represented 50 percent of the total number of urban unemployed, they usually received the more limited direct assistance payments. Only later, as the private sector improved and put whites back to work, would there be an increase in the percentage of blacks on work relief rolls.[10]

The administration of FERA relief in Tennessee and particularly in its westernmost city was a different story altogether. A political machine dominated affairs in Memphis, but unlike the situation in New Orleans, the Crump organization was not involved in a showdown against a powerful rival. Crump cooperated with federal administrators from the outset and continued to do so throughout the 1930s. The boss named local relief personnel, just as he appointed all municipal employees. His key ally in Washington, D.C., Senator McKellar, clearly intervened in the relief process by firing the Tennessee Emergency Relief Administration (TERA) director for not allowing the agency to take sides in the 1934 elections. But within Shelby County, Crump's power was absolute and unchallenged, and political maneuvers had little direct effect on the relief process. There were some instances of duplicate payrolls and relief payments to persons in private employment, although the Division of Investigation of the Public Works Administration (PWA) in 1934 cleared the city of charges that its work

---

10. E. Foster, Field Report: Birmingham, Alabama, February 2–4, 1934, in FERA, Alabama Field Reports; Williams to Algernon Blair, January 11, 1934, memorandum, Holt to John Darmody, January 25, 1934, Roberta Morgan to Loula Dunn, May 9, 1934, all in RG 69, Records of the Civil Works Administration, Alabama File, NA, hereinafter cited as CWA; Gaston, "A History of the Negro Wage Earner," 357; Atlanta *Daily World*, January 5, 1934; Joseph A. Pierce, *The Negro: A Collection of Data on the Negro Population of Atlanta, Georgia* (Washington, D.C., 1940), 89–92.

relief foremen were demanding kickbacks from relief labor. More noteworthy, there was no evidence that ERA funds became tools to influence votes, in Memphis or for that matter in New Orleans, probably because of the many nonvoting blacks on relief.[11]

Beginning in late summer, 1933, the unemployed began registering for public works placement, initially through the FERA, and later through the Civil Works Administration (CWA). The CWA opened in November to help temporarily with wage relief because of the fast approach of what would be another "crisis winter." Furthermore, the flow of federal dollars through the several bureaucratic levels had proceeded slowly, causing delays in the parent program, and even the best-organized and best-managed FERA offices had too many kinds of programs to inaugurate too soon. Case loads were rapidly expanding with the simultaneous listing of RFC project transfers, new clients, and those already on relief rolls but previously unassigned. Plans called for a cooperative effort between local and federal authorities in all emergency works. Washington, D.C., financed labor costs while states and municipalities furnished equipment and materials and paid the cost of workmen's compensation insurance. Officials also hoped to supplement relief wages with direct assistance in the form of clothing and surplus commodities.[12]

The CWA established a uniform national wage policy of one dollar per hour for craftsmen and forty cents per hour for the unskilled for a maximum 30-hour week. Officials in the southern cities, however, paid little attention to such rates because wages in the private sector were far lower than those elsewhere. In Birmingham, 85 percent of the 14,000 CWA workers in December, 1933, were earning the "common wage," as skills were disregarded, while the 8,000 CWA workers in Memphis, and also Atlanta's 14,000, never earned more than a rural, regional hourly rate of thirty cents. When the CWA ceased operations in the spring of 1934, moreover, the AERA works division immediately reduced wages and maximum work hours by 20 percent and then wages again by another 50 percent when federal authorities officially approved a "prevailing sectional rate" policy.[13]

11. S. B. Bratton to McAlister, March 1, 1935, in Hill McAlister Papers, Box 83, Tennessee State Archives and History, Nashville; Memphis *Press Scimitar*, February 1, 8–10, 17, 23, April 4, 11, 1934; Overton to Kenneth Markwell, September 15, 1934, and Markwell to Overton, November 20, 1934, both in Mayor's Correspondence File, Drawer 5, Memphis and Shelby County Archives, Memphis; New Orleans *Item*, February 28, 1934.

12. New Orleans *Times-Picayune*, July 15, 26, 1933; Louise Gambill, *The Public Works Program, 1930–1938: Its Benefits to Memphis* (Memphis, 1938), 8.

13. Atlanta *Journal of Labor*, December 8, 1933; Birmingham *Age-Herald*, November 23, 1933; New Orleans *Times-Picayune*, November 19, 1933; Holmes, "The New Deal

Of all the southern cities, New Orleans afforded the best opportunity for emergency employment. Twenty-four thousand CWA
employees there represented one-third of the state's quota. Still, less
than half of those certified for work obtained it, while the Birmingham,
Memphis, and Atlanta relief offices placed less than one-third of those
registered. And beginning in the spring of 1934, when the CWA closed,
opportunities for emergency employment were even fewer. Typical was
the situation in Atlanta, where the GERA allocated a total of one
million dollars for public works between January and November, 1934,
although the CWA had spent almost an equal amount each month
during its four-month tenure. Total CWA spending in the cities ranged
from just over two million dollars in Memphis to a high of nearly four
million dollars in Birmingham. Local relief officials were thus selec-
tive in the placement of clients; applicants in Memphis, although
jobless, were rejected because they owned a radio or held a mortgage or
made an automobile payment.[14]

Despite the cutbacks in 1934, the urban communities genuinely
benefited from the relief labor. Workers in Birmingham constructed
four new sewage plants, repaired miles of sewer lines, improved school
buildings and their playgrounds, remodeled the municipal auditorium, modernized the airport, and graded almost one hundred miles
of roads. In New Orleans, relief workers aided in the expansion of City
Park, the largest in the city, and in the construction of new recreational
sites, including Leman Park. The new facility, located adjacent to a
congested downtown neighborhood, included separate but "roughly
equal" playgrounds for whites and blacks. Also significant were the
beginnings of a new residential area along Lake Pontchartrain and the
restoration of a number of historic buildings in the Vieux Carré
district.[15]

in Georgia," 165–70; Foster, Field Report: Birmingham, Alabama, February 2–4, 1934, in
FERA, Alabama Field Reports; Overton to Crump, January 8, 1934, April 25, 1934, in
Watkins Overton Papers, Box 2, Memphis State University Library; Memphis *Press
Scimitar*, January 13, 1934; Memphis *Commercial Appeal*, November, 1937.

14. Holt to Hopkins, April 14, 1934 (Alabama Administrative Correspondence),
Final Report of the CWA in Louisiana (Final Reports), both in CWA; CWA of Jefferson
County, *Report on the Civil Works Administration in Alabama* (Birmingham, 1934), 6;
Birmingham *Post*, March 10, 1934; Birmingham *News*, August 31, 1934; Memphis *Press
Scimitar*, February 21, March 19, 22, April 2, 1934; Memphis *Labor Review*, May 25,
1934, January 4, 1935; Atlanta *Constitution*, March 18, November 15, 1934; Atlanta
Georgian, March 25, 1934; Atlanta *Daily World*, December 30, 1934; New Orleans *Times-
Picayune*, December 10, 1933, April 1, 1934.

15. Roland R. Pyne to Perry Fellows, May 6, 1935 (Alabama Work Relief), Pyne to
Fellows, May 6, 1935 (Louisiana Work Relief), both in FERA; Henderson, "Public Relief in
Jefferson County," 40–43; Birmingham *Post*, February 16, 1934; Birmingham *News*,
March 25, 1934; New Orleans *Times-Picayune*, December 10, 1933.

Atlanta enjoyed similar benefits, including construction at Chandler Airport and Grady Memorial Hospital, the partial development of ninety-two-acre North Fulton Park, and the remodeling of several schools. But the early relief programs, as had the RFC, rejected as too costly the city's application for a multi-million-dollar sewerage system. ERA offices also supervised garden projects, through which relief gardeners raised vegetables for their own consumption and for direct relief recipients. Statewide, the GERA provided more than four million plants and almost two hundred tons of seed, and through June, 1934, the yield of forty million pounds of produce had reached 200,000 people.[16]

Memphis too realized a large number of construction projects, and like Atlanta, the city had a garden program, transforming 41,000 former cotton acres in the county into more than 50,000 separate gardens. In addition, the Memphis TERA bureau sponsored a malaria control project, which put to work as many as 1,000 men clearing ditches and sewers throughout the city. In 1933, local health officials had estimated that malaria infected at least 10 percent of Shelby County school-children; statistics released a year into the mosquito-control effort showed that malaria deaths had decreased by 35 percent and that the number of active cases had declined by almost half.[17]

Of course there were projects that failed because of bureaucratic delays or mismanagement or both. In mid-1934, the federal government put 45,000 head of cattle on Island Number 37 north of Memphis under TERA jurisdiction as a relief canning plant was being readied in the city. Plans called for the employment of 600 to 1,200 and the distribution of processed meat to direct assistance cases. The slaughtering began on schedule, but delays in plant construction led to the contamination of the first 60,000 pounds of beef, enough to give several pounds to every needy family in Shelby County. Federal investigators also discovered that cattle were dying of starvation as island underbrush choked off all suitable grazing substances. The ill-fated venture lasted only until January, 1935, during which time relief workers canned more than 600,000 pounds of beef but disposed of half of that amount owing to spoilage.[18]

16. Joseph H. Pratt to Fellows, May 9, 1935, in FERA, Georgia Work Relief; Minutes of the Fulton County Commission, V, December 6, 1933, pp. 27–28, Fulton County Commission Office, Atlanta; Atlanta *Constitution*, December 3–5, 12, 20, 28–29, 1933, July 1, 1934; Melvin W. Ecke, *From Ivy Street to Kennedy Center: Centennial History of the Atlanta Public School System* (Atlanta, 1972), 243–44.

17. H. L. Baddoux to Fellows and Martin Brown to Fellows, May 3, 1935, both in FERA, Tennessee Work Relief; Memphis *Press Scimitar*, September 16, November 16, 1933; Memphis *Commercial Appeal*, February 15, 1934, February 27, 1935.

18. Memphis *Commercial Appeal*, August 15, October 6, 1934, January 22, 30,

An important aspect of early federal relief was women's professional projects, directed at first by the Civil Works Service and later by special divisions within ERA offices. Relief employment for women generally involved sewing, nursing, and clerical or, in the case of blacks, domestic labor, with such positions paying between twenty-five and forty-five cents per hour. The program began slowly, for urban residents, as well as relief officials, were initially suspicious about the placement of women on work relief rolls. According to federal officials in the Memphis area, the director of women's work inherited a program in which "most of the quotas are almost if not entirely filled by men." Even in Georgia, where a woman supervised all relief efforts, progress beginning in 1933 was not swift, although the Atlanta area ultimately realized one of the most active white-collar and service relief divisions anywhere in the South. The few hundred at work in late 1933 increased to five hundred within a year, and by June, 1935, the women's force throughout the state numbered in excess of fifteen thousand. Among the most successful undertakings was the Atlanta home visitation program, prompting Shepperson to conclude that "women in America today may be nearer the economic independence of their dreams than at any other period of history."[19] The first women's activities, which included special programs designed for the handicapped, proved so worthwhile that they undoubtedly paved the way for more vigorous social service divisions under later New Deal agencies.

In addition to ERA and CWA jobs divisions, the PWA helped ease urban relief burdens. Established under the National Industrial Recovery Act, and the only part of that statute to escape the effects of the Schechter decision, the PWA funded projects through a combination of grants and loans, setting wage scales equal to prevailing local rates for skilled and unskilled labor. All authority within the program rested at the top despite the opening of state and county PWA offices. PWA hospital and harbor improvement projects employed more than six thousand men in Memphis in 1934, while Birmingham and Atlanta reported about one thousand men each month through 1935 on similar projects. Later in the decade, PWA activities expanded when Secretary of the Interior Harold Ickes reluctantly agreed to fund jointly with the

---

1935; Memphis *Press Scimitar*, January 29, September 20, 25, 1935.

19. Ira Scherrebeck to Ellen S. Woodward, December 25, 1933, in FERA, Tennessee Women's Projects; Memphis *Commercial Appeal*, February 4, 1934; Jane Van De Vrede to Woodward, November 23, December 5, 1934, July 19, 1935 (Georgia Women's Projects), Weber to Woodward, September 10, 1934, Report on Special Projects in Alabama, in Francis Stephenson to Woodward, June 17, 1935 (Alabama Women's Projects), all in FERA; Atlanta *Journal*, January 21, February 16, 1934.

WPA a number of large construction ventures, several beneficial to the southern cities.[20]

Unfortunately, the available ERA and CWA works programs numbered too few to handle demands, especially in the cities. As a result, the unpleasant task of applying for direct assistance faced thousands of urban residents, with the acceptance of meager "charity" being the only alternative. In some counties, where case loads were small, almost all relief recipients earned their assistance checks, but in the cities, ERA allotments for direct relief generally made up from 50 to 75 percent of total monthly expenditures. Between July, 1933, and November, 1935, the five urban counties in Georgia accounted for more than 70 percent of all direct relief payments in the state.[21]

The number of families on direct relief varied monthly. In early 1934, 7,500 cases in Memphis and up to 20,000 in Atlanta and in Birmingham were receiving direct aid, and when the CWA closed in the spring, those figures jumped sharply. Monthly assistance, moreover, was less than could be earned on emergency jobs, although extra clothing, canned food, and fresh vegetables were sometimes available through the Federal Surplus Commodities Corporation or local relief gardens. In Memphis, monthly per-case allotments ranged from about $7.00 for a family of two to $25.00 for a family of eight or more. The other southern cities reported comparable or lower figures—all below the pitifully low national monthly average of $25.43 per family.[22]

Because of chronic unemployment in Birmingham, where local relief officials were described as "tense, tired, and discouraged," that city was selected for a study of the feasibility of public welfare commissaries. The operation of a special dispensary system was

---

20. Overton to Paul V. Betters, June 1, 1935, Betters to Overton, June 3, August 25, 1935 (Drawer 4), Persons Working on PWA and WPA Projects, November 30, 1935–March 5, 1937 (Drawer 7), all in Mayor's Correspondence File; Birmingham *News*, May 21, July 11, 1934; Atlanta *Constitution*, July 25, 1935, October 3, 1937; Holmes, "The New Deal in Georgia," 349–51. In addition to PWA projects, other state and federal special works programs benefited the cities. Included were an RFC-funded Mississippi River bridge construction project in New Orleans; emergency highway work in Birmingham, funded by the Alabama Highway Department; and a handful of projects for the urban jobless relocated in rural counties and camps, funded by the Civilian Conservation Corps and the Tennessee Valley Authority.

21. Georgia Emergency Relief Administration, *Monthly Review of Relief Statistics* (Atlanta, 1935), 10–14, 21.

22. Memphis *Press Scimitar*, January 5, 16, 1934; Atlanta *Constitution*, August 28, November 20, 1933, March 21, 1934; Brooks, *A Half Century of Progress*, 66–68; Alabama Relief Administration, *Two Years of Federal Relief in Alabama* (Wetumpka, Ala., 1935), 45, 54; Henderson, "Public Relief in Jefferson County," 14; Schlesinger, *The Coming of the New Deal*, 294.

unique; similar programs functioned elsewhere only in Cincinnati and Los Angeles. Normally, community retailers filled ERA food orders, but in the test areas, the needy purchased food coupons in one of several area ERA-subsidized warehouses. In Birmingham, the newly created Jefferson County Department of Public Welfare, working with local AERA personnel, staffed the commissaries.

Relief officials favored the new system; store owners did not because they suffered from the loss of direct food orders. Grocers also complained that relief recipients, especially blacks, would come to think that they could obtain free food. The latter possibility, the retailers grumbled, would be detrimental to the community and its thousands of honest, hardworking residents. Others complained that the relief outlets handled inferior produce and that those in charge profited at the expense of the indigent. Yet through 1934, the public dispensaries recorded a monthly business volume of several hundred thousand dollars, proving so successful that the county welfare bureau maintained them after the FERA ended.[23]

Still, direct welfare dollars did not stretch far. FERA benefits were larger and more regular than what the jobless had known in 1932, but demands remained great, as did legitimate needs. Moreover, the program was untried, and much of its local personnel lacked experience in the administration of public assistance.

In addition to the works programs and direct relief, the FERA operated a number of special divisions, perhaps explaining many of the operating delays and other bureaucratic inefficiencies. Accounting for more than 30 percent of a state's ERA budget, special programs included rural rehabilitation, mainly to help small farmers; reemployment efforts for all the jobless; student aid to maintain school enrollment; and emergency education courses to advance adult literacy.[24] Two such programs were particularly noteworthy in southern urban areas—the transient care network and, to a lesser extent, the organization of experimental self-help business cooperatives.

FERA administrators hoped that a self-help program, directed by a separate division within the parent agency, would prove a viable alternative to public relief. But throughout the South, the idea attracted scant attention, except in Alabama. There, the AERA financed seven

23. Aubrey Williams to George Huddleston, June 13, 1934, Dunn to Josephine Brown, October 15, 1934, and Williams, Field Report: Alabama, September 13, 1933, all in FERA, Alabama File; Hugh A. Locke to Jefferson County Department of Public Welfare, September 18, 1934, in James M. Jones, Jr., Collection, Drawer 2, Alabama Archives and History, Montgomery.

24. Whiting (comp.), *Final Statistical Report*, 194, 198, 202, 222.

separate enterprises, including one in its industrial center—the only one in any of the major Dixie cities. Local businessmen, the white-collar jobless, and voluntary relief recipients joined together to use available dollars to remodel an old industrial section of Birmingham. In 1935 they opened a canning plant, a woodworking shop, a blacksmith shop, a barber shop, a beauty parlor, a truck farm, and a cafeteria. Hopes were initially high that the cooperative venture would quickly flourish on its own. The basic principle of all such units was an exchange of labor for subsistence, with goods and man hours being acceptable mediums of exchange.[25]

The constitution of the Birmingham unit, officially called the Alabama Cooperative Industrial Group Number 6 (ACI), declared that participants "shall share in the projects of the association according to the productivity of the enterprise as a whole." Prospective members served a probationary period of three months, "during which time every effort is made to adopt such applicant to his appropriate sphere of capability." Voting members, or those who averaged a minimum of six hours of work each week, constituted the general assembly of the unit and elected a board of directors and other officers. An internal judicial system, complete with judge, prosecutor, and public defender, settled all disputes. The single objective of the nonstock, nonprofit corporation was the acquisition of jobs for members. Dues were simply whatever one had to offer the operation and the donation of forty hours of labor for the benefit of the whole. Members invested no cash, and memberships were not sold.[26]

The first chairman of the Birmingham operation was C. F. Ward. A former "mechanical and efficiency engineer for various big corporations," the Birmingham native was described by FERA officials as a "hard worker and forceful manager" whose "dictatorial trends are tempered by his sincere devotion to the common cause and his very humane desire to rehabilitate the membership." Ward's enthusiasm indeed seemed contagious; he launched ACI Number 6 on an optimistic note with an initial enrollment of three hundred. At first, the project was locally popular, with AERA field inspectors speaking of its ultimate success despite the absence of "positive proof that such will

25. Itjalmar Rutzebeck, Handbook on Self-Help Cooperative Activities, n.d., and Tage Palm, Report on the Inspection of Alabama Self-Help Cooperatives, June 12, 1935, both in FERA, Self-Help Cooperative Division Records, Box 1.
26. Constitution of Alabama Cooperative Industrial Group No. 6, n.d., Palm to Udo Rall, August 12, 1934, and Frank Aaltonen to Rall, August 23, 1935, all in FERA, Self-Help Cooperative Division Records, Box 25.

be the case." Objections came only from craft unions, which charged that cooperative wages would fall below union scales.[27]

The first applicants eagerly donated their mandatory hours of labor, and for every work hour over forty, they received credits redeemable at cooperative stores. The canning plant, which handled produce from AERA gardens and from the ACI's own thirty-acre farm, was the largest employer. Helping the plant was the American Can Company, which provided a free advisory service on canning processes while assisting with the installation of machinery. Within the cooperative, members exchanged goods and services, with stores transacting business for others just like regular retail establishments. By late June, 1935, the membership had increased to 450, with approximately 200 holding jobs at any one time. A uniform wage scale of thirty cents per hour prevailed.

Unfortunately, what began as an ambitious experiment quickly proved a great financial bust. Sufficient capital never circulated within the cooperative, and from the beginning, most establishments failed to turn profits. The AERA, moreover, hesitated to pump thousands of dollars into what proved an unstable operation. Apparently the relief bureau expected immediate success; therefore, it delayed and even withheld funds during the formative period when self-help shops and plants were sure to struggle.

Problems began in July, 1935, when Ward purchased a ten-year lease on a coal mine and involved ACI Number 6 in its largest and most disastrous venture. The cooperative operated the mine at a heavy loss for one year and then abandoned and later subleased it. Most of the members, who were relief clients, also became discouraged when the enterprise failed to redeem their work credits. Furthermore, audits later showed that officials had squandered small amounts of cooperative funds through what the AERA described as the "unbusinesslike handling of petty cash." No prosecutions resulted, but allegations diminished an already foundering reputation.[28]

Conditions and suspicions became so serious that in late 1935 Ward submitted his resignation. The AERA in turn accepted the offer, as administrators had come to believe that only new management, if anything, could save the Birmingham experiment. No doubt Ward's early supervision had been beneficial, but the chairman's business

27. Rall to Palm, June 20, 1935 (Box 1), Aaltonen to Rall, August 23, 1935 (Box 25), both in FERA, Self-Help Cooperative Division Records.

28. Albert Wheelon, Field Report: Alabama Cooperative Industrial Group No. 6, n.d., in Wheelon to Rall, September 4, 1935, and G. R. Parks to Rall, January 21, 1937, both in FERA, Self-Help Cooperative Division Records, Box 25.

sense was not the best, as the mining gamble had clearly indicated. According to the state self-help director, Ward had simply entered too many "foolish contracts and purchases." Even worse, the Birmingham native had slowly developed an "exaggerated ego and his general attitude toward the membership changed to such an extent . . . that working under him became almost impossible."[29] The state director further noted that while experienced management might save the project, federal regulations prohibited the hiring of persons who were not on relief, even if they were experts.

Following Ward's resignation, ACI Number 6 was supervised by two new managers and underwent one major reorganization of stores and departments, all for naught. In fact, indicated one field investigation in early 1936, only the woodshop was providing "an opportunity for employment . . . which can be construed as productive labor" because of its outside contracts with local companies. In general, FERA examiners were far from hopeful. Chief inspector Tage Palm concluded, also in early 1936, that there were "no great hopes for the ultimate success of the Birmingham cooperative from a business standpoint." He went on to say that "the once apparently invincible spirit is badly shaken and that the organization today is without outstanding leadership and lacks faith in the future to an appalling extent." The Birmingham unit struggled on a few months longer, as did projects throughout Alabama and elsewhere in the country, finally ceasing operations when the FERA closed in mid-1937.[30]

One other cooperative experiment was contemplated, likewise in the Birmingham area. Working with the Jefferson County Department of Public Welfare, local relief officials in late 1933 procured a special $1 million federal allocation to fund a "back-to-the-farm" project. At first, it seems, many southerners agreed with the thinking of the Atlanta *Constitution* that "three-fourths of the unemployed in the cities" once resided on farms and that joblessness would be cured only by "the repopulation of the once prosperous agricultural sections of the country."[31] The abundant land surrounding Birmingham and other southern cities no doubt fostered this attitude, although the chances of the successful resettlement of urban residents were not very good.

Project leaders in Birmingham proposed that the abandoned mine

29. Parks to Rall, December 18, 1935 (Box 25), Memorandum and Field Report, n.d., in Eric Orf to Rall, April 24, 1937 (Box 1), all in FERA, Self-Help Cooperative Division Records.

30. Field Report: Birmingham, Alabama, n.d., in Orf to Rall, February 29, 1936, Palm to Rall, March 12, 1936, Rall to Parks, June 11, 1936 (Box 25), Parks to Rall, December 1, 1936 (Box 1), all in FERA, Self-Help Cooperative Division Records.

31. Atlanta *Constitution*, July 8, 19, 1935.

town of Bayview, located four miles from the city, be transformed into an agricultural and industrial community. The detailed plan, which took more than a year to formalize, pointed to Bayview's several thousand acres of wooded hills and tillable farmland and to the number of standing homes and the availability of electric and water facilities. Settlers were to work either on a community farm or in the agricultural manufacturing plant; the AERA was to contribute monetary aid while situating doctors, dentists, and recreation personnel in the town. The ultimate goal was community self-sufficiency.

The only such community designed for a southern urban area never became a reality. A number of AERA bureaucrats were skeptical of collective experiments, causing continual bickering among state and local relief administrators. The idea resurfaced periodically throughout the decade but in the end Bayview remained a blueprint. A number of Atlanta area residents took part in the experimental Pine Mountain Valley rural industrial community, located in Harris County. Opened by the Interior Department through the Georgia Rural Rehabilitation Corporation, and later directed by the Farm Security Administration from 1937 to 1942, the short-lived endeavor ultimately proved impractical in a region committed to a rural, free-enterprise life-style.[32]

The federal transient program was by far the most active of the FERA special divisions in the southern cities. Until 1933, community chest agencies such as the Salvation Army and the Travelers Aid Society cared for the homeless who passed through the urban areas. But as the depression caused increasing numbers of individuals and families to flock to the larger cities in search of assistance, the number of "hobo jungles" and flophouses multiplied, threatening community health and safety. Of twenty-six low-rent hotels (ranging in price from ten to fifteen cents per night) inspected by Birmingham relief officials in mid-1933, only three offered clean linens, while blankets were unwashed, and mattresses and pillows were mildewed in all of them. None had bathing facilities, few were heated, and toilet facilities were inadequate. And with cities throughout America so affected, the need for federal assistance was clear.[33]

In the fall of 1933, as part of the initial 261 centers and 40 camps nationwide, FERA transient divisions opened in each of the southern

32. Morgan to Williams, April 10, 1935, in FERA, Alabama File; Georgia Emergency Relief Administration, *Pine Mountain Valley, Harris County, Georgia* (Atlanta, 1935), 9–84; Paul Conkin, "It All Happened in Pine Mountain Valley," *Georgia Historical Quarterly*, XXXVII (March, 1963), 1–35.

33. Kenneth E. Burnhart, Supplement to a Study of the Transient and Homeless in Birmingham, Alabama, January–July, 1933, in FERA, Alabama Transients; Hannah, "Urban Reaction to the Great Depression," 123.

cities in question. A separate staff within the local ERA office operated a central registration bureau, a medical clinic, a number of shelters for the homeless, a family unit, and a works program, while organizing educational and recreational activities. Especially important was health care; Memphis employed local medical students, and New Orleans hired a full-time physician and staff. At first, single men and women lived in separate dormitories, and families resided in hotels under special contract. Central cafeterias provided meals at an average cost of only a few cents each day per person, although the homeless in Memphis received meal certificates for fifty cents each, redeemable at designated restaurants. Those able to work usually performed small tasks for the city and earned weekly cash allowances of $0.90 to $2.70.[34]

Initial plans called for only the temporary feeding, clothing, and housing of families and individuals before they were sent on their way. But by mid-1935, the problem of overcrowding in the inner-city shelters began to take its toll. By then, Birmingham had handled more than 32,000 cases, while in March of the same year, Memphis was caring for 8,000 individuals and had provided more than 55,000 days of care for unfortunate wanderers—nearly four times more than any of the state's other major municipalities. It seems that Memphis became a haven for the homeless from the entire mid-South area, because no transient center existed either north of Jackson, Mississippi, or east of Little Rock, Arkansas. Special problems also plagued New Orleans because of the large number of unemployed seamen who passed through and who were unhappy about waiting weeks before shipping out again. In early 1934, the Crescent City was caring for more unattached men than any other urban area in the country except Los Angeles. An overflow crisis likewise affected Atlanta when Florida governor David Sholtz in mid-1934 dispatched patrols to his northern border to prevent further transient migration into the Sunshine State. The result was that many Florida-bound transients stayed in Georgia, with many congregating in the larger urban areas.[35]

34. Heber Hiton to Joseph L. Rhodes, September 15, 1933, Hopkins to R. B. Pitley, September 19, 1933, J. K. Byrne to Williams, October 2, 1933 (Louisiana Transients), Hopkins to C. C. Menzler, September 19, 1933, Elizabeth J. Scheiblich to Morris Lewis, October 16, 1933, L. Heiskell to Walter Chandler, February 4, 1935 (Tennessee Transients), Hopkins to Ronald Ransom, October 3, 1933 (Alabama Transients), all in FERA; F. F. Newcomb to [?] Hawkins, May 1, 1935 (Box 36), Keller F. Melton to W. O. Wheary, March 2, 1935, J. A. Flynn to Elizabeth Wickenden, March 12, 1935 (Box 37), Report on the Memphis Transient Bureau, n.d., Helen C. Mawer to William J. Plunkert, June 6, 1934 (Box 52), all in FERA, Federal Transient Bureau Records, hereinafter cited as TBR; Dixie Brooks Jones, "A Study of Twenty Boys Registered with the Atlanta Transient Bureau, May and June, 1935" (M.A. thesis, Emory University, 1935), 4.
35. Henderson, "Public Relief in Jefferson County," 36–37; Scheiblich to Plunkert,

The rapid influx of transients into the cities beginning in 1934 only served to generate public fears, as most communities disliked the nonresidents, who competed with local labor for private and relief work. One critic of the program, the Memphis *Labor Review*, called for the removal of the Memphis center not just from the county but from the state. An uneasiness among locals also surfaced when relief officials first attempted to replace a number of contract hotels with transient camps. In Birmingham in September, 1934, the announcement of a plan to open a camp in Lane Park, located one mile from the city, drew loud and frequent criticism. Citizen groups such as the American Legion argued that inhabitants would use the park stream as a bathroom facility and that the vicinity would be unsafe for women and children who walked through it on their way to and from school. In fact, Birmingham was the city most intolerant of the transient problem, perhaps because of its own depression joblessness. The Jefferson County work relief director was especially uncooperative with transient personnel. He refused to approve cash allowance projects for the homeless, maintaining that "transients were unfitted [*sic*] for work."[36]

Elsewhere, efforts to relocate transients encountered fewer obstacles as crowded inner-city conditions dictated the movement of men and some families into larger camps. But to avoid incidents like that involving Lane Park, administrators located the new facilities on abandoned military bases or similar sites well beyond city limits. The new program in Memphis called for the reconstruction of the barracks at the World War I pilot training school in Park Field, a 911-acre area located 20 miles from the city, in Millington. In Atlanta, a 325-acre former prison-camp site became the new home for transients, with the men themselves building a dining hall, a recreational facility, and 36 living huts to complement buildings already standing.[37]

New Orleans also opened a camp removed from the inner city when the Department of the Navy in May, 1934, approved a request for use of several abandoned buildings at the Algiers Naval Station. The

August 18, 1934, George Bell to Wickenden, May 3, 1935 (Tennessee Transients), Plunkert to H. J. Early, February 14, 1934, Early to Plunkert, February 15, 1934, Converting Seamen into Regular Transients, January 8, 1935, Early to Williams, January 10, 1935 (Louisiana Transients), Mawer to Plunkert, December 18, 1934, Gay Shepperson to Plunkert, December 24, 1934 (Georgia Transients), all in FERA.

36. Memphis *Labor Review*, May 25, 1934; First Annual Report of the Bureau of Transients, August 1, 1934, in TBR, Box 30; Newcomb to Plunkert, July 3, 1934, in FERA, Alabama Transients; Newcomb to Hawkins, May 1, 1935, in TBR, Box 36; W. B. Leddy to Lewey Robinson, September 14, 1934, in James M. Jones, Jr., Collection, Drawer 2.

37. Scheiblich to Lewis, December 4, 1933, Scheiblich to Mawer, December 5, 1933, M. D. Wheller to Director of FERA Transient Activities, May 28, 1934 (Tennessee Transients), Shepperson to Plunkert, October 10, 1934 (Georgia Transients), all in FERA.

new facility, which allowed the city to close its three major downtown shelters, could accommodate 3,000 at one time, and through 1934 handled between 1,500 and the maximum in most months. Later in the same year, the Crescent City obtained permission from the Department of Labor to open a transient hospital and an isolation ward in the former immigrant center at Algiers.[38]

These developments in the New Orleans area transpired despite the opposition of LERA director Harry Early. Early was hostile to any form of care for transients, even offering unsolicited advice to Hopkins. First, said Early, Washington, D.C., should abandon all transient centers and force every man to establish a legal residence and carry an identification card that included a photograph and fingerprints. To limit movement even more, no one should be allowed to cross state lines unless he had a job waiting. The state director concluded that such a federal program would discourage family desertion, encourage the able-bodied to earn a living, and force single and homeless men to attend mandatory vocational training schools. The plan was not unlike compulsory school attendance, he indicated; besides, it would be for the transients' own good. Attached to Early's written recommendations was a brief response by Hopkins that he did not "think much of the idea."[39]

Early's objections notwithstanding, the new transient camps opened, offering room and board and greater opportunity for the homeless to earn cash in exchange for worthwhile labor. Of course all transients were not forthright, and the frequency of turnover in the camps, as well as the large numbers involved, precluded thorough investigations of all who sought assistance. Inexperience also plagued bureau personnel. According to federal field examiners, the Memphis transient director was "extremely sympathetic towards the transients" and created "a kindly atmosphere for the clients and the staff" but simply did not "possess the necessary executive abilities to put over this very complicated job."[40]

One unfortunate incident involved an unshaven, poorly dressed young man from Pittsburgh who arrived in New Orleans in mid-1934. His story was typical of many—he had left home in search of work in order to ease the burden on his jobless parents. Following a routine

38. Plunkert to H. L. Roosevelt, March 19, 1934, Early to Plunkert, April 23, 1934, telegram, Roosevelt to Wickenden, May 2, 1934, Hopkins to Early, October 29, 1934, all in FERA, Louisiana Transients; Report of the Engineering Department: Estimated Cost of Proposed Buildings for Bureau of Transients, E. R. A. of Louisiana, n.d., in TBR, Box 39.

39. Early to Hopkins, November 25, 1934, in FERA, Louisiana Transients.

40. Report on the Memphis Transient Bureau, n.d., in Mawer to Plunkert, January 6, 1934, in TBR, Box 52.

medical examination, the young man was sent to a transient "boarding hotel," where for a week or so he received a bed and two hot meals daily in exchange for cutting wood for the community woodpile.

Yet all was not as it appeared. Ten days after his arrival, the once hapless and destitute young man suddenly packed his knapsack and took a cab to the city airport. Without explanation, he wired for money that allowed him to charter a private plane to take him home. The episode clearly embarrassed relief officials who later discovered that the youth had been "shelter hopping" on a sightseeing excursion across the country. All had gone well until he reached New Orleans, where he learned from a newspaper that his millionaire father had passed away. The news caused him to drop the masquerade and return to Pittsburgh for the funeral.[41]

Despite the Pittsburgh caper, camp directors rarely complained of misrepresentation—the majority of the homeless were apparently in genuine need. Most were more than willing to work in return for food, lodging, and limited wages; men in Atlanta's Fulton Camp, for example, aided in the development of a 315-acre park. The Atlanta project also operated a "subsistence homestead" program in cooperation with the Department of the Interior. The camps provided the manpower and wages, while the Interior Department purchased the necessary land and supervised the actual labor. In Memphis, some of the Park Field campers cared for five hundred head of cattle for use in the bureau's contract restaurants, and in New Orleans, playground construction and cleanup proved most common. The transients at Algiers in the New Orleans area were able to construct their own dairy facility and with leased equipment instituted a purification process that conformed with the local milk ordinance.[42]

Most programs for transients offered, in addition to wage labor, a variety of educational and recreational opportunities. The Algiers camp, for example, opened its own high school and conducted a number of classes for boys and men. Attendance was voluntary but averaged 97 percent each week for those registered. Subjects ranged from American literature to basic English and from fundamental mathematics to algebra, and there were even a few advanced courses available for college students. For those interested in vocational skills,

41. Walter F. Craddock to Ella Charls, July 15, 1934, in Charls to Wickenden, July 16, 1934, in FERA, Louisiana Transients.

42. First Annual of the Bureau of Transients, August 1, 1934, in TBR, Box 30; W. H. Robin to H. B. Woodcock, May 14, 1935 (Louisiana Transients), Lewis to Shepperson, January 5, 1934 (Georgia Transients), Plunkert to Department of Interior, July 6, 1934, J. H. Jenkins to Newcomb, August 18, 1934 (Alabama Transients), Scheiblich to Plunkert, July 2, 1934 (Tennessee Transients), all in FERA.

the Atlanta unit opened a crafts school. Individual projects were sold, and profits were returned to the builder. Leisure activities in turn ranged from community singing to athletics, all under the supervision of experienced recreation directors. In some cases, transient athletic teams entered into community competition. The large urban shelters in Birmingham and Atlanta organized a weekly newspaper to keep transients informed of educational, recreational, and other opportunities.[43]

Of course hospital wards were available for the transients, and medical personnel were always on call. The facility at Algiers, able to accommodate more than one hundred men, was the best single unit in the region. It included three doctors in addition to nurses and other medical aides. In Birmingham, the transient division inaugurated a successful venereal disease treatment project that set an example for bureaus elsewhere. That unit also first arranged with local hospitals for maternity care, establishing a ward for expectant mothers in an apartment building next to central headquarters. Clearly the extensive medical programs helped control the spread of disease. One close call with meningitis among transients frightened officials in Memphis in late 1934, but local doctors and the public health department quickly identified the strain, isolated the infectious, and successfully averted an epidemic.[44]

Included in each urban transient network was a registration unit for blacks, although local relief officials were in no hurry to open the Negro centers. In Birmingham, for example, no black division existed until January, 1934, and then only after local black leaders petitioned several times for a bureau "staffed with Negro personnel." Although FERA director Hopkins eventually heeded the pleas, an active program in the steel center never functioned as it should have. Its supervisor, Nelson C. Jackson, was from the North and so disliked the South that he spent most of his time trying to obtain a transfer to another region. All southern cities by mid-1934 were operating Negro units, but the separate facilities offered little more than temporary shelter and food, sending blacks quickly on their way. Only a regional Negro camp at Fort Benning, Georgia, provided more than minimum assistance, and no

43. Wickenden to D. E. Proctor, March 6, 1934, in FERA, Louisiana Transients; First Annual Report of the Bureau of Transients, August 1, 1934, and Report on the Alabama Transient Bureau, n.d., both in TBR, Box 30; Jones, "A Study of Twenty Boys," 49; Atlanta *Georgian*, April 28, 1934.

44. Plunkert to Lewis, October 11, 1933, Newcomb to Plunkert, February 1, 1934 (Alabama Transients), Frances K. Strong to Scheiblich, February 11, 1935 (Tennessee Transients), all in FERA.

southern urban black unit ever compared to the elaborate camps available to whites.[45]

The beginning of the dismantlement of the FERA in 1935 meant the end of the local transient bureaus. Camps and centers throughout the nation curtailed activities in the fall of that year and either assigned transients to other federal agencies or else transferred them as general relief cases to the care of public welfare departments or private organizations. Certainly those placed with the WPA were more fortunate than those transferred to the new county agencies. The public departments did not organize transient programs, and during the remainder of the decade, there were no shelters or camps for the homeless, except a unit in Atlanta for single women. Black transients after 1935 struggled to even a greater degree than before. They received nothing from private organizations and therefore relied solely on the underfinanced public bureaus.[46]

Indeed, the entire FERA program was only a little more than two years old when New Dealers became convinced of its inadequacy. By 1935, the NRA had proved ineffective and was on its way out, depression still gripped the nation, and millions still depended on emergency relief. More importantly, it was obvious that the economic downturn was not temporary and that piecemeal federal relief plans were neither the best stopgap measures nor the basis for a permanent remedy. The situation in the urban South clearly demonstrated that the problem of unemployment and relief demanded a new look. About 20 percent of the Atlanta population in mid-1935 still received assistance, mainly in direct form, while in New Orleans, more than thirty thousand cases, or 15 percent of the city's residents, were listed on relief rolls. Even in Memphis, where the burden had never been as great as in the other cities, an independent survey reported thirty thousand persons in July, 1935, on direct relief and a like number "living from hand to mouth, selling matches, magazines, and doing other miserably paid jobs."[47]

If numbers caused Washington, D.C., to alter its approach to relief,

45. Tony W. Walker to Hopkins, January 9, 1934, Jackson to Plunkert, February 5, 1934, Report of the Central Transient Department of Alabama, n.d., and Plunkert to Williams, October 20, 1933, all in FERA, Alabama Transients; Report on the Alabama Transient Bureau, n.d., in TBR, Box 30; *Louisiana Weekly,* October 28, 1933.

46. C. C. Block to Hopkins, October 3, 1935, Charles Alspach to Block, April 17, 1936 (Louisiana Transients), Newcomb to Alspach, October 11, 1935 (Alabama Transients), F. F. Athearn to Alspach, October 22, 1934, Shepperson to Wickenden, April 6, 1935, Athearn to Alspach, March 3, 1936 (Georgia Transients), A. Malone to Alspach, November 26, 1935 (Tennessee Transients), all in FERA; M. Starr Northrup *et al., A Survey of the Transient and Homeless Populations in 12 Cities, September, 1935 and September, 1936* (Washington, D.C., 1937), 51.

47. John C. Petrie, "Demand Justice for Negroes," *Christian Century,* July 4, 1935, p.

funding was an equally important consideration. Under the FERA, federal dollars financed almost all relief activities in the southern cities, with the federal government contributing 86 percent of total expenditures in Atlanta and 97 percent in New Orleans. The national average was 70 percent. Southern statehouses contributed almost nothing, with Alabama leading the way by allocating only $65,000 to the Birmingham area through 1935. From the GERA's inception to its demise, the Georgia legislature provided only one "unintentional contribution" of $4.95 to the relief network in the form of a reimbursement payment. Tennessee and Louisiana lawmakers provided nothing in supplementary aid to any locality.[48]

Obtaining city contributions to the ERA system was sometimes equally difficult. Relief administrators often threatened localities with the termination of federal funds; Shepperson in Georgia resorted to such a tactic on several occasions. Her periodic warnings forced Atlanta and Fulton County together to allocate $75,000 monthly for GERA purposes. Compared to municipal spending elsewhere in the South, the Atlanta area's $1.7 million total expenditure was actually generous, although quite limited when compared to Boston's contribution, which through 1934 amounted to two-thirds of all relief expenditures. For the same period, between April, 1933, and April, 1935, Jefferson County and Orleans Parish appropriated less than one-third as much as Atlanta, while Shelby County released only about $300,000 in four years. Compared to total FERA spending in the southern urban counties, which was $5 million in Shelby, $12 million in Jefferson, $13.7 million in Fulton, and $18.3 million in Orleans Parish, local contributions were indeed paltry.[49]

Still, the overall impact of the early federal assistance programs in the southern cities was significant. FERA efforts proved the worth of public works projects, while demonstrating the need for a workable and permanent welfare structure operating locally. After 1935, therefore, a new federal works agency modeled on the FERA experiment but requiring matching sponsor (local) contributions directed a broader

910; U.S. Department of Labor, Bureau of Labor Statistics, *Family Income in the Southeastern Region* (2 vols., 1939), I, 137; Chandler to McKellar, July 8, 1935, in Kenneth McKellar Papers, Box 337, Memphis Public Library, Downtown Branch; Thelma Fite to Sam Jackson, December 17, 1936, in Mayor's Correspondence File, Drawer 7; Whiting (comp.), *Final Statistical Report*, 225, 256, 240, 247.

48. Whiting (comp.), *Final Statistical Report*, 194, 198, 202, 222, 251, 257, 267, 287; Holmes, "The New Deal in Georgia," 71.

49. Atlanta *Constitution*, December 29, 1933, March 11, 13, 1934; Atlanta *Georgian*, April 1, August 19, 1934, March 21, 1936; Atlanta *Journal*, January 21, 1934, February 28, 1938; Minutes of the Fulton County Commission, V, October 6, 1934, p. 275; Memphis *Press Scimitar*, February 18, 1935.

emergency jobs program. The Works Projects Administration (WPA) would function for eight years, during which time the southern municipalities realized more elaborate construction and service projects than the FERA had ever considered. Furthermore, new county public welfare departments, most having emerged under FERA auspices, assumed responsibility for remaining indigent cases. Between the scaling down of the FERA in 1935 and its official closing in 1937, the agency's main function was to assist in the development of local welfare agencies by absorbing initial administrative costs and by aiding those waiting for WPA assignment.[50] And as the municipal bureaus expanded each year, the concept of public responsibility for welfare grew as an accepted function of local government in the urban South.

50. Whiting (comp.), *Final Statistical Report*, 327, 331, 343; Overton to Crump, September 15, in Watkins Overton Papers, Box 2; J. H. Crutcher to Robert Maestri, March 30, 1937, in Robert Maestri Papers, microfilm roll 405B, New Orleans Public Library.

 5

THE WORKS PROJECTS ADMINISTRATION
AND THE IMPACT OF PUBLIC WORKS

The operation of various federal relief programs notwithstanding, sufficient assistance was still unavailable for millions of former jobholders as the unemployment rate remained high in the mid-1930s. Few could do anything but accept their plight, although one out-of-work electrician from Atlanta journeyed to Washington, D.C., to stage his own shocking demonstration. Selecting the White House Executive Office Building as a forum, the young man slashed his wrists and, while bleeding from both arms, ran into the building and demanded to see a presidential aide. Neither federal nor local relief officials had helped him, he later informed a New York *Times* reporter; therefore, he hoped to get the chief executive's personal attention by turning to "the most dramatic method he could think of."[1]

The young Georgian's story was hardly commonplace, but his inability to obtain either local or federal assistance was not unusual for countless depression victims. Wage relief benefits remained uncertain, even after the WPA became active in late 1935. Case-load quotas were constantly changing, while pay scales varied according to geographic section. Assistance for those unable to work was even more uncertain because after 1935 federal appropriations for direct relief depended on matching local and state contributions.

The new relief network was a dual one. The federal role in it was most apparent in the WPA, which the Roosevelt administration intended to be far broader than either the CWA or the FERA. The second part of the revamped program concerned direct assistance for "unem-

1. New York *Times*, October 8, 1936.

ployables," the disabled, and the able-bodied who could not obtain WPA positions. Plans called for the expansion of county welfare departments through increased municipal and state funds, supplemented by federal matching contributions provided in the Social Security Act of 1935. Under WPA guidelines as well, federal funds could absorb a maximum of only 70 percent of a project's cost, with the remaining portion being financed by either state or local sponsors. This strict requirement for joint funding distinguished the WPA from its predecessors. The WPA funding scheme, it has been suggested, "marked new departures of utmost significance in federal policy," even as it left the federal structure fundamentally intact.[2]

Under the new program, work relief funds continued to flow from Washington, D.C., through state and ultimately local county offices, but federal authorities appointed state and local WPA staffs and closely supervised area offices. The former state ERA executive commissions, many of which remained as advisors to the WPA, no longer requested or distributed relief funds. In turn, the state offices, which consisted of seven or eight inner-office divisions, directed a number of WPA district units also subdivided into individual task departments. Work relief administrators on all levels cooperated with federal and developing state employment services, just as they did during the CWA and ERA projects.[3]

For eight years, the WPA employed thousands of men and women who labored on emergency projects in cities and small towns nationwide. Through December, 1936, in New Orleans the WPA allocated more than $12.5 million, while Atlanta by mid-1937 had realized almost $15 million for more than 150 projects. WPA appropriations varied annually, but in the next two years in the Georgia metropolitan area, federal and sponsor spending increased to more than $25.6 million. By the time the WPA ended in 1943, agency spending in the southern states ranged from $126 million in Louisiana to almost $200 million in Alabama, with Birmingham receiving nearly $42 million.[4]

2. Dumas Malone and Basil Rauch, *War and Troubled Peace* (New York, 1960), 223; William E. Leuchtenberg, *Franklin D. Roosevelt and the New Deal* (New York, 1963), 124–25.

3. New Orleans *Times-Picayune*, February 2, 1935; Birmingham *News*, June 14, 1942; Holmes, "The New Deal in Georgia," 204–206; R. L. Pittman to Jones, December 1, 1939, in James M. Jones, Jr., Collection, Drawer 2, Alabama Archives and History, Montgomery; Georgia State Department of Public Welfare, *Report for . . . 1935* (Atlanta, 1936), 10.

4. New Orleans *Times-Picayune*, January 1, 1937; Atlanta *Journal*, August 21, 1940; U.S. Federal Works Agency, *Final Report on the W. P. A. Program, 1935–1943* (1943), 124–25; Birmingham *News*, June 14, 1942; S. T. Pease to Overton, September 29, 1937, in

Such figures resulted in construction activity, social service programs, and professional art, music, and theater ventures, each contributing greatly to the overall attractiveness, physical development, and maturity of the southern cities.

Especially noteworthy was the WPA's effect on developments in community planning in the urban South. The "relief" dollars stimulated building of all sorts, which left municipal leaders with a choice of either the rapid, piecemeal expansion of their cities or the establishment and revival of urban institutions to supervise orderly growth. Based on their business-efficiency sentiments, leaders in Atlanta, Birmingham, Memphis, and New Orleans opted for the latter. The commitment to city planning suggests once again the advancement of an urban consciousness, although clearly within the bounds, at least for now, of the prevailing urban ethos.

The concept of urban planning in the Dixie municipalities was somewhat familiar as of 1930. City officials in the 1920s, for example, had realized that expansion need not be disorderly and that an attractive community was a key ingredient in the booster creed. They also saw that social control, especially patterns of segregation, could be better maintained in a planned environment. Early in the predepression decade, therefore, planning and zoning commissions officially appeared as part of the government structure in Memphis, Atlanta, and New Orleans. Most of the original planners were local business leaders, whose shortsighted interests accounted for the implementation of street, transportation, and recreational improvements but little in terms of slum clearance or housing developments. The "commercial elites," as they have been labeled, owned much of the city's land and thus worked diligently to preserve the security of property rather than restrict the privileges of real estate. They believed that their welfare, and that of their property, was always in the city's best interest.[5]

But with the depression, city administrations trimmed their already inadequate planning budgets, halting what little work the commissions were doing. Mel Scott, in his comprehensive study of city planning in America, states that nearly 95 percent of all localities with populations over 2,500 remained unplanned as of 1929. Although some cities, such as those in the South, had confronted the issue in the 1920s, Scott concludes, until the New Deal "generally the country was

Mayor's Correspondence File, Drawer 7, Memphis and Shelby County Archives, Memphis.

5. Blaine Brownell, "The Commercial-Civic Elite and City Planning in Atlanta, Memphis and New Orleans," *Journal of Southern History*, XLI (August, 1975), 363; Charles E. Patterson, Jr., "The Organization and Administration of the Metropolitan Planning Commission, Atlanta, Georgia" (M.A. thesis, Emory University, 1958), 24.

wholly unprepared to entertain the question." And when New Dealers opened a series of national planning commissions, which functioned under four different names from 1933 to 1943, the purpose was not to make Washington, D.C., a problem solver in the field of urban development but to assist in the establishment of state and local planning agencies. Clearly the concept of central planning was never truly embraced, suggests both Otis Graham in his provocative survey of that issue and Mark Gelfand in his recent analysis of federal urban policy. Instead, New Deal policies gave rise to what Graham calls the "broker state."[6]

Locally, the federal planning agencies clearly had measurable effects. Municipal leaders in Memphis first revived their planning commission, which was all but inactive in the early 1930s, and in 1935, the city's legislative delegation in Nashville sponsored the creation of the Tennessee State Planning Commission. The state bureau subsequently opened regional offices, including one in Memphis, and, in cooperation with WPA authorities, hired relief and nonrelief personnel as local staff. Thereafter, state and city planners together examined proposed public works, surveyed local business and residential areas, and with the assistance of the new Memphis Housing Authority implemented a modern building code, which for the first time required approved sanitary plumbing in all new buildings. In 1940 the city commission invited the participation of county representatives, thereby creating the Memphis-Shelby County Regional Planning Commission. When Congress ended the National Resources Planning Board (NRPB) in 1943, the Tennessee unit, as well as city bureaus by now operating in Nashville, Chattanooga, and Johnson City, remained functional.[7]

In addition to reorganizing the New Orleans Development Planning Board and staffing it with local businessmen, Mayor Robert Maestri in 1936 appointed the first Vieux Carré Commission. According to *American City*, popular sentiment in the Crescent City in the

6. Mel Scott, *American City Planning Since 1890* (Los Angeles, 1969), 260–68; Otis L. Graham, *Toward a Planned Society: From Roosevelt to Nixon* (New York, 1976), 68; Gelfand, *A Nation of Cities*, 65–70. Also see Blake McKelvey, *The Emergence of Metropolitan America, 1915–1966* (New Brunswick, 1968), 100.

7. E. D. Coppedge to Woodward, August 18, 1936, in Record Group 69, Records of the Works Progress Administration, Tennessee Planning Projects, National Archives, hereinafter cited as WPA; text of a speech by Mayor Overton, April, 1937, in Watkins Overton Papers, Box 3, Memphis State University Library; William Gardner to McAlister, January 23, 1935, in Hill McAlister Papers, Box 34, Tennessee State Archives and History, Nashville; Eleanor K. Guess, *The First Fifteen Years: A History of the Tennessee State Planning Commission* (Knoxville, 1949), 52.

mid-1930s was "growing in favor of a greater control of the landscape and of public buildings in public view, in order to prevent ugliness and promote beauty." The bureau established architectural standards for the preservation of the historic French Quarter and controlled construction activity in and around that section. Representatives from the state historical society, the Louisiana Museum, and the American Institute of Architects were included on the nine-member commission. Voters approved the new board as part of a 1937 constitutional amendment, and the courts later upheld its authority. It worked in harmony with WPA personnel, while cooperating with the Louisiana Planning Commission and the State Department of Public Works, established in 1936 and 1940, respectively. Even those who argue that planning in New Orleans "languished during the depression and war periods" agree that its partial revival prepared the city for the construction and planning boom later in the 1940s.[8]

Federal authorities likewise assisted in the resurgence of planning in the Atlanta area. Not only did the dormant city planning board of Atlanta resume operations in mid-decade, but similar agencies in Decatur and in Dekalb County were newly organized. Most important was the opening of the Fulton County Planning Commission in 1938, although initially its influence was limited. According to one of its members, the commission for six years had "no power—only persuasion" and "our decisions were overruled and reversed so often that half the time we didn't know whether we were coming or going." Nevertheless, the county unit worked with the businessmen's Civic Improvement Committee to propose public works projects, and it cooperated with the Fulton County Building Inspector's Office and the Georgia Planning Commission, both established in 1937, to complete a survey by census tract of land use and construction trends, which facilitated future zoning regulations and building codes. The formation of the commission was also the first step toward the establishment in 1947 of the Metropolitan Regional Planning Council. According to Scott, the Atlanta area commission was "the first official metropolitan planning agency supported from the beginning by public funds."[9]

8. Monthly Report of the Women's Professional Project Division, Orleans Parish, May, 1937, in Mrs. Leo G. Spofford to Charley Tidd Cole, June 15, 1937, in WPA, Louisiana Women's Projects; "Esthetics—Preservation of Buildings Having Architectural and Historical Value," *American City* (April, 1942), 103; Louisiana State Planning Commission, *First Progress Report* (Baton Rouge, 1938), 11–14; Louisiana Department of Public Works, *First Progress Report* (Baton Rouge, 1942), 11; L. Vaughn Howard and Robert S. Friedman, *Government in Metropolitan New Orleans*, Tulane University Studies in Political Science, VI (New Orleans, 1959), 35.

9. Harry J. Toombs, "City Planning in Atlanta: Urbanization Without Concentration as an Objective," *Landscape Architecture*, XLIII (April, 1953), 101; Scott, *American City*

The concept of urban planning made the slowest progress in Birmingham. The steel center had not experimented with a planning council in the 1920s, and its weak zoning adjustment board was little more than a paper bureau. Still, as elsewhere, the federal building activity demonstrated a need for order, and the planning divisions of the PWA and CWA and the NRPB were active in the state. The state legislature in 1935 created the first Alabama state planning commission, although this agency was not really the result of state direction. It was part of a WPA project, financed through the office of the United States comptroller-general. Its staff consisted mainly of relief workers, who opened small offices in Birmingham and other cities in 1939. Unfortunately, reduced WPA expenditures each year after 1938 limited their activities.

So between 1935 and 1943, planning throughout Alabama was piecemeal and related only to specific federal building projects. State and local leaders embraced the planning movement slowly, and as long as New Deal agencies were active and money from Washington, D.C., was available, they showed little inclination to establish a planning network. Not until 1940 did Alabama lawmakers adopt the necessary legislation enabling subdivisions to organize local commissions. Even then, two more years elapsed before county leaders in the Birmingham area organized the Jefferson County Regional Planning Commission, which was empowered to "make, adopt, amend, extend, and add to a master plan for the physical development of the county." Finally in 1943, city officials created the Birmingham Planning Board, although developments thereafter continued to be slow. As of 1945, the Birmingham board had no permanent staff and only one part-time employee.[10]

Birmingham's hesitancy to embrace the planning movement, despite federal encouragement and direction (including government studies on the efficient use of local resources), in no way indicated a rejection of the New Deal. The urban New South leadership had little difficulty accommodating the various programs, which operated

---

Planning, 442–43; "Rebuilding Atlanta: A Fifteen Year Effort in Progress," *American City* (February, 1940), 79; Patterson, "The Organization of the Metropolitan Planning Commission," 24–26; Minutes of the Fulton County Commission, X, September 7, 1938, pp. 120–25, Fulton County Commission Office, Atlanta.

10. R. W. Torras to Birmingham City Commission, February 13, 1934, in James M. Jones, Jr., Collection, Drawer 2; Thad Holt, "Establishment of Unemployment Relief Agencies in the Hoover-Roosevelt Era" (Typescript, Alabama Archives and History, Montgomery), 9–10; National Resources Committee, *Proceedings of the Third Southeast Planning Conference* (Atlanta, 1938), 6–9; Alabama State Planning Board, *First Annual Report . . .* (Montgomery, 1944); Cooper, *Metropolitan County*, 26–29.

within the federal structure while providing funds to modernize and make their cities more attractive to outside business and manufacturing interests. Most importantly, sponsorship funding requirements meant local control, in that city officials through their planning and zoning agencies applied for grants and loans on their own terms and for their own advantage. Thus, they were able to maintain as much of the established, traditional order as possible.

If there was one area that remained intact throughout the depression period, it was the urban political structure. Commercial and business interests remained in control in Atlanta and Birmingham through the offices of William Hartsfield and James Jones respectively, and certainly there were no "last hurrahs" in either Memphis or New Orleans. The Crump machine in Memphis operated during the 1930s without serious challenge, while the administrative reshuffling in New Orleans was mainly the result of municipal and state politics, although federal programs often became entangled with local political affairs. Still, New Orleans business and commercial interests retained influence in city hall, first through Mayor Walmsley and then through Mayor Maestri when Huey Long's conservative successors replaced the Old Regulars in mid-decade. One machine followed another, both reliant on business support. "Reformers" would be unsuccessful in the Crescent City until 1946, despite their triumph in the statehouse over the Longs in 1940.

The voting records of southern urban congressmen also suggests the compatibility of New South conservatism and the New Deal. The urban representatives generally supported federal public works, just as they approved most New Deal policies, never identifying with the conservative coalition, which V. O. Key has argued was primarily rural in makeup. Although no outburst of political liberalism was apparent, the southern urban congressmen in the 1930s and thereafter were increasingly supportive of government action that addressed problems of modern industrial and urban life.[11] Throughout the depression decade, they worked to obtain maximum public funding for their cities and even had little difficulty supporting labor legislation, including wage and hour laws, so long as sectional differentials were in part preserved.

The story was the same in machine and nonmachine city alike.

11. V. O. Key, *Southern Politics in State and Nation* (New York, 1949), 378–80. Also see James T. Patterson, *Congressional Conservatism and the New Deal: The Growth of the Conservative Coalition in Congress, 1933–1939* (Lexington, 1967), 343–46; James E. Titus, "Urbanism and Southern Politics," in Rupert B. Vance and Nicholas J. Demeruth (eds.), *The Urban South* (Chapel Hill, 1954), 230–51.

From Birmingham and Atlanta, congressmen Luther Patrick and Robert Ramspeck followed a New South philosophy almost exclusively. Their negative votes were mainly on proposed business regulatory laws, such as the Public Utilities Holding Company legislation and the Guffey-Snyder Coal Act. Somewhat more supportive of the Roosevelt line were Memphian Walter Chandler and New Orleans congressmen Joachim O. "Bathtub" Fernandez and Paul H. Maloney.[12] All represented political machines that found the decentralized nature of federal agencies with all intendant patronage to their liking. Fernandez was an especially interesting character. He survived the transfer of power in New Orleans from the Old Regulars to the Longs in 1935 but then lost, along with his colleague Maloney, in 1940 to a reform candidate in the wake of the Louisiana "hot oil and kickback" scandals.

The congressmen clearly reflected the general attitudes of their constituencies. Voters in Birmingham, for example, turned out anti–New Deal and twenty-year incumbent congressman George Huddleston in 1936 in favor of Luther "no promise" Patrick, endorsed by Jim Farley and New Deal senator Hugo Black. Similarly, Atlanta residents voted in far greater numbers proportionately than Georgians in general for New Deal candidate Lawrence Camp in Roosevelt's misguided effort to "purge" conservative Democratic senator Walter George in 1938. In that election, George carried Atlanta, as well as the entire state, but Camp ran a strong second in the city, while anti–New Dealer Eugene Talmadge ran second statewide. According to the Atlanta *Constitution*, George's victory was not a rejection of the New Deal but a vote for its continuation within a moderate, constitutional framework.[13]

The major city newspapers, with their New South inclinations, were also cautiously supportive of the New Deal, just as were their subscribers. Editorials from the long-established Birmingham *Age-Herald* and the Atlanta *Constitution* endorsed the necessity of temporary relief, the principle of social security, the concept of public welfare, federal slum clearance and insured housing, a wage and hour law with regional differentials, the right of collective bargaining (but with a weaker labor board), and the Tennessee Valley Authority (TVA), while opposing the utilities "death sentence," the undistributed-profits tax, any long-term movement away from a balanced budget, and the court-packing fiasco. Similar in tone were the long-standing New Orleans *Times-Picayune* and Memphis *Commercial Appeal*, at least until late

12. *Congressional Record*, 74th Cong., 1st Sess., Vol. 79, part 3, p. 3060; *ibid.*, part 10, pp. 1637–39; *ibid.*, part 13, pp. 13666–67.

13. Birmingham *News*, September 5, 1937; Roy E. Fossett, "The Impact of the New Deal on Georgia Politics, 1933–1941" (Ph.D. dissertation, University of Florida, 1960), 96; Atlanta *Journal*, September 9, 1938; Atlanta *Constitution*, September 1, 16, 18, 1938.

in the decade. As part of their editorial crusades against the Longs and Boss Crump respectively, these newspapers became increasingly critical of federal relief programs under machine influence.[14]

Among the other southern urban dailies, which were separate publications (unlike today) of more recent origin, the Atlanta *Journal* was more enthusiastic about New Deal policies than was the *Constitution*. The *Journal* was even supportive of the Judiciary Reorganization Act, a position that went beyond the sentiments of its counterparts, the Birmingham *Post*, the Memphis *Press Scimitar*, and the New Orleans *Item*. Yet while these newspapers were less cautious overall about the expansion of new federal programs than their New South rivals, they too reserved foremost support for local business and real estate interests and the maintenance of regional industrial advantages. This clearly reflected the continuity of conservative business influence in municipal affairs during the thirties, later a factor in the reemergence of Republicanism in the urban South in the post–World War II years as white-collar professionals began arriving from the North and other sections of the country and as blacks began registering as Democrats. As early as 1940, the Atlanta *Journal* joined the three Scripps-Howard newspapers (the two Memphis dailies and the Birmingham *Post*) in endorsing Republican Wendell Willkie's presidential bid, although specifically in this instance because of the editor's vehement opposition to Roosevelt's quest for a third term.[15]

News coverage and editorials also reflected general support for federal work relief among the majority of southern city residents and their leaders, at least as long as needs remained great. But because the public works effort was designed to be temporary, there was neither steady nor sufficient assistance available for those who qualified for emergency jobs. The number of relief openings fluctuated almost monthly, and for those who received assignments, the work was demanding for wages that did not provide the minimum necessities of

14. Atlanta *Constitution*, November 16, 1934, July 3, 1935, February 17, July 16, September 1, 9, 1937, May 25, 1938; Birmingham *Age-Herald*, May 15, 17, August 12–14, 1935, June 27, 1936, May 26, June 8, 15, 1938; Birmingham *News*, May 25–26, 1938; Thomas H. Coode, "The Presidential Election of 1940 as Reflected in the Tennessee Metropolitan Press," *East Tennessee Historical Society Publications*, XL (1968), 83–100; Memphis *Commercial Appeal*, June 2, 25, September 1, 21, 1935; New Orleans *Times-Picayune*, May 10, 1938.

15. Atlanta *Journal*, May 24, 1935, June 28, 1936, February 7, March 29, April 4, 6, 1937, July 17, 1938, July 18, 1940; Birmingham *Post*, August 8–9, 1935, June 27, 1936, May 17, June 7, 11, 1938, July 12, 16, November 4, 1940; New Orleans *Item*, December 6, 1937, January 17, 21, 1939; Memphis *Press Scimitar*, November 14, 1937; Coode, "The Presidential Election," 93; Bernard Cosman, "Republicanism in the Metropolitan South" (Ph.D. dissertation, University of Alabama, 1962).

life. Established labor organizations throughout the urban South, moreover, opposed public works and thus lent little support to relief workers. And if emergency jobholders flirted with would-be "relief unions," they invited the wrath of municipal authorities, local WPA foremen, and other relief officials. Clearly a relief position was not, as some WPA critics have suggested, the receipt of charity for merely leaning on a rake or a shovel.

Although established in April, 1935, WPA machinery did not become operable in the southern cities until the fall. The transfer of clients from ERA rolls was especially slow, as was the certification of additional jobless persons. In Georgia, for example, federal administrators approved an initial $10.5 million for the state in early July, and plans called for 15,000 in Atlanta to be on the job as of August 1. Yet by mid-November, the first public jobs remained unfilled. The situation was little different in other cities, as WPA applicants often faced a period of six months when little or no aid was available. An additional problem involved the assignment of unemployed craftsmen or skilled and professional workers to appropriate positions. Until later in the decade, when the WPA established white-collar programs and joined the PWA in large building ventures requiring craftsmen, only manual jobs with accompanying lower pay scales were available. Ultimately, white-collar programs in the Dixie cities would absorb more than 25 percent of total WPA expenditures.[16]

Fortunately, transfer delays did not last long, and by the winter of 1935, the WPA had reached thousands who were assigned to scores of projects. By mid-1936, 15,000 were working in Atlanta and more than 20,000 in the Birmingham corporate limits, while in Memphis about 7,000 were active. The program peaked slightly earlier in New Orleans, where administrators reported more than 25,000 on WPA payrolls in December, 1935. Within weeks, the level had increased to 34,000, a number representing one-half of those assigned throughout Louisiana. Clearly the new federal agency directed its greatest efforts in the nation's devastated cities; the urban areas also did their part, sponsoring a sufficient number of projects to reach maximum employment levels. In 1936, for example, Louisiana voters approved a constitutional amendment allowing New Orleans to collect a two-cent gasoline tax for emergency works. In all of the southern cities in question through 1939, sponsors accounted for an average of 31 percent of project

16. Atlanta *Constitution*, June 23, July 3, November 21, 1935; New Orleans *Times-Picayune*, September 7, 1935; Memphis *Commercial Appeal*, September 12, 21, 1935; Birmingham *Post*, July 4, 1935; text of speech to Rotary Club, n.d., in Watkins Overton Papers, Box 1; U.S. Works Progress Administration, *W. P. A. Projects: Analysis of Projects Placed in Operation Through June 30, 1937* (1938), 100.

funding, compared to a national figure of 25 percent.[17]

The peak WPA employment levels lasted barely a year, as federal authorities in early 1937 suddenly and sharply reduced work relief rolls. By midyear, the southern city quotas had declined by more than 50 percent. Municipal leaders in attendance at the United States Conference of Mayors protested vociferously, and Memphis mayor Watkins Overton was especially aghast when his city's new quota was set equal to that of the smaller and less devastated Tennessee urban areas. The timing of the cutbacks suggests political manipulation, with Roosevelt's safe return to the White House having been assured the previous November. And despite the recession of 1937 and 1938, it is curious that New Dealers revitalized the program to former levels just prior to the 1938 congressional elections. The New Orleans *Times-Picayune*, suggesting that expanded public works could only help those in power locally and nationally, noted that "relief expenditures during the depression years have shown the interesting if not edifying habit of rising during election years."[18]

Of course economic conditions as of 1937 had shown improvement, and the federal government had theretofore invested millions in the economy. Still, joblessness remained a serious problem in the southern cities and elsewhere. A federal census bureau investigation in early 1938 found that more than 50,000 former Birmingham-area jobholders had located, at best, part-time work in the private sector, or none at all. In Atlanta, the unemployment rate continued at 15 percent (22 percent of the black work force and 12 percent of the white work force), while more than 30,000 and nearly 20,000 former jobholders remained idle in New Orleans and Memphis respectively. In fact, even when the WPA was operating at its maximum, thousands of certified cases were without assignment; Birmingham reported 5,000 such cases (representing 20,000 individuals) in December, 1938. Furthermore, local relief officials did not always move expeditiously to keep quotas filled. According to the Memphis City Engineer's Office, which

17. Atlanta *Constitution*, July 3, 1937, February 16, 1938; E. E. McDaniel to John Garvey, May 16, 1936, in WPA, Alabama Labor Complaints; Memphis *Commercial Appeal*, August 9, 1936, December 31, 1939; Pease to Overton, January 10, 1938, in Mayor's Correspondence File, Drawer 7; New Orleans *Times-Picayune*, December 8, 1935; "The Federal Work Relief Program in New Orleans," *City Problems* (New Orleans), January 25, 1939, p. 3.

18. New Orleans *Times-Picayune*, September 13, 1938. Also see Overton to Betters, May 17, 1937, Overton to McKellar, June 14, 1937, Overton to Chandler, July 12, 1937, telegram, Overton to Harry S. Berry, July 12, 1937, Overton to Crump, July 19, 1937, all in Mayor's Correspondence File, Drawer 7; Atlanta *Journal*, April 11, 1937; Atlanta *Constitution*, February 16, July 20, 1938; Hardy Scott to Hopkins, March 9, 1938, in WPA, Georgia Labor Complaints.

sponsored many area projects, the local WPA director moved cautiously because he was a "senile old man" who was too old "to keep up with the details."[19]

Throughout the remainder of the decade, WPA quotas all across the country varied according to annual appropriations, which continued through 1942. In Atlanta, for example, the 1938 Emergency Appropriations Act provided for fifteen thousand workers, with that number being gradually reduced to about one thousand four years later. And of course WPA efforts did not solve depression joblessness. The Alabama relief director in early 1940 noted that "the employment situation in Birmingham remains most serious" and "is worse than at any other time during the history of the relief program." He added that area landlords were evicting those tenants cut from WPA rolls and that many of the indigent were contracting "pneumonia as the result of inadequate shelter, clothing and food." Similarly, Congressman Walter Chandler of Memphis, a city that had never known the worst of the depression, protested the WPA's second retrenchment, suggesting that it was not "a wise thing to do under the circumstances."[20]

As federal authorities in 1939 trimmed WPA allocations, southern urban residents increasingly showed less enthusiasm for public works. Most seemed to agree with the ever-cautious Atlanta *Constitution* that the economy would have survived without the agency only "at a cost greater than the cost of having it," but that now federal relief programs had outlived their usefulness. Birmingham and Atlanta voters in the late 1930s, despite endorsements from municipal officials and the local press, rejected bond issues that would have raised substantial matching funds for additional public employment. Only New Orleans after 1940 continued any kind of ongoing special funding for emergency works — a local 2 percent sales tax that had replaced the gasoline tax abolished in 1939 because of pressure from city dealers. Furthermore, nowhere

19. Overton to Crump, July 19, 1937, William Fowler to Berry, n.d., Persons Working on PWA and WPA Projects, November 30, 1935, to November 28, 1936 (Drawer 7), Pease to Chandler, May 14, 1940 (Drawer 10), all in Mayor's Correspondence File; Memphis *Commercial Appeal*, September 10, 1936, January 19, 1938; Memphis *Press Scimitar*, April 8, 1938; Jefferson County Department of Public Welfare to Hopkins, December 22, 1938, telegram, John L. Donovan to Williams, December 22, 1938, both in WPA, Alabama Labor Complaints; Arner Hermanson, Open Letter on the Relief Situation in Jefferson County, March 2, 1939 (Drawer 2), U.S. Conference of Mayors, A Report on the Existing Relief Situation Covering 100 American Cities, n.d. (Drawer 3), all in James M. Jones, Jr., Collections.

20. Chandler to Overton, January 18, 1939, in Watkins Overton Papers, Box 1; Henderson to Malcolm Miller, January 25, 1940, in WPA, Alabama Labor Complaints; Holmes, "The New Deal in Georgia," 236; Atlanta *Constitution*, June 26–27, 1938; Atlanta *Journal*, July 9, 25, 1939.

were city leaders willing to contribute to work relief directly from regular tax revenues, suggesting that New South efficiency sentiments were little changed. They supported the WPA as an emergency measure only, although it allowed them to modernize their cities and maintain the prevailing order in the midst of a devastating economic crisis.[21] Still, attitudes toward a role for Washington, D.C., in municipal affairs did seem to be changing, even in the South; clearly, the public works effort overall, as a major part of the New Deal, was the cornerstone of the direct relationship that continued to evolve between the federal government and the nation's cities.

A concern for social order explains why the southern cities sponsored more opportunities for women and included more blacks on the WPA than on earlier work relief rolls. Jobless women, for example, found public employment in libraries, in sewing rooms, as secretaries, and in social service fields, accounting for 15 to 25 percent of a southern city's WPA quota. Unemployed blacks throughout the agency's eight years held more than one-half of the public jobs, a figure comparable to their percentage among the total number of unemployed. Of course blacks rarely received anything but low "common" labor wages, and pressure from planters often meant their displacement during cotton-picking season for available work in the fields. Official policy "guaranteed" a relief position once the picking season ended, although relief officials in New Orleans demanded proof of "verifiable employment" upon reapplication. The catch was that domestic or seasonal work was considered "unverifiable."[22]

Complementing the WPA was the agency's junior partner, the National Youth Administration (NYA), which designed two types of programs to assist young people from indigent families. The first was a student aid project to keep needy youngsters in school. High school and college students worked for a few hours each week on school maintenance and groundskeeping jobs, earning between six and fifteen dollars a month. The second was a regular works division for unem-

21. Atlanta *Constitution*, April 19, 1940; Birmingham *Post*, December 2, 1936; Betters to Overton, July 1, 1939, in Mayor's Correspondence File, Drawer 7; New Orleans *Times-Picayune*, December 7, 13, 31, 1940.

22. Fred R. Rauch to Chandler, July 26, 1939, in WPA, Tennessee Labor Complaints; WPA of Georgia, *A Statistical Study of the Social and Economic Pattern of the City of Atlanta, Georgia* (Atlanta, 1939), 106; Holt to Overton, September 10, 1936, E. C. Klaiber to Holt, September 10, 1936, Pease to Berry, November 3, 1936, Memphis Welfare Commission to Overton, August 30, 1938, all in Mayor's Correspondence, Drawer 7; New York *Times*, September 10, 13, 1936; Memphis *Commercial Appeal*, August 26, 1935, September 27, 1939; Memphis *Press Scimitar*, September 9, 1936; *Louisiana Weekly*, December 7, 1935.

ployed youth already out of school, paying a maximum of thirty-four cents per hour. Like WPA policy, the policy of the NYA required local sponsor contributions. Among the southern cities, New Orleans reported the largest number of young relief laborers, reporting a monthly average of at least 1,200 throughout 1938.[23]

While quotas, cutbacks, and the uncertainty of finding employment affected WPA labor throughout the nation, the problem of non-uniform pay schedules had special relevance for southern urban relief workers. The WPA's first wage scale, little modified for four years, lumped states into four groups and established a pay chart for each group. In the Northeast / Northwest division, unskilled workers earned from $40 to $55 per month and skilled labor from $65 to $85 per month, with the higher rates generally prevailing in the cities. In the Deep South, where wages in the private sector were low, monthly pay scales were $14 to $30 for unskilled workers and $35 to $68 for skilled labor. Typical of the southern cities was Memphis, where 80 percent of all WPA workers fell among the unskilled; their maximum monthly rate was 25 percent below the minimum wage paid manual laborers in rural Oregon and in Vermont. New Orleans was the only exception among the cities under discussion ($21 to $35 a month for unskilled workers)—it fell into the WPA's Southwest division. Although southern administrators in 1936 and again in 1938 raised monthly rates slightly for urban workers, a $40 figure was never reached.[24]

WPA workers in the southern cities, moreover, rarely received support from established labor organizations. Only occasionally did the urban trades councils speak out for the unskilled, as they did for skilled emergency workers in 1936. In that year, labor leaders helped bring about a WPA provision allowing local offices to hire 10 percent of their quotas as nonrelief personnel at local union scales. In a rare incident in Birmingham in the same year, the city's construction unions helped oust local relief administrator W. D. Twing. Labor sources reported that Twing and his foremen carried firearms on the job and treated all WPA workers as slave labor. In a petition to relief officials in Washington, D.C., union leaders referred to the boss as "the big Mongul and Ruler over unfortunates on relief," concluding that he "be given a shovel and placed in a ditch at 27 cents per hour." It was further suggested that "our government will not have to go to Europe to get a

23. "The Federal Work Relief Program in New Orleans," 3; New Orleans *Times-Picayune*, October 16, 1935; Memphis *Commercial Appeal*, September 22, 1935.

24. Atlanta *Constitution*, May 21, 1935; George L. Googe to A. Steve Nance, October 15, 1935 (Georgia Labor Complaints), Ray Crow to William O'Neil, February 26, 1936 (Alabama Labor Complaints), both in WPA; Memphis *Commercial Appeal*, July 23, 1935, August 16, 1939; Atlanta *Journal*, November 11, 1935.

Mussolini or a Hitler" because "we are sure that you have Mr. Twing to call on."[25]

Still, the established urban labor federations never fully endorsed the concept of federal works that paid less than union scales. Unionists, for example, opposed the special bond issue referenda in Birmingham and Atlanta that would have increased sponsorship revenues. The Memphis Trades Council, in fact, adopted a resolution in late 1935 calling for an immediate halt to all plans for future WPA construction and for all current work to be transferred to the PWA, which paid prevailing local wages of thirty-five to forty cents per hour for a 130-hour month. The Tennessee Federation of Labor, in which the Memphis trades organization wielded much influence, indicted federal and state administrators as "reaction [sic] politicians" and "low wage employers." One prominent leader in the Birmingham-headquartered Alabama Federation of Labor concluded that the WPA through its low wage scale "has done more damage to the citizens of Alabama than any other agency ever created."[26]

The failure of local labor unions to support either ERA or WPA workers in part prompted the activities of outside organizations among relief labor. As early as 1934, would-be organizers attempted to bring some type of union to unskilled workers. In New Orleans, for example, the short-lived Relief Workers Protective Union led a number of demonstrations against low emergency wages, while similar groups did the same in the other southern municipalities. Not surprisingly, civic authorities watched the agitators closely and, whenever disturbances seemed imminent, quickly arrested the leaders for vagrancy or on any fabricated charge. Such was the case with Jack Welch and Boris Israel in Memphis in late 1933. Police jailed the two men for circulating among the jobless and for advocating the "communist doctrines of the destruction of the Christian church and the overthrow of the American government," and for promoting racial equality.[27]

25. William Van Hauten to Shepperson, October 10, 1935, and Robert Ramspeck to Jacob Baker, November 7, 1935, both in WPA, Georgia Labor Complaints; Memphis *Commercial Appeal*, November 15, 1935; Atlanta *Journal*, November 11, 1935; Birmingham *News*, July 1, 1936; New Orleans *Times-Picayune*, June 27, July 2, 1938; petition enclosed in Ray Copeland to Holt, February 29, 1936, in WPA, Alabama Labor Complaints; Birmingham *News*, June 14, 1942.

26. T. M. Ray to Roosevelt, November 25, 1935, in WPA, Tennessee Labor Complaints; Memphis *Press Scimitar*, September 8, 1936; James A. Hodges, "The Tennessee Federation of Labor, 1919–1939" (M.A. thesis, Vanderbilt University, 1959), 154; W. O. Hare to Birmingham City Commission Council, July 20, 1938, in James M. Jones, Jr., Collection, Drawer 3.

27. Memphis *Press Scimitar*, October 31, 1933, January 29, 1934; New Orleans *Times-Picayune*, May 2, 1933.

Later in the 1930s, the Workers Alliance became active among WPA labor throughout the urban South. Its leaders had recorded a few union victories in the private sector, as a result of the National Labor Relations Act, and hoped to capitalize on those gains and organize relief workers. Local workers councils, affiliated with the central alliance, appeared in each city in 1936, although their efforts produced little for emergency jobholders. In New Orleans, the alliance failed to obtain even WPA recognition of job stewards on individual projects. WPA foremen remained in charge, with absolute authority to settle nearly all labor complaints in the field. Despite repeated demonstrations by the Workers Alliance, attempts to procure a higher pay scale in the southern urban areas also failed.[28]

Incidents in Birmingham and Atlanta exemplified the organization's few victories in the South. In 1936, the Alabama WPA director ordered a temporary 20 percent cut in wages for several thousand Jefferson County relief workers. He planned to use the savings to support welfare programs for widows with children and for the handicapped—the responsibility of state authorities, not the federal jobs agency. The Birmingham Workers Alliance immediately joined with a number of other civic groups protesting the reductions, which were clearly illegal. The state WPA chief, who at one time had considered a 50 percent pay cut, ultimately restored wages in full. In Atlanta, a local workers' council in 1938 won the right to present its grievances each week to Georgia WPA officials. The meetings lasted for just sixteen months, terminating in late 1940 because of insufficient business to warrant regular gatherings.[29]

The "radical" identity of the Workers Alliance was the organization's greatest handicap in the South. Although few card carriers were active in the Dixie cities, it was no secret that Communist sympathizers worked within the group nationally. Consequently, city officials perceived a threat, or at least manufactured one in the public mind, to justify their opposition to any organizational activity among local relief labor. Urban officials maintained that welfare demonstrations were the first steps toward social disorder, especially if whites and blacks worked together. Officials in Atlanta, for example, successfully

28. New Orleans *Times-Picayune*, April 28, 1938; Carl Bendvus to Roosevelt, May 24, 1938, David K. Nile to Bendvus, June 9, 1938, memorandum, W. F. Oakes to R. B. Fowler, June 23, 1939, Selene Gifford to Rauch, July 11, 1939, all in WPA, Louisiana Labor Complaints.

29. McDaniel to Garvey, May 16, 1936 (Alabama Labor Complaints), Miller to David Lasser, November 18, 1940 (Georgia Labor Complaints), both in WPA.

linked the local Urban League with the relief union, which only intensified popular antipathy toward both.[30]

In Birmingham in 1939, City Commission Council president James Jones refused to meet with the Workers Alliance because its local delegation was racially mixed. Through the press he bluntly informed the group that "I do not like your organization." Police in Birmingham were especially quick to use blackjacks and guns against relief demonstrators, whom relief authorities described as "ungreatful [sic] swine" and "the most illiterate and misguided persons in their communities." In mid-1936, the City Commission Council ordered the police chief to "pin anything possible on persons thought to be communists." During an alliance-led strike at one Birmingham construction site, Public Safety Commissioner Eugene Connor declared the disturbance a health and fire hazard and called on police to remove demonstrators from the unfinished building. Connor announced that the strike leader was a "Greek letter man from Columbia University" who "ought to have known better than to allow humble, ignorant W.P.A. workers to act as they did."[31] He apparently changed little during the next thirty years, reflecting Birmingham's general stagnation during the post–World War II years of growth and diversification in other southern cities.

Similar incidents transpired outside of Birmingham; one of the most interesting was the Maurice Clark case in New Orleans. In 1936, police apprehended the alliance organizer, also the leader of the local Non-Partisan Labor Council, for planning a strike in protest of WPA quota reductions. Later released after suffering much physical abuse, Clark remained on the Gulf Coast; from there, his organization bombarded Roosevelt and national administrators with petitions demanding a federal investigation into the situation in the Crescent City. His letters attributed police tactics to the "fascism of the Southern Bourbons," while referring to Roosevelt's presidency as truly a "Jeckyl-Hyde performance." Yet what Clark and others never understood was that the hostility of urban authorities only reflected the suspicions of the vast majority of workers in the southern cities, whether black or white. Few southerners were inclined to join any organization with a "foreign" label, and even a group called the United WPA Union, which required

30. Atlanta *Daily World*, December 18, 1938, November 2, 1939. Only in Memphis, where Workers Alliance rhetoric was more moderate in tone, did the organization escape constant harassment, notwithstanding Boss Crump's disdain for unionism. See Pease to Berry, August 25, 1936, in WPA, Tennessee Labor Complaints.

31. Birmingham *Post*, April 18, 1936; Birmingham *News*, April 19, 1936; Birmingham *Labor Advocate*, September 3, 1938, February 4, 1939; WPA of Alabama, *Final Report of the W. P. A., Alabama* (1943), 12; John L. Williams, "Struggles in the Thirties in the South," in Sternsher (ed.), *The Negro in Depression and War*, 176–77.

that its members take an oath "on God's Holy Bible" to "uphold Americanism in its truest form," had no success in the cities.[32]

Not until July, 1939, did the WPA adopt a wage scale that accounted for urban versus rural as well as sectional differentials. The reason was not altogether clear, but there is no evidence that the new policy resulted from any "relief union" pressure. Under the Emergency Appropriations Act of 1939, states remained divided into geographic sections, although wages now varied according to county population within each group. The revised scale established the southern urban worker's maximum at least above the rural northeastern jobholder's minimum. The former still earned less than his counterparts in northern and western cities ($48 and $55 per month respectively), but the new schedule somewhat narrowed previous inequities.[33]

The 1939 statute also contained the infamous eighteen-month rule, which forced a relief worker after a year and a half to forfeit his position. If the individual still desired emergency employment, he had to submit again to the WPA certification process and then wait for an opening. Although the policy created positions for some unassigned cases, it adversely affected an equal number who surrendered the work. In New Orleans, for example, the reapplication process often lasted a month, and as of August, 1939, the "new" applicant joined a waiting list of twelve thousand seeking three thousand jobs.[34]

The traditional, somewhat worn belief that living costs in the South, even in the major cities, were much lower than elsewhere determined WPA wage guidelines, as did wage levels in the private sector. New South business and civic leaders championed this thinking. They used their influence in Washington, D.C., to include the principle of sectional differentials in all monetary policies, such as the ones written into the NRA codes in 1933 and 1934. Prevailing wages in private employment also determined low relief scales in order to keep those with jobs from being tempted to leave for emergency work. Figures in Atlanta were representative. In 1939, the average white worker earned about $1,050 annually ($88 per month), while employers paid blacks about half as much.[35]

32. Petition, Non-Partisan Labor Council of New Orleans to Roosevelt, November 1, 1936, in Brian McMahon to Roger Bounds, November 20, 1936 (Louisiana Labor Complaints), C. R. Carter to Roosevelt, January 21, 1936 (Alabama Labor Complaints), Ester Avery to F. C. Harrington, October 26, 1939 (Georgia Labor Complaints), all in WPA.

33. Birmingham *News*, August 29, 1939; Betters to Overton, August 29, 1939, in Mayor's Correspondence File, Drawer 7; Rauch to Frank Ingram, October 2, 1940, in WPA, Louisiana Labor Complaints; Citizens Fact Finding Movement of Georgia, *Public Welfare: Appraisal and Proposals* (n.p., 1940), 15.

34. Holmes, "The New Deal in Georgia," 236; New Orleans *Item*, August 20, 1939.

35. WPA of Georgia, *Report on the Real Property, Land Use and Low Income*

Emergency jobholders in the southern cities, therefore, received wages that covered only 33 to a maximum of 65 percent of the national average emergency standard-of-living expense established by the federal government using depression prices. National administrators judged that WPA wages for Atlanta's unskilled, relative to the city's cost of living, were the lowest in the nation, and that those on public works in the region's other urban areas fared little better. Atlanta labor leaders, reflecting conservative craft union hostility to the WPA, bitterly resented this disparity as "legalized peonage."[36] Because of the differentials factor, few wage earners in private employment even earned the minimum standard.

Reliable studies showed, however, that living costs in the southern cities were not significantly lower than in urban areas elsewhere. This fact, generally ignored by federal authorities, had contributed to the overall ineffectiveness of the NRA program and to labor's dislike of the blue eagle codes. It clearly limited the worth of wage relief throughout the decade, and it would also undermine the thrust of federal minimum wage and hour legislation adopted in 1938. According to a WPA survey in 1935, the living cost in Atlanta was higher than the average for all American cities, while in New Orleans and Memphis it equaled the average. Only Birmingham reported a lower than average figure, although residents there still faced living expenses of more than 90 percent of the national urban average. An additional study completed in 1937 again found only slight cost differences between southern and nonsouthern urban areas. Average maintenance costs in the former were barely 4 percent lower than the average in the latter. The cost of living in Atlanta, Memphis, New Orleans, and Birmingham compared to that in such cities as Philadelphia, Providence, Seattle, Indianapolis, Portland, and Columbus, Ohio, all of which recorded significantly higher factory wage and work relief scales.[37]

Clearly WPA employment never gave steady, sufficient assistance to depression victims, although thousands of the southern urban jobless welcomed the opportunity to earn their "relief." The major problem involved the availability of emergency positions, which varied almost monthly depending on federal appropriations, the abilities

---

Housing Area Survey of Metropolitan Atlanta (Atlanta, 1940), 51.

36. Howard, *The W. P. A. and Federal Relief Policy*, 178; Holmes, "The New Deal in Georgia," 213, 237.

37. "Cost of Living Figures," *City Builder* (Atlanta) (March, 1934) 21; Margaret L. Stecker, *Intercity Differences in Cost of Living in March, 1935, Fifty-Nine Cities*, WPA Research Monograph, XII (Washington, D.C., 1937), 158–59. H. M. Douty, "Are Living Costs Lower in the South," *Southern Economic Journal*, V (January, 1939), 363–70; Lumpkin, *The South in Progress*, 69–70.

or the whims of local relief officials, and the willingness of municipal sponsors to contribute their share. As well, approximately 70 percent of all WPA jobholders, and more than 90 percent of all blacks, were classified as unskilled and thus earned a pitiful existence that could not satisfy even minimum needs. And in the southern cities, at least, relief workers could not find support from the established urban labor councils, which refused to accept them as their own. Yet in spite of such conditions, and the feelings of some that emergency jobholders were receiving something for nothing, the laborers were responsible for new construction, repair work of all kinds, and social services that benefited the cities. This in turn generated an increasing awareness of the complexities of twentieth-century urban life and beginning efforts to address those intricacies through community planning.

 6

POLITICS AND PUBLIC WORKS: MODERNIZING THE SOUTHERN CITIES

The millions of dollars released through the public works programs in the 1930s were responsible for a host of large and small construction projects in the southern cities. Emergency laborers completed hundreds of worthwhile new structures while improving a greater number of old ones. A press release in February, 1936, described one unique Memphis WPA project as "modernistic in design, with curtained windows, shower baths, spacious runways, individual rooms, and [offering] a daily change of bedding." The mayor of nearby Rankin, Arkansas, congratulated Memphis mayor Overton on the project, although he lamented at the same time that he had been unable to procure federal dollars for his town for such necessary works as hospital improvements, park extension, school repairs, and street paving. The recently completed structure in Memphis suggested that Overton could obtain money for almost anything.

Opened in early 1936, the WPA project in question was a modern dog pound. The federal government and the city had jointly sponsored the endeavor, which ultimately became the target of adverse publicity from local and state officials and newspapers all across the country. Because relief money was limited, perhaps the outcry against the Tennessee project should not have been surprising. Still, Mayor Overton resented the criticism and steadfastly defended the new structure as an improvement to life in his city. The mayor was particularly outraged when the New York *Times* called the project a "$25,000 Boondoggling Dogpound" and when the Associated Press circulated a poem appropriately entitled "It's A Dog's Life." It concluded with the stanza:

Fido, you should greatful [*sic*] be
To the new democracy;
What a home for you to win!
Hey! One side! I'm moving in![1]

While there were a few "boondoggling dogpounds," the majority of
federal projects were of much greater value to communities throughout
America. The first three decades of the twentieth century had been a
time of both population growth and physical expansion, especially in
the urban South, with the Dixie cities beginning to look less like
oversize regional towns and more like twentieth-century metropolitan
areas. Temporarily, the depression downturn retarded the pattern of
modern development, although the millions of dollars made available
through the relief agencies launched the trend anew. According to the
Birmingham WPA director, the construction work of the 1930s, which
accounted for 60 to 70 percent of emergency employment, moved the
city ahead thirty years in building improvements, based on past growth
rates.[2] The politics involved in the acquisition of emergency projects in
the southern cities suggests that New Deal administrators were more
generous to their friends than to others—as the renovation of the
Memphis dog pound makes clear. Yet it is equally clear that municipal
authorities hoped that the improvement and modernization of their
physical surroundings would help attract outside businesses while
providing assistance for the jobless at minimal local cost, all supportive of the existing political and social order.

When the first public works programs became operable in 1933,
civic leaders in Atlanta showed a determination to acquire as much
federal money as possible. By midyear, a city council subcommittee
had completed an investigation of area needs and priorities for possible
PWA, FERA, and CWA projects. Throughout the decade, this special
municipal group maintained a dialogue with administrators of several
federal programs, and its efforts in 1935, for example, brought to
Atlanta one-half of Georgia's entire WPA allocation for building activities. Within one week of the group's organization, moreover, city
officials approved an initial list of programs, including $18 million in
school repairs, hospital improvements, the construction of a new
police station, and park and playground development. At the top of the
list was the city's most urgent need—a new, $10 million metropolitan
sewerage system.[3]

---

1. Memphis *Commercial Appeal*, February 14, 23, 1936; Memphis *Press Scimitar*,
February 11, 1936.

2. Birmingham *News*, June 14, 1942.

3. Atlanta *Constitution*, June 19, 22, 28–29, 1933, July 6, 16, August 13, 1935,

The New South capital entered the 1930s as one of the fastest-expanding urban areas in the nation, but its physical facilities had not kept pace with population and industrial growth. In particular, the city's sewerage system was a disgrace. Human and industrial waste polluted streams well within the corporate limits, so that most of the waterways were offensive to sight and smell. By late 1930, many court cases were pending against city hall, several brought by area farmers who used the creeks for their livestock. Local disposal plants, as well as private septic tanks, were overloaded, and poor drainage caused street and cellar flooding during even moderate rainstorms. The archaic sewers were also a serious health hazard. The director of the state health department reported in 1933 that Atlanta ranked first among all American cities in diphtheria deaths and that the local typhoid rate was twice the average for the fifteen largest urban areas in the country. He attributed much of the problem to inadequate sewer facilities.[4]

Clearly, municipal officials were interested in solving current drainage and health problems; there was also a concern about the city's future growth. City hall had initially sought RFC assistance for a new facility, but to no avail, and when the New Deal agencies appeared, Atlanta councilmen immediately bombarded them with funding requests. First, the city appealed to the CWA, and in 1933 Washington, D.C., released more than one million dollars for the beginnings of a modern sewer trunk line to be sponsored jointly by the municipality and the Fulton and Dekalb county commissions. The work ended when the agency closed in mid-1934. The city next turned to the GERA, but its works division would not allocate the necessary finances. Plans called for construction to span the decade, and FERA director Hopkins favored neither large projects nor proposals that required a long-term financial obligation. Secretary Ickes of the PWA was likewise unimpressed with the sewer project. He was not convinced that the city had the means to repay the 70 percent loan portion of the project's cost. The fate of the Atlanta proposal clearly demonstrated Ickes's commitment to deliberate decision making.[5]

Throughout the depression decade, the PWA was never as active in

---

September 18–19, 1938; Atlanta *Journal*, July 24, 1935; Atlanta City Council Minutes, XXXIV, September 8, 1933, p. 309, City Hall, Atlanta.

4. Atlanta *Journal*, October 12, 1930; T. F. Abercrombie to Editor, Atlanta *Constitution*, July 14, 1935.

5. Atlanta *Constitution*, October 19–20, 1933; Minutes of the Fulton County Commission, V, January 19, 1934, pp. 56–59, Fulton County Commission Office, Atlanta; Clark Howell to Hopkins, January 17, 1934, in Record Group 69, Records of the Civil

Georgia as in the other southeastern states. From 1933 to 1936, the presence of anti–New Deal governor Talmadge made an ever-cautious Ickes even more uneasy, and in 1935, the agency director actually suspended all PWA aid to the state at the same time that Hopkins was "federalizing" FERA work in Georgia. Another problem was a state constitutional provision preventing the state and its localities from borrowing to repay federal loans. The restriction was certainly out-of-date—the work of defeated Confederates who had opposed Reconstruction bonds. But even after Eurith D. Rivers replaced Talmadge as governor, PWA funds were never readily available. President Roosevelt, for example, halted agency aid to the state for nearly a year after Rivers failed to support New Deal candidate Lawrence Camp against conservative incumbent Walter George in the 1938 senatorial primary. As of mid-1939, the PWA had appropriated only twenty million dollars to Georgia—less than 5 percent of its total spending in the Southeast.[6]

The Atlanta sewer project, therefore, would have surely encountered untold delays had the New Deal not altered its work relief network in 1935. When the WPA became functional, the city council applied for a grant, and in November, local voters approved a million-dollar bond issue to provide the sponsor's initial share. At the same time, Fulton County commissioners set aside $400,000 as their portion of the cost, and soon thereafter WPA chief Hopkins gave his approval. Ultimately, the project became a joint effort of the WPA and the PWA, when Secretary Ickes demanded partial control because of the heavy construction that fell within his program's jurisdiction. Work finally began on the $11 million venture in late 1935. Thousands of WPA laborers extended and enlarged pipelines, while PWA efforts went into the building of several large treatment plants. Later, city and federal authorities added a new water purification system. Like the sewer lines, the old system had become a health hazard, incapable of handling the volume of water consumed each month in the Atlanta area.[7]

More than in Atlanta, the fate of federal construction projects in

Works Administration, Georgia Administrative File, National Archives, hereinafter cited as CWA; Shepperson to Hopkins, November 16, 1934, and Perry Fellows to Howell, November 22, 1934, both in RG 69, Records of the Federal Emergency Relief Adminstration, Georgia Projects, NA, hereinafter cited as FERA.

6. Holmes, "The New Deal in Georgia," 351–57; "PWA and Georgia: The State's No-Debt Policy Rouses the President's Ire," *Newsweek*, December 5, 1938, p. 12.

7. Atlanta City Council Minutes, XXXVI, December 2, 1935, pp. 227; Minutes of the Fulton County Commission, V, November 13, 1935, pp. 607–609; David L. Browne to J. C. Capt, October 1, 1935, and Ralph Langely to R. W. Crawford, July 12, 1937, both in RG 69, Records of the Works Progress Administration, Georgia Projects, NA, hereinafter cited as WPA; Holmes, "The New Deal in Georgia," 358–60.

New Orleans became entangled in state political maneuvers. For example, in late 1933, city officials requested more than $2.5 million in PWA loans and grants for a project to be supervised by the local sewerage and water board. Through 1934, the federal government delayed the application, as Secretary Ickes mistrusted Huey Long and his lieutenants in the Louisiana legislature who claimed authority over all state contract work. In March, 1935, however, the PWA chief reluctantly approved the city's request as a test case. But as Ickes probably guessed would happen, the project immediately became entwined in a political showdown between Long and Mayor Walmsley's Old Regulars, who still dominated New Orleans.[8]

As soon as the federal government released the grants and loans, Louisiana governor Oscar K. Allen obtained a court order preventing the city from spending the money. The governor then turned to the legislature, which created a new sewerage and water board for New Orleans—a move that was only one part of Long's legislative assault on the city machine. At the same time, lawmakers were giving the state organization total control of Crescent City finances. A complicated judicial struggle followed. One state court declared the new board unconstitutional, but the Louisiana Supreme Court reversed the decision, declaring that the state was simply exercising its lawful police powers. The question was then taken up by the federal courts, where District Judge William E. Borah ruled that the wording of an 1899 law prohibited either the city or the state from appointing members to a new board. Only the commission as established in 1899 could legally allocate federal funds.

The confrontation remained unsettled until July, 1935, when the existing New Orleans sewerage and water board, on its own, surrendered to the Kingfish. By the summer, Long was in control of city finances as well as local police and fire department personnel. Municipal leaders could not even collect local taxes, as Louisiana lawmakers had transferred that power to the state. Capping the victory, the Old Regulars throughout 1935 were steadily deserting Mayor Walmsley; among them were members of the sewerage board who finally capitulated to Long's terms. In an effort to keep their jobs, they appointed a

8. Data on the water and sewerage board controversy from Thomas Martin, *Dynasty: The Longs of Louisiana* (New York, 1960), 126–28; C. H. Campbell, "Huey Long Chokes New Orleans," *Nation*, July 24, 1935, pp. 93–95; Arnold Fulton, "First Month of Dictator Long," *Nation*, August 14, 1935, pp. 179–81; New Orleans *Times-Picayune*, December 14, 1934, April 11, 16, 1935; New York *Times*, January 2, 5, August 7, 11, November 18, 1934, January 6, 15, April 11, 19, June 22–23, July 17, 21, 1935. For a comprehensive analysis of the machine struggle throughout Louisiana, see Williams, *Huey Long*, 266–67, 756–79, 891–94; Allan P. Sindler, *Huey Long's Louisiana: State Politics, 1920–1952* (Baltimore, 1956), 118–36.

pro-Long director and agreed to operate under a new state civil service commission. Although the mayor stubbornly held on until early 1935, the Long organization's sweep of state and municipal elections in that year left him little choice but to resign.

Walmsley's replacement was Robert Maestri, elected in August, 1936, without opposition. A businessman, Maestri ruled New Orleans for ten years. He lowered taxes, balanced the budget, centralized purchasing, and generally conducted an efficient, businesslike administration. Until 1946 he held together a coalition of Long leaders and former Old Regulars, while winning the support of the city's business and financial community.[9]

Two days after Judge Borah's decision, Secretary Ickes froze the New Orleans sewer project. In so doing, he informed the New Orleans *Times-Picayune* that "the trouble with Long is that he is suffering from halitosis of the intellect." Then in July, Ickes acted again, ending all PWA aid to the state, including money earmarked for projects already under construction. The Interior boss was clearly retaliating against the state's attempted control of federal funds, and no doubt he hoped to trigger a popular reaction against the Kingfish by halting PWA expenditures. Other New Deal agencies were likewise prepared to intervene in state political affairs. There was evidence that Louisiana ERA and WPA chief Frank Peterman opposed the machine throughout 1935 by appointing anti-Long relief officials in several Louisiana parishes.[10]

But after Long's death in September, 1935, the project situation in Louisiana suddenly changed. Within two months, Ickes reversed the freeze and released the sewer and water funds once again, this time to test Long's successors. Unlike their former boss, the new machine leaders—Earl Long, Governor Richard Leche, and Mayor Maestri—represented mainstream Democrats within the organization who endorsed the New Deal. They hoped to use the federal programs to bring millions of dollars into the state and strengthen their political base. Thus, in 1936 New Orleans received its $2.5 million for sewer and water improvements, and soon thereafter, the city and state began gathering additional millions. The so-called Second Louisiana Purchase had begun, with federal authorities exchanging relief funds for machine support within the Democratic party. According to Louisiana

9. Don Eddy, "Kingfish the Second: Robert Sidney Maestri," *American Magazine* CXXVIII (November, 1939), 16; New York *Times*, September 29, 1935, March 10, 1936; Hermann B. Deutsch, "New Orleans Politics: The Greatest Show on Earth," in Hodding Carter *et al.* (eds.), *The Past as Prelude: New Orleans, 1718–1968* (New Orleans, 1968), 326–28; Edward F. Haas, "New Orleans on the Half-Shell: The Maestri Era," *Louisiana History*, XIII (Summer, 1972), 283–310.

10. New Orleans *Times-Picayune*, April 17, July 19, 1935; New York *Times*, July 19, 1935.

scholar Edward Haas, "In private conversation the mayor [Maestri] often declared the WPA a money tree that he shook whenever the city needed revenue."[11]

The honeymoon between the New Deal and the state organization lasted until mid-1939, when syndicated columnist Drew Pearson uncovered a number of illegal dealings involving machine leaders who had profited handsomely from public works. Subsequent investigations, which involved as many as nine federal agencies between 1939 and 1942, discovered graft, kickbacks, bogus contracts, and noncompetitive bidding on a huge scale. The most newsworthy scandal involving WPA dollars was the Louisiana State University building program, which resulted in the school president's resignation and flight from prosecution. Not all of the illegalities involved the New Deal; the "hot oil" leasings, which led directly to the resignation of Governor Leche, were unassociated with the federal relief program.[12]

Not surprisingly, the scandals had statewide political repercussions, and in the 1940 elections, reform-minded governor Sam Jones defeated the Long organization. Yet throughout it all, investigations never linked Mayor Maestri of New Orleans directly to the payoffs, despite the involvement of many of his friends and business associates. Maestri's "efficient administration" was too popular to suffer from the scandals—or perhaps city voters were still recovering from a decade of political fireworks—and the mayor retained his office until 1946.[13]

The rebuilding of Charity Hospital, which contained the only indigent wards in Louisiana, also reflected the entanglement of politics and federal projects in New Orleans and throughout the state. The multi-building complex dated from 1736, when a local philanthropist willed his large estate to the city for the establishment of a hospital for the poor. Although the unit had provided excellent medical treatment for many years for the Louisiana needy, by the early 1930s most of its physical structures were too old to handle the increasing volume of

11. Haas, *DeLesseps S. Morrison*, 17; New Orleans *Times-Picayune*, November 1, 18, 1935; New Orleans *Tribune*, July 8, August 16, October 25, 1936, March 26, 1937. For a general discussion of the "second Louisiana Purchase" years, see Field, "The Politics of the New Deal in Louisiana," 246–310; Hamilton Basso, "Can New Orleans Come Back?" *Forum* (March, 1940), 124–28.

12. For thorough analyses of the Louisiana scandals, see Field, "The Politics of the New Deal in Louisiana," 100–408; Martin, *Dynasty*, 169–71; Harnett T. Kane, *Louisiana Hayride: The American Rehearsal for Dictatorship* (New York, 1941), 280–82.

13. Haas, *DeLesseps S. Morrison*, 290–91; Joseph Parker, *The Morrison Era: Reform Politics in New Orleans* (Gretna, La., 1974), 56–69; Michael Kurtz, "Earl Long's Political Relation with the City of New Orleans," *Louisiana History*, X (Summer, 1969), 241.

patients.[14] The State Board of Health had condemned the main build-ing as unsafe because the 1,756-bed hospital was caring for more than 2,500 patients each day. According to federal relief inspectors, 90 patients shared 42 beds in one ward, leaving some of the sick to sleep on the floor for weeks at a time.

Additional problems involved the Kingfish, who insisted on tam-pering with the facility for political ends. The Louisiana boss con-trolled the board of directors, extorted contributions from employees, and offered free medical care to his lieutenants. He also thought he could move large medical buildings at will, ordering in the early 1930s the 5-story, 10-year-old Female Medical Building moved 162 feet to make room for a combined pharmacy and dental unit, which was to become part of a new medical college. Long planned an entirely new school to humble the surgical faculty at Tulane University for refusing to admit the director of Charity as a full professor in their department. To accomplish the move, bulldozers razed the Vincent Memorial Contagious Building, which stood in the path, and the state transferred the patients into unheated wooden structures, where they remained for almost a year. The move also destroyed the basement of the women's clinic, which work crews two years later moved back to its original location to make room for a new main hospital building funded by the PWA. The episode cost the state more than $500,000 and adversely affected the quality of medical care available in New Orleans.

Recognizing a need to modernize the health complex, hospital administrators in late 1933 applied for PWA loans and grants totalling nearly ten million dollars. The original plan, which included the establishment of a number of pay wards to help repay federal loans, stirred more controversy than officials had envisioned and led to its rejection by a state PWA advisory committee. The New Orleans Tax-payer's Association argued that tax monies would ultimately repay the loans, pay wards notwithstanding, and the Orleans Parish Medical Society raised legal technicalities, questioning the authority of the hospital to borrow money or alter health services through the pay-ward scheme. Private hospitals were also critical, indicating that the present public facility was sufficient, especially if it halted free health care to

14. Data on the Charity Hospital project from S. R. Winters, "The New Orleans Charity Hospital," *Hygeia*, XV (November, 1937), 990–92; Field, "The Politics of the New Deal in Louisiana," 122–24, 150–52; Stella O'Conner, "The Charity Hospital of Louisiana at New Orleans: An Administrative and Financial History, 1736–1941," *Louisiana Historical Quarterly*, XXXI (January, 1948), 88–94; "Double Bed Charity," *Time*, Novem-ber 29, 1937, p. 53; "New Orleans Hospital," *Time*, April 15, 1940, pp. 70–72; New Orleans *Times-Picayune*, July 16, 1935, March 10, 1936, July 1, 1937; New Orleans *Item*, September 22, 1938.

Long's cronies. In fact, the threat of a new indigent hospital caused the city's five largest private medical units to institute a unique health insurance program. Employee groups of ten or more were eligible at a minimal annual cost of nine dollars per family. The American Hospital Association endorsed the idea as a means of bringing health care to families who might otherwise turn to charity in the event of prolonged sickness.

The project remained unsettled until late in 1934, when Senator Long revived it. The boss first had Louisiana lawmakers legalize the accrual of a federal debt; and then to appease the medical profession, he dropped the pay-ward scheme and offered an annual state subsidy of $400,000 to repay the necessary loan. The $10 million venture, however, was too large for WPA consideration; it still required the approval of Secretary Ickes. Not until after Long's death did the Interior Secretary in 1937 finally approve the building of the new $12 million public hospital.

Once completed, the health facility was truly a magnificent structure. It included a new, 20-story main hospital of 2,700 beds, which complemented the 850 beds still in use in 4 separate memorial clinics. The central building provided separate but roughly equal wards for whites and blacks, a gymnasium for interns, a drug manufacturing department, a cafeteria, a printing shop, and laundries. Each ward was a complete unit with treatment rooms and doctors' offices, and a pneumatic tube system connected each of the fifty operating rooms to the pathology laboratory. A fourteen-story school of nursing, training laboratories, and classrooms for medical students from Tulane and Louisiana State University, an ambulance garage, and several warehouses and workshops were also part of the multi-building complex. The modern hospital opened as the second largest in the United States and the largest state health facility in the world for the treatment of acute and contagious diseases.[15]

Leaders in Birmingham, like their counterparts in the other southern cities, believed that continued industrial growth depended upon the availability of modern facilities and services for both established and prospective manufacturers. Thus, officials in the steel center were especially quick to request millions from the New Deal for small and

15. The Charity Hospital project was also involved in the Louisiana scandals of the late 1930s, although there was no evidence of actual construction fraud (materials or workmanship). Investigators did discover that employees were subject to political kickbacks, that the administration was inefficient, and that contractors who had not received bids had received compensation from a general fund set up by all bidders. After the election of reform governor Jones in 1940, the hospital was placed under a new, more efficient administration. See O'Conner, "The Charity Hospital of Louisiana," 95–96.

large projects alike. Beginning in July, 1933, City Commission Council president Jones bombarded PWA and later CWA administrators with applications for building programs, and in 1934, commissioners applied for their largest proposed venture—a $7 million PWA grant and loan for a new industrial water supply unit. Jones appointed a permanent civic engineering commission to take charge of the planned project. Specifically, the engineers sought the construction of a major dam, distribution resources and lines, and chemical treatment plants, all of which would create jobs for thousands of area laborers.[16]

Local hopes remained high until October, 1934, when Secretary Ickes rejected the city's application. The secretary understood that local leaders had designed the project in order to attract new industry, but he worried about the repayment of the federal loan portion because the established plants, which would be the principal customers in the short run, already had water supplies. Even the lobbying efforts of Alabama senator John Bankhead failed to change the PWA chief's decision, as did pledges by local manufacturers to use the new system, with municipal supplements if necessary, and city guarantees that all federal loans would be repaid on schedule. It was later suggested that Ickes delayed the venture until assured through the office of Senator Hugo Black that Birmingham voters would replace conservative congressman George Huddleston with Luther Patrick, the national administration's candidate, in the 1936 Democratic primary.[17]

Municipal leaders by mid-1935 had become discouraged with Ickes's deliberateness. They especially failed to understand why he opposed their project when late that year he approved a similar one for Little Rock, Arkansas, which was one-third Birmingham's size. But upon the opening of the WPA, when Birmingham commissioners opened negotiations with Hopkins, the possibility of WPA involvement quickly prodded the Interior Secretary, always protective of his jurisdiction over large-scale construction, to reconsider his decision. The end result was that the two works agencies reached an accommodation, as they did in Atlanta. In January, 1936, Ickes approved a PWA loan for the purchase of dam and pipeline materials, and the WPA

16. Birmingham *Age-Herald*, June 21, 1933; Birmingham *News*, July 29, November 15, 1933.

17. Clinton Decker, "The Birmingham Industrial Water Supply," *Journal of the American Water Works Association*, XXX (January, 1938), 56–66; Birmingham *Age-Herald*, October 10, 1934; Birmingham *News*, October 3, 1934; Birmingham *Post*, October 5, 1934; Horatio B. Hackett to Jones, May 24, 1935 (Drawer 2), Harold Ickes to Bankhead, June 21, 1935 (Drawer 3), in James M. Jones, Jr., Collection, Alabama Archives and History, Montgomery.

agreed to cover labor costs for the three thousand men who gained emergency employment.[18]

Construction began in February, 1936, and emergency work crews completed the modern industrial supply system in December, 1939. The unit's largest component was a 180-foot dam, erected at Blackburn Fork of the Warrior River, 32 miles above Birmingham. The dam created a 22-billion-gallon reservoir covering 6,000 acres, which supplied the city with a daily capacity of 40 to 60 million gallons of water. From the lake, water moved through steel and cast-iron pipes, purchased with PWA loans from local industries. By 1939, more than 40 area firms had tapped into the new system, receiving water at one-third the cost charged by the municipal waterworks company. After less than two years of operation, the system was producing one-half of all water consumed in Birmingham, and from the outset, the venture proved self-liquidating. An important by-product of the water system was the area that became Blackburn Lake. The city later transformed the area into a recreation center and leased a portion of the lake frontage to owners of summer camps.[19]

No doubt Birmingham officials had hopes that the water project would appeal to outside manufacturers. Municipal elites believed, as one reporter from *American City* magazine concluded, that a lack of inexpensive water had "hampered the growth of the manufacturing district" and that such a supply was "essential in attracting new industry to consume Birmingham's products of raw materials." The city even operated the system with leaking pipelines, despite the warnings of federal inspectors that damages were "much in excess of allowable tolerances for economic operation." The booster motive became even more apparent when the Birmingham chamber of commerce opened a ten-year crusade to lure manufacturing to the area. The campaign hoped to attract all types of industry and thus lessen the city's dependency on steel and coal. Especially high on the list were chemical, clothing, farm implement, and heavy machine manufacturers. The crusade and its advertising stirred much local interest and raised expectations of future expansion. The Birmingham *Labor Advocate*, for example, announced in bold print in 1938 that "Birmingham Is

18. "Birmingham's Industrial Water Supply," *American City*, (May, 1936), 66; Birmingham *News*, January 3, 6, 1939; Birmingham *Age-Herald*, January 7, 1937, May 8, 1938.

19. "Industries Cooperate with City to Build a Separate Water Supply," *Engineering News-Record*, April 22, 1937, p. 591; Florence Hawkins Woods Moss, *Building Birmingham and Jefferson County* (Birmingham, 1947), 198; Birmingham *Age-Herald*, June 25, 1938.

Going Forward! Nothing Can Stop Her—Nobody Can Stop Her."[20]

The campaign never succeeded as planned. By the 1930s, it seems, industries had developed area resources almost to their maximum. In the postdepression years, TCI and other established firms periodically expanded or renovated their operations, but no companies that would bring in a large number of employees relocated in Birmingham. And the city did not keep pace with overall southern urban population growth. Birmingham began falling behind during the depression decade, growing by less than 4 percent, while the growth rates for Atlanta, New Orleans, and Memphis averaged nearly 12 percent. This disparity continued, and as other southern urban areas became increasingly metropolitan in structure with more diverse populations—a trend led by the more recently expanded Sun Belt cities—Birmingham remained stagnant, essentially unchanged. As a result, the steel city became increasingly hesitant to embrace social progress and reform, doubtless contributing to its recent reputation as "America's Johannesburg."[21]

The combined resources of two New Deal agencies, the PWA and the TVA, were similarly responsible for the largest building project in Memphis. The result was that the city became eligible for inexpensive TVA power, generated from nearby federal hydroelectric stations; and in the process, the city gained control of electrical distribution lines and other utilities. By 1940, Memphis was the fifth largest city in the country with a municipal gas system and the largest city to own both gas and electrical facilities.[22]

Within months of the TVA's opening in 1934, Memphis joined other area municipalities in expressing an interest in inexpensive power. The privately owned Memphis Power and Light company controlled the flow of electricity in Memphis, with civic officials noting that consumers paid twice as much for power as did homeowners in the Muscle Shoals area in the heart of the TVA region. Also, Boss Crump recognized the political implications of the issue. In early 1934, he indicated to gubernatorial candidate Hill McAlister that the matter would be a "spectacular campaign issue" and that McAlister should

20. H. A. Gray to F. C. Harrington, July 12, 1938, and B. B. Gauld to Fellows, August 26, 1938, both in WPA, Alabama Projects; Birmingham *News*, January 15, 1936; Birmingham *Labor Advocate*, June 25, 1938.

21. J. Allen Tower, "The Industrial Development of the Birmingham Region," *Bulletin of Birmingham Southern College*, XLVL (December, 1953), 13; *Sixteenth Census of the United States* (1940), I, 325, 336, II, 375, 383, III, 427, 435, VI, 710, 741.

22. Ralph C. Hon, "The Memphis Power and Light Deal," *Southern Economic Journal*, VI (January, 1943), 344.

"lose no time in advocating the stringing of TVA wires into every city, town, village and hamlet in the state."[23]

The local electric company did not concede easily, joining several private firms in opposition to the new federal program. Leaflets, newspaper advertisements, and other propaganda pieces labeled the TVA as "creeping socialism." In addition, Memphis Power and Light even lowered its rates by as much as 15 percent as part of a campaign to stall the growing TVA movement in the western Tennessee area.[24]

The company's tactics were not successful. In March, 1934, Mayor Overton opened negotiations with the federal commission while obtaining state legislation enabling the municipality to construct its own distribution lines for the transmission of TVA power. Within weeks, the mayor began meeting with TVA director David Lilienthal, and by midyear, the federal authority approved the financing of a distribution system up to the city limits. In November, Memphis residents voted seventeen to one in favor of bringing TVA power to the city and of public ownership of distribution facilities. The vote authorized a $9 million bond issue for either the purchase of private power lines or the building of new ones. The turnout was three times larger than for any other bond issue referendum in Memphis history. One year later, federal and municipal officials signed a twenty-year contract, allowing the flow of TVA power to Memphis as soon as the municipality constructed or purchased distribution lines within its corporate limits.[25]

To finance the acquisition or the building of distribution lines, the mayor in 1935 applied to the PWA for substantial grants and loans and called on Senator McKellar to help expedite the negotiations. The Crump organization maintained a direct line to the president through the senator's office, the kind of advantage that project sponsors in Birmingham, Atlanta, and, at least through 1935, New Orleans did not have. In the Memphis-TVA deal, McKellar at one point even telegrammed the vacationing chief executive at Hyde Park, asking that Roosevelt involve himself personally "in having said project approved." Still, a year went by, showing that Ickes was as deliberate as ever, although in October, 1936, the secretary approved the release of initial loans and grants totaling seven million dollars for the electrical system. Three years later, after rising costs forced the city again to call

23. Crump to McAlister, March 23, 1934, in Hill McAlister Papers, Box 14, Tennessee State Archives and History, Nashville.

24. Memphis *Press Scimitar*, September 24–25, December 18, 1933; Miller, *Mr. Crump of Memphis*, 224, 230.

25. Memphis *Press Scimitar*, March 6, 30, May 7, October 7, 1934, November 23, 1935.

on McKellar for assistance in securing federal monies, the PWA agreed to cover the venture's entire final estimated cost of nearly eighteen million dollars.[26]

Indeed, the Crump machine worked closely with New Deal administrators throughout the 1930s, just as the Long organization did in the later years of the decade. In return, the Memphis boss controlled more than a few federal positions in his county, as well as in the state. Tennessee WPA director Harry Berry was a Crump confidant, as was Memphis district relief director S. T. Pease. Other officials likewise owed their appointments to Crump, including local social security board administrators, federal housing personnel, a United States marshall, and federal district attornies in several western Tennessee counties. The relatively slow rate of population growth in the 1930s contributed as well to the Crump machine's continued presence and strength. Not until the late 1940s would Crump's power crumble, owing mainly to post–World War II demographic changes and active labor and black opposition.[27]

The cooperation between Crump and national administrators was in evidence in other matters as well. In the Tennessee Democratic primary of 1938, for example, Crump and McKellar combed the state relief rolls for votes and campaign funds for their gubernatorial and senatorial candidates, Prentice Cooper and Tom Stewart, respectively. An investigation directed by the Senate Committee on Campaign Expenditures later found evidence of wrongdoing. But despite proof of what the New York *Times* called a "vigorous effort throughout the state to raise funds by contributions from WPA and other Federal employees for the coalition [machine] ticket," Cooper and Stewart won the primary and the election, and took their seats without challenge.[28]

Once PWA and TVA funds were procured, Memphis set out to

26. Telegram, McKellar to Roosevelt, September 9, 1935, in Kenneth McKellar Papers, Box 411, Memphis Public Library, Downtown Branch; telegram, N. L. Bachman to Overton, October 10, 1936, in Watkins Overton Papers, Box 4, Memphis State University Library; Approval Sheet for Non-Federal Projects, n.d., in Record Group 135, Records of the Public Works Administration, microfilm roll no. 7244, National Archives; Thomas Allen to McKellar, February 22, 1939, E. K. Burlew to McKellar, March 14, 1939, in Kenneth McKellar Papers, Box 411.

27. Peterson, *The Day of the Mugwhump*, 205. The Crump and Long (after 1935) organizations were not the only Democratic machines to develop working relationships with New Deal administrators. See Bruce M. Stave, *The New Deal and the Last Hurrah: Pittsburgh Machine Politics* (Pittsburgh, 1970).

28. R. B. Fowler to McKellar, n.d. (Box 411), McKellar to Crump, April 9, 23, May 20, 1937, Crump to McKellar, June 24, 1935, June 7, 1939 (Box 3), all in Kenneth McKellar Papers; Patterson, *The New Deal and the States*, 84; William R. Majors, "Gordon Browning and Tennessee Politics, 1937–1938," *Tennessee Historical Quarterly*, XXVIII (Spring, 1969), 57–67; William D. Miller, "The Browning-Crump Battle: The Crump

construct what federal examiners described as the "largest distribution system ever built at one time." Memphis Power and Light still objected, and when it refused to sell its facilities, the city began building duplicate lines and transformers to rival the existing system. The private company countered by lowering its rates by as much as 40 percent in an effort to compete with the city operation, and in January, 1939, it rejected an $18.1 million proposal for both its gas and electrical facilities. Meanwhile, construction on the municipal lines continued, and by early 1939, the city was distributing power to 6,000 Memphis homes through the PWA project. Ultimately, the popularity of the expanding municipal system, as well as its supply of inexpensive TVA electricity, forced the private concern to agree on a purchase price of $17.4 million for all of its properties.[29]

To operate the new municipal system, Memphis officials combined the administration of light, gas, and water under one commission appointed by city hall. The operation remains basically the same today, with three commissioners supervising a utilities board consisting of an attorney, engineers, and other paid personnel. With the commission's approval, the board establishes all rates, purchases power and gas, and recommends bond issues when necessary. After the new system began operating, utility expenses for all Memphis consumers were lower, despite some loss of property tax revenue owing to the city's acquisition of the former private holdings. Bureaucratic costs were also lower under the municipal system, and the construction of new distribution lines, in addition to improvements later made on the old ones, brought emergency jobs as well as increased electrical consumption to Shelby and adjacent counties.[30]

Memphis was the only southern city under examination to benefit from TVA power, although the possibility of inexpensive electricity generated interest elsewhere. The Atlanta City Council in 1933 and

Side," East Tennessee Historical Society Publications, XXXVII (1965), 77–88; New York Times, June 20, 1935, July 26, 28, August 29, 1938, January 4, May 11–12, 1939.

29. "Memphis Power Defi," Business Week, December 10, 1938, p. 20; George W. Sneed to W. J. O'Brien, December 29, 1938 (Box 391), Thomas Allen to O'Brien, January 12, 1939 (Box 411), both in Kenneth McKellar Papers; Minton, "The New Deal in Tennessee," 307; Memphis Press Scimitar, June 27, 1939; Hon, "The Memphis Power and Light Deal," 373–74. For an analysis of the issue of public power throughout the state, see James David Bennett, II, "Struggle for Power: The Relationship Between the Tennessee Valley Authority and the Private Power Industry, 1933–1939" (Ph.D. dissertation, Vanderbilt University, 1969), 172–236.

30. "Memphis and the TVA," National Municipal Review, XXVII (May, 1939), 385; Bobbie Joe Williams, "Let There Be Light: History of the Development of Public Ownership of Electric Utilities in Memphis" (M.A. thesis, Memphis State University, 1972), 88–91.

again in 1934, for example, authorized a subcommittee to meet with TVA administrators. The idea of bringing public power to the city never developed beyond the talking stage and never reached a public vote.

In Birmingham, the City Commission Council in mid-1933 considered the construction of distribution lines to bring power from Muscle Shoals to the area. At the movement's forefront was the Jefferson County chapter of the League of Municipalities, the Birmingham Trades Council, and even City Commission Council president Jones, who initially indicated that it would be "an unforgivable calamity" for Birmingham not to participate in the TVA venture. Jones was mainly interested in the issue's political value, as it might affect his reelection bid that year. He was also hoping to squeeze the Birmingham Electric Company, then engaged in a dispute with the city over streetlight contracts. The private firm vehemently opposed public power, but even a 25-percent reduction of its rates in midyear failed to keep the issue off the ballot on October 9, 1933.[31]

Participation was light, but of those voting, nearly 60 percent rejected the municipal power proposal. By larger majorities, residents also voted down plans for city ownership of the local waterworks, streetcar lines, and steam-heating facilities. The pro-business Birmingham *Age-Herald*, which had called the public power movement "half-baked and irrational," rejoiced at the outcome, as did the Birmingham *News*, which concluded that voters did not want their government "to engage in business which common experience in this country has shown is best left to private enterprise." No real surprise was the change of heart of Jones, who had won his election in an August primary. Throughout the critical September weeks of debate, his once vocal support for the TVA and public ownership steadily diminished. He later became an outspoken opponent of public power, and without the backing of city officials, the idea had little chance of resurfacing.[32]

To preserve its victory, the local electric company continued to reduce its rates throughout the decade—seven cuts in the next six years. By 1939, the press was reporting that the "TVA yardstick was practically met." Despite the later construction of the Guntersville Dam, which brought electricity through public facilities to several communities in the Birmingham area (Bessemer, Tarrant City, and

31. Birmingham *Post*, July 13–14, 22, 26, 28–29, October 7, 1933; Birmingham *Age-Herald*, July 29, August 4, 1933.

32. "An Alabama Defeat for Public Ownership," *Literary Digest*, October 28, 1933, p. 45; Birmingham *Age-Herald*, October 10–11, 1933; Birmingham *News*, October 10, 1933.

Irondale), the city itself did not acquire any utility until 1951, when it purchased the local waterworks.[33]

In addition to the "headline" and sometimes politically controversial construction ventures, the federal works programs funded numerous less newsworthy but significant projects. Hospital improvements were among the top priorities in the southern cities. Atlanta health authorities, for example, described Henry Grady Hospital in the early 1930s as "in deplorable condition physically" and "not on any accredited list." Although a new main building for Grady was ten years away, significant renovations in the late 1930s improved the facility, as did thousands of hours of work on John Gaston Hospital in Memphis. One major setback to urban hospital improvement was the failure, despite federal approval, to remodel and triple the size of Atlanta's Albert Steiner Cancer Clinic. Fearing that its members would lose their fees, the Fulton County Medical Society won a court order blocking a plan to operate the institution for thirty-five years as a tax-free charity in exchange for public works allocations. Still, municipal and county officials in 1941 established the nine-member Metropolitan Hospital Authority to coordinate health care throughout the Atlanta area.[34]

Birmingham, too, benefited from hospital construction. Through 1939, forty-year-old Hillman Hospital was the only facility in the Birmingham district for indigent care. The population boom during the predepression years had placed a great strain on the medical unit; furthermore, there had been no major renovations since its opening. The situation improved significantly in 1940, however, when the new sixteen-story Jefferson Hospital opened its doors. Constructed through PWA grants and RFC loans totaling $2.5 million, Jefferson operated on a private basis, billing patients according to their ability to pay. The two health units later merged to become part of the Medical College of the University of Alabama at Birmingham.[35]

Federal agencies also aided the cities in school building and renovation projects. Almost every school in Memphis needed and benefited from WPA labor. Workers improved, among others, the Manassas High building, described by the principal as having "stood so

---

33. Cooper, *Metropolitan County*, 65–68; Birmingham *Post*, September 5, 1936; Birmingham *Age-Herald*, August 12, 1939; Birmingham *News*, November 28, 1939.

34. S. C. Dobbs to L. W. Robert, Jr., March 22, 1934, and J. B. Franklin to Dobbs, March 22, 1934, both in CWA, Georgia Administrative File; Atlanta City Council Minutes, XXXVI, October 21, 1935, p. 152; Atlanta *Constitution*, October 18, November 4, 1938, August 12, 1941; Atlanta *Journal*, October 20, 1939; Memphis *Press Scimitar*, November 6, 1939.

35. Jack D. L. Holmes, *A History of the University of Alabama Hospitals* (Birmingham, 1974), 37–55.

long that its foundation of sills and studs has dry-rotted rendering it extremely hazardous for the safety of the pupils." Designed to hold 500, the building by 1937 was accommodating more than 2,300 students each day. Between 1930 and 1945, public relief supplied much of the labor and more than $4 million for work in Memphis on seven new schools and for structural improvements on five existing buildings. In Atlanta, public school projects for the decade were valued at more than $6 million, including $1.6 million in PWA grants and loans for work at the Georgia Institute of Technology. New Orleans relief labor renovated more than 200 area educational buildings between 1933 and 1937.[36]

Birmingham's educational facilities were in equally deplorable condition, especially those for area blacks; yet the city failed to benefit to any great extent from federally sponsored school construction. In mid-decade, the Negro community of nearly 100,000 had only one school with space for more than six grades, and in a number of elementary buildings, more than 100 pupils crowded into each classroom. Outside the corporate limits, more than 11,000 black students and their 275 teachers met daily in 55 county-owned rooms, 26 church classrooms, and 174 private rooms. The WPA's construction of Carver High in 1937 barely dented the problem. City commissioners were simply not committed to educational projects for either blacks or whites. In 1936 they rejected a proposed $7 million PWA school building program by vetoing a bond issue necessary to finance a 55 percent share. A nationwide survey in 1938 found that Birmingham students held their own scholastically compared to the national average but that area school buildings were in such poor repair that "conditions endanger the health and safety of the children."[37]

The federal works agencies were responsible as well by decade's end for thousands of dollars worth of work on airports, sports stadiums, state and municipal government buildings, community recreation centers, public libraries, military training grounds, and countless

36. J. A. Hayes to McKellar, June 1, 1937, R. H. Neville to McKellar, June 1, 1937, E. C. Jones to McKellar, June 1, 1937, W. J. Overscott and E. C. Ball to McKellar, May 31, 1937, Ball to Overton, March 28, 1928, all in Mayor's Correspondence File, Drawer 5, Memphis and Shelby County Archives, Memphis; David Moss Hillard, "The Development of Public Education in Memphis, Tennessee, 1848–1945" (Ph.D. dissertation, University of Chicago, 1946), 61; Atlanta *Journal*, July 25, 1937; Atlanta *Constitution*, September 18, 1938; Ecke, *From Ivy Street to Kennedy Center*, 245; *Louisiana Weekly*, July 19, 1938.

37. Application of Jefferson County Board of Education for Funds for the Construction of Rural School Houses, n.d., in FERA, Alabama Projects; Jap Bryant to Alabama League of Municipalities, September 9, 1937, in WPA, Appraisal Reports: Alabama; Ambrose Caliver, "The Largest Negro High School," *School Life*, XVII (December, 1931), 73–74; "The Birmingham School Situation," *School and Society*, September 17, 1938, pp. 363–64.

historical sites. Included was the construction of a municipal slaughterhouse and a public grain elevator with a 1.4 million bushel capacity in Memphis. Both projects withstood the ire of private businesses, and upon completion they made Memphis more attractive to area farmers as a livestock and grain center rather than merely as a cotton market. Municipal leaders in New Orleans went so far as to propose the building of a $14 million city-operated railroad station. The plan triggered strong protests from railway unions, which referred to it as "national socialism." WPA budget cuts after 1938 led to the plan's rejection in Washington, D.C. The PWA-funded Fulton County jail was equally controversial. Advertised as escape-proof when completed in 1935, embarrassed officials announced two successful breakouts within a month of the prison's opening because of structural weaknesses undetected by building inspectors.[38]

Perhaps less visible than the many new large buildings were the modern parks and playgrounds opened in the cities in the 1930s. The WPA allocated thousands of relief dollars for Overton Park in Memphis for the renovation of equipment, a new concert amphitheater, and the expansion and improvement of the zoo. The complex, covering many acres, still operates today. Likewise, emergency jobholders in Atlanta completed the development of the Atlanta zoo and the modern Grant Park facility, which the city immediately placed under a new Jim Crow ordinance, federal protests notwithstanding. In Birmingham, WPA labor modernized baseball fields, tennis courts, open-air theaters, picnic areas, and swimming and wading pools in the city's three largest parks. In conjunction with TCI, which provided the land, the federal government was also responsible for the construction of Red Mountain Park and the placement of the Vulcan statue that still stands over Birmingham today. That city lost its zoo during the depression period, however, when the City Commission Council in 1934 closed the animal displays described by the local press as "a disgrace to the city." The only protest came from area schoolchildren, who had recently raised money to purchase "Miss Farcy," the zoo's only elephant. City authorities in turn threatened to "turn Miss Farcy over to . . . members of the board of education and let them look after her."[39]

38. Allen to Overton, January 25, 1934, August 17, 1934, William Fowler to Overton, July 13, 1935, Markwell to Overton, April 24, 1935, January 27, 1936, all in Mayor's Correspondence File, Drawer 5; New Orleans *States*, October 28, 1938; New Orleans *Item*, September 8, 1939; Atlanta *Constitution*, December 30, 1933, March 23, 1934, June 9, 1935.

39. Copy of Press Release, n.d., in Mayor's Correspondence File, Drawer 5; Bryant to Alabama League of Municipalities, September 9, 1937, in WPA, Appraisal Reports: Alabama; Birmingham *Post*, October 8, 1934; Birmingham *Age-Herald*, July 25, 1935; "Iron Man: Birmingham's 'Vulcan,'" *Time*, August 17, 1936, p. 68.

New Orleans recorded the most impressive park work, channeling more than 50 percent of its WPA funds into new recreational facilities. In April, 1936, more than 10,000 relief laborers, one-half of the city's total WPA force, were involved on projects in City Park. New Orleans and federal agencies together appropriated more than $10 million to convert the park from an ordinary facility into one of the most magnificent recreational centers in the country. The area, in excess of 1,500 acres, was formerly part of a local plantation. The city had acquired the land, part by purchase and part as a gift, from local philanthropist John McDonough. Until WPA work, only 400 acres were in use, but by 1940, federal dollars had funded the development and reclamation of more than one-third of the remaining portion. Included in the effort was the construction of a 26,000-seat stadium, golf courses, clubhouses, greenhouses and gardens, tennis courts, roadways and sidewalks, drains and bridges, and a beautiful mall area named in honor of President Roosevelt.[40]

The extension of the Lakefront Park residential area was another major WPA project in New Orleans. Plans to develop a modern housing subdivision on the south shore of Lake Pontchartrain dated from the 1870s, and when the Louisiana legislature in 1918 finally authorized the construction of a necessary seawall, the idea gained momentum. Residents in the 1920s approved a $9 million bond issue for the reclamation of more than 1,200 acres of land, and in 1931, private developers completed the multi-million-dollar levee. The depression stalled the work until 1936, when nearly 5,000 WPA workers began developing the land now filled with thirty million cubic yards of sand. Some of the men constructed sewers, streets, sidewalks, gardens, parks, and community recreation centers, while others surveyed and cleared 1,500 lots and planted 4,000 trees. What had been a breeding ground for malarial mosquitoes, and a place where only fishermen could be found, became a modern residential development, accommodating 1,200 families.[41]

General road improvements represented a final category for public works dollars, absorbing about 25 percent of all local WPA expendi-

40. U.S. Works Progress Administration, *W. P. A. Projects: Analysis of Projects Placed in Operation Through June 30, 1937* (1938), 100; R. B. Ritely to Jacob Baker, August 29, 1933, in FERA, Louisiana Work Relief; New Orleans *Times-Picayune*, August 6, 1933, June 28, 1936, March 6, September 28, 1938; New Orleans *Item*, August 15, 1937.

41. New Orleans *Times-Picayune*, October 9, 1935, January 17, June 10, 1936; New Orleans *Item*, August 15, 1937; United States Community Appraisal in the City of New Orleans, n.d., in WPA, Appraisal Reports: Louisiana; James Crutcher, "The WPA Program in Louisiana" (MS in Robert Maestri Papers, microfilm roll 420B, New Orleans Public Library, June 10, 1936); H. Van Chase, "Shores of Historic Pontchartrain Made Beautiful," *American City* (November, 1937), 101; New Orleans *Tribune*, September 18, 1936.

tures. In New Orleans, and typical of all southern cities at the time, pavement topped barely one-third of the city's streets. Although each paving project required only a few weeks of labor, their collective cost was in the millions, and they put to work the bulk of the WPA unskilled laborers. Between 1935 and 1940 in the Crescent City, road work totaled more than $18 million, which included street surfacing and the construction of bridges, curbs, sidewalks, and drainage ditches. In Birmingham through 1942, relief workers paved more than 800 miles of streets and erected nearly 150,000 highway markers. For street improvements in Memphis and Atlanta, Washington, D.C., set aside for each almost $8 million through 1938. The effort in Memphis was especially important, because street and drainage projects supported the malaria control program begun under the ERA and CWA and then continued with WPA personnel.[42]

In all of the Dixie cities under examination, perhaps the best measurement of the building activity in the 1930s was the increase in the value of residential and commercial construction permits. Their value had reached a nadir in 1933, having declined in four years by 33 percent in New Orleans and by 65 percent in Birmingham—the most in any of the cities. In part because of the public works programs, values began to increase in 1934, and with the exception of temporary setbacks during the recession in 1937 and 1938, advances continued throughout the decade. In 1940, the southern cities recorded permit values between 50 and 300 percent higher than those listed a decade earlier. Of course the rising value of building permits did not reflect an employment boom, as much of the labor came from the relief rolls. The unemployment rate among building craftsmen in the urban South remained high, although below the national average for that group, while the general unemployment rate in the Dixie cities ranged between 12 percent in Atlanta and nearly 19 percent in New Orleans, compared to a national urban average of 15 percent.[43]

Clearly the New Deal works programs fell short of reviving a depressed economy, and they did not fundamentally alter any city's

42. James Lee Reilly, "Street-Cleaning Problems in a Semi-Tropical City," *American City* (November, 1937), 53–56; "Concrete Street Signs . . . ," *ibid.* (May, 1938), 65; William Fowler, "Traffic Safety, Civic Beauty," *ibid.* (November, 1938), 95; New Orleans *Times-Picayune*, February 2, 1937, September 1, 1938, May 12, 1940; Memphis *Press Scimitar*, September 14, 1938, November 6, 1939; McKellar to Crump, July 19, 1935, August 7, 1939, in Kenneth McKellar Papers, Box 3; Birmingham *News*, August 14, 1941, April 13, 1943.

43. U.S. Bureau of Foreign and Domestic Commerce, *Statistical Abstract of the United States* (1935), 789–90; and (1942), 987–88; Memphis *Labor Review*, January 1, 8, 1937; *Sixteenth Census of the United States* (1940), I, 47, 336, 386, 438, 744; "Report on Craft Unemployment," *American Federationist* (July, 1938), 752, (May, 1939), 493, and (January, 1940), 67.

economic base. Yet emergency construction valued at millions of dollars for cities large and small had an effect on the private sector. Building meant additional tax revenue for the operation of municipal services as well as contracts for many local businesses producing necessary materials. CWA drainage and sewer projects in Birmingham, for example, created local orders for cast-iron pipe and other products, which according to TCI sources provided employment for 2,600 new men in the firm's rail mills and red-ore mines. Federal and city officials indicated that the Birmingham industrial water project brought nearly $3.5 million in benefits to local industries. Furthermore, it was common for store owners and homeowners to cooperate with WPA road surface programs. In 1935, a group of Birmingham retailers purchased paving materials for use by public jobholders on street improvements around their places of business. Similar efforts were in evidence in the other cities.[44]

Indeed, New Deal–sponsored construction had a tremendous impact on the southern cities. Work was made available for thousands of jobless men on scores of worthwhile community projects, generally coordinated by the newly developing city planning agencies. Even when an assignment was temporary and pay was low, a work position at least allowed an individual to earn his way, while his efforts facilitated the expansion and modernization of municipal health, recreation, education, and transportation services. And because federal funds went to the cities with few strings attached, especially if officials were supportive of the Democratic administration, civic boosters found that the works programs modernized their cities at minimal local cost and left the existing political and social order intact.

44. Carole E. Scott, "The Economic Impact of the New Deal on the South" (Ph.D. dissertation, Georgia State University, 1969), 194–200; Birmingham *Age-Herald*, January 7, 1936; Birmingham *Southern Labor Review*, December 6, 1933; Lewey Robinson, "Unpaved Streets Surfaced by Relief Labor," *American City* (November, 1935), 53–54.

 7

THE EXPANSION OF MUNICIPAL SERVICES

For years after the depression, southern urban residents made use of the scores of new buildings, the miles of paved roads, and the many playgrounds and large parks funded by the New Deal works agencies. Thousands of depression victims who had once held jobs in the expanding cities' private sectors labored on public building projects each day during the 1930s, and no doubt other certified but unassigned men and women would have gladly joined them had the federal government expanded the emergency programs. While construction activity was clearly the largest category of relief employment for skilled and unskilled workers, a number of public service ventures particularly accommodated jobless women, as well as white-collar workers of both sexes, whom the economic crisis had also left very much in need.

The contributions of service relief personnel were not as immediately visible as were the many new hospitals and schools. Service projects included sewing, canning, book repair, and school lunch programs, in addition to more sophisticated skilled projects—community health services, adult and child education, recreational leadership training, and a variety of vocational training clinics for young people. These had an immediate effect on thousands of workers and on an even greater number of individual recipients of the services. Equally important, the federal effort promoted active state and municipal health, recreation, and education programs that continued to operate in succeeding years. Such services addressed the general welfare of the public and were indicative of the advancing urban consciousness in the South. Referring to one unpublicized beautification project in Birmingham, the Alabama WPA service director seemed to summarize the overall worth of such endeavors. "No broad economic dilemmas are ended" and "no political problems are thus solved," she remarked; yet "here is a grand undertaking . . . which will be ministering to the spirits of men, women and children long after present problems have been forgotten and succeeded by other questions and troubles."[1]

The Division of Women's and Professional Projects (later changed to the Community Services Program) within the WPA's engineering and construction section was mainly responsible for implementing and supervising relief service programs. In Atlanta, Birmingham, and Memphis, professional projects absorbed nearly 25 percent of WPA allocations. A like dollar figure was set aside in New Orleans for the training and employment of hundreds of men and women who staffed new and rejuvenated community services. The NYA was active as well in the service sector. The youth agency's in-school program placed students from welfare families in after-class jobs. In the late 1930s, elaborate NYA training projects opened in many new building facilities constructed by young people through the agency's regular works program. By mid-1940 in Birmingham, more than $2.5 million had assisted 20,000 individuals, both white and black, in work and training endeavors.[2] One important feature of the NYA was Mary McLeod Bethune's active Division of Negro Affairs. It ensured the inclusion of some blacks in the youth programs, even if facilities and projects in the southern cities remained separate and not always equal.

The relief positions categorized as exclusively "women's work" were not glamorous, but they were important. Sewing and book repair projects had proved successful earlier; consequently, WPA officials offered similar opportunities to thousands of jobless women, most of whom provided for a family. Adverse economic conditions among women clearly dictated the organization of special programs for them, and nowhere was the situation more desperate than in the South. Of all certified clients in Georgia, as well as in the other states under consideration, nearly one-third were women. This figure compared to a national rate of less than 16 percent. Furthermore, while southern women represented 17 percent of the region's economic heads, they

1. Report of the Division of Women's and Professional Projects, January, 1939, in Mary Weber to Blanche Ralston, February 23, 1939, in Record Group 69, Records of the Works Progress Administration, Alabama Women's Projects, National Archives, hereinafter cited as WPA.

2. U.S. Works Progress Administration, *W. P. A. Projects: Analysis of Projects Placed in Operation Through June 30, 1937* (1938), 89–100; Birmingham *Post*, September 2, 1935, October 5, 1938; Birmingham *News*, April 14, 1940.

averaged less than 15 percent of the total WPA work force, even with the special projects.[3]

In the cities, where joblessness was the greatest, women faced more acute problems than in outlying areas. Those without previous employment experience were in especially uncertain positions because many service projects required some skill or at least in-service training. Between 70 and 80 percent of the women's relief force in the Dixie municipalities was unskilled, compared to a national rate of 46 percent. The large number of jobless black domestics in the southern labor force accounted for the disparity, and in Georgia, their plight was made even worse when lawmakers attempted to limit relief to women with the education, experience, or training to secure private employment in available work relief fields. Fortunately, Georgia WPA director Gay Shepperson circumvented the legislative effort, and throughout the 1930s, she operated one of the most active women's divisions in the country. Still, black women often received "pick and shovel" jobs, particularly in places where whites filled "women's work" quotas. According to the Atlanta *Daily World*, black women were often "forced to work in overalls at labor . . . exceeding their strength." WPA supervisors denied the charge, explaining that the overalls protected the women's clothing and that much of the "work was not terribly strenuous."[4]

The problem of securing sponsors, and thus the local government or private funding required, constantly plagued the women's programs. Such projects were not highly visible, and municipal officials in particular showed little enthusiasm for allocating city revenues for them. This was especially true in New Orleans. The WPA office there spent far fewer dollars proportionately for service work than relief administrators working with civic leaders in the other southern cities under examination, themselves far from generous. The WPA hot lunch project in the Crescent City, for example, was active through 1935 under school board sponsorship, providing more than 500,000 free meals to underprivileged children. But in early 1936, following a court order banning the participation of educators in welfare activities, the city abandoned sponsorship responsibility. Between 1935 and 1940, WPA lunches reached schools in every section of the state except New Orleans.[5]

3. Atlanta *Constitution*, July 15, 1937; Howard, *The W.P.A. and Federal Relief Policy*, 281, 452–53.

4. Atlanta *Daily World*, November 3, 1936; John Donovan to Williams, October 3, 1938, and Phyllis W. Francis to David K. Nile, October 15, 1938, both in WPA, Alabama Labor Complaints; Katherine D. Wood and Gladys L. Palmer (comps.), *Urban Workers on Relief: The Occupational Characteristics of Workers on Relief in 79 Cities, May 1934* (2 vols.; Washington, D.C., 1934), II, 90.

5. New Orleans *Times-Picayune*, February 18, November 14, 1935, May 12, 1940.

Locating sponsors became even more difficult later in the decade, when enthusiasm for the relief effort waned in general. In mid-1938, the Tennessee WPA director returned to the federal government more than one million dollars that national administrators had earmarked for service programs in Memphis. He reported that present women's quotas were full and that prospective sponsors would not submit new projects when they learned that a financial contribution was necessary. Only the newly developing city and county welfare bureaus seemed willing to sponsor as much "women's work" as possible. Yet their inadequate budgets, which barely allowed them to manage their direct relief case loads, limited the number of projects that could be subsidized at any one time.[6]

Difficulties notwithstanding, including opposition from those who sought to keep the mythical southern lady on her pedestal, the women's programs provided countless benefits for many indigent individuals and families. The sewing program was the largest and the most important. In New Orleans, Atlanta, and Birmingham, between 1,000 and 2,000 WPA seamstresses labored each day in the middle and late 1930s, with Atlanta women distributing more than four million garments to area welfare recipients, public hospitals, and sanitariums. Even in Memphis, where the total number of relief workers was never as large as in the other cities, several hundred women between 1936 and 1938 repaired or made clothing valued at more than $250,000. The work brought an annual payroll of $200,000 to the city. The sewing program, moreover, cost communities very little; Washington, D.C., appropriated 85 percent of all operating expenses in Memphis.[7]

School-related projects were also important. In Birmingham through 1939, the hot lunch program had served more than 3.5 million meals, and 20,000 were still being prepared each day. In Orleans Parish, where the lunch program reopened in 1940, relief officials discovered that 140 schools and more than one-fifth of the pubic school enrollment qualified for free lunches. The food came from the Federal Surplus Commodities Corporation and WPA gardens. Through 1942 in Memphis, workers stored an average of 100,000 cans of vegetables each year, using more than 70 percent of them for school lunches. All remaining

6. Telegram, Crump to McKellar, May 25, 1938, in Kenneth McKellar Papers, Box 3, Memphis Public Library, Downtown Branch.

7. Henderson, "Public Relief in Jefferson County," 43–44; Birmingham *News*, December 18, 1933, August 3, 1941; New Orleans *Times-Picayune*, August 21, 1938, May 12, 1940; Virginia Robinson to Overton, September 6, 1935, Pease to Overton, May 5, 1936, October 11, 1938, Sam Jackson to Overton, November 18, 1938, all in Mayor's Correspondence File, Drawer 7, Memphis and Shelby County Archives, Memphis; Minutes of the Fulton County Commission, X, July 21, 1939, p. 489, Fulton County Courthouse, Atlanta.

products went to direct relief cases. Another school-related activity was library work. In New Orleans through 1940, WPA women renovated or cataloged more than 3 million volumes, while through 1939 in Birmingham, more than 1 million books were repaired. The federal government absorbed 98 percent of those expenditures, which provided daily employment for nearly 800 women.[8]

Some WPA women served as housekeeping aides, especially unemployed domestics, who were usually unskilled blacks. The women visited needy families and helped with cooking, cleaning, and other homemaking duties, even providing live-in care on occasion. Furthermore, a host of WPA nursery schools offered employment for women as well as valuable preschool training for eligible children. Classes opened for whites and for blacks in all southern cities. Typical was the Atlanta program, which according to WPA officials stressed a child's "physical, mental, social, and emotional growth." All students received physicals, dental examinations, and the proper immunizations, and teachers used materials that encouraged "self-expression, the acquisition of information" and that taught even "the youngest . . . to live happily with one another" and "to conform without sacrificing their own individuality." Teachers visited homes and conducted well-attended study groups in order to work directly with parents.[9]

Not all women's service projects were so far-reaching. An example was the Birmingham matrons' project, which employed women as lavatory supervisors in the schools. The program opened in 1939 and operated until the spring of 1941, when most remaining WPA projects became affiliated with the national defense effort. In an attempt to save the "restroom patrol," as the program was called, one high school principal suggested that "there is nothing more devastating to morale than untidy restrooms, especially when there is writing on the walls or partitions." Another educator argued that "very few laymen realize that the school lavatories are the most fertile source of the beginning of delinquencies that occur in the schools" and that when "salacious writing appears on the walls [it] becomes a source of undesirable sex

8. Report on WPA Activities in Alabama, March 24, 1940 (Appraisal Reports: Alabama), H. Reed Hunter, Report and Appraisal Federal Education Project, City of Atlanta, n.d. (Appraisal Reports: Georgia), Mrs. Leo G. Spofford to Ellen Woodward, July 8, 1937 (Louisiana Women's Projects), Alma Hammond to Florence Kerr, September 4, 1941 (Louisiana Public Health), all in WPA; Memphis *Commercial Appeal*, September 12, 1936; New Orleans *Times-Picayune*, May 12, 1940; Jones to T. B. Hudson, September 9, 1937, in James M. Jones, Jr., Collection, Drawer 7, Alabama Archives and History, Montgomery.

9. Report and Appraisal . . . City of Atlanta, n.d., in WPA, Appraisal Reports: Georgia. Also see Birmingham *News*, June 14, 1942; Atlanta *Constitution*, July 26, August 2, 1936.

knowledge to younger students."[10] Despite such pleas, federal officials discontinued the program as planned.

In addition to women's activities, the WPA service division sponsored a variety of professional and white-collar projects that required greater skills. Unemployed technical and professional laborers of both sexes were eligible, although no small number of unskilled workers secured emergency employment through active in-service training programs. The purpose of these endeavors was more than wage relief. Between 1933 and 1939 in Birmingham, the more than forty white-collar health projects employed a total of four thousand, whose field-work in turn reached a far greater number of area indigent.[11] National administrators hoped that such ventures would promote the local development or expansion of community services, particularly in the urban South, where health, recreation, and similar programs were lacking in the 1930s.

Public health projects were especially needed in the Dixie municipalities in question. Health services there had not kept pace with urban growth, even during recent reform periods. Progressive leaders in early twentieth-century Atlanta, for example, generally ignored public health matters; consequently, throughout the 1920s and into the 1930s the city was without adequate clinics, a dispensary service, a venereal disease control program, a health education plan, and suitable public hospital facilities. Similar situations existed in Memphis, Birmingham, and New Orleans, where death rates from tuberculosis, heart defects, and infant mortality were twice the national average. The depression then brought reduced funding for the already inferior community health services. Between 1929 and 1934 in Birmingham, where a city health program only dated from 1917, local officials cut health expenditures by 63 percent, while total municipal receipts fell only 27 percent. The United States Public Health Service, moreover, reported that minimum health care required annual per capita spending of at least one dollar and that the national average in 1934 stood at just seventy cents. The per capita figure in Birmingham was only seventeen cents, which in part explained increases in both the infant mortality rate and the incidence of communicable diseases in the early depression years.[12]

Efforts such as the Memphis malaria control project, which in 1936 employed 25 percent of all Shelby County relief workers, and sewer

10. J. F. Byrne to Kerr, April 1, 1941, in WPA, Alabama Public Health.

11. "Public Health and the 'White Collar' WPA," *Birmingham Health* (May, 1939).

12. Alton T. Dial, "Public Health in Atlanta During the Progressive Era" (M.A. thesis, Georgia State University, 1970), 103–106; "Civic Candor," *Survey* (April, 1934), 132.

renovations in Atlanta contributed to preventive health care. A rat eradication project in New Orleans occupied several hundred exterminators and laboratory workers during the late 1930s and was especially significant because of the number of stagnant swamps and marsh areas surrounding the Crescent City. WPA personnel turned rat catching into a science of sorts, and reassignment awaited those who failed to master the correct techniques. Crews reported that large rats and stray cats shared trash piles in some slum areas. One worker concluded that rats had become almost "pampered pets of the occupants," while one species was "particularly swank" and could eat eggs and birds and "climb like a squirrel."[13]

In addition to preventive ventures, relief officials expanded existing ERA nursing programs, supplementing them with projects involving skilled and even unskilled workers who received pre-service and in-service training. The WPA nurses were either registered nurses without jobs or women soon to be graduated and enrolled in the National Organization of Public Health Nursing. As relief employees, they provided bedside care to welfare recipients, especially prenatal and pediatric services, and staffed first aid stations that treated WPA construction crews. More importantly, they immunized thousands of school-age children against diphtheria and other diseases. The incidence of diphtheria in New Orleans in the early 1930s had nearly reached epidemic proportions.[14]

An active nursing aide program trained men and women to staff newly constructed neighborhood health clinics and city hospitals. Usually, municipal or county administrators, public hospitals, or the various health bureaus (county, state, or federal) contributed the necessary equipment, first aid supplies, and office space. The director of Grady Memorial Hospital in Atlanta reported that without WPA aides his facility would have operated with "25 percent less efficiency in every way." Health workers also conducted special testing in the schools. One of the most impressive efforts occurred in Birmingham in 1938, when twenty thousand children in seventy schools received free hearing and vision tests, with a local fraternal club donating free glasses to students unable to afford them. Private physicians occasionally mounted publicity campaigns against the public programs;

13. New Orleans *Times Picayune*, September 27, 1935; New Orleans *Item*, October 6, 1938; Final Report of the CWA of Louisiana, n.d., in RG 69, Records of the Civil Works Administration, Final Reports, NA; J. Roth to Pease, September 2, 1936, in Mayor's Correspondence File, Drawer 7.

14. Spofford to Woodward, March 13, 1937 (Louisiana Women's Projects), Mrs. Charles Cole to Mrs. John G. Gilman, August 23, 1936 (Tennessee Women's Projects), Report and Appraisal . . . City of Atlanta, n.d. (Appraisal Reports: Georgia), all in WPA.

nevertheless, local residents and the press generally applauded the health projects.[15]

To complement the field services, relief and local health officials in each city launched public education projects, hoping to awaken a general health consciousness in their communities. At first, publicity was limited to printed materials, but it was quickly realized that pamphlets and newspaper advertisements were of little value among the most indigent, many of whom could not read and among whom there were often deep-rooted superstitions to overcome. In New Orleans, for example, public health authorities confronted the primitive belief that evil spirits caused venereal disease and that special charms could bring about a cure. Well-known voodoo doctors sold small bags containing crushed bone, peach seeds, toadstools, and other ingredients to the uneducated for as much as fifty dollars apiece. According to medical personnel, the voodoo treatment was "occasionally accompanied by chants and by dances and other primitive maneuvers."[16]

Clearly, health officials needed an appealing campaign if they hoped to direct the infected to local venereal disease clinics supervised by state and federal medical authorities and staffed by WPA workers. So in place of printed leaflets, officials in mid-1937 turned to radio broadcasts and plays, marionette shows, motorized exhibitions (including photographs, posters, and sound equipment), lectures in community centers and schools, and special health films. The education project in Birmingham and throughout the rest of Alabama was one of the most active. Relief personnel presented materials under the direction of a professionally licensed public relations agency, and by the end of 1937, a special troupe of twelve actors and musicians had presented more than seventy radio dramas on health-related topics. The group toured area schools and community centers, presenting skits that promoted fire, traffic, child, and general home safety.[17]

The radio dramas and educational materials were intended as well to publicize new medical clinics established in the southern cities in the 1930s. The modern Slossfield Health Center in Birmingham, completed in 1939, exemplified the WPA-sponsored clinics, initially staffed by emergency workers and later by local, state, and United

15. Van De Vrede to Mildred T. Law, April 28, 1941 (Georgia Public Health), Final Report of the Women's Professional and Service Projects, Alabama, n.d. (Final Reports of Women's Projects), both in WPA.

16. Hammond to Kerr, February 16, 1940, in WPA, Louisiana Public Health.

17. Final Report of the Women's Professional and Service Projects, Alabama, n.d., in WPA, Final Reports of Women's Projects; Birmingham News, April 16, 1939, June 14, 1942; Hudson to Jones, November 29, 1937, in James M. Jones, Jr., Collection, Drawer 3.

States Public Health Service employees. The city donated the land for the clinic; NYA officials provided orderlies and educational and recreational workers; the state health department allocated social security funds to pay for physicians and health care services; WPA labor constructed the buildings; and the American Cast Iron Pipe Company contributed additional space in the area community center it had built in the 1920s. The Julius Rosenwald Fund in Chicago also contributed grants for the purchase of heavy equipment and for the funding of community education programs and training seminars for local medical personnel. By 1941, the Slossfield unit contained clinics for maternity care, pediatrics, child health, dentistry, venereal disease, tuberculosis, and general diagnosis. It opened as one of five health centers in the Birmingham corporate limits, located in a black neighborhood desperately in need of expanded medical facilities.[18]

The establishment of such clinics was among the lasting results of the health service projects. Children gained the most, as low-cost preventive vaccines and treatment became widely available in many cities and towns for the first time. Special child-care provisions included in the Social Security Act later ensured that federal grants, combined with local and state matching contributions, continued to support all public health activities. The number of visits to clinics steadily increased throughout the later New Deal period, and most importantly, all cities began allocating larger percentages of their annual budgets for health work. Typical was Birmingham, where local public health expenditures increased 100 percent between 1935 and 1940, while total municipal spending increased by only 22 percent. Of course the new medical units did not solve urban health problems entirely; New Orleans in the mid-1940s ranked sixth among the nation's largest cities in the prevalence of venereal disease. Many area girls turned to prostitution during the war, and according to one health official, many of them thought they were "doing their bit for morale."[19]

In addition to health work, the federal service programs sponsored community educational activities. The most active emergency school project involved student aid, an idea first conceived, as were so many New Deal efforts, under the FERA. The NYA in 1935 expanded the availability of student aid, and throughout the remainder of the decade, the aid program was indeed important in the southern cities, which

18. Walter H. Maddox, "The Slossfield Health Center," *American Journal of Public Health*, XXXI (May, 1941), 481–86; Cooper, *Metropolitan County*, 93–97.

19. Jones to J. D. Dowling, October 9, 1930, and Birmingham Budget Statements for Fiscal Years Beginning September 1, 1933–1939 and Ending August 31, 1934–1940, both in James M. Jones, Jr., Collection, Drawer 1; Final Report . . . Alabama, n.d. (Final Reports of Women's Projects), Spofford to Kerr, July 23, 1940 (Louisiana Public Health), both in WPA; Amelia Hardesty, "Juvenile Delinquency in the Orleans Area," *Louisiana Welfare*, III (July, 1943), 6.

according to a 1938 federal survey had slightly more serious dropout problems than urban areas elsewhere in the United States. A nation-wide study revealed that in Birmingham, for example, more than 70 percent of all employed blacks under 25 years of age and 50 percent of the young white work force had left school for financial reasons. The national urban average was 48 percent.[20]

The NYA school program in Memphis was typical of that venture throughout the country. Students in twenty high schools and junior high schools received assistance while working each day after class on public projects. Local college students were likewise eligible—they could earn up to fifteen dollars per month while continuing in their studies at Memphis State Teachers College, the University of Tennessee College of Medicine, Southwestern College, or LeMoyne College. In Atlanta between 1936 and 1938, temporary wage relief helped more than eight thousand students, and in New Orleans, NYA grants assisted an average of 12 percent of the local college enrollment.[21]

Special education programs were also made available to thousands of adults long out of the classroom. Many of the returning students desired additional training for job placement; others enrolled in WPA-sponsored literacy courses. Indeed, the problem of illiteracy was a substantial one throughout the South. The 1930 census reported a 4.3 percent illiteracy rate in the nation as a whole, with the largest category of those unable to read and write being black Americans, among whom the rate averaged about 16 percent. Southern state averages ranged from Georgia's 10 percent to Alabama's 13 percent; for blacks those figures were double. Among the region's cities, where schooling was more accessible, the federal survey found a 5.4 percent illiteracy rate (14 percent among blacks) in New Orleans, while corporate Atlanta and Memphis each recorded levels almost equal to the overall national average. In Birmingham, where blacks accounted for more than 80 percent of all illiterates, the rate was twice the national average. Alabama's illiteracy rate ranked fifth in the nation, and only heavily populated New York and Texas recorded a greater real number of individuals unable to read and write.[22]

20. Williams to A. P. Morgan, Jr., May 7, 1934, in RG 69, Records of the Federal Emergency Relief Administration, Alabama File, NA; "Youth in Industry," *Monthly Labor Review* (November, 1939), 1102; Birmingham *News*, September 14, 1938.

21. NYA of Tennessee, *National Youth Administration in Tennessee, 1935–1936* (Nashville, 1936), 22; NYA of Georgia, *Report on the NYA of Georgia* (Atlanta, 1939), 9; Report and Appraisal . . . City of Atlanta, n.d., in WPA, Appraisal Reports: Georgia; Betty and Earnest K. Lindley, *A New Deal for Youth: The Story of the National Youth Administration* (New York, 1958), 189; Memphis *Commercial Appeal*, September 1, 23, 1936, March 8, 1942; Atlanta *Constitution*, September 22, 1935; New Orleans *Times-Picayune*, June 21, August 30, 1936.

22. See numerous undated reports on illiteracy (Alabama, Georgia, Louisiana

The effort in adult education was the most impressive of the educational projects, which put to work many unemployed teachers and vocational instructors. Through 1940 in Birmingham, over 14,000 area residents learned to read and write, while in Atlanta, where statistics typified the effort in all southern cities, more than 50 instructors worked, on the average, with 2,500 "pupils" each day during the 1930s. Included in the adult program were elementary education courses and general instruction in reading, mathematics, English, and other academic subjects. In cooperation with the Atlanta Urban League's Opportunity School, one of the largest vocational endeavors in the South, there were programs in home and family education and specialized job training. Extension services in all cities reached shut-ins as well as prisoners in local correctional facilities. Naturalization classes for aliens were also offered. When the WPA ended in 1943, many of these continuing education programs remained available entirely under local supervision and funding.[23]

WPA education projects were active in the black communities in each of the Dixie cities in question. The *Louisiana Weekly*, published in New Orleans and usually skeptical of federal relief activities, concluded that adult instruction "has been a boon to underprivileged Negroes, and will show great returns as the days go by." Black teachers gained relief employment in far greater numbers than did jobless Negro professionals in other WPA service fields, where skilled jobs were often restricted. Forty percent of Tennessee's WPA teachers were black, and at its peak in New Orleans, the program was reaching more than ten thousand black children nearly every day. Of course classes remained separate, in the tradition of Jim Crow, and instruction for blacks was generally confined to reading and writing, vocational programs, or, in the case of black girls, training as domestics.[24]

Reaching an even greater number of individuals than either the

Education Projects), L. R. Alderman to Berry, January 19, 1939 (Tennessee Education Projects), all in WPA.

23. Report on WPA Activities, March 24, 1940 (Appraisal Report: Alabama), Report and Appraisal . . . City of Atlanta, n.d. (Appraisal Reports: Georgia), Judson Snead to Dr. G. L. Maxwell, February 17, 1939 (Alabama Education Projects), M. S. Robertson to Woodward, June 22, 1936 (Louisiana Women's Projects), all in WPA; Holt, "Establishment of Unemployment Relief Agencies in the Hoover-Roosevelt Era," 14; Atlanta *Constitution*, July 5, 1936; Ecke, *From Ivy Street to Kennedy Center*, 244–45; New Orleans *Times-Picayune*, May 12, 1940; Birmingham *News*, August 3, 1941, June 14, 1942; "The Birmingham School Situation," *School and Society*, September 17, 1938, p. 363.

24. *Louisiana Weekly*, April 30, November 12, 1938; Robertson to Alderman, January 9, 1939 (Louisiana Education Projects), E. R. Lingerfelt to Alderman, January 9, 1939 (Tennessee Eduction Projects), both in WPA; Atlanta *Daily World*, June 4, 19, 1934.

health or education projects was the WPA effort in recreation. Publicly funded leisure-time programs already existed in the South, as most large cities supported parks commissions of some kind. Still, the New Deal relief network moved such services ahead by several years. Like most white-collar projects, the recreation endeavor had its beginnings under FERA and CWA direction. In Atlanta in 1934, one program directed by these agencies boasted the slogan, "Fill Up Playgrounds and Empty the Jails." Similar ventures functioned elsewhere, promoting better supervision of park and community centers, which offered activities ranging from creative dramatics to athletic leagues.[25]

When the WPA assumed work relief responsibility in 1935, among its top priorities was the expansion, in the nation's cities especially, of what Atlanta newspapermen were calling "a most remarkable piece of work and a power of good in the community." More than 70 percent of Louisiana's recreation budget at that time went to New Orleans, while the program in Atlanta had become so complex that Georgia relief officials had placed it under a separate director, apart from the overall state project. State recreation supervisors cooperated with city planning commissions and park personnel, and as in other service fields, the federal government contributed up to 90 percent of all expenditures. In Birmingham, relief dollars accounted for more than half of all funds set aside in the city for recreation each year during the late 1930s. The hundreds of thousands in federal appropriations covered the wages of WPA workers, who augmented local recreation staffs, and financed training workshops for all personnel. Municipal funds in turn purchased equipment for the implementation of new activities and the expansion of existing ones.[26]

At first, the program moved quite slowly, at least in the southern cities, where workers on municipal payrolls were hesitant to share authority with emergency labor. The parks bureau in Birmingham delayed the opening of the project for six months, demanding that Washington, D.C., pay several supervisors of the city's choice, who were already regularly employed, to direct all relief labor. Instead, national officials appointed one such overall director of relief personnel for the steel city and later ordered that all individual playground supervisors, paid directly from federal funds, come from the ranks of the unemployed who had attended special WPA training camps. The Louisiana

25. Atlanta *Constitution*, March 25, 1935; Atlanta *Daily World*, April 2, 1935; A. R. Brousseau to Arthur Goldschmidt, June 25, 1935, in WPA, Louisiana Recreation Projects.

26. Atlanta *Constitution*, March 25, 1935; Paul Unger to Eduard Lindeman, March 24, 1939 (Louisiana Recreation Projects), Harold Meyer to Irma Ringe, n.d., August Fisher to Meyer, August 15, 1936, Lindeman to Shepperson, August 19, 1935 (Georgia Recreation Projects), Ruth Ray to Lindeman, February 20, 1937 (Tennessee Recreation Projects), all in WPA; U.S. Works Projects Administration, *Social Group Work Agencies in Birmingham and Jefferson County, 1939* (1939), 4, 69–76.

WPA chief reported that because the New Orleans division had confronted local "indifference and in some cases open hostility," the Crescent City program as of mid-1936 had advanced little beyond the daily supervision of public playground activities. Similarly in Memphis, and as late as 1939, conflicts between relief and regularly employed staff members weakened recreation work. One federal investigator reported that the facilities in Memphis were "magnificent compared to the usual recreation centers" but that local fieldwork did not "hold a candle to the program I saw in a one-room shack in East Chattanooga."[27]

A series of regional conferences conducted in the summer of 1936 finally pushed recreation projects ahead. Sponsored by national relief officials and conducted throughout the country by Harold Meyer, regional director of a federal program called the Community Organization for Leisure, the meetings brought municipal and WPA leaders together and encouraged the expansion of recreational services. The hope was to provide immediate training and emergency employment for white-collar jobless individuals who would in turn supervise activities for thousands of residents. Meyer emphasized the future, pointing out that modern labor-saving devices were creating additional leisure hours for everyone and that it was the responsibility of the government on all levels to ensure that individuals knew how to spend those hours. Participants argued that planned recreation was important for current depression victims as well as for all residents of large cities, where space was limited. According to one Alabama journalist, planned recreation programs would soon "be devoted more and more to finding occupations for the leisure hours of the regularly employed."[28]

Finally in late 1936, municipal officials began organizing special clinics for all local recreation supervisors. The New Orleans clinic was typical, conducting daily classes for more than five years. All playground directors from WPA rolls, as well as many employees on the city's regular payroll, received instruction each morning in first aid and in several activities categories. Workers then reported to area parks and community centers and directed programs with the help of assistants

27. Agnes Couglin to Hopkins, September 9, 1935, Weber to Bruce McClure, September 18, 1935, Frances Stephenson to Lindeman, February 24, 1935 (Alabama Recreation Projects), Crutcher to Lindeman, September 1, 1935 (Louisiana Recreation Projects), Ray to Kerr, March 8, 1939 (Tennessee Recreation Projects), all in WPA; New Orleans *Times-Picayune*, September 20, 1938.

28. Fisher to Ringe, May 25, 1936 (Georgia Recreation Projects), clipping, August 13, 1935 (Alabama Recreation Projects), John A. Zimmerman to Lindeman, August 1, 1935 (Louisiana Recreation Projects), all in WPA; New Orleans *Times-Picayune*, July 25, 1936.

likewise from the relief lists. Administrators in New Orleans also structured a scheme for promotion up the job hierarchy based on hours of training and success in the field. Those who failed to improve were either dropped from the project or else demoted to the ranks of the unskilled. In 1938, the Crescent City training center reached an agreement with Louisiana State University, allowing workers to earn college credit for training received.[29]

Recreation leaders remained in the parks in both the winter and summer months and involved thousands of southern urban residents in programs designed for young and old. From handicraft classes to dance instruction to participation, in Birmingham, on one of 60 softball teams or 48 basketball teams, activities were never lacking. During one month in Atlanta, nearly 400 WPA playground supervisors in 90 area facilities reached more than 215,000 individuals. Emergency recreation personnel also took charge of public and parochial school playgrounds in the summers, recording a total attendance in New Orleans in 1935 of one million. Furthermore, most Christmas parades and Easter festivals in the late 1930s were work relief efforts at least in part, with floats, costumes, street decorations, and toys for the underprivileged resulting from WPA services. Additional undertakings included work with boys clubs and similar organizations, the sponsorship of small park construction projects using volunteer labor, and the supervision of recreation in the new federal housing complexes.[30]

A number of sleep-away and day camps, established in cooperation with state parks departments and the National Forest Service, represented another facet of the relief effort in recreation. Four such facilities served the Atlanta area, including a state music camp with sessions for young people and adults, a children's summer camp, a training center for key recreation personnel, and a special mothers' camp, offering a temporary change of pace at a cost of ten cents a day for many WPA certified women. Camp Sky-Hi in the Birmingham area was

29. Zimmerman to Dorothy I. Cline, October 25, 1935, Zimmerman to Lindeman, January 18, 1937, October 10, December 28, 1938, Spofford to C. E. Triggs, October 15, 1940, all in WPA, Louisiana Recreation Projects; New Orleans *Times-Picayune*, January 24, 1936, September 20, October 2, 1938.

30. Report of Georgia's State Recreation Project, April, 1935, Robert Bradford to Shepperson, May 6, 1936, Mildren Mitchell to Fisher, July 6, 1936 (Georgia Recreation Projects), Malvina Allen to Lindeman, June 22, 1938, Weber to Ralston, November 17, 1939, March 22, 1940 (Alabama Recreation Projects), George Simons to William Hartsfield, March 10, 1938 (Appraisal Reports: Georgia), all in WPA; Atlanta City Council Minutes, XXXIX, January 3, 1939, p. 81, City Hall, Atlanta; Jones to Birmingham WPA Office, January 17, 1938, in James M. Jones, Jr., Collection, Drawer 3; "From Market to Art Center," *Recreation* (March, 1935), 600; Atlanta *Constitution*, April 3, 1939; Atlanta *Journal*, February 16, 1938; New Orleans *Times-Picayune*, June 16, 1939.

typical of the several children's camps opened in the South. It operated for three months each summer at Oak Mountain, an 8,200-acre national recreational site located fifteen miles southwest of the city. In 1939 and again in 1940, the facility served more than 800 Jefferson County boys and girls from families on work relief or direct assistance. Parents or groups sending youngsters to camp paid only seven dollars per child. The Birmingham Board of Education cooperated by providing transportation, and federal subsidies kept city and county contributions at a minimum.[31]

Regular contact between recreation personnel and concerned residents was perhaps a more important aspect of the relief effort in recreation than employment opportunities or the implementation of playground activities. Local advisory councils first appeared in Birmingham in early 1935, with similar groups soon following elsewhere. Working together, recreation leaders and interested residents procured buildings for recreation centers while determining activities to be made available in various neighborhoods. In the Birmingham area in 1938, forty-six separate groups were meeting weekly, and the local citizenry was coming to understand that recreation was not a temporary phenomenon caused by depression unemployment but a permanent need resulting from modern technology. According to one staff report, the community councils "assisted materially in building sentiment and understanding toward the permanency of the . . . Recreation Program."[32]

By the late 1930s, a trend toward improved recreational services was in evidence in all southern cities. In Atlanta, where no official recreation commission existed prior to the New Deal period, the city council in 1939 organized a separate division within the parks department responsible for activities programming. Federal investigators reported that "although the sums appropriated are not large, they are important as indicators . . . that the Recreation Program which has been carried on by the W. P. A. is a vital need and is recognized as such in a most substantial way by appropriations from tax funds for the purpose of further administering the program." Relief officials further noted that "sentiment is crystallizing in favor of a substantial contribution."

31. Reports on Recreation Projects, in Spofford to Walter Kiplinger, March 13, April 4, 1941 (Alabama Recreation Projects), Camp Sky-Hi Report, n.d., in Final Report of Alabama Recreation Program, n.d. (Final Reports of Women's Projects), Van De Vrede to Kerr, June 1, 1939, February 18, 1941, E. L. Bothwell to E. M. Lisle, April 3, 1940 (Georgia Recreation Projects), all in WPA.

32. Monthly Report, November, 1938, in Fisher to Ringe, January 11, 1939 (Georgia Recreation Projects), Alabama Recreation Program, January–June, 1936, (Alabama Recreation Projects), Unger to Lindeman, March 24, 1939 (Tennessee Recreation Projects), all in WPA; Memphis *Commercial Appeal*, June 14, 1937.

In Birmingham, as well as in Memphis, officials strengthened existing bureaus financially, which made additional manpower and equipment available. The Alabama and Tennessee cities in 1938 set aside respectively 4.3 and 5.4 percent of their budgets for recreation, compared to a national average for all major urban areas of less than 3 percent. In both Birmingham and Memphis, the percentage had doubled since the 1920s. Although recreational activities in New Orleans were not centralized until 1946—before which the Playground Community Service Commission supervised an overlapping system consisting of the City Park Improvement Association, the Audubon Park Commission, and the Parks and Parkway Commission—at least the city began allocating additional funds annually for such services.[33]

Another emergency service effort was the opening of a series of NYA training centers for unemployed youths from families on relief. It too was impressive. This program allowed young people to earn minimum wages while learning skills and producing finished goods. One of the most active projects was in Birmingham, where young men reported to either a downtown workshop or a resident center near Bessemer for training in carpentry, drafting, and metalwork. Instruction at the women's sites included lessons in sewing, canning, gardening, and secretarial and domestic work. Sponsors also provided health, recreational, and educational activities in all complexes. Because acquired skills were transferable to jobs in the private sector, Birmingham city commissioners and the local school board established their own "little NYA" after the federal venture closed in 1943.[34]

Facilities in Atlanta were comparable to those in Birmingham, although imagination and effort were often more responsible than equipment for a program's success. One enthusiastic Atlanta *Journal* newsman commented that the local NYA staff was the "youngest, brightest and the liveliest of all [area] federal staffs." After visiting Memphis, one field examiner was so impressed that he remarked that the local NYA office was operating "the best project that I have seen" and "the work is an outstanding success." Similar reports described

33. Monthly Report, January, 1939, in Fisher to Ringe, February 15, 1939, and Monthly Report, February, 1940, in Van De Vrede to Kerr, May 16, 1940, both in WPA, Georgia Recreation Projects: *Financial Statistics of Cities over 100,000 Population* (1937), 186–87; Cooper, *Metropolitan County*, 73–74; Jones to Linton E. Allen, June 15, 1939, in James M. Jones, Jr., Collection, Drawer 2; Ray to Kerr, March 8, 1939, in WPA, Tennessee Recreation Projects; Howard and Friedman, *Government in Metropolitan New Orleans*, 138–43; "Recreation in New Orleans," *Louisiana Municipal Review*, IV (May-June, 1941), 99.

34. Birmingham *Post*, February 12, 1941, February 16, 1943; NYA of Alabama, *Report of Programs, National Youth Administration in Alabama* (Montgomery, 1941); Birmingham *Age-Herald*, April 9, 1939, July 21, 1941.

the New Orleans training project, opened in 1937, although Crescent City welfare officials occasionally complained that their NYA program was "the smallest in the United States."[35]

There were countless other NYA and WPA white-collar projects that affected thousands of residents in every community. A toy-making program in Birmingham, for example, employed men past the age of sixty-five and distributed more than 30,000 items to needy children. Another project, the WPA records survey, put to work 500 emergency clerical workers in New Orleans in the mid-1930s in salvaging and preserving municipal, county, and state archival materials. The workers also published local guidebooks from documents uncovered, being careful that their efforts did not duplicate the work of the separate Federal Writers Project. In New Orleans, and perhaps best demonstrating the wide variety of relief service projects, a WPA marine weather program trained workers in the use of modern office equipment and machines.[36]

More impressive than the large construction projects, at least in terms of human impact, WPA and NYA service programs in some way touched almost everyone in every locality in which they operated. The major endeavors—health, education, recreation, and youth training—employed hundreds of depression victims and reached a far greater number through fieldwork. The relief programs promoted home health care and better treatment facilities, made vocational and adult educational instruction more accessible, and for the first time in many cities sponsored planned recreation for a generation gaining additional leisure hours, if not by joblessness then by technological advancement. At the same time, countless numbers of young people received either employment or job training that benefited them for years thereafter. Some efforts even reached more than marginally into black residential areas—especially those by which the city as a whole stood to gain, such as the public health endeavor. Most importantly, service programs addressed the health and welfare of the overall community, and many

35. Beatrice Denmark to Richard Brown, November, 23, 1936, in Mayor's Correspondence File, Drawer 5; Richard Foster to Maestri, May 18, 1937, in Robert Maestri Papers, microfilm roll 404B, New Orleans Public Library; Atlanta *Journal*, July 15, 1942. Also see Report on NYA Projects in Memphis, n.d., in Mayor's Correspondence File, Drawer 5; A. J. Sarro to Maestri, June 9, 1939, in Robert Maestri Papers, microfilm roll 405B; NYA of Georgia, *Report on the NYA of Georgia*, 4–5; Lindley and Lindley, *A New Deal for Youth*, 30–31, 48, 55–57.

36. Birmingham *News*, December 11, 1940; Atlanta *Constitution*, January 10, 14, 1937; New Orleans *Times-Picayune*, September 20, 1936; Leslie Smith, Report on Marine Weather Project, n.d., in Spofford to Ralston, October 25, 1937, in WPA, Louisiana Women's Projects; William F. McDonald, *Federal Relief Administration and the Arts* (Columbus, Ohio, 1969), 52.

continued to operate in some form under municipal direction and funding when New Deal agencies closed. These new or expanded public service commitments advanced—and their continuation in later years was indicative of—a growing urban consciousness in the South, which increasingly aimed at improving the general quality of urban life.

 8

PUBLIC WELFARE
AND THE ADVANCING URBAN CONSCIOUSNESS

Prior to the 1930s, departments of public welfare had never existed in most urban areas of the South. The combination of conservative New South leaders and residents who remained "small town" at heart had no doubt worked against the establishment of such institutions. The one exception among the cities was Birmingham, which from 1916 to 1924 operated a relief bureau, first as part of the Department of Safety and later under the Department of Health and Education. Its directors spent eight years trying to obtain a steady flow of municipal funds; never did they receive more than eighteen thousand dollars annually. Finally in 1924, the city disbanded the operation, and thereafter a family relief agency within the community chest, dependent upon public generosity each year and a small annual city subsidy, became the area's principal welfare institution.[1] Although brief, the Birmingham experiment certainly suggests that a sense of public responsibility was evolving among urban southerners and that in time the region's major cities would have established permanent public relief commissions. Yet it is equally certain that the combination of economic conditions and federal policy in the mid-1930s accelerated that development and forged new attitudes about it.

Just as thousands of unemployed urban residents relied on WPA and NYA emergency wages, large numbers of needy families after 1935 depended on aid from the second arm of the revised relief network. As the FERA machinery stopped, federal guidelines dictated that states and localities absorb much of the relief burden, including relief funds

1. Cooper, *Metropolitan County*, 100.

for all those unable to work and the able-bodied waiting for emergency positions to become vacant. To assist the subdivisions in paying the costs, and to ensure a system funded by federal, state, and local contributions, the administration provided matching disability grants for the blind, the disabled, and dependent children as part of the Social Security Act of 1935. Although criticized by some historians as a piecemeal effort, and thus an example of broker statism, the establishment of a decentralized relief apparatus that operated nationwide was as close as New Dealers could come, or wanted to come, to a national welfare system. And, as the depression continued to magnify the complexities and the needs of modern society, federal policy was significant, at least as it affected the southern cities. It ended the reliance on private and community chest charitable agencies for indigent care, with that service commitment being forever absorbed into the public sector. Even the staunchest New South conservatives had to accept the reality of public welfare as a function of local government and accommodate it, however modestly, into their vision of an efficient, orderly urban environment.

To qualify for federal assistance, a locality first established a public bureau responsible for welfare. The leader among the southern cities was Birmingham, where officials in 1933, two years before such a requirement, organized the Jefferson County Department of Public Welfare, staffed by workers from the old Red Cross Family Service Society. At first, the new agency did little more than support local AERA activities, but when federal lawmakers passed social security legislation in 1935, the city had only to reorganize the bureau slightly to meet specified standards. In proposing the new charter, local welfare leaders included the important clause "In the creation of the Public Department, [the] words 'Emergency' or 'Temporary' [should] not be used" because the commission "must be made an integral part of local government and by local government full responsibility taken therefor."[2]

Similarly in New Orleans, a public welfare bureau was functional prior to 1935. A fifteen-person voluntary committee became active in early 1934, but like its counterpart in Birmingham, its duties were initially limited to the coordination of private philanthropic work. The activities of this first bureau were so few that federal officials were skeptical of the Crescent City's motives. Investigators reported that "without denying the usefulness of this first step," there must be "a more orderly process of dealing with destitution and other extreme

2. Roberta Morgan to Jones, August 23, 1934, and W. J. Wynn to Jones, September 9, 1935, both in James M. Jones, Jr., Collection, Drawer 2, Alabama Archives and History, Montgomery; Brooks, *A Half Century of Progress*, 58.

social problems." Officials in the statehouse in Baton Rouge, moreover, thought that the federal government was bluffing, at least at first, and would never transfer relief cases back to state and local care. They were somewhat dismayed upon discovering that federal policy was no idle threat. Yet despite its limited beginnings, the New Orleans department, like the Birmingham unit, was ready to assume responsibility for more than ten thousand cases when the FERA ended.[3]

The situation in Atlanta and Memphis was different. In neither city were leaders quick to establish public welfare machinery, with the result that they assumed that burden at the same time they were receiving their first FERA transfers. Atlanta took no action until December, 1934, when municipal and county officials finally activated the Fulton County Department of Public Welfare. The metropolitan unit immediately became responsible for several thousand former federal relief clients. In addition, it took charge of all municipal appropriations to juvenile and correctional institutions. It also became a clearinghouse for private charities so as "to consolidate welfare" and handle "the entire problem with a minimum expenditure of moneys." Not until a year later did leaders in Memphis organize the Memphis Welfare Commission. Its early development differed slightly from the pattern in the other cities, but in the end it too would become a permanent civic institution.[4]

Public financing distinguished the new urban welfare networks from past charitable endeavors. For several months into 1936, FERA dollars assisted the agencies by absorbing their administrative costs and by donating used equipment. Also, social security disability payments eventually flowed to all communities. Yet the municipal commissions were officially part of local governmental bureaucracies, and cities had to find a means of financing them. Civic officials generally solved the problem in one of two ways. In Birmingham and Memphis, relief personnel received monthly appropriations from general city and county revenues. In each case, state dollars supplemented

3. Scott, Confidential Report on New Orleans, Louisiana, April 12, 1934, in Alcorn to Williams, April 14, 1934, in Record Group 69, Records of the Federal Emergency Relief Administration, Louisiana File, National Archives, hereinafter cited as FERA; Crutcher to Howard Hunter, April 22, 1936, in RG 69, Records of the Works Progress Administration, Louisiana File, NA, hereinafter cited as WPA; William J. Guste, "The Orleans Parish-City Board of Public Welfare," Louisiana Welfare, IV (April, 1944), 8, 19; Howard and Friedman, Government in Metropolitan New Orleans, 97; New Orleans Department of Public Welfare, Three Year Report, 1934–1936 (New Orleans, 1937), 17.

4. Minutes of the Fulton County Commission, V, December 5, 1934, May 31, 1935, pp. 300, 476–78, Fulton County Commission Office, Atlanta; Memphis Commercial Appeal, January 25, 1936, January 13, 1937; Ralph Picard, "Centralizing Welfare Work in Memphis," American City (June, 1936), 105.

local funds, and in Memphis, legislative appropriations became the city unit's primary means of support. Municipal and Shelby County leaders hesitated to allocate significant sums for welfare; Mayor Overton assured his constituency that the "city welfare commission is not an organization for using tax money to buy groceries."[5]

Officials in New Orleans and Atlanta, ever mindful of New South efficiency, turned to a different means of relief financing. The Crescent City was the first to obtain legislative authority to levy special taxes in support of welfare activities. Beginning in 1934, a small amusement tax and a gasoline tax of one to two cents per gallon was in force, and in 1936, lawmakers in Baton Rouge added a statewide 2 percent luxury tax. Municipal relief officials handled funds collected in their own localities until 1938, when legislators authorized the new state welfare bureau to distribute all welfare tax revenue according to need and without regard to individual parish collections. A 1 percent state sales tax replaced the luxury tax at that time, although state law also allowed Orleans Parish to place a 2 percent tax on theater admissions and a 5 percent tax on entrance fees to other places of entertainment for relief purposes.[6]

There were no designated welfare taxes in the Atlanta area until 1937. For two years, city and Fulton County officials had set aside funds for relief directly from general revenues, but when the state finally empowered counties to levy up to three mills to finance local welfare activities, Fulton County commissioners moved immediately. Their actions at least guaranteed steady funding, even if it remained inadequate. The city continued its direct annual appropriations for a time to augment the special tax revenues; yet throughout the 1930s, the new relief bureau continually sought funds above those available.[7]

The municipal agencies extended aid to three types of relief clients. First, with the assistance of social security allocations, the commissions cared for the elderly, the handicapped and blind, and dependent children. Once these groups were determined eligible for

5. Memphis *Commercial Appeal*, December 14, 1935. Also see Birmingham *News*, September 35, 1933; Robert Morgan, Sr., "Public Relief in Louisiana from 1928–1960," *Louisiana History*, IV (Fall, 1973), 373; Shepperson to Williams, March 7, 1936, Charles Alspach to Shepperson, March 9, 1936, both in FERA, Georgia Transients; Atlanta *Constitution*, June 7, 16, 28, 1935.

6. Miller to Williams, October 15, 1934, in FERA, Louisiana Field Reports; New Orleans *Tribune*, August 22, 1936; Amelia Hardesty, "General Assistance in New Orleans," *Louisiana Welfare*, VI (April, 1940), 17.

7. Minutes of the Fulton County Commission, V, February 19, May 22, 1935, pp. 382, 477, and X, March 31, 1939, p. 341; Atlanta City Council Minutes, XXXVI, January 6, 1936, p. 29, City Hall, Atlanta; Atlanta *Constitution*, December 3, 1936, February 1, 1937, November 20, 1938.

federal grants, and once the required local welfare units were fully operational, social security provided matching funds in the amount of one-half of the combined state and local appropriations for the three categories. According to welfare officials in New Orleans, the federal provision "had the effect of crystallizing public consciousness of these groups, and of stabilizing, in-so-far as funds would permit, assistance to them."[8]

Second, with only state and local monies, the urban departments extended direct relief to "unemployables," many of whom were ineligible for social security disability. Third, and also without federal aid, the commissions cared for residents and transients who were WPA certified but unable to obtain work assignments. Whether or not an individual was "unemployable" caused some confusion, because one person could be employable in one job and not in another. The New Orleans bureau indicated that it had many applicants "desperate in need, trying to determine where the best chance of aid lies, and then trying to prove their employability or unemployability as the case might be."[9]

Of the last two categories, "employables" who failed to locate WPA work received by far the fewest benefits. State law in Louisiana prohibited the use of state funds for them, leaving thousands dependent on surplus commodities and inadequate private financial support. In the Pelican State, according to one contemporary study, the "inability to work was considered an indication of need," but state policy dictated that "unemployability could be due only to physical or mental incapacity, or because a person was needed at home to care for ill or dependent members of the family, or was without a work record and had no employment opportunities." Officials considered the federal works program, or even one's acceptance by the state or national reemployment services, as a job opportunity. Rarely did the state make a special allocation for the "employable" category.[10]

Similar situations existed in Atlanta, Birmingham, and Memphis, although state laws were not always to blame. The welfare bureaus operated on limited resources; consequently, caseworkers had no choice but to consider persons who could not work a higher priority than applicants who were temporarily jobless. In 1938, Birmingham

8. New Orleans Department of Public Welfare, *Three Year Report*, 21.
9. *Ibid.*, 22.
10. Amy C. Dunlap, "A Study of Temporarily Unemployable Persons Receiving Assistance in the Others Assistance Category of the Orleans Department of Public Welfare" (M.S.W. thesis, Tulane University, 1942), 18–19; Donald V. Wilson, *Public Social Services in Louisiana* (Monroe, La., 1943), 79–85; M. H. Gehan to Maestri, August 28, 1936, in Robert Maestri Papers, microfilm roll 405B, New Orleans Public Library.

reported more than nine thousand individuals and families receiving no aid except in the form of food surpluses.[11]

Working with the Federal Surplus Commodities Corporation, the local welfare departments provided hundreds of pounds of canned and dried products to direct relief clients, as well as to many WPA families. The amount of aid per case was never high, mainly because the food had to be distributed among thousands of residents. In Memphis, for example, the welfare commission in late 1936 was caring for about 2,500 families with surplus goods alone. Case loads in the other municipalities were larger, but the amount of assistance available per family in each city was about the same. The average welfare family received little more each week than several pounds of flour and five pounds of potatoes, plus limited quantities of canned vegetables and two bars of soap.[12]

The policy of direct distribution of food surpluses changed in 1940, when New Orleans, Birmingham, and Memphis became part of a nationwide experimental food stamp program. The plan was successfully tested in Rochester, New York, in the spring of 1939, and when implemented elsewhere later that year, all direct relief recipients and many WPA workers were eligible. In the Memphis area, the program included almost 14,000 families initially, and through 1940, officials there had issued more than $1 million in stamps to more than 25,000 city residents. Welfare departments made available both orange and blue stamps. For every dollar spent on the former at face value, the government offered the relief client fifty cents worth of the latter for free. The orange stamps could purchase any food in participating grocery stores, while the blue ones were good for surplus produce designated by the Department of Agriculture (butter, rice, pork, corn, eggs, wheat flour, and several kinds of vegetables). Grocers then redeemed the stamps with wholesalers, who in turn converted them to cash at the relief bureaus. Both retailers and distributors earned the same profits as if a cash transaction had transpired.[13]

The new welfare departments had additional responsibilities as well. The New Orleans bureau acted as a clearinghouse for out-of-town inquiries, such as those concerning relief applicants in other states

11. Alabama Department of Public Welfare Statistics, April, 1938, in James M. Jones, Jr., Collection, Drawer 2.

12. Memphis *Press Scimitar*, November 11, 1936; C. E. Moore to Maestri, n.d., in Robert Maestri Papers, microfilm roll 405B; Atlanta *Journal*, January 15, 1937; Birmingham *Age-Herald*, July 31, 1934.

13. Memphis *Commercial Appeal*, November 25, 1939, February 6, 1940; Memphis *Press Scimitar*, January 8, 1941; Report of the Jefferson County Department of Public Welfare, September 30, 1939, in James M. Jones, Jr., Collection, Drawer 2; Alma Hammond to Florence Kerr, August 31, 1940, in WPA, Louisiana Professional Projects; New Orleans *Times-Picayune*, June 28, 1940.

who resided permanently in the Crescent City. The departments assisted in the certification of emergency workers and in the distribution of clothes and other garments from WPA sewing projects. In Memphis, the popularity of the food stamp program triggered an experimental cotton stamp plan to provide welfare recipients with clothing while—it was hoped—increasing employment in area manufacturing plants and decreasing southern surpluses. With motion picture cameras recording the first transaction, welfare officials issued or sold at minimal cost special decals to twelve thousand eligible families, who redeemed them at retail outlets for unsold cotton garments.[14]

The New Orleans department also operated a boardinghouse project for elderly persons not ill enough for institutional care. In addition, that bureau directed a youth care program for children awaiting transfer to private agencies and a training facility for social work students from Tulane and Xavier universities. The Birmingham welfare board supervised the administration of Indigent Hospital and Jefferson County homes for the needy, while in 1940, the Atlanta relief commission became active in the operation of publicly financed Grady Memorial Hospital. In cooperation with federal authorities and state employment bureaus, the urban welfare commissions aided in the organization of an unprecedented unemployment compensation program. As provided in social security, jobless persons who had paid into the insurance plan became eligible after 1938 for eight to fifteen dollars in weekly benefits. During the system's inaugural year in New Orleans, recently unemployed residents, many affected by the downturn of 1937 and 1938, collected more than $1.3 million.[15]

A related duty was the coordination of local reemployment services that had operated since 1933 under the direction of the National Reemployment Service (NRS). Created by the Wagner-Peyser Act in June of that year, the NRS was an emergency program in the Department of Labor. The service operated local offices and through a system of matching funds was designed to support the work of state employment commissions. But in the South, where state employment agencies did not exist in 1933, federal authorities offered assistance directly to cities and towns and their private or, in rare cases, municipal job registration programs. Thus, until later in the decade throughout Dixie, city governments rather than state offices allocated funds annually in

14. New Orleans Department of Public Welfare, *Three Year Report*, 28; Memphis *Commercial Appeal*, May 8, 1940, May 7, 1941.

15. New Orleans *Times-Picayune*, September 15, 1936, July 2, 1937, January 14, 1938; Cooper, *Metropolitan County*, 101; Zell B. Miller, "The Administration of E. D. Rivers as Governor of Georgia" (M.A. thesis, University of Georgia, 1958), 39–41; Memphis *Commercial Appeal*, September 5, 1938; Memphis *Press Scimitar*, January 4, 1938.

order to be eligible for NRS services—an example of new, direct relationships between the federal government and urban communities. Memphis provided about forty thousand dollars each year.[16]

Provisions called for all unemployed individuals to register with the NRS, showing a prospective relief recipient's willingness to work while clearing an ERA and WPA investigation. NRS officials then sought either public or private employment for the registrants. In Atlanta in early 1934, more than 30,000 names appeared on reemployment rolls, including some names of employed workers who simply hoped to locate new or better-paying jobs. In Memphis, where conditions were never as desperate as in other urban areas, more than 40,000 enrolled in the first year, and in August, 1934, more than 24,000 active applications remained on file. The Memphis operation, perhaps the best managed among the southern urban units, included programs for men, women, and even young people. The staff was dedicated and hardworking, especially the agency's junior placement division, which studied, according to field reports, "the interests, aptitudes and personality traits of boys and girls out of school" and then furnished "free guidance as to vocation and training."[17]

Elsewhere, bureaus were not as efficient as the Tennessee unit, nor did they maintain as many contacts with prospective employers on behalf of the jobless. A federal investigation in New Orleans discovered that while the placement director there voiced concern for the jobless, his actions and policies did "not include any evidence of constructive thinking in respect to unemployment." The chairman doubted his own figures on unemployment, indicated the same report, and consciously neglected the plight of "young stenographers, Negro women, and large numbers of others" whom he believed "normally would not be considered as wage earners." It was further concluded that the director "seemed to think that everything would come out all right and that the one hope is the revival of industry and that no other planning is necessary." Not until later in the decade would the success of the NRS in the private sector be more than minimal. Between June, 1933, and the same month in 1935, the Alabama NRS claimed a placement rate of

16. Georgia Department of Labor, *Second Annual Report* (Atlanta, n.d.), 43–44; McAlister to W. Frank Persons, November 2, 1933, and March LaDame to McAlister, November 7, 1933, both in Hill McAlister Papers, Box 76, Tennessee State Archives and History, Nashville; Report from C. P. Noah on Reemployment in Memphis, n.d., in Mayor's Correspondence File, Drawer 2, Memphis and Shelby County Archives, Memphis.

17. "Reemployment Figures," *City Builder* (Atlanta) (March, 1934), 4; Georgia Department of Labor, *Third Annual Report* (Atlanta, n.d.), 23–25, 33; Memphis *Labor Review*, April 30, 1934; "Reemployment Service," *National Municipal Review* (December, 1937), 602.

50 percent; yet 87 percent of those placed had secured public work, and many of the others had received only part-time assignments. Similar were results in Memphis. City commissioners in mid-1937 indicated that "we have not been entirely satisfied with the results to date" because most of the "reemployed" had only gained federally funded emergency positions.[18]

Federal reemployment personnel continued to render support to urban placement bureaus until state employment agencies finally appeared in mid-decade. The trend began in 1935 in Louisiana and Alabama. The new state departments in turn opened district and city divisions to work with the newly developing local departments of welfare, which assumed the burden of the investigation and certification of relief and reemployment applicants. Finally in early 1939, the NRS officially terminated operations and relinquished functions entirely to the states and localities in cooperation with a more active United States Employment Service within the Department of Labor.[19]

By taking charge of all relief activities, the new public welfare commissions freed private charities and community chest organizations to expand efforts into other social service fields. The Atlanta Social Welfare Council, which had first evolved as a relief organization in 1931, adopted in mid-decade the new title of Social Planning Council. Directed by Rhoda Kaufman and other social work activists, the agency began consolidating social services in the Georgia metropolitan area. It became involved in recreation and playground supervision, and in cooperation with the Family Service Society, it operated a consultation service for anyone under strain because of family disturbances. The council maintained a network of contacts with area physicians, psychologists, the courts, and schools, and it took the lead in the establishment of a city-sponsored corrective speech center. The association of social workers also joined with the Humane Society, the Urban League, and other local groups in surveying community problems, leading an effort to generate a new social consciousness in the Atlanta area.[20]

18. Ralph Picard to A. B. Foust, April 24, 1937, in Mayor's Correspondence File, Drawer 2; Scott, Confidential Report on New Orleans, April 12, 1934, in Alcorn to Williams, April 14, 1934, in FERA, Louisiana File. Also see Birmingham *Labor Advocate*, June 27, 1936; P. J. Charley to Maestri, May 27, 1937, in Robert Maestri Papers, microfilm roll 404B; New Orleans *Times-Picayune*, January 13, 1935; Memphis *Commercial Appeal*, October 11, 1935, May 19, 1937.

19. Report of the National Reemployment Service in Alabama, n.d., in James M. Jones, Jr., Collection, Drawer 2.

20. Atlanta *Georgian*, October 26, 1935; Social Planning Council Report, n.d., in Rhoda Kaufman Papers, Georgia State Department of Archives and History, Atlanta; Atlanta *Daily World*, February 28, 1937.

Similar developments occurred in the other cities, with the new social work agencies receiving limited manpower assistance from NYA and WPA programs. By 1939 in Birmingham, concerned residents had organized the Community Welfare Council, which began as an informal alliance of voluntary groups and continued its operations into the 1940s. In 1948 it became permanent with a paid director, and in 1955, the city and county officially transformed it into the publicly financed Family Counseling Association of Jefferson County. The Memphis community chest, which had disbanded in 1932 because of insufficient collections, reorganized in mid-decade, and affiliate organizations became active in areas other than the disbursal of charity.[21]

In New Orleans, according to one contemporary source, the local Travelers Aid Society, which had been primarily a relief bureau, reorganized to "give more specialized and professionalized case work service to a limited number of persons who lived in Louisiana for less than one year." The city's Family Service Society and Association of Catholic Charities became involved in marital, domestic, and family counseling. Public welfare also allowed community chest funds to support the reorganization and expansion of the Mental Hygiene Institute, operated by municipal funding through the Tulane University School of Social Work. The unit had evolved from an old clinical guidance center, opened in 1929, which through 1937 had functioned almost entirely through the efforts and finances of local philanthropist Samuel Zemurray. The new center offered a guidance program for children and adults, and by January, 1939, the institute had a full-time staff available for psychiatric, medical, social, or psychological diagnosis and consultation. The service operated in a building at the university until 1941, when the WPA provided it with its own headquarters.[22]

Notwithstanding their promising beginnings, the new public agencies still faced numerous problems in the 1930s and thereafter. Few residents in 1935 fully comprehended the concept of public responsibility, which affected financial arrangements. According to one contemporary study, the southern cities initially sponsored the new bureaus "not because of any conviction of the public at large that relief was a responsibility of the whole people rather than a philanthropy to

---

21. Annie L. Fulcher, *The History, Structure and Program of the Family Counseling Association of Jefferson County, Alabama* (Birmingham, 1957), 9.

22. Ada B. Jarman, "The Progress of the New Orleans Guidance Center with Special Reference to Referrals from the Orleans Parish Department of Public Welfare" (M.S.W. thesis, Tulane University, 1941), 9–23, 145; Lucile Bruner, "The Travelers Aid in New Orleans," *Louisiana Welfare*, V (October, 1945), 12; Federal Writers' Project of Louisiana, *New Orleans City Guide* (Boston, 1938), 70.

be supported by a few individuals . . . [but] because of the availability of federal funds through a public department."[23]

A major problem was the unwillingness of some states to partici- pate in the social security program. Federal policy required active public agencies at the local level, as well as supervisory state commis- sions. Prior to the depression, most southern states had developed only skeletal welfare boards, which were advisory to city, county, and private charitable endeavors. Typical was the Georgia bureau, estab- lished in 1919. The unit operated in the early 1930s on an annual budget of $44,000, covering only salaries and administrative expenses. Throughout the South, only Mississippi, North Carolina, and Alabama were among the twenty-one states nationwide to receive federal grants in social security's first year.[24] In Georgia, Louisiana, and Tennessee, the establishment of municipal departments in the major cities pre- dated state action by two years. During the interim, meager local and state appropriations were the only monies available for all direct assistance work.

Birmingham was the only Dixie city in question to become imme- diately eligible for social security grants, but there was a catch. The Alabama legislature in August, 1935, created a state department that adhered to federal guidelines, yet the enabling legislation, signed by Governor Bibb Graves in September, tied the amount of state aid to the localities to the level of city and county contributions, which in turn limited federal matching allocations dependent on the state funds. Between October, 1938, and September, 1939, Washington, D.C., spent less than $200,000 in Jefferson County, although much more was available had not Alabama law minimized the flow of state appropria- tions. The dilemma led to the resignation of several key administrators from the Birmingham welfare office. Especially critical was the depar- ture of Roberta Morgan, who had supervised relief for the poor in the steel city through various private and public programs for more than twenty years.[25]

Late in 1935, New Orleans became eligible for social security allocations. The antics of Huey Long no doubt delayed matters for a few

23. As quoted in Anita Van de Voorf, "Public Welfare Administration in Jefferson County, Alabama" (M.A. thesis, Tulane University, 1933), 99.

24. Social Planning Council Report, n.d., in Rhoda Kaufman Papers; Atlanta *Journal of Labor*, March 6, 1936.

25. Raymond E. Thomason to Williams, June 29, 1938, in WPA, Alabama Labor Complaints; Alabama Department of Public Welfare, *First Annual Report* (Montgomery, 1936), 11–16; Brooks, *A Half Century of Progress*, 75–78; Report of the Jefferson County Department of Public Welfare, September 30, 1939, in James M. Jones, Jr., Collection, Drawer 2; Birmingham *News*, August 29–30, 1935, April 21, 1936; Birmingham *Post*, March 27, 1937.

months during that year, but following the boss's death in September, his successors moved quickly to make amends with the federal administration. They proposed the opening of a state welfare commission despite not being able to organize such a unit officially until voters approved a constitutional amendment in the fall, 1936, elections. To show good intentions, the state channeled emergency aid to parishes for more than a year prior to the vote through a special bureau directed by former LERA chief Harry Early.

The New Orleans bureau operated on only state and local welfare tax collections until the November, 1936, referendum, which brought in the first federal dollars. Soon thereafter, city and parish leaders reorganized their welfare network, with the two-year-old city department becoming part of the revamped Orleans Parish Department of Public Welfare under the new supervisory state agency. The two local committees, both appointed by the mayor, met together and acted as one unit in the administration of funds from relief taxes collected within parish borders. As in Alabama, Louisiana lawmakers until 1938 limited state contributions, which in turn minimized federal grants; in that year, a second legislative statute revised the system, making parish bureaus advisory to state-appointed welfare commissioners. City relief personnel maintained direct authority only in the direction of private charities and in the administration of public hospitals, foster homes, and similar institutions.[26]

Welfare workers in the capital of the New South waited even longer than their New Orleans counterparts for social security payments. Once again, delay resulted from inactivity at the state level, because through 1936 Eugene Talmadge was waging his war on Washington, D.C. The anti–New Deal governor vetoed an old-age pension plan in early 1935, then later in that year refused to summon a special legislative session to organize the necessary state welfare machinery. In 1936, he blocked a proposed constitutional amendment containing an enabling clause for the establishment of a new Georgia relief unit. During the Talmadge years, the average monthly direct relief allowance statewide was only six dollars, mainly in the form of surplus commodities. Only 10 percent of those eligible received even this limited aid.

Finally, under the "little New Deal" administration of Governor E. D. Rivers, Georgia in 1937 adopted the required legislation bringing the first federal grants to the Atlanta welfare unit. The statute also

26. New Orleans Department of Public Welfare, *Three Year Report*, 20–26; Wilson, *Public Social Services in Louisiana*, 34–38; Mary Raymond to Alfred Danzieger, November 25, 1936 (microfilm roll 405B), Foster to Maestri, May 17, 1938 (microfilm roll 414B), both in Robert Maestri Papers; New Orleans *Times-Picayune*, February 19, June 24, November 23, December 9, 1936.

legalized the establishment of local relief councils in counties other than Fulton—the organization of an Atlanta welfare commission had predated the state system because of a 1922 law authorizing counties with a population in excess of 100,000 to form welfare units. The 1937 Georgia legislation was perhaps the most progressive in the South. It required only a 10 percent local contribution for relief, with the state allocating more than one-half of all total welfare appropriations and Washington, D.C., providing the remainder. Even Rivers could make no financial guarantees, however, and in 1939 a revenue crunch caused the governor to reduce state expenditures drastically, abandoning much of his "little New Deal."[27]

Welfare officials in Memphis faced a similar dilemma. They too received no federal grants until 1937, when lawmakers in Nashville finally organized the Tennessee Department of Institutions and Public Welfare. Even then, the Tennessee network authorized the dispersal of federal disability payments through the county courts or through regional representatives appointed by the state. As a result, the two-year-old Memphis Welfare Commission still handled on its own the distribution of commodities and garments, the certification of WPA labor, and direct relief payments to those not eligible for social security disability. Not until 1939 did the state welfare system assume direct responsibility for all general assistance cases, and not until the next decade did a Shelby County welfare apparatus officially replace the Memphis Welfare Commission.[28]

Even after becoming eligible for federal grants, municipal welfare units continued to struggle. State appropriations were never substantial and often irregular, while local allocations—which in Birmingham, and for a short while in New Orleans, determined the amount of social security assistance—remained minimal. The situation in Atlanta exemplified those financial uncertainties when Georgia in 1939 sharply reduced welfare spending because of looming deficits. At the same time, Georgia's leading city cut its financial support for welfare by

27. Georgia State Department of Public Welfare, *Report for... 1935*, (Atlanta, 1936), 8–9; "Georgia Constitution Changes but Public Thirst Stays the Same," *Newsweek*, June 19, 1937, p. 13; "State News: Georgia," *Southern Economic Journal*, VII (July, 1940), 114–15; Fossett, "The Impact of the New Deal on Georgia Politics," 232; Young Allen Beall, "The Organization and Administration of the Department of Public Welfare of the State of Georgia" (M.A. thesis, Emory University, 1950), 21–29; Miller, "The Administration of E. D. Rivers," 35–36.

28. Governor's Report on the Relief Situation, November, 1935, in Hill McAlister Papers, Box 84; Tennessee Department of Public Welfare, *First Annual Report ... June 30, 1939* (Nashville, 1939), 5–6; Memphis *Commercial Appeal*, September 12, 1936; Robert C. Lowe, *State Public Welfare Legislation*, WPA Research Monograph, No. 20 (Washington, D.C., 1939), 368.

50 percent, explaining that its decision was determined by improving economic conditions and the special three-mill county relief tax established in that year. The result was an immediate reduction in monthly per case assistance for needy area families, from an average of $9.52 in mid-1938 to $5.08 by December, 1939. Available direct assistance in the city stood only pennies above the statewide average, and only three states in the country (Mississippi, Arkansas, and Oklahoma) offered fewer benefits. Less state and local money also meant fewer social security dollars, which caused the Fulton County welfare unit to cut in half the number of federal disability recipients.[29]

Welfare workers in Birmingham faced equally serious financial problems when the city in 1940 slashed its relief appropriations by 50 percent. Municipal officials had long argued that the county received revenues from state gasoline, sales, and liquor taxes that could be used for welfare. Thus, it was argued, the city "would be justified in discontinuing its contribution to the Department of Public Welfare entirely; if not it certainly should contribute a very small amount." Local reductions in turn triggered curtailed state and federal allocations, with the result that in 1940 the Birmingham welfare unit spent only $0.31 per capita for direct relief work, compared to a national urban figure of $5.19. For those on social security disability in the Alabama city, the per capita allowance in 1940 was equally dismal in comparison with national and even with regional urban allowances, which were five to seven times greater. According to the chairman of the local welfare office, the reductions substantially increased the incidence of sickness and malnutrition among welfare families. A group of concerned leaders accurately concluded that "the Birmingham program is particularly weak at this point."[30]

In 1938, cities throughout the country allocated, on the average, 18 percent of their total expenditures for welfare activities. Spending for relief ranked just below education as the top cost item in most urban budgets. In the Dixie cities, however, appropriations for welfare ranged from a high of 10 percent in Atlanta to a low of 1 percent in New Orleans. Indicative of scant local and state spending, the average

29. Georgia State Department of Public Welfare, *Georgia Public Welfare Statistics, December 1938* (Atlanta, 1938), 22–32, and *Georgia Public Welfare Statistics, January, February, March, 1940* (Atlanta, 1940), 25; Citizens Fact Finding Movement of Georgia, *Public Welfare: Appraisal and Proposals* (n.p., 1940), 10; Minutes of the Fulton County Commission, X, September 28, 1939, p. 576; Atlanta City Comptroller, *Report of the City Comptroller of Atlanta, Georgia, 1930–1940* (Atlanta, 1941), 43–60.

30. Wynn to Jones, May 27, 1937, in James M. Jones, Jr., Collection, Drawer 2; Birmingham Housing Authority, *Social and Economic Survey of the Birmingham, Alabama District for 1940* (Birmingham, 1943), 48–50; Thomason to Jones, November 19, 1938, September 2, 1939, in James M. Jones, Jr., Collection, Drawer 2.

welfare payment per capita in cities nationwide in 1937 was $8.81, while comparable figures in the southern municipalities fell between $0.02 per capita in Memphis and $0.99 in Atlanta. The situation in the southern cities, moreover, reflected conditions throughout the region. In 1939, more than 27 percent of the total number of relief cases nationally were receiving local and state financial assistance, while the percentage in the Southeast stood at less than 4 percent. Between 1929 and 1938, cities nationwide on the average quadrupled appropriations for welfare in proportion to their total expenditures. During the same period, comparable allocations in the urban South doubled.[31]

Local officials kept their relief contributions at a minimum for the same reason that they hesitated to sponsor WPA projects later in the decade. The conservative leadership had organized the new public welfare departments, but their New South efficiency sentiments prevented such institutions from advancing far under their direction. Municipal authorities in the 1930s, as they would do again during the civil rights era, sought to temper new social trends first by accepting, ever so cautiously, as few new, outside ideas as possible and then by controlling them so as not to threaten the prevailing urban ethos. In 1936, for example, New Orleans mayor Maestri replaced social workers and religious leaders on the board of the city's welfare agency with individuals more to his liking, a number of prominent area businessmen. Among the new appointees were the presidents of the Maison Blanche Department Store, Bernhardt Paint Company, National Food Products, and Foster Manufacturing Company. The new directors retained their predecessors as assistants, yet the revised unit was clearly less social work–oriented than the old one.[32]

The restructured New Orleans relief unit operated efficiently under its new directors with the limited resources available. In 1937, federal social security authorities judged it as "the outstanding department in the South and probably one of the more efficient in the country." The nonpolitical New Orleans Bureau of Government Research, a local citizens' lobby, praised city officials for "permitting the welfare directors to direct the destinies of the department and for not dividing the department's jobs between ward leaders as patronage." The relief apparatus included a personnel committee and a merit plan

31. *Financial Statistics of Cities over 100,000 Population* (1937), 122–23, 186–87; U.S. Bureau of Foreign and Domestic Commerce, *Statistical Abstract of the United States* (1929), 232–34, and (1941), 256–57; Howard, *The W.P.A. and Federal Relief Policy*, 552; Alvin H. Hansen and Harvey S. Perloff, *State and Local Finances in the National Economy* (New York, 1944), 169; "Employment Conditions and Unemployment Relief," *Monthly Labor Review* (September, 1937), 604.

32. New Orleans *Times-Picayune*, December 22, 1936; Martin, *Dynasty*, 153; Perry S. Howard, *Political Tendencies in Louisiana* (Baton Rouge, 1957), 267.

for employment and promotion based on training, ability, and experience. Field workers, even if not the directors, were found to be dedicated, concerned, and qualified social workers, who experienced few of the problems that had undermined relief operations during the days of the Long versus Walmsley confrontation.[33]

Nowhere was a New South attitude in welfare more apparent than in Memphis. The Crump machine, especially its leading lieutenant, Mayor Overton, applauded the involvement of Washington, D.C., in welfare while organizing a local relief apparatus only marginally sympathetic to the jobless and indigent. More so than the other municipalities, Memphis balked at requirements that it contribute its own resources to the effort. Delay and unwillingness confirmed the charges of federal examiners that "local concern is atrophical" and that the municipal and county leadership welcomed "absolution from responsibility—moral and financial." Investigators also reported that "the old aristocratic attitude toward the slave has its hangover and now prevails in respect to the black and only to a less degree to the white working class." The same study concluded that "the lower stratum is tolerated to the extent of granting it the right to live" and that social concerns in Memphis were "quite cowed." The elites "were very sorry for the mass"; nevertheless, they believed that "the betterment of this mass could only arise out of the prosperous operation of industry."[34]

Memphis was the last of the major southern municipalities to establish a permanent welfare department, and the city relied almost solely on state funding of its relief commission. In 1937, Memphis allocated only one-tenth of 1 percent of its budget for welfare work, setting aside more funds for the maintenance of public golf courses than for indigent care. Eventually, requirements included in the state statute creating the Tennessee welfare department forced Memphis to contribute proportionately more of its revenues for relief. Although Boss Crump paved roads and improved parks and playgrounds for Memphis residents, the so-called benevolent despot showed little public welfare responsibility.[35]

In Birmingham as well, a strong business presence in civic affairs determined the course of public welfare. City hall appointed the relief

33. Minutes of the Orleans Parish Department of Public Welfare, April 14, 1937, in Foster to Maestri, May 3, 1937, in Robert Maestri Papers, microfilm roll 404B; New Orleans Department of Public Welfare, *Three Year Report*, 31; New Orleans *Times-Picayune*, March 30, December 22, 1936.

34. Scott, Confidential Report on Memphis, n.d., in FERA, Tennessee Field Reports.

35. *Financial Statistics of Cities over 100,000 Population* (1937), 186–87. For the "benevolent despot" thesis, see Peterson, *The Day of the Mugwhump* and Miller, *Mr. Crump of Memphis*.

commissioners, men and women who generally represented the upper classes and whose attitude toward the unfortunate combined regional paternalism with New South sentiments. Such attitudes certainly influenced local welfare personnel when they withheld assistance from striking miners seeking union recognition under the provisions of the National Labor Relations Act. In the past, federal authorities had aided strikers in securing relief, but under the new welfare system, labor was at the mercy of a locally operated relief bureau. And the management of large industrial outlets in Jefferson County was influential with City Commission Council president Jones. TCI apparently kept a full-time representative in city hall—he even had his own desk— as an advisor on matters that might affect the company. In the case of strikers, it was easy to justify a policy of no aid because the applications placed an added burden on already limited resources.[36]

Although the new public departments proved permanent, even if ill funded, most urban residents by the turn of the decade had not fully accepted the fundamental issue of community responsibility for welfare. More than a few men and women continued to eye the bureaus with misgivings, and frequent, highly publicized accusations of wrongdoing only enhanced the skepticism, complicating the task of relief work. It was not surprising that the loudest indictments against welfare operations were heard in New Orleans, where one of the first critics was the city's Housewives' League. The women feared that public financing would deprive social clubs of organizing future fundraising benefits for charity. The most vehement opposition came from anti-Long politicians, who charged Mayor Maestri and his welfare directors with using relief payments for political advantage. The New Orleans *Times-Picayune*, which by the late 1930s had become an antimachine press, gave these charges banner headlines.

Even the clean bill of health given the New Orleans unit by federal authorities and the local citizens' lobby did not assuage the Long opposition. Long's successors through Mayor Maestri controlled the Crescent City's relief apparatus, and by 1940, corruption had become a trademark within the organization. The oil scandals and WPA irregularities, which drove Governor Leche from office, did little to nurture the concept of public responsibility. Still, field workers apparently refrained from manipulating votes with welfare funds, despite charges to that effect. Federal grand jury and social security investigations in 1940 found no evidence that the machine had used welfare payments to force relief clients to vote for its gubernatorial candidate, Earl Long.[37]

36. Birmingham *News*, November 15, 1935; interview with Reuben Farr, Birmingham area labor leader, May 2, 1975.

37. New Orleans *Times-Picayune*, January 13, 1934, May 6, 1938, February 6, 1941.

In other cities as well, periodic inquiries into welfare operations by local fraternal groups, whether to probe the expenditure of public money or just to generate self-publicity, enhanced public skepticism. In Birmingham, the American Legion led a crusade to purge out-of-state caseworkers and administrators from local relief offices. Their charges earned newspaper headlines when so-called irregularities were uncovered—such as white stenographers taking dictation from black welfare personnel. This inquiry ultimately forced a number of resignations from the county welfare department, as well as from both the city transient bureau and the area CWA office. The Birmingham Real Estate Owners Association likewise launched several relief investigations. Local landlords believed that welfare officials were urging relief clients to withhold rent payments and also that large numbers of blacks were exchanging welfare checks for gasoline and liquor. Demanding the reorganization of local relief machinery, the property owners eventually brought their well-publicized case to officials in Montgomery, who proved uncooperative. Instead, the state joined city hall in questioning whether depression conditions in Birmingham warranted additional federal aid to help tenants maintain rent payments.[38]

Similar welfare investigations occurred in Atlanta. In 1937, the Fulton County chapter of the Ku Klux Klan demanded that local officials cease all appropriations to the area welfare commission. Klansmen had discovered that many indigent black families were receiving aid equal to that available to white relief clients, and blamed the situation on bad management. A grand jury investigation in 1939 further enhanced suspicions of public welfare activities. Jurors reported that the department had "in several cases failed to recognize its obligation to the taxpayers of the county, in that the use of public money has not been limited to the paupers of the county." The legal inquiry returned no indictments because the alleged irregularities, it was later found, resulted not from conscious graft but from the inexperience of personnel. Nonetheless, damage to the public welfare image had been done.[39]

Lingering public skepticism suggests that the concept of public welfare responsibility limped into the postdepression years. Yet there is little doubt that New Deal policy advanced the concept, for support for the new relief networks was not entirely lacking. During the last several years of the decade, for example, city and county officials in Atlanta were locked in a struggle over who should contribute more to

38. Birmingham *News*, January 5, 19, June 15, 24, 26, 1934; Birmingham *Age-Herald*, June 23, 1934.

39. Minutes of the Fulton County Commission, W, March 3, 10, 1938, pp. 533, 548; Atlanta *Constitution*, July 1, 1939.

the local welfare bureau. More than 90 percent of those on relief were city residents, yet the county rather than the city government possessed the authority to levy special taxes. At one point, Mayor Hartsfield announced that he would retaliate against any reduction of county allocations for welfare by curtailing municipal fire, water, and library services to persons living outside the incorporated area. Commenting on the controversy, the conservative and always cautious Atlanta *Constitution* endorsed the principle of public welfare, indicating that "it is unthinkable that because of these differences of opinion even worse suffering and deprivation than already being borne by a large group of Atlanta citizens should be unnecessarily forced upon them." The same editorial concluded that financial issues must never cloud the more important concern of "whether unfortunate men, women and children who, through no fault of their own, are unable to supply themselves with food, shelter and clothing shall be permitted to suffer."[40]

Thus, a new public assistance network, and with it new attitudes, began to emerge during the New Deal period. In the southern cities and major urban areas elsewhere, the result was the organization of what would become permanent public welfare institutions. The system's survival depended not only upon state and federal funding but to a great extent as well upon local generosity; and throughout the 1930s, municipal officials began setting aside more of their total expenditures for such work. The machinery remained decentralized; the New Deal's intent all along was to generate local responsibility. Toward that end, federal statutes required the establishment of local relief bureaus, directed and financed by city and state authorities, which over time advanced the concept of public responsibility for care of the indigent. No doubt the process also helped launch a new, permanent relationship between the federal government and municipalities throughout the nation, including those in the South. While the region's urban ethos— including the values of social order, efficiency, tradition, and expansion—remained in evidence throughout the 1930s, new social commitments, even if accommodated grudgingly and from necessity, were forthcoming and would never be undone.

---

40. Atlanta *Constitution*, February 3, 1937, March 30–31, April 1, 1939.

 9

FEDERAL HOUSING PROGRAMS
AND THE BOOSTER ENVIRONMENT

If municipal services in the southern cities were lacking in the 1930s, residential housing conditions were more disgraceful, and slum clearance programs were desperately needed. Joblessness forced either the abandonment of homes or the forgoing of improvements; even those employed could barely maintain their dwellings. The vast majority of southern urban workers earned less than one thousand dollars per year, with the annual average for blacks being several hundred dollars lower. And while regional wage differentials narrowed somewhat during the depression, urban living costs negated the small gains, so that adequate housing remained an elusive goal for most. Thousands of substandard homes lined southern city streets, typified by the Beaver Slide housing development, located adjacent to one of Atlanta's black colleges. In September, 1934, the Atlanta *Daily World* described Beaver Slide as an area in which "little barefoot children, skipping along the muddy allies, dodging bottles thrown at them by estranged lovers, were the victims of a social environment that has led hundreds to disgrace, poverty and criminal careers. While there were many fine young ladies . . . there were many of the don't care types, barelegged, half-naked, puffing cigarettes and offering their person on the auction block of licentious and loose living."[1]

Even the operation of several New Deal housing and slum clearance programs, beginning with a PWA housing division and culminating with the United States Housing Authority (USHA), created in 1937, barely dented the problem in the southern cities. New Deal efforts did

1. Atlanta *Daily World*, September 25, 1934.

not constitute a national housing plan and brought no basic transformation of metropolitan structure. Urban historian Zane Miller suggests that housing projects, as well as the low-interest improvement loans made available to homeowners, "all fit neatly into the pattern of sprawling growth in and around cities that had developed after 1880." The housing program of the 1930s failed to alter the pattern of flight from urban to suburban areas prevalent throughout the period and thereafter in cities north, west, and south. At the same time, argues Howard Preston in *The Automobile Age in Atlanta*, the increasing availability of the automobile was reinforcing both that trend and established Jim Crow practices particular to the southern municipalities.[2]

Still, federal funds made possible the razing of many of the worst slum areas, such as Beaver Slide, emergency employment for the jobless, subcontract work for local builders, and a flow of dollars into city treasuries that more than offset tax revenues previously collected on dilapidated properties. Furthermore, the organization of local housing authorities, and the acceptance of environmental determinist theories by some, once again demonstrated that an urban consciousness was advancing throughout the region. Of course, like other New Deal programs—perhaps even more so than work relief efforts—the federal slum clearance projects fit nicely into the southern booster creed. It was important to enhance the value of real estate, much of which civic leaders owned and which they believed reflected the overall well-being of their communities. Many conservative urban elites thus endorsed some federal involvement in at least this area of municipal affairs—a trend in evidence in cities nationwide. And in later years, during more prosperous times, that support continued. The growth of public housing caused Atlanta's leading housing expert to remark, somewhat tongue in cheek: "At long last Uncle Sam caught up with himself. When General Sherman's Federal Troops were a bit careless with fire in Atlanta in November, 1864, they burned 3500 of the 4000 structures then in the city. Federal funds replaced them in full measure with 4,996 low-rent homes by 1940. After 76 years, Uncle Sam helped rebuild more than Sherman burned."[3]

The many federal and state surveys in the 1930s showed that municipalities throughout Dixie contained the nation's most serious housing problems. A CWA study in Memphis, directed by social

2. Zane L. Miller, *The Urbanization of Modern America: A Brief History* (New York, 1973), 168–69; Howard Preston, *The Automobile Age in Atlanta: The Making of a Southern Metropolis, 1900–1935* (Athens, Ga., 1979), 74–112.

3. Charles R. Palmer, *Adventures of a Slum Fighter* (Atlanta, 1955), 237.

activist John Petrie, compared conditions in that city to those in Chicago, Boston, and New York. Petrie concluded that he had never "seen anything to equal the filth, squalor, and misery of what pass for homes in Memphis." He discovered that "in many cases ventilation is unknown, in others there is nothing but ventilation." More than 50 percent of the city's population lived in housing below federal minimum standards, and more than one-third of all Memphians resided in structures judged too dilapidated for repair. Nearly one-fourth of the city's inhabitants lived in what were considered slum conditions. "One hears much about Southern pride," Petrie wrote, "but it does not display itself in any attempt to hide the slums of Southern cities."[4]

Similar situations existed in Atlanta and Birmingham. In the former, a 1934 census tract survey of inner-city residences reported that 54 percent of all homes were substandard, with 30 percent unfit for occupancy or in need of major structural repairs. Less than one-third of the 83,000 houses in Birmingham had both hot and cold running water, while more than 32,000 had no heating system and 53,000 had no bathing facilities. A 1936–1937 federal study of 64 urban areas nationwide reported that only five had worse slum conditions on the whole than the steel city.[5]

Federal studies likewise revealed poor conditions in New Orleans. Half of the city's 516,000 residents lived in substandard complexes, representing 40 percent of all city residences. This figure compared to a 1930 federal census statistic that judged one-fourth of all non-farm houses nationwide as substandard. Also, private housing construction in New Orleans had not kept pace with recent population growth. Between 1929 and 1935, the city's population grew by 60,000, while only 2,000 new residences were built, doubtless explaining the low 1 percent vacancy rate reported in the late 1930s. In comparison, vacancy rates in the other southern cities were 10 percent or higher.[6]

4. John C. Petrie, "Survey Shows Housing Scandals," *Christian Century*, February 21, 1934, p. 265; D. M. Graves and Alfred H. Chandler, "Developing a Housing Program in a Southern City," *American Journal of Public Health*, XXXVII (July, 1937), 649.

5. WPA of Georgia, *A Statistical Study of the Social and Economic Pattern of the City of Atlanta, Georgia* (Atlanta, 1939), 70; "Housing Authorities Describe Local Conditions," *American City* (November, 1938), 58; Paul Pearson to Charles Palmer, October 17, 1936, in Charles R. Palmer Papers, Housing File, Robert Woodruff Library, Emory University, Atlanta; Jefferson County Board of Health, *Final Statistical Report of Surveys . . .* (Birmingham, 1937), 7, 54–58; Birmingham Housing Authority, *Social and Economic Survey of the Birmingham, Alabama District for 1940* (Birmingham, 1943), 20, 44.

6. New Orleans *Times-Picayune*, September 8, 1938; Atlanta *Journal of Labor*, August 10, 1934; Peter Edward Arnold, "Public Housing in Atlanta" (M.A. thesis, Georgia State University, 1970), 22–23; Nelwyn E. Huff, "The Immediate Dysgenic Effect of An

The blighted urban areas contributed little except disease and crime to the overall community, costing the cities far more than tax revenues collected. Birmingham's nine worst housing districts, where 12 percent of the population resided, recorded 50 percent of the city's crime, 33 percent of all typhoid cases, and more than 30 percent of all tuberculosis deaths. In all southern cities, police costs per person in substandard sections doubled the average spent per capita in other areas. Housing conditions, moreover, reflected a city's economic plight. In Birmingham, more than 60 percent of all residents earned less than $1,000 per year, and 80 percent of all rental units, representing 60 percent of all local dwellings, leased for less than $15 per month.[7]

Inadequate housing was a way of life in black residential urban areas. Ninety-four percent of all black Memphians paid less than three dollars per week for dilapidated wooden shacks or rooms in run-down tenement houses. Black families in New Orleans rented, or in rare cases owned, two-thirds of the occupied substandard residential structures. In Memphis, federal investigators judged only 3,000 of 35,000 black residences to be standard; in Atlanta, one-third of the homes in black residential sections were unfit for occupancy and most others had no running water, no electricity, and no gas. Twenty-two blighted districts in Birmingham represented 10 percent of the city's total area but contained 50 percent of its black population (23 percent of all families) and 66 percent of its slum dwellings.[8]

Two-story tenement "arks" were prevalent throughout the urban South. In these structures, sixteen or more families crammed onto each floor, where rooms rented for five to seven dollars per month. According to federal surveys, most families had "a single room entered from a balcony hanging miraculously to the side of the building." Students at the Tulane University School of Social Work described one of the largest tenement areas in New Orleans as follows:

> Many of the housing areas are characterized by fantastic names such as the Pepper, the Yellow Dog, the Lizard, the Ark and the Red Devil. The Red Devil located at 2816 Faret Street is a long narrow two-story building. Rows of houses surround it on all sides. This tenement is divided into thirty-six

---

Economic Depression . . . During the Years 1929 Through 1935" (M.S. thesis, Birmingham Southern University, 1936), 32–33.

7. "Selling Birmingham," *Business Week*, May 9, 1936, pp. 32–34; Memphis *Press Scimitar*, January 14, 1938; Arnold, "Public Housing in Atlanta," 11.

8. Memphis *Commercial Appeal*, April 13, 1937; Memphis *Press Scimitar*, November 5, 1941; Housing Authority of New Orleans, *Report of the Housing Authority . . . 1939* (New Orleans, 1940); WPA of Georgia, *Statistical Study*, 60–66, 70; Jefferson County Board of Health, *Final Statistical Report*, 7.

rooms. There are four toilets in the front yard for the use of the occupants of the building. On the lower gallery are six sinks with cold running water. None of the rooms have electricity or gas. One tenant stated that there are approximately 115 individuals in the tenement. The rooms rent for one dollar a week.[9]

Not surprisingly, the prospect of federally funded buildings, paved roads, and modern sewers and housing generated much excitement among urban elites in the South. This excitement was reflected in the organization of the Birmingham Industrial Recreation Association in 1934, a cooperative venture between industrial employers, who donated money and property, and the FERA to improve a large run-down neighborhood where many steelworkers resided. The result was the construction of a community park, the building or remodeling of 1,100 homes, and the installation of new gas distribution facilities.[10] City business and government leaders were aware of the necessity of an attractive community if they hoped to revive what had been a nation-wide interest in the region. They were also sympathetic to the health and social problems of the poor, yet their first concern was their city's future economic and industrial expansion.

The determined efforts of Charles R. Palmer, Atlanta businessman, realtor, and past president of the National Association of Building Owners and Managers, were largely responsible for the coming of the first federal housing projects to the southern cities. In 1933, the Atlantan organized influential business and community leaders into a group known as Techwood Incorporated. Included were the editors of the three Atlanta daily newspapers, Mayor Key, and representatives from Georgia Tech University, the chamber of commerce, and the AFL. The "dividend corporation" then opened negotiations for a $3 million housing program with the PWA housing division, directed by Secretary of Interior Ickes. Plans called for the renovation of a slum area adjacent to Georgia Tech. Initially, Ickes approved and even encouraged the idea of an economic stake for locals, believing that it would ensure an operation's efficiency. At the same time, Palmer's group sought an additional $2 million for a 675-unit black project, with the new apartments to be constructed in the dilapidated Beaver Slide area. A Negro advisory committee, directed by Atlanta University president John Hope, cooperated with Techwood Incorporated in planning the

9. Tulane University School of Social Work, "A Housing Study of the Flinnt-Goodridge Hospital Area, July 1, 1934" (Typescript in Louisiana Collection, Howard Tilton Memorial Library, Tulane University, 1934), 7.

10. "Slum Clearance in Birmingham, Alabama," *American City* (November, 1935), 43.

latter venture. PWA authorities ultimately agreed to contribute 85 percent of all costs for each project.[11]

Despite Palmer's influence, Atlanta real estate interests were against the federal housing plan. More than a few realtors, many of whom stood to profit as urban property values increased, seemed to endorse the sentiments of Georgia governor Talmadge: "Slums don't hurt anybody. In fact, slums are good for people, Makes 'em stronger." The result was that the first projects often faced stern, organized opposition, such as that of Atlanta's Apartment House Owners Association. Claiming a 25 percent vacancy rate among local rental dwellings, the group invested thousands in a campaign against Palmer and Techwood. Referring to the Atlanta plan as "Palmer's Paradise," the association charged that Palmer had a direct financial interest in Techwood. A subsequent PWA investigation found that while Palmer owned land near the project, he had acquired it long before the advent of this slum clearance effort, and there was no evidence of wrongdoing. The property owners also pleaded their case before the city council, but in the end only delayed construction and never blocked it. Municipal officials initially endorsed the federal program and facilitated the building by closing streets for work crews and by financing sidewalk and road improvements in designated public housing areas.[12]

The government housing effort also faced a problem of unreasonable prices placed on slum properties. Federal regulations stipulated that the acquisition of land could absorb only 20 percent of a project's resources, and urban slumlords often refused to sell at the appraisal price. According to Palmer's own account, delays troubling the Techwood and University projects came from a conspiracy of "owners of slum properties who had been collecting extortionist rents for years, brokers who managed slum properties, trust companies, or dummy real estate corporations that concealed the identity of prominent people, and agents or home office representatives of certain insurance and mortgage companies." The situation was little different in Birmingham and Memphis, where federal slum clearance likewise gained early PWA approval.[13]

11. Palmer to Brame Hood, October 27, 1933, in Charles R. Palmer Papers, Housing File; Arnold, "Public Housing in Atlanta," 2–9; Mark B. Lapping, "The Emergence of Federal Public Housing: Atlanta's Techwood Project," *American Journal of Economics and Sociology*, XXXII (October, 1973), 379–80; Paul Pearson, "Federal Housing Projects for Negroes," *Southern Workman*, LXV (December, 1936), 376–77; Atlanta *Constitution*, September 2, 1936.

12. Palmer, *Adventures of a Slum Fighter*, 135, 18–20, 27; Garrett, *Atlanta and Environs*, III, 908–909; Atlanta *Constitution*, March 30, July 3, 1934.

13. Palmer, *Adventures of a Slum Fighter*, 19; Birmingham *Post*, April 22, 1935; Birmingham *News*, December 11, 1937.

Even the threat of court action did not always hasten the process of land acquisition. Ickes hoped that the threat of condemnation proceedings would force owners to sell at reasonable prices and thereafter improve land and structures adjacent to the project sites. However, despite one court victory against Atlanta realtors in control of Beaver Slide, the judiciary often decided against the government and in favor of private ownership of property. Such was the case in Louisville, Kentucky, in 1935, where the sixth circuit court ruled that Washington, D.C., could not claim the right of eminent domain to acquire property for government housing. For a time thereafter, slum clearance programs moved slowly.[14]

In March, 1934, New Dealers modified the housing program with the passage of the National Housing Act, transferring the ownership of ongoing and future slum clearance projects to the Federal Emergency Housing Corporation (FEHC). The two Atlanta complexes, while continuing to receive PWA construction funds, thus became exclusively federal property, which meant the liquidation of Techwood Incorporated as a dividend corporation. Palmer thereafter devoted his energies to planning additional projects for his city (11,000 family structures at a cost of $31 million by late 1934) and assisting municipal leaders throughout the South with their housing plans. In mid-1934 and again in 1936, the Atlantan toured Europe and studied low-rent government housing, gathering blueprints from Italy, France, Great Britain, and Germany, as well as from eastern European nations. He also sponsored an international housing conference held in Atlanta in December, 1934. By the 1940s, Palmer had become a leading authority on subsidized housing and slum clearance, and during World War II, President Roosevelt appointed him director of the national emergency wartime housing program.[15]

The other major southern municipalities were not far behind in seeking PWA slum clearance dollars. In mid-1933, Birmingham businessman J. C. DeHoll (later to be chairman of the Birmingham Housing Authority) and a group of realtors prodded the City Commission Council to sponsor a series of residential surveys, leading in 1934 to an official request of $4 million for a Negro project to be constructed in a twenty-eight-acre downtown area. A thorough PWA study followed,

14. New York *Times*, April 22, 1934; Leuchtenberg, *Franklin D. Roosevelt and the New Deal*, 135.

15. Lapping, "The Emergence of Federal Public Housing," 381; A. C. Montgomery to Palmer, October 24, 1933, Palmer to Elizabeth Lanagan, November 6, 1934, Palmer to Angelo Cass, June 17, 1935, Palmer to Robert Wagner, June 25, 1935, all in Charles R. Palmer Papers, Housing File; Atlanta *Constitution*, July 1, 1934; Palmer, *Adventures of a Slum Fighter*, 31–100, 144–204.

after which Ickes approved the building of Smithfield Court at a cost of $2.5 million in federal loans and grants. The work began in 1935, and the first tenants arrived in 1938. Likewise in Memphis, where Boss Crump's lieutenants worked closely with FEHC director Robert Kohn to survey area slums, housing conditions more than justified PWA approval in mid-1935 of $7 million for more than 1,400 dwelling units in two projects, one for whites (Lauderdale Court) and one for blacks (Dixie Homes). By that time as well, housing efforts had advanced in other southern urban areas, including Montgomery, Louisville, Charlotte, Nashville, Miami, and Jacksonville.[16]

Of the large southern cities, only New Orleans failed to benefit from the first public housing efforts. Like other PWA proposals in 1934 and early 1935, housing plans became entangled in the controversy between the Interior Secretary and Senator Long. This resulted in the rejection of a five-million-dollar proposal for two housing projects in mid-1935. Then, following the death of the Kingfish, the city's resubmitted bid was rejected when President Roosevelt ordered the PWA housing division closed late in October of the same year. The president was disappointed with the first federal housing experiment. The opposition of realtors and court delays had blocked the acquisition of slum properties, in turn preventing the jobless from obtaining needed work. Only seven projects nationwide were then under way, and only forty-nine others had received PWA approval. Even Ickes by late 1935 had become disillusioned, agreeing to the investment of all unused slum clearance funds in WPA and other relief endeavors. Construction went ahead on previously approved projects, such as those in Atlanta, Birmingham, and Memphis, but no new building was begun. All subsequent housing proposals remained in limbo for two years.[17]

During this two-year period, the FEHC tackled another obstacle affecting urban slum clearance—the entanglement of rental payments, local property taxes, and municipal services. Having its southern origins in Atlanta, the conflict nearly jeopardized the scheduled opening of Techwood Homes in 1936 and the completion of the complexes in the other cities. Clearly, the Techwood and University projects were responsible for the elimination of two of Atlanta's worst

16. W. J. Wynn to W. O. Downs, May 7, 1934, in James M. Jones, Jr., Collection, Drawer 2, Alabama Archives and History, Montgomery; Birmingham *News*, September 17, 1934, August 13, 1935, November 2, 1937, February 8, 1938; Birmingham *Post*, April 22, 1935; Memphis *Press Scimitar*, March 19, August 17, 1934, February 5, 1935, January 12, 1936, November 12, 1937; Memphis *Commercial Appeal*, April 19, May 17, June 18, July 25, August 18, 1935.

17. New Orleans *Times-Picayune*, September 18, 1934, September 8, October 9, 1935, February 18, July 9, 1936; Atlanta *Georgian*, September 8, 1935; Memphis *Commercial Appeal*, September 17, 1935; Memphis *Press Scimitar*, September 26–27, 1935.

slums, and the housing effort between 1934 and 1937 rid Memphis of as many dilapidated dwellings as were razed in all of New York City during the same period. Yet the replacement of slums with modern apartments by itself was not always satisfactory to local governments. City leaders demanded the right to tax the former slum areas as improved properties in return for municipal services. Birmingham city attorney W. J. Wynn argued that FEHC authorities should turn over to municipal governments "the amount which would be paid on the property as presently improved were it in the hands of private ownership."[18] Technically, FEHC ownership exempted the federal projects from local taxation; still, urban officials saw the issue as one of expanding federal authority versus local autonomy.

The conflict's opening round occurred in March, 1934, when the Atlanta city attorney ruled that Techwood would be ineligible for services unless the project paid municipal taxes. United States Attorney General Homer Cummings immediately overruled the local decision, which in turn generated a municipal threat to deny residents police protection, garbage collection, and other services. The matter remained unsettled for more than a year, during which time the city sought the support of Georgia senators Richard Russell and Walter F. George. Then in October, 1935, the city presented Washington, D.C., with a bill for $9,200 for services so far rendered at the project site. In response, United States Comptroller-General J. R. McCarl ruled that such a bill was tantamount to the illegal taxation of federal property.

Finally in late October, the Interior Department announced a plan to pay Atlanta and other municipalities 5 percent of annual project rentals in lieu of taxes for services. Georgia congressmen had been pressuring housing authorities for more than a year to find a satisfactory solution, and by now, even Attorney General Cummings was endorsing the idea of payments to cities in some form. The arrangement also stipulated that public housing residents pay all local and state personal taxes and be required to purchase business licenses from city hall. Congress subsequently formalized the 5 percent scheme in July, 1936, in the George-Healy Act. To keep rentals as low as possible, the federal law also applied PWA grant (45 percent) and loan (55 percent) guidelines to the housing program. The result was that Techwood opened on schedule in September, 1936. Official dedication ceremonies had occurred nearly a year earlier, involving an impressive array of dignitaries, including President Roosevelt, the governors of Ala-

18. Wynn to Jones, May 29, 1937, in James M. Jones, Jr., Collection, Drawer 1. Also see text of a speech by Mayor Overton, April, 1937, in Watkins Overton Papers, Box 3, Memphis State University Library.

bama, Florida, and South Carolina, and Georgia senators George and Russell. The only absentee of note was Georgia governor Talmadge, who purposely left the city that day to visit his farm in Telfair County.[19]

The George-Healy Act, however, did not settle the broader issue of the future of the slum clearance program. That was determined in 1937 with the creation of the USHA. The plan had only lukewarm presidential backing, and according to William Leuchtenburg, even its cosponsor Congressman Henry Steagall thought it "socialistic and financially reckless." And like most later New Deal measures, it touched off months of legislative debate. A key participant in the congressional hearings was Atlantan Charles Palmer, who in April, 1937, testified to the worth of low-rent government housing as he had studied it in western Europe. Again in September, Palmer journeyed to Washington, D.C., this time to attend the opening planning sessions for the organization of the USHA as signed into law by President Roosevelt earlier that month.[20]

The Wagner-Steagall Act established the USHA within the Interior Department and authorized the new housing agency to appropriate a maximum of $800 million for additional slum clearance work. Federal loans could absorb up to 90 percent of the cost of the new complexes, with repayment extending over 60 years at an interest rate of 0.5 percent. Local bonds would provide the remaining 10 percent of the cost, and cities would receive 5 percent of rents in lieu of taxes. Of primary importance in urban development, the statute limited USHA assistance to cities with permanent housing commissions, which would administer the new, low-rent units.[21]

Memphis was prepared for the USHA even before the passage of the enabling legislation. Mayor Overton had appointed the Memphis Housing Authority in August, 1934, to oversee the Lauderdale and Dixie projects, and by 1937, that commission had become an integral part of municipal affairs. The local bureau initially included PWA-

19. Arnold, "Public Housing in Atlanta," 10–16; Palmer, *Adventures of a Slum Fighter*, 141; Atlanta *Journal*, February 17, March 17, 26, October 18, 23, November 29, 1935; Atlanta *Constitution*, January 28, May 31, June 21, 1936; C. H. Grayson to Jones, June 23, 1938, in James M. Jones, Jr., Collection, Drawer 2; Birmingham *Post*, January 12, 1937, June 21, 1938; Birmingham *Age-Herald*, July 2, 1938; Birmingham *News*, August 27, 1938.

20. Leuchtenberg, *Franklin D. Roosevelt and the New Deal*, 135; Palmer, Statement Before the Senate Committee on Education and Labor, April 15, 1937, Ickes to Palmer, September 15, 1937, and Palmer to Ickes, September 17, 1937, all in Charles R. Palmer Papers, Housing File.

21. Robert M. Fisher, *Twenty Years of Public Housing: Economic Aspects of the Federal Program* (New York, 1959), 74, 106, 123–24; Arnold, "Public Housing in Atlanta," 25–30; New Orleans *Times-Picayune*, August 9, 1938.

appointed advisors, which triggered protest against what Boss Crump called outside interference in "our purely local matter." Yet local personnel had gained valuable experience working with the first slum clearance program, and the Memphis authority was ready to lease the two PWA complexes, opened in 1938. Within months, the USHA approved funding for three additional projects (Le Moyne Gardens, Lamar Homes, and Foote Homes) at a total cost of more than ten million dollars, and by the early 1940s, the Memphis Housing Authority was operating public housing units for more than three thousand low-income families. Other Tennessee cities, including Nashville, Chattanooga, Knoxville, Jackson, and Kingsport, were not far behind.[22]

Birmingham likewise had an active housing agency prior to the USHA's opening, established under state statute in August, 1935. By 1946, similar groups were operating in seven municipalities adjacent to the steel city, in addition to the Jefferson County Housing Commission, organized in 1941. Construction began in late 1938 on the first USHA project approved for Birmingham, the $4.5 million Elyton Village complex, and in succeeding years, the federal agency funded the Central City, Eastwood, and Southampton projects. Including Smithfield Court, which the Birmingham group leased from the PWA in 1938, the five contained more than 3,100 dwelling units with 12,000 rooms. National administrators set conditions for the selection of tenants, established guidelines for occupancy, and supervised local operating budgets, which were largely comprised of federal loans and subsidies. In turn, local personnel in Birmingham and elsewhere surveyed area slums and recommended projects, channeled federal and local bond money to contractors, hired residential superintendents and directed tenant activities.[23]

Anticipating the Wagner-Steagall Act, the Housing Authority of New Orleans (HANO) began operations in March, 1937, under a Louisiana housing statute passed the previous year. Controlled by Mayor Maestri and other prominent commercial and business leaders,

22. Crump to McKellar, January 28, 30, 1938 (Box 3), Walker Jones to Nathan Straus, February 14, March 29, 1939, Straus to McKellar, March 30, 1939 (Box 411), all in Kenneth McKellar Papers, Memphis Public Library, Downtown Branch; Overton to A. R. Clas, August 28, October 26, 1935, memorandum by Overton, January 29, 1936, all in Mayor's Correspondence File, Drawer 3, Memphis and Shelby County Archives, Memphis; Memphis *Press Scimitar*, November 20, 1937, April 25, September 12, 1938, November 2, 1939, April 16, 1941.

23. J. C. DeHoll, Report of the Housing Authority of the Birmingham District, April 27, 1938, and Frank Spain to R. A. Coale, January 28, 1939, both in James M. Jones, Jr., Collection, Drawer 2; Cooper, *Metropolitan County*, 83–87; Birmingham *News*, August 24, 1937, February 8, June 3, August 26, 1938; Birmingham *Age-Herald*, July 2, 1938; Birmingham *Post*, February 20, 1939.

the Crescent City group sought to make up quickly for projects lost during Huey Long's regime. Louisiana senators Allen Ellender and John Overton joined the effort, and as part of the Second Louisiana Purchase, President Roosevelt in March, 1938, personally approved $7.2 million for the construction of the Magnolia (black) and St. Thomas (white) projects, totaling 1,400 units. The housing program in New Orleans expanded rapidly thereafter, although for years HANO and its counterparts throughout the South remained without labor, minority, or professional welfare representation.[24]

Construction on the first complexes began in mid-1939, following an inspection tour of the city by USHA director Nathan Straus. As he examined area slums, Straus remarked that "never have I seen worse, even in Honolulu, and they have some classics there." Even before the visit, USHA officials had announced the approval of $20 million for an additional five projects (Iberville, Florida Avenue, Lafitte, Calliore Street, and St. Bernard), and by mid-1942, the seven Crescent City projects, totaling almost 5,400 units, were either fully occupied or accepting their first tenants. Monthly rents in New Orleans were similar to those elsewhere—$8 to $23 for a one- to four-bedroom dwelling.[25]

The Crescent City program functioned with fewer problems and delays than did projects in the other southern cities. Local real estate interests there offered only token resistance, and most property owners settled for HANO's appraisal figure. Of course a political machine that endorsed the federal program and that controlled key executive, legislative, and judicial personnel facilitated the process. Furthermore, the privately owned New Orleans Public Service Company cooperated in supplying gas and electricity for the low-rent complexes, whereas the problem of providing utilities for the projects in Birmingham and Atlanta precipitated long negotiations. HANO simply threatened to construct small power plants at each housing project site. Also, New Orleans authorities accepted rent payments in lieu of taxes without argument. In a letter to housing officials in Utica, New York, HANO's attorney remarked that "there seems to be a complete attitude of

24. Housing Authority of New Orleans, *Annual Report, 1937–1938* (New Orleans, 1939), 3–13; Howard and Friedman, *Government in Metropolitan New Orleans*, 47–49; Don Eddy, "Kingfish the Second: Robert Sidney Maestri," *American Magazine*, CXXVIII (November, 1939), 82; New Orleans *Tribune*, March 16, 1937; New Orleans *Times-Picayune*, December 14, 1937.

25. New Orleans *Tribune*, March 1, 1939; *Hearings Before a Joint Committee on Housing*, 80th Cong., 1st Sess., Part 2 (1948), 1823; New Orleans *Times-Picayune*, September 9, December 11, 14, 1937, February 15, March 18, April 27, September 8, 30, December 16, 1938, May 24, July 18, November 2, 1939.

cooperation, interest and desire for the carrying into effect of the projects contemplated."[26]

Once the southern leader in slum clearance, Atlanta in late 1937 fell from the front ranks. Palmer returned to the Georgia capital in September of that year, having assisted in the USHA's organization and hoping to become director of a local housing commission that would rank among the best in the nation. But a new administration was now in charge in Atlanta, and a cautious Mayor Hartsfield was in no hurry to qualify the New South capital for the USHA program. Hartsfield vetoed the first proposed municipal housing commission, noting that Atlanta was "not going to be the guinea pig in this matter." The mayor understood that many realtors opposed government housing and that some influential Atlantans had become weary altogether of the federal alphabet agencies. The conservative Atlanta press, usually quite cautious concerning federal programs, called the city's inaction "little less than tragic." Nevertheless, concluded Palmer, the mayor continued to move slowly "until he felt sure that at least 150 percent of the voters wanted him to set up a local body."[27]

A tragic incident in March, 1938, ultimately prodded the Hartsfield administration to act. On the morning of March 27, a fire burned out of control for hours in the center-city slum area next to Grady Memorial Hospital. Not only did it destroy all residences adjacent to the hospital, but flames damaged several businesses and warehouses, as well as part of the public medical center. The tragedy demonstrated exactly what the lack of slum clearance could mean to a city, and in May, 1938, the mayor and council finally approved an ordinance creating the Atlanta Housing Authority. Hartsfield named Palmer as director of the commission of prominent business leaders, and the group quickly won the endorsement of Governor Rivers. Local housing agencies were already active in Savannah, Columbus, Macon, Rome, Athens, and Augusta, and in early 1940, Fulton County commissioners appointed a county housing board to bring the federal program into rural sections around the city.[28]

Once organized, the Atlanta Housing Authority immediately assumed management of Techwood and University homes and gained approval for additional work costing more than $15 million. The Clark

26. William Guste to Vincent R. Corrov, June 7, 1938, in Robert Maestri Papers, microfilm roll 409B, New Orleans Public Library; New Orleans *Times-Picayune*, April 14, 1938.

27. Palmer, *Adventures of a Slum Fighter*, 229; Atlanta *Constitution*, March 15, 1938; Palmer, "Who's to Blame" (Typescript in Charles R. Palmer Papers, Housing File, April 13, 1938).

28. Atlanta *Constitution*, September 4, 22, April 4, 1940.

Howell complex, named for the editor of the Atlanta *Constitution*, was the first USHA project, followed in order by State Capitol, John Hope, John Egan, Grady, and Herndon homes. The eight complexes represented a total investment of $25 million and included more than 5,000 units situated on over 230 acres of former slum properties. Half of the projects in Atlanta, as in the other major southern cities, were for blacks. Yet while John Hope's "colored advisory committee" continued to cooperate with Palmer and Atlanta housing personnel—and was especially involved in the placement of slum residents in dwellings outside the building area during construction—there were no blacks appointed to the housing authority itself.[29]

A completed project transformed a slum area into a modern, landscaped residential complex. Where old wooden shacks had lined the streets, new two- to six-room brick dwellings now stood. Federal subsidies ensured low rents, and monthly charges ranged from a low of ten dollars for a small apartment at Birmingham's Smithfield Court to a high of thirty-eight dollars for a larger residence in Atlanta's Techwood Homes. Housing officials also set limits on tenant income, allowing a family to earn no more than five times its rent. Each residence contained a gas range, an electric refrigerator, electric lights, hot and cold running water, indoor toilets, and other conveniences considered luxuries by most low-income families. The cost of electricity was usually included in the rent, with tenants paying separately for gas for cooking and heating. Housing authorities in Birmingham allowed the use of inexpensive coal rather than a gas furnace system.[30]

Living quarters in the new complexes occupied less than one-fourth of the available space. Thus there was ample room for the construction of administrative offices, community centers, laundries, wading pools, first aid clinics, and playground and picnic facilities. Smithfield Court spread over six city blocks (twenty-eight acres) and included all of the above features in addition to its seventy-four residential buildings. Techwood Homes, besides apartments and row

29. Arnold, "Public Housing in Atlanta," 31–33, 45; Margaret A. Hamrick, "Changes the Clark Howell Housing Project Is Bringing in the Group Life of Its Tenants" (M.A. thesis, Emory University, 1942), 17–19; Atlanta Housing Authority, *Second Annual Report* (Atlanta, 1940); Atlanta *Constitution*, November 20–21, 1937, February 16, 1939, April 26, 1940; Atlanta *Journal*, July 2, 1938, March 3, August 21, 1940; Atlanta *Daily World*, November 19, 1939.

30. Birmingham *Post*, March 1, 1937, January 24, 1938; Birmingham *News*, November 2, 1937, June 27, 1939; Atlanta *Constitution*, July 7, 1936; Atlanta *Journal*, March 14, 1937; "Techwood Homes Is a Working Reality," *American City* (October, 1936), 58–59; Memphis *Press Scimitar*, January 14, 1938, March 7, 29, May 24, 1940; Dorothy C. Cole, "The New Orleans Housing Projects as Seen by Their Tenants" (M.S.W. thesis, Tulane University, 1945), 63–64.

houses, contained a variety of stores and shops, a three-story dormitory for Georgia Tech students, and a recreation building with a library and rooms for kindergarten classes. Project community centers allowed residents to join planned social clubs as well as to participate in special functions organized through tenant associations and publicized in weekly newsletters, such as the *Techwood News* or the University Homes's *Tenant Builders Association*, or *TAB*. Residents of the New Orleans Iberville project, with the assistance of the city's Council of Social Agencies and the Council of Jewish Women, opened Teen Town in 1944, a modern recreation facility for local young people. And despite the many construction delays created by opposition to black projects that fell too near white housing areas, black and white complexes had the same conveniences and programs.[31]

The millions invested by the federal government in public housing had some local economic impact. Under USHA guidelines, municipal housing commissions contracted with private construction firms for much of the building, and often local contractors presented the lowest bids. Seventeen of the nineteen subcontractors engaged at Smithfield Court, for example, were local companies, while nineteen other area firms received orders for materials. An average of 650 men, who might have otherwise been unemployed, worked each day for nearly three years and earned annual wages totaling almost $500,000. In Memphis, the Dixie and Lauderdale projects released $1.65 million in wages over two years, while the six housing complexes in New Orleans meant more than $11.5 million for payrolls and building supplies. In addition, the cities found that annual USHA subsidies and the 5 percent plan brought in up to 8 times more revenue than had taxes collected on the unimproved slum properties that would otherwise still have been among the most crime- and disease-infected areas.[32]

31. Birmingham *Post*, March 1, 1937; Birmingham *News*, November 2, 1937; Atlanta *Journal*, March 14, 1937; Lapping, "The Emergence of Federal Public Housing," 382–83; Hamrick, "Changes the Clark Howell Housing Project Is Bringing," 158–62; Alonzo Morton to Straus, January 18, 1940 (Georgia Recreation), B. S. Hovde to G. Ott Romney, August 25, 1939 (Tennessee Recreation), in Record Group 69, Records of the Works Progress Administration, National Archives; Beulah Sterbcon, "History and Development of Teen Town (Bienville Youth Center)" (M.S.W. thesis, Tulane University, 1947), 51–52; Pearson, "Federal Housing Projects for Negroes," 371–75; Atlanta *Daily World*, August 24, 1937; *TAB: 25th Anniversary Edition, 1962*, in Charles R. Palmer Papers, Housing File.

32. DeHoll to Jones, November 5, 1937, in James M. Jones, Jr., Collection, Drawer 2; Birmingham *Southern Labor Review*, February 2, 1938; Birmingham *News*, December 27, 1937; *Hearings Before a Joint Committee on Housing*, 80th Cong., 1st Sess., Part 2 (1948), 1184, 1819, 1967; Memphis *Labor Review*, April 25, 1939; Memphis *Press Scimitar*, July 12, 1935; Memphis *Commercial Appeal*, January 12, 1938; Housing Authority of New Orleans, *Annual Report, 1940* (New Orleans, 1941), 17.

Of course the federal housing program had shortcomings. For example, the sites on which municipal agencies resettled local residents during the construction period too often became permanent homes for the poor. Local and national administrators feared the possibility of uncollected rents and therefore established a minimum earnings base of three times the rent for all tenants. While a maximum earnings guideline reserved the projects for the needy, the minimum guideline had the effect of ruling all jobless persons, all WPA workers, and the lowest-income families ineligible for public dwellings. Studies in Memphis found that a white family of four had to earn $950 a year to qualify for Lauderdale Courts, while a black family of the same size, whose earning capacity was far less, had to make nearly $900 annually to be eligible for a residence in Dixie Homes. Tennessee city engineers in 1941 reported that the federal housing projects catered to the "top of the bottom 30 percent of Memphians in terms of salary but not to the bottom 10 percent." The same study concluded that slum clearance "does nothing for the man or his children who live in a dilapidated house" and that most of those resettled during the construction of the public apartments could not afford the new low-cost complexes.[33]

Similar situations prevailed in the other cities. In Atlanta's John Hope Homes for blacks, the earnings of residents averaged $735 per year, a figure substantially higher than the average income for Atlanta Negroes, $576. Forrester B. Washington, NAACP activist and director of the Atlanta School of Social Work, suggested that the words used in tenant newspapers "would split the palates of the mightiest slum dwellers if they would attempt to pronounce them."[34] All federal housing applicants had to clear a welfare investigation, prove a good credit rating, and according to the Birmingham Housing Authority, have a "steady income sufficient to meet the project rentals without denying themselves other essentials of life." Public school teachers in Birmingham, as well as New Orleans, did not earn enough to qualify. And in the Crescent City, the earnings of as many as one-third of the public housing residents had increased by the mid-1940s to well above the allowable maximum. But because of a lack of private homes, a

33. L. M. Graves and Alfred H. Fletcher, "Problems of a Housing Enforcement Program," *American Journal of Public Health*, XXVIII (June, 1938), 704; USHA to Memphis Housing Authority, n.d., in Mayor's Correspondence File, Drawer 3; Memphis *Press Scimitar*, September 8, 1936, November 18, 1937, January 14, 1938; Memphis *Commercial Appeal*, July 7, 1936, November 20, 1937, January 2, 1938.

34. Atlanta *Daily World*, November 30, 1937. Also see Arnold, "Public Housing in Atlanta," 17–18; WPA of Georgia, *Report on the Real Property, Land Use and Low Income Housing Area Survey of Metropolitan Atlanta* (Atlanta, 1940), 51.

congressional committee reported, there was little turnover in the low-rent apartments, further depriving families most in need.[35]

Perhaps the major problem with the USHA program, especially in the southern cities, was that it was a limited effort in the face of overwhelming odds. By the mid-1940s in Atlanta, officials still reported more than one-third of the population "living in filthy dirty slums, cess pools, human junk yards, breeding places for juvenile delinquency and disease, immorality and crime." They found that the worst slums, which represented 20 percent of the city's total area, continued to absorb half of the tax dollars spent on fire, disease, and crime while providing less than 5 percent of local tax revenues. The 1940 census confirmed the grim situation there, while showing that conditions in Birmingham, Memphis, and New Orleans were equally bad or worse. At least half of all residences in all of the southern cities in question fit the description of Atlanta housing offered by Palmer in 1940—substandard "by reason of dilapidation, overcrowding, faulty arrangement or design, lack of ventilation, light or sanitation facilities."[36]

The overall value of the few completed USHA projects proved less than expected. Sponsors such as Palmer subscribed to notions of environmental determinism and thus provided planned recreation, clubs, and tenant groups on the slum clearance sites. They argued that the incidence of crime and delinquency in once-deprived neighborhoods would decline with the organization of activities that strengthened family life and enhanced a feeling of community. Their objective was to instill a sense of pride among low-income families in their new surroundings. And a few projects, such as Techwood Homes, were in part responsible for a decrease in area burglaries, fires, syphilis and tuberculosis rates, disease-related deaths, and various childhood illnesses.[37]

The majority of low-rent units, however, were not situated around a leading regional university but were instead constructed adjacent to slums unaffected by the scant federal funds. A few scattered apart-

35. Birmingham *Post*, January 20, 1938, January 1, 1940; Birmingham Housing Authority, *Real Income . . . Land Use Survey of Birmingham* (Birmingham, 1939), 134–35; Housing Authority of New Orleans, *Annual Report, 1939*, 35–37; New Orleans *Times-Picayune*, August 16, 1938; *Hearings Before a Joint Committee on Housing*, 80th Cong., 1st Sess., Part 2 (1948), 1280, 1821.

36. "Rebuilding Atlanta: A Fifteen Year Effort in Progress," *American City* (February, 1940), 79. Also see *Hearings Before a Joint Committee on Housing*, 80th Cong., 1st Sess., Part 2 (1948), 1819–20; U.S. Bureau of Foreign and Domestic Commerce, *Statistical Abstract of the United States* (1942), 1019.

37. Michael L. Porter, "The Development and Amelioration of Housing Conditions in the Techwood Housing Area (1890–1938) and the University Housing Area (1930–1950)" (M.A. thesis, Atlanta University, 1972), 23–26.

ments, even with active tenant programs, could have only a minimal social impact on the entire neighborhood. Officials in New Orleans, for example, reported that the Magnolia project and its planned recreational outlets had no effect on the local gang problem. Guns and liquor prevailed among teenagers, random shooting was common, and groups such as the Wildcats and Black Peacocks "have so terrorized the neighborhood that people are afraid to leave their homes at night for fear of being attacked."[38]

As well, the USHA effort of the late thirties was not sustained during the succeeding two decades, even with the additional emergency housing of the World War II years. New Orleans, among the southern cities, received the most attention during the war. But in the later 1940s and the 1950s—critical years for all American cities—the slow advance of federal slum clearance and building programs made former USHA accomplishments look spectacular by comparison. The Atlanta Housing Authority, twenty years after the construction of the first PWA-sponsored projects, was managing only ten public residential developments. Six had opened before the war, and despite reports during a 1947 congressional investigation on housing of an immediate need of 20,000 additional units and an expectation of needing 75,000 more in the next ten years, federal funds between 1942 and 1955 financed just four more complexes. Officials from New Orleans reported similar needs during those hearings, but as late as 1962, HANO was operating just thirteen public developments, one-half of which were former USHA or emergency wartime units. The Crescent City in the early 1960s ranked fourth nationally in terms of public housing activity.[39]

Among the other New Deal housing programs was the Federal Home Loan Bank system, established late during Hoover's administration and supplemented by the opening of the Home Owners' Loan Corporation (HOLC) in 1934, which established offices in every southern city. HOLC loans were available to distressed homeowners for the payment of local property taxes, for the installation of plumbing or other equipment to conform to municipal building regulations, or simply for the payment of mortgages to prevent foreclosure. Memphis area residents between 1933 and 1936 received nearly $6.8 million from the HOLC, while qualified Atlantans during the same period

38. Amelia Hardesty, "Juvenile Delinquency in the Orleans Area," *Louisiana Welfare*, III (July, 1943), 7.

39. Atlanta *Constitution*, October 15, 1944; Housing Authority of New Orleans, *Public Housing in New Orleans* (New Orleans, 1947), 3–6; Maurice d'Arlan Needham, *Negro Orleanian: Status and Stake in a City's Economy and Housing* (New Orleans, 1962), 176.

borrowed nearly $10 million of the $24 million released in Georgia. It was estimated in western Tennessee that HOLC loans saved 35 percent of all residences after foreclosure, most of which were situated in Memphis.[40]

When the HOLC ceased operations in June, 1936, the Federal Housing Authority (FHA), established under the Wagner-Steagall Act, took charge of the homeowner loan program. By 1940, the FHA had insured mortgages on 4,000 Memphis homes for more than $15 million, and on 4,600 Atlanta residences for more than $20 million. In all cities, the low-interest loans triggered home improvement and buying campaigns, generally sponsored by private developers in cooperation with the FHA's Federal Home Building Service Plan. Federal inspectors registered new houses on the market, assuring purchasers, according to officials in New Orleans, that "factors of obsolescence have been eliminated and that sound construction minimizes physical depreciation."[41]

Home building and improvement activity in the 1930s was also responsible for underwriting several modern residential subdivisions in the southern cities. One example was Oak Knoll, opened in Atlanta in 1937, with Charles Palmer as one of the primary realtors. There, a family could purchase a $4,000 home for a $300 down payment with a twenty-year mortgage. Homeowners found sewerage, electric, water, and gas facilities, paved streets, sidewalks, and playgrounds, as well as schools and churches, within a short distance. Another example was the Pontchartrain Lakefront development in New Orleans, where WPA workers cleared and filled low-lying areas, and private contractors built new homes. There were even low-cost subdivisions opened for blacks, such as Hunter Hills in the Atlanta University area. Lots sold for $5 down and $5 per month. Even so, the availability of HOLC and FHA loans in the 1930s and thereafter affected only marginally the percentage of owner-occupied residences in the southern cities, which stayed below the national average. In the early 1950s in New Orleans, less than 25 percent of all dwelling units were owner occupied, compared to a national rate of 35 percent.[42] And certainly the continuation of middle-income homeowner loans, together with the relocation of low-income families in renovated, but inner-city, dwellings, did not address the

40. John Bullington to Overton, August 5, 1933, May 14, 1934, Overton to Bullington, August 21, 1933, May 12, 1934, all in Mayor's Correspondence File, Drawer 3; Crump to McKellar, January 15, 1937, in Kenneth McKellar Papers, Box 3; Walter G. Cooper, *The Story of Georgia* (4 vols., New York, 1938), III, 558.

41. New Orleans *Times-Picayune*, April 30, 1939. Also see Memphis *Commercial Appeal*, June 2, 1935, January 8, 1937; Memphis *Press Scimitar*, June 9, 1939; *Hearings Before a Joint Committee on Housing*, 80th Cong., 1st Sess., Part 2 (1948), 1938; Atlanta *Journal*, April 6, 1940.

42. Atlanta *Journal*, July 4, 1937; Atlanta *Daily World*, October 16, 1938; Forrest E. La Violette and Joseph Taylor, *Negro Housing in New Orleans* (New Orleans, 1957), 23.

problems of suburban flight and the clustering of the poor in downtown areas, most acute in the South in post–World War II and more
recent years.

Still, it is doubtful that reformers and national administrators
could have accomplished more, at least in the 1930s. Although the
nation's cities, including those in the South, developed a new, direct
relationship with the federal government during the decade, there was
no farsighted, national urban plan, just as there never was a commitment to broad social or central economic planning at the federal level.
Instead, New Dealers were working with twenty years of untested
conservative and reformist housing theories, many of which assumed
that urban populations would decrease rather than multiply over the
next generation.[43] As well, it is not realistic to think that lawmakers in
the 1930s would have accepted a comprehensive urban policy, cen-
trally managed from Washington, D.C., nor is it conceivable that
municipal leaders, especially those in the South, would have favored a
proposal adding more federal controls. Just their support for existing
efforts was beyond the endorsement they would have given ten years
earlier.

Indeed, city leaders throughout the depression South supported
the housing endeavors, perhaps more so than any of the other new
federal programs, and continued to do so in later years. Birmingham
authorities joined several civic organizations in 1945, for example, in
denouncing those real estate interests backing a state law preventing
Alabama cities from participating in the federal housing effort. Local
newspapers the next year led a successful campaign to replace all
incumbent Jefferson County legislators with men who favored the bill's
repeal. During the congressional hearings on housing in 1947, municipal officials from all of the major southern cities joined with chambers
of commerce, labor organizations, and the American Legion in an
unqualified endorsement of public housing and federal improvement
and construction loans. After all, the programs continued to operate
within the bounds of boosterism and the prevailing urban ethos.[44]

Overall, the New Deal housing projects razed hundreds of substandard structures in each major city of the South, provided jobs and
payrolls, resettled thousands of low-income families (although not
always the most needy) in modern dwelling units, and made millions

43. Miller, *The Urbanization of Modern America*, 164; Graham, *Toward a Planned
Society*, 68; Charles Glaab and Theodore A. Brown, *A History of Urban America* (2nd
ed., New York, 1976), 274–75; McKelvey, *The Emergence of Metropolitan America*, 90.

44. Irving Beiman, "Birmingham: Steel Giant with a Glass Jaw," in Robert S. Allen
(ed.), *Our Fair City* (New York, 1947), 119–20; *Hearings Before a Joint Committee on
Housing*, 80th Cong., 1st Sess., Part 2 (1948), 1161, 1279–85, 1821.

of dollars available for structural improvements and new building. Furthermore, the decentralized operation of the USHA program—like other federal ventures—required local involvement that resulted in the establishment of municipal housing agencies that proved permanent and that worked closely with the new or revamped city planning and zoning commissions. Such groups were all controlled by conservative, New South interests, always attracted by the prospects of increased property values and a modern environment conducive to future economic expansion, if within the bounds of efficiency and the existing social order, especially patterns of segregation. Yet there was increasing concern that impoverished environments trapped thousands and adversely affected the overall attractiveness, health, safety, and welfare of the cities. The problems of urban blight and poverty in general were beginning to be confronted as a public responsibility, requiring the mobilization of municipal, state, and even federal resources against private real estate or other forces unconcerned with community well-being.

10

NEW FOOTHOLDS FOR ORGANIZED LABOR

As the country experienced the economic upheavals of the Great Depression, the plight of labor, including shameful conditions in general throughout the urban South, became more evident than ever before. In the major southern cities, few unions with more than minimal clout existed in the building trades, and in the large industrial plants, there was no organization at all. With few exceptions, employers simply did not recognize the principle of collective bargaining for fair wages and job security. Municipal leaders with booster sentiments had long discouraged labor organization, and many urban workers themselves, some of whom were recent arrivals from small towns or rural areas, were also skeptical of unionism. They were especially suspicious of organizers who came from national union offices in the North.[1]

Even the conservative southern urban trades councils and the few long-standing railroad crafts, according to labor historian Irving Bernstein, were "weak and ineffective" as of the early 1930s. A federal relief investigator noted in 1934 that labor in Memphis "still has its horizontal layers and petty aristocracies" and that even the established crafts were not forceful on labor's behalf. In 1929, the city's chamber of commerce was assuring outside manufacturers that "non-union men are employed in the building trades" and that "there is a small likelihood of strike disturbances, because of Anglo-Saxon stock and the Negro. The latter is an excellent laborer when properly handled and is not prone to organize." Similar situations were in evidence in Atlanta,

1. The history of union activity in the South, including organizational efforts in the region's cities at least until the 1930s, magnifies the conclusions of Wilbur Cash made nearly fifty years ago. See Cash, *The Mind of the South* (New York, 1941), 428–29.

Birmingham, and New Orleans, where labor was unable to obtain the employment of union men at fair wages on municipal jobs.[2]

A need for collective action was as visible as labor conditions were shameful. Southern industrial positions paid between 30 and 50 percent less than the national average for similar manufacturing jobs. In the cities, pay scales were only slightly, if at all, above those in rural areas, although urban living costs in the South nearly equaled those in cities of comparable size elsewhere. According to a Department of Labor survey in the mid-1930s, between 30 and 43 percent of all employed labor in the southern cities could not afford an adequate diet. Rent, clothing, and carfare absorbed the bulk of the employees' money. Furthermore, living costs escalated during the depression years faster than did wages. Between 1933 and 1939, the Alabama Industrial Union Council reported, the cost of living in Birmingham increased more than 18 percent, while earnings increased only 10 to 15 percent. In all the southern cities, spendable income after cost-of-living adjustments failed to increase equally with the national average, even while sectional wage differentials were declining.[3]

In addition, employer-owned commissaries and houses still prevailed. Company stores were especially numerous in Birmingham, where, according to federal examiners in 1934, prices were as much as 40 percent above retail value. Bosses often paid labor in scrip or clacker (metal tokens) and deducted for so-called welfare items, such as medical treatment, religious services, and education. Also, it was common for several part-time workers to fill each full-time position, and during depression times, employers maintained greater control. Upon announcing a 50 to 75 percent wage reduction in 1932, officials at TCI in Birmingham attached the following to plant bulletin boards: "No scale will be posted. No question will be answered. Any employee who talks or discusses the new scale, either in or around the plant or anywhere outside, will be fired if word gets back to the office."[4]

2. Bernstein, *The New Deal and Collective Bargaining Policy*, 1; Confidential Report on Memphis, n.d., in Record Group 69, Records of the Federal Emergency Relief Administration, Tennessee Field Reports, National Archives, hereinafter cited as FERA; Memphis Chamber of Commerce, *Report . . . 1929* (Memphis, 1929), 11; John H. David to Maestri, March 20, 1937, in Robert Maestri Papers, microfilm roll 399B, New Orleans Public Library.

3. "Labor Conditions in the South," *Monthly Labor Review* (October, 1938), 747–52; Birmingham *Labor Advocate*, September 26, 1939; Clarence Heer, *Income and Wages in the South* (Chapel Hill, 1930), 42; Irving Bernstein, *A History of the American Worker, 1920–1933: The Lean Years* (1960; rpr. Baltimore, 1966), 10.

4. Field Report: Birmingham, February 2–4, 1934, FERA, Alabama Field Reports; Birmingham *Southern Labor Review*, February 3, 1937.

Although labor had attempted to consolidate support among disgruntled workers in the early depression years, organizing drives in 1930, as well as in 1933 and 1934 under NRA provisions, had gained little. The urban crafts increased their numbers slightly, but the Alabama UMW was the only large industrial group in the South to benefit directly from NRA codes. The New Orleans waterfront workers remained without strong organization, and the collapse of the 1934 textile strike defeated the UTW in city and mill village alike.

The Wagner Act and subsequent nationwide organizing drives led to significant victories in the southern cities, laying a foundation for later efforts in the region. Without New Deal guarantees, according to southern labor activists, Dixie unionists would have never recruited workers in large numbers, despite depressed economic conditions. Labor gains in the South seemed to parallel the pattern nationwide, at least in part. Irving Bernstein has concluded that "metropolitan influences were much more significant than either state or regional factors" in determining union successes during the depression period. Unionists hoped to initiate a ripple effect from city to small town; their plan in the 1930s proved more successful in the East and in the north central states than in either rural New England or the South.[5] Even the UMW, perhaps the most entrenched industrial union in the late 1930s, had little success with large employers in rural counties adjacent to Birmingham. Still, more than a few southern urban employers by World War II were bargaining with legitimate unions that represented thousands of wage earners, many of whom had even set aside traditional racial attitudes for the prospect of economic betterment.

Much of the southern opposition to organized labor lay in the notion that Communists were manipulating black wage earners in order to seize control of American workers. Employers and their allies in municipal government had skillfully exploited this anxiety for years, and in the 1930s, the issue intensified in the wake of the split between the conservative AFL and John Lewis' more militant Committee of Industrial Organization (CIO). Reports from the House Un-American Activities Committee, which exaggerated the presence of communism among southern blacks and American workers in general, further enhanced fears, as did the inflated claims of radical groups. The Young Communist League, for example, boasted fifteen thousand dues-paying members in Birmingham, although reliable studies never

5. Interviews with Maurice Allen and Reuben Farr, Birmingham labor organizers, May 1–2, 1975. Also see David Brody, "The Emergence of Mass-Production Unionism," in John Braeman, Robert H. Bremner, and Everett Walters (eds.), *Change and Continuity in Twentieth Century America* (Columbus, Ohio, 1964), 262; Irving Bernstein, *A History of the American Worker, 1933–1941: The Turbulent Years* (Boston, 1970), 770–71.

uncovered more than a handful of Communist sympathizers in any of the Dixie cities. The Birmingham *Southern Labor Review*, the voice of the local trades council and itself suspicious of mass unionism, concluded that police and industrialists together were "trying to pass the buck on to the communists . . . by saying 'the Niggers are the guilty party, down with the Niggers.'" This was clearly "an effort by operators and their lawyers to discredit labor . . . so the public won't see the truth that the real cause of strikes is the defiance of employers."[6]

A regenerated Ku Klux Klan was another problem for the urban labor movement in the 1930s. The rebirth centered in Atlanta, the headquarters of Imperial Wizard Hiram Evans. In 1936, Evans moved his office from the city's rural outskirts to Peachtree Street in the downtown area. Klan parades and floggings (numbering about fifty between 1937 and 1940) were once again prevalent in the New South capital, with the vigilantes directing their intimidation mainly against industrial unionists who worked among blacks. Editorials in the *Kourier* argued that imported labor organizers would bring unwanted ways into the region and that southern blacks would begin to agitate for more freedoms, like their counterparts in the North.[7]

There was little official opposition to the Klan's antilabor outburst. Municipal authorities did little to halt the night-riding; in 1939 Atlanta city councilmen tabled an ordinance banning the wearing of hoods on the grounds that it would prevent the appearance of Santa Claus on the streets at Christmas. According to policeman Herbert Jenkins, later to be Atlanta's police chief, Klan membership for a lawman was "an ID card, the badge of honor within the in-group, and it was unfortunately often an allegiance stronger than the policeman's oath to society."[8] When the Atlanta press published editorials against the Klan's activities, a public protest by six hundred Klansmen followed, claiming that the Atlanta *Constitution* printed only unfair Klan stories. The reborn organization remained highly visible in Atlanta until the late 1930s when new wizard James Colescott moved it into the small textile towns throughout the region. There it found greater public support.

The Klan reappeared in the other southern cities as well, but was not as active as in Atlanta. Louisiana anti-Klan legislation, which dated

6. Birmingham *Southern Labor Review*, May 9, 1934; Birmingham *News*, May 3, 1935; Birmingham *Post*, May 16, 1935; Cayton and Mitchell, *Black Workers*, 338–41; John L. Williams, "Struggles in the Thirties in the South," in Sternsher (ed.), *The Negro in Depression and War*, 174–75.

7. *Kourier*, IX (September, 1933), 29.

8. Herbert Jenkins, *Keeping the Peace: A Police Officer Looks at His Job* (New York, 1970), 4; New York *Times*, November 27, 1939; David M. Chalmers, *Hooded Americanism: The First Century of the Ku Klux Klan, 1865 to the Present* (Garden City, 1965), 317. For an analysis of KKK activities throughout Georgia, see Clement C. Mosely, "Invisible

from 1924, deterred the group's rise in New Orleans, while in Memphis, the Crump machine's extralegal efforts against labor seemed to preclude the need for vigilante activity. Memphis Klan boss Clarence Howell, however, maintained a dialogue with municipal authorities, urging them to protect whites against "cheap negro labor." He informed Mayor Overton that he was pursuing a "watchful, waiting policy." Klan leaders in Birmingham mobilized when unionists appeared in the steel mills, but their activities were limited when white UMW members joined local klaverns and gained control of most operations. Other, similar groups included the Loyal American Guard of Memphis and the White Legion of Birmingham, which led a reign of terror against miners during the UMW strikes of the 1930s.[9]

Industrial employers at first reacted to union organizers by reviving or strengthening company unions. In Atlanta, several small textile plants challenged the UTW through Good Will clubs. Mill owners permitted Good Will solicitors on their property during work hours, a freedom not given to UTW organizers. Workers who refused to join Good Will as dues-paying members were subject to discharge or to increased work loads.[10]

In the Birmingham manufacturing district, independent coal operators challenged the UMW with the Progressive Mineworkers' Association. Officials promised good-faith bargaining with the company organization, which longtime Birmingham labor leaders referred to as a "popsicle union" because of the iced refreshments served at meetings in hot months. TCI president J. L. Perry also endorsed a company union, the United Association of Iron, Steel and Mine Workers, joining together the Plan of Industrial Relations in the mills and the Brotherhood of Captive Mine Workers in the firm's red ore and coal mines. In a later congressional investigation of antilabor activities, TCI steadfastly defended its association as an "effective medium for us to use in settling any differences we may have and, in addition, to work out together the ways and means of making better steel." In 1937, at the same time that steel union activities peaked locally and nationwide,

---

Empire: A History of the Ku Klux Klan in Twentieth Century Georgia, 1915–1965" (Ph.D. dissertation, University of Georgia, 1968).

9. Howell to Overton, July 14, September 12, 1934, in Watkins Overton Papers, Box 3, Memphis State University Library; Northrup, *Organized Labor and the Negro*, 165; Cayton and Mitchell, *Black Workers*, 339; Dorothy Siegel, "The Growth of Coal and Steel Unions in Two Companies in Birmingham, Ala., 1918–1941" (Honor's thesis, Brandeis University, in possession of Birmingham Public Library, 1969), 22; Louie Thompson, "Southern Terror," *Crisis* (November, 1934), 328; Kenneth E. Harrell, "The Ku Klux Klan in Louisiana, 1920–1930" (Ph.D. dissertation, Louisiana State University, 1966), 361–62.

10. Atlanta *Journal of Labor*, January 17, March 20, 1936.

TCI launched a public relations blitz in Birmingham as it increased wages and reduced the work week. The new benefits proved to be short-lived, however, as the company withdrew them all just two days after United States Steel signed with the Steel Workers' Organizing Committee (SWOC) of the CIO.[11]

The New Orleans waterfront situation best revealed the persistence of company unionism.[12] Early in the 1930s, the New Orleans Steamship Association, composed of local dock employers, established two segregated independent unions to block the resurgence of black and white locals of the ILA. The independent leaders were Leo Tujage, president of National Fruit Products, which used waterfront facilities extensively, and Paul Hortman, longtime boss of black dock workers. The Negro independent group was particularly strong, and its leaders, who had controlled waterfront hiring since the early 1920s, refused to honor ILA-proposed boycotts and strikes. Black bosses and workers also mistrusted President T. J. Darcy of the New Orleans ILA white local, who was also international ILA vice-president. Darcy had earlier supported Mayor Walmsley's dock ordinance restricting Negro employment on the wharves. ILA strikes in 1933 and in 1934 had accomplished little, and even when NRA officials called for an open election among Crescent City longshoremen, employers rejected the plan and continued to work with the company unions.

In September, 1935, the struggle among employers and the independent and ILA locals intensified when the east Gulf Coast ILA leadership called strikes in New Orleans, Gulfport, Mobile, and Pensacola. The union sought contracts in these cities and also hoped to defeat the many company labor groups, now joined throughout the region in the Independent Longshoreman's Gulf Coast Dock Association. When the first pickets appeared in New Orleans on October 1, the steamship association called on a cooperative local police force to protect strikebreakers and disperse ILA protestors. Later, a federal

---

11. *Hearings on Violations of Free Speech and Rights of Labor Before a Sub-Committee on Education and Labor* (1938), 75th Cong., 2nd Sess., 6323–29; New York *Times*, March 3–6, 1937; Birmingham *Southern Labor Review*, May 12, 1937; interview with Maurice Allen, southeastern regional labor organizer, May 1, 1975; Birmingham *Labor Advocate*, January 9, April 24, 1937; Siegel, "The Growth of Coal and Steel Unions," 31–33.

12. Information on the dock strike in New Orleans from New Orleans *Times-Picayune*, May 3, December 5, 1934, March 7, June 6, July 11–12, August 1, September 12, 25, October 1, 6, 9, 12–18, November 9, 20, December 6, 13–17, 1935, December 22, 1936; Robert C. Francis, "Dock Troubles in New Orleans," *Crisis* (December, 1935), 373; Carroll G. Miller, "A Study of the New Orleans Longshoreman's Union from 1850–1962" (M.A. thesis, Louisiana State University, 1962), 29–48; Marshall, *Labor in the South*, 204–206.

district court enjoined the ILA from blocking the handling of cargoes. Dock employers never acknowledged the strike, claiming that they had valid contracts with the two independent unions through 1937. Thus, work on the wharves was not interrupted.

The Gulf Coast strike lasted sixty-two days, during which time police and company guards attacked pickets indiscriminately in all regional ports, killing four men in New Orleans. When a settlement was finally reached in December, the result of federal mediation and pressure applied on southern employers by a number of New York owners, the Crescent City ILA locals found themselves in no better position than before. The New Orleans Steamship Association refused to surrender, despite the promises of many east Gulf dock employers to raise wages equal to pay scales in Texas ports and agreements made by Pacific operators with offices on the Gulf Coast to recognize ILA bargaining rights. Instead, the New Orleans group continued to deal with the independent unions, as did most local dock companies, who remained loyal within the "fraternity." The result was that in March, 1936, the international ILA leadership, working with national and regional AFL bosses, revoked the New Orleans ILA charters and issued new ones to the independent unions headed by Tujage and Hortman. The ILA convention then replaced Darcy with Hortman as its international vice-president, and the members of the New Orleans Steamship Association immediately signed contracts with the new ILA locals.

In 1937 and 1938, the National Maritime Union of the CIO challenged the ILA of the AFL. Organizers from both unions resorted to intimidation and violence on occasion. In October, 1938, the AFL won an overwhelming NLRB election victory over the CIO and a third group, the Stevedores and Longshoremen's Benevolent Association, directed by T. J. Darcy. Although the CIO later gained bargaining status among New Orleans port and warehouse owners, the ILA continued to represent Crescent City dock workers in the late 1930s and thereafter. The ILA locals faced future problems, most notably a host of financial irregularities, and it took a long time for management's influence to disappear.

Also to deter union efforts, southern mill owners rarely hesitated to use local strikebreakers, protected by imported company goons, just like their counterparts in the North, where labor upheavals received a greater number of newspaper headlines. Strong-arm squads in the Dixie cities cooperated quite often with industrial spies supplied by Pinkerton Detectives; the Philadelphia-based Railroad Audit and Inspection Company, a subsidiary of United States Steel; and the Forrest C. Pendleton Bureau of Investigation. Between 1933 and 1934,

Pinkerton agents infiltrated twelve international unions in five leading southern cities, and in 1935, General Electric even hired Pinkerton operatives to investigate previously employed spies. The *CIO News* reported that between 1933 and 1937, 2,500 American businessmen invested nearly $10 million in labor espionage. Of course steel, automobile, rubber, and other industrial operations all reserved portions of their strikebreaking funds for their southern outlets.[13]

Birmingham steel mill owners were especially prepared to use strong-arm tactics against the SWOC, which replaced the Amalgamated Association of Iron, Tin and Steel Workers in local plants in 1936. TCI earned the most notoriety for such tactics, but smaller firms, such as Woodward Iron Company and Sloss-Sheffield Steel and Iron, were equally bold in arming company guards and hiring spies to keep organizers off their grounds and racial anxieties stirred up. The bosses realized that Amalgamated had failed in 1933 and 1934 and earlier not only because of employer resistance but because of the association's failure to enlist black support. The SWOC, however, was following John L. Lewis' "racial formula" of integrated locals with black and white officers, and blacks were joining the CIO affiliate in large numbers. According to Reuben Farr, president of the first Birmingham steelworkers local: "I told them [whites] how I felt about taking colored and everybody; they still went ahead and elected me president."[14]

The LaFollette Committee investigations in 1936 and 1937 discovered that TCI throughout the decade poured thousands of dollars into a strike expense fund. Special deputies appeared on the company payroll (five thousand dollars expended just for deputy badges), and management purchased revolvers, machine guns, shotguns, rifles, gas equipment, and ammunition. Company thugs patrolled the mills and also guarded housing areas, where residents could not grow gardens higher than a man's head. Outside lights burned through the night to make movement between the guarded houses more visible after sundown.[15]

The most notable incident associated with the Birmingham steel-organizing drive involved outsider Joseph Gelders, representing the

13. Lumpkin, *The South in Progress*, 107; New Orleans *Times-Picayune*, May 30, 1934, August 13, 1936; Atlanta *Constitution*, September 23, 1936; *CIO News*, December 29, 1937.

14. Siegel, "The Growth of Coal and Steel Unions," 30. Also see Herbert R. Northrup, "The Negro and Unionism in the Birmingham, Ala., Iron and Steel Industry," *Southern Economic Journal*, X (July, 1943), 27–40.

15. *Hearings on Violations of Free Speech and Rights of Labor Before a Sub-Committee on Education and Labor* (1938), 75th Cong., 2nd Sess., 6343–44; Siegel, "The Growth of Coal and Steel Unions," 8.

National Committee for the Defense of Political Prisoners.[16] He arrived in the city in September, 1936, determined to organize area steelworkers and to win the release of several local labor leaders who had been imprisoned and sentenced without benefit of counsel or jury trials to county chain gangs. Antilabor forces proved to be equally resolute. On an evening in late September, a group of TCI guards, led by Walter Hanna, captain of a local National Guard unit and chief of the company's special police force, apprehended Gelders, beat him with pipes and pistol butts, stripped him, and drove him out of town. The organizer later identified his abductors, but local grand juries on three occasions failed to return indictments. One frightened grand juror claimed that TCI owned "15/16 of the Birmingham district," and several later testified before the LaFollette Committee that management's influence reached deep within the legal process. This was further demonstrated when powerful southern congressmen, following the publication of the committee's report, led a successful effort to reduce the investigative team's operating budget and limit the inquiry.

Despite such resistance, the SWOC was ultimately successful in enrolling a majority of Birmingham steelworkers. In early March, 1937, United States Steel signed with the union, and fifteen days later, the firm's Birmingham affiliate agreed to bargain with SWOC local number 1,013, the first of its kind in the South. For more than six months, organizers had moved among workers in the mills and at their homes, publicizing activities with sound trucks and window posters. While the March victory was mainly the result of the parent company's capitulation, as TCI was prepared to hold out much longer, local efforts were responsible for generating an interest in unionism among workers, not an easy accomplishment, and for ensuring the viability of the organization in later years. As well, organizers immediately established the Birmingham Steel Council to coordinate activities in the three main TCI plants, and then secured a contract that included wage increases, an eight-hour day, the first paid vacations, and official company recognition. Furthermore, TCI management within six weeks dropped support of its Plan of Industrial Relations. Although the

16. Information on the struggle to organize TCI, including the Gelders case, from *Hearings on Violations of Free Speech and Rights of Labor* (1937), 75th Cong., 1st Sess., 805; Birmingham *Labor Advocate*, September 26, 1936; New York *Times*, January 15, 16, March 18, April 27, 1937; Birmingham *News*, November 18, 1936; Jerald S. Auerbach, *Labor and Liberty: The LaFollette Committee and the New Deal* (Indianapolis, 1966), 94–96; Bernstein, *The Turbulent Years*, 459; John D. Bevis, "Frank M. Dixon: Alabama's Reform Governor" (M.A. thesis, Samford University, 1968), 191; Frank T. DeVyver, "Status of Labor Unions in the South," *Southern Economic Journal*, V (April, 1939), 489; Robert P. Ingalls, "Antiradical Violence in Birmingham During the 1930s," *Journal of Southern History*, XLVII (November, 1981), 521–44.

settlement was not union shop, a later NLRB election confirmed that the union was the exclusive bargaining agent for TCI employees. By 1942, more than 75 percent of the company's wage labor force was enrolled in the SWOC, now called the United Steelworkers of America.

White workers in Birmingham, even if reluctantly, accepted black participation in the union movement. Increasing numbers were beginning to realize the sense in Lewis' doctrine that "if a company hires them, we'll organize them." Yet like the impact of many of the New Deal relief and recovery programs, changes that seemed to be coming were often cut short. The first contract, for example, froze TCI's occupational structure at a time when, because of the depression, black workers were lower on the job ladder and weaker numerically than they had been for more than twenty years. Furthermore, whites were quick to discover that the racial caste system, and particularly segregated jobs and patterns of promotion, could be safeguarded through the very machinery that was supposed to increase every worker's clout with management. Recent studies have argued that "white workers used the power gained in the organizing struggles of the 1930s to maintain and even to expand their economic advantage in the mills." It was a harsh irony that "unionization made possible by interracial solidarity now yielded greater restrictions on black opportunity than existed before the 1930s" and tightened the bond between segregation and economic well-being.[17] Clearly, the SWOC bosses were in no hurry to challenge fundamental regional traditions, even if the union, as it claimed, backed both black and white workers against individual discrimination and harassment. After all, local labor leaders had been raised within the same Jim Crow system, with its assumptions and cultural norms, as had the rank and file.

Throughout the nation, the SWOC followed its victory over United States Steel with organizing drives against "little steel" operations. A new wave of terror resulted, and in Birmingham, the small companies only slowly came to terms. Some continued their dealings with independent labor groups, or none at all, for years thereafter; not until 1974 did the last Birmingham plant sign with the United Steelworkers of America. There were few immediate ripples into rural areas, although TCI's capitulation was not the only major victory for steel organizers in the region. Atlantic Steel Company in Atlanta came to terms in 1941.[18]

17. Robert J. Norrell, "Caste in Steel: Jim Crow Careers in Birmingham, Alabama," *Journal of American History*, LXXIII (December, 1986), 679, 694.

18. Interview with Allen, May 1, 1975; Siegel, "The Growth of Coal and Steel Unions," 33; Glenn Gilman and James W. Sweeney, *Causes of Industrial Peace Under Collective Bargaining: Atlantic Steel Company and the United Steelworkers of America* (Washington, D.C., 1953), 2–24.

Besides hostile management, organizers in the southern cities confronted municipal authorities with strong anti-union sentiments. Including the machine bosses in Memphis and New Orleans, urban leaders were determined to combat mass unionism, which threatened regional advantages, the expansion of manufacturing, local traditions, and the social and economic order. Mayor Overton, for example, told newsmen bluntly that Memphis wanted more industry and payrolls and would forever oppose unionism in all local industrial operations.[19] Local police played on "red black" anxieties, justifying their ruthlessness as a defense against Communist insurgency among blacks, which they claimed was instigated by the CIO. The city leaders, however, did not oppose AFL trades councils, which at that time were also opening organizing campaigns under the Wagner Act, but rarely in the large industrial plants.

Negotiations in 1936 and 1937 between Memphis City Hall and Firestone Tire and Rubber demonstrated the attitude of many urban elites. The company in 1936 was about to open a $3 million plant in the Tennessee city, which would employ 1,500 workers. Management more than once expressed concern about the labor situation in Memphis, with the president of the company even outlining carefully to Mayor Overton that "we have no formal organization—we do not believe in any form of self-government in our shops." To assure the arrangement, Crump and his lieutenants promised to keep unions out of the rubber operation as well as other local manufacturing establishments. (Local officials also changed the name of White Avenue, the building site, to Firestone Boulevard.) Writing to the boss, who at the time was resting at Battle Creek Sanatarium, Overton remarked that "I am afraid Firestone won't expand much here if CIO gets busy." He added that "we will have to form a definite policy of some kind" and concluded by asking the boss, "Have you any suggestions?"[20]

The Memphis "policy" unfolded later in 1937 in an incident involving UAW organizer Norman Smith. In the fall of that year, the UAW of the CIO opened a nationwide drive against Ford and General Motors, which brought Smith to Memphis to organize workers at the local Ford and Fisher body (Chevrolet) plants, employing a total of four thousand men. Before Smith's arrival, "unidentified assailants" twice beat local labor leader Ben McCullough for advocating unionism in the Memphis factories. During the same month, moreover, Boss Crump's

19. Memphis *Commercial Appeal*, September 22, 1937.

20. Overton to Crump, April 13, 1937, in Watkins Overton Papers, Box 2; F. F. Doyle to Overton, January 4, 1937, and Overton to Doyle, January 15, 1937, both in Mayor's Correspondence File, Drawer 3, Memphis and Shelby County Archives, Memphis; Memphis *Press Scimitar*, November 24–25, 1936.

police commissioner boasted to the Memphis *Press Scimitar* that "we can't help but brag a little about our record in labor matters this year. We want to maintain that record."[21]

They did. The Smith affair began on September 20 when Mayor Overton announced to the press that "imported CIO agitators, communists and highly paid organizers are not welcome in Memphis." He concluded that "they care nothing for Memphis—only to use us if they could" and that "we don't [want them] and won't tolerate them." The next day, the police commissioner endorsed Overton's sentiments, claiming that "we have started today and will free Memphis of these unwanted people," and the Memphis *Commercial Appeal* reported the existence of a secret anti-union plan in city hall.[22]

On the evening of September 21, a group of masked men abducted Smith and several other labor activists and beat them senseless with pistols and hammers. Lawmen continued their intimidation, even after jailing Smith on vagrancy charges, and when the first beatings failed to discourage union activity, local police repeated them in early October. Tennessee governor Gordon Browning, no friend of labor either, refused to investigate, as did the United States attorney general. An independent investigation by John Petrie of *Christian Century* concluded that Pinkerton agents were responsible for the beatings, with the full backing of municipal authorities. Within four months of the affair, Crump was able to announce to Senator McKellar that the UAW had left Memphis and that "everyone has forgotten the CIO down this way. Don't hear anything about it."[23] That the Tennessee senator had earlier cast his vote for the Wagner Act clearly demonstrates the politics of the period.

Police forces in all southern cities organized "red squads" responsible for protecting strikebreakers, guarding company property, and intimidating labor organizers. Periodically, they even raided local bookstores to confiscate "dangerous literature," such as *Nation, New Republic, Redbook Magazine,* and during one raid in Atlanta, the pamphlet *Are Petting Parties Dangerous?* In the New Orleans and Birmingham areas, county sheriffs still employed the fee system and profited handsomely by loaning special deputies to companies. Jeffer-

---

21. Memphis *Press Scimitar*, April 11, 25, 1937.

22. Memphis *Commercial Appeal*, September 19–22, October 6, 1937; George Lambert, "Memphis Is Safe for Ford," *Nation*, January 22, 1938, pp. 93–94.

23. Crump to McKellar, April 6, 1938, in Kenneth McKellar Papers, Box 3, Memphis Public Library, Downtown Branch; Chester R. Pedro to Browning, October 8, 1937, in Gordon Browning Papers, Box 11, Tennessee State Archives and History, Nashville; John C. Petrie, "Memphis Makes War on the C. I. O.," *Christian Century*, October 13, 1937, p. 1273.

son County sheriff Milton McDuff leased so many men that at one point he ran out of badges. According to LaFollette Committee testimony, TCI even indemnified each deputy to protect McDuff against possible damage claims. Birmingham authorities were opposed to picketing as well; the city's young commissioner of public safety, Eugene (not yet known as "Bull") Connor, informed union leaders that there was no such thing as a peaceful demonstration. Connor and his fellow commissioners feared that interracial labor activities in particular would have unfavorable social consequences. In the words of the Birmingham chief of police: "Why, before the radicals began scattering such stuff, the nigger would come holding up his hands when a white man called. Now the niggers are uppity." City Commission Council president Jones, an active Ku Klux Klan member, banned all integrated labor meetings and disrupted more than one with armed police.[24]

In New Orleans, police strong-arm tactics on the docks caused AFL organizer Holt Ross to describe Crescent City law authorities as "one of the most vicious strikebreaking forces in the world." Yet during a later AFL versus CIO showdown on the wharves, New Orleans police joined forces with Ross and other trades council leaders to oppose industrial union sympathizers with force. They raided CIO headquarters, confiscating membership records and other materials with the tacit approval of United States District Court Judge Wayne Borah. Borah refused to enjoin the police raids and other strong-arm, extralegal methods. Furthermore, during a transportation strike in 1938, Mayor Maestri ordered that police ride as extra passengers to keep all taxicabs in operation no matter the cost. When a Department of Labor investigative team arrived, resulting in a victory for the CIO's United Transportation workers, the mayor closed city offices to them and also attempted to keep them out of local federal buildings. Maestri's predecessors, Walmsley and his Old Regulars, had acted similarly, and from time to time Governor Leche joined in as well, providing state patrolmen to help usher union leaders from the state.[25]

24. Jones to Charles DeBardeleben, December 13, 1935, in James M. Jones, Jr., Collection, Drawer 1, Alabama Archives and History, Montgomery. Also see Tindall, *The Emergence of the New South*, 514–15, 527; *Hearings on Violations of Free Speech and Rights of Labor* (1937), 75th Cong., 1st Sess., 762, and (1938), 75th Cong., 2nd Sess., 6301; Birmingham *News*, August 24, 30, 1936; Siegel, "The Growth of Coal and Steel Unions," 9, 17–20; Atlanta *Constitution*, February 4, 1938; Atlanta *Journal*, October 25, 1934; Atlanta *Journal of Labor*, July 14, 1939.

25. New Orleans *Times-Picayune*, October 5, 1935, September 26, 1936, June 12, 1937, June 23, 29, July 8, 13, 16, 1938, March 24, 1939; New Orleans *Item*, January 15, May 28, June 11–12, 1937; New Orleans *Tribune*, July 1, 1937; New York *Times*, July 9, 12, 1938; *CIO News*, August 6, 1938; Kane, *Louisiana Hayride*, 295; Haas, "New Orleans on the Half-Shell," 305–306, and *DeLesseps S. Morrison*, 23–24.

Police and company opposition did not prevent labor unions from gaining an urban foothold in the 1930s, and the evidence suggests that the cities on the whole were not supportive of the strong-arm, anti-union tactics. For example, the urban press was uneasy about industrial unionism, condemning radical influences within the CIO, but a "wait and see" policy toward federal labor guarantees showed that it was beginning to recognize that workers needed protection in some form. The Memphis *Press Scimitar* went so far as to call the Wagner Act "one of the most important pieces of legislation ever laid before congress." The conservative Birmingham *Age-Herald* and the Atlanta *Constitution* accepted the notion of labor guarantees as well, with the Alabama journal even tolerating UMW and SWOC presence in the coalfields and steel mills. Press editorials also opposed the intimidation directed against union members and organizers. The Memphis *Commercial Appeal*, almost always supportive of New South interests, took a tough stand against the beating of Norman Smith, although an important factor in its stance was its emerging anti-machine posture. Still, if a choice had to be made, city editors in general preferred "order"—even if some compromises were necessary—as opposed to Crump and his lieutenants, who seemed steadfastly committed to "tradition." There was the fear of further interference from outside the region, especially from Washington, D.C., and the belief that a tranquil environment would be attractive to industries and businesses looking to relocate in the South.[26]

The newspaper most hostile toward labor was the New Orleans *Times-Picayune*, described by one AFL leader as "the No. 1 foe of organized labor and champion of the scab shop," with "no peer in the art of lying" and "no peer as an enemy of the laboring man." Yet when Mayor Maestri unleashed his "red squad," the community response was not altogether supportive. Some residents applauded the extralegal police activities, and one congratulated the mayor for his "determined and intelligent stand in combatting unionism and subversive activities of communists." But at least an equal number of residents condemned municipal antilabor policies. The New Orleans *Item* and its morning affiliate, the *Tribune*, sided with the mayor's critics, printing editorials sympathetic to labor. The Atlanta *Journal* and the Birmingham *Post* also adopted editorial policies more sympathetic to

26. Memphis *Commercial Appeal*, September 23, 1937; Memphis *Press Scimitar*, March 2, 1934; Atlanta *Constitution*, February 7, 11, April 14, June 20, September 5, 1937, June 18, 1938; Birmingham *Age-Herald*, August 25, 30, 1936; Billy Hall Wyche, "Southern Attitudes Toward Industrial Unions, 1933–1941" (Ph.D. dissertation, University of Georgia, 1969), 69–92.

labor than those of their hometown rivals, accepting labor legislation and the inevitability of even industrial unionism.[27]

The attitude that unionism was a permanent, even if a distasteful, movement became increasingly evident among urban employers as well as among municipal officials. The Atlantic Steel Company in Atlanta revealed this attitude during the "little steel" organizing drives. An NLRB election in 1941 authorized the United Steelworkers of America to be the official bargaining agent for the Atlantic Steel work force. Only 114 of the firm's 1,100 employees were then union members, but management approved the vote to avoid future trouble. From a 10 percent enrollment in 1941, the Atlanta local continued to expand, and by the early 1950s, 90 percent of the company's workers were dues-paying members.[28]

The preservation of what were seen as regional industrial advantages ultimately made the labor movement less threatening from the standpoint of urban leaders. The final version of the 1938 Fair Labor Standards Act, while establishing needed wage and hour guidelines, exempted numerous labor categories and delayed wage adjustments in selected industries, most notably southern textiles, for several years. Even more important were state right-to-work laws, passed when rural and small-town legislators in control of Dixie statehouses joined urban manufacturing interests in the 1930s and 1940s to embrace the open-shop movement. The Birmingham Chamber of Commerce in 1938 reported to outside manufacturers that despite a union presence, the central Alabama industrial district was not a union shop area. The bureau further concluded: "Our people are physically large and accustomed to hard work. All are acclimated to hot weather. Both white and black stand the heat well in industrial labor." Although the state statutes weakened southern unions in comparison with labor groups elsewhere, some organizations, such as the Atlanta steel local, circumvented the laws in part through informal agreements with management that all new workers would receive applications for checkoff dues upon their employment.[29]

27. *Progress* (Hammond, Louisiana), n.d., in Robert Maestri Scrapbooks, X, New Orleans Public Library; Donald Bruce to Maestri, June 29, 1938, in Robert Maestri Papers, microfilm roll 411B; New Orleans *Tribune*, September 20, 1937, January 14, 1938; Atlanta *Journal*, March 27, 1934, February 12, 1937. Even the New Orleans *Times-Picayune* eventually tempered its anti-union sentiments. See *Times-Picayune*, July 31, 1937, October 12, 24, 1938.

28. Gilman and Sweeney, *Causes of Industrial Peace*, 2–24; Kuniansky, "A Business History," 140–42; Marshall, *Labor in the South*, 187.

29. Birmingham Chamber of Commerce, *Birmingham Industrial Information* (Birmingham, 1938), 48; Hodges, "The New Deal Labor Policy," 449–50; Gilman and Sweeney, *Causes of Industrial Peace*, 22–23.

In addition to federal guarantees and depression conditions, the rift within labor's own ranks stimulated union activity in the southern cities. When AFL president William Green ordered the expulsion of CIO affiliates from all state and local trade organizations, John Lewis' followers in turn formed industrial union groups as alternatives to existing state federations of labor. Industrial councils appeared in each of the southern states in question, to which AFL leaders responded by intensifying their own organizational efforts. Municipal trades councils added craft locals as well as groups of industrial employees brought together in new "federal unions." In 1939, the Memphis *Labor Review* claimed that the Tennessee city had become the "union capital of the South." Even the newspaper guilds were bargaining with both conservative dailies, although not under closed-shop agreements. Some of the new locals were technically CIO affiliates, but the Memphis Trades Council found them acceptable when their leaders repudiated national industrial union policies.[30]

Atlanta's central AFL committee more than doubled the number of affiliate locals between 1937 and 1939, publishing an exaggerated figure of sixty-five thousand individual members. The Georgia city was not "a union town in the full sense of the word," as one study has suggested, yet local craft organizations had become stronger while many manufacturing plants were organized for the first time. Trades councils reported similar gains in New Orleans and Birmingham, where numbers had decreased during the early depression years. Urban unionists were responsible in part for the organization of state departments of labor throughout the South; for the passage of the Factory Inspection Act, new unemployment insurance, and improved workman's compensation policies in Georgia; and for more effective child labor statutes in most states.[31] Clearly a new economic and even political force was taking shape—a consideration for municipal elites and the prevailing order.

30. New York *Times*, March 29, 1937; Memphis *Press Scimitar*, June 10, 17, August 15, September 21, 1937; Memphis *Labor Review*, August 31, 1939; Paul Cappock to Overton, September 15, 1937, in Mayor's Correspondence File, Drawer 5; Minton, "The New Deal in Tennessee," 224–27.

31. Gilman and Sweeney, *Causes of Industrial Peace*, 1–2; *Federationist* (New Orleans), October 8, 1937; Atlanta *Journal of Labor*, April 12, 1940; Birmingham *Southern Labor Review*, December 29, 1937, September 10, 1938; Alabama State Federation of Labor, *Official Year Book and Buyer's Guide, 1931* (n.p., 1931), 3; Louisiana State Federation of Labor, *Proceedings of the 25th Annual Convention* (n.p., 1937), 40–43; J. B. Pate, "Half Century of Progress: Georgia Labor Pulls Itself Out of the Mire," *American Federationist* (September, 1949), 1819; Birmingham *Labor Advocate*, September 21, 1935, July 11, 1936; Bevis, "Frank M. Dixon," 174–75; Addison T. Cutler, "Labor Legislation in Thirteen Southern States," *Southern Economic Journal*, VII (January, 1941), 297–316.

Active industrial unionism also made AFL leaders throughout the country realize that they had either to become more active among blacks or else to lose them to CIO competitors. Craft unions thus expanded segregated locals, organized new ones, or created integrated locals in occupations wherein blacks outnumbered whites. The AFL's Tobacco Workers Industrial Union, for example, which won agreements from most manufacturers in the southern cities, organized racially mixed locals because blacks represented between 50 and 75 percent of all employees. In addition, the AFL was active among Negro dock workers in New Orleans and Memphis; and unions for carpenters, bricklayers, electricians, and plasterers in all of the large Dixie cities openly recruited black craftsmen. The coordinator of the AFL campaign was B. C. Baskerville, the first black AFL regional representative ever sent to the South. According to Herbert Northrup, the scattered victories for blacks in labor unions demonstrated to other Negro leaders, especially in the cities, the necessity of organization in the pursuit of social, economic, and political advancement.[32]

Yet the conflict between the AFL and the CIO had a negative side as well, forcing wage earners too often to take sides against one other rather than against employer resistance. In 1938 and 1939, AFL representatives in the Birmingham area challenged the UMW and the CIO's Smelter Workers by recognizing the Progressive Mineworkers' Association and the Brotherhood of Captive Miners, both former company unions. During the nationwide coal strike in 1939, the AFL filled grocery orders for members, and when the work stoppage ended and Alabama miners had not secured a union shop agreement, the Progressive Mineworkers' Association attracted several hundred dissatisfied men into its fold. The UMW survived the ordeal, which included an AFL promise to restore lost wages to all who enrolled and an active campaign against the CIO, spearheaded by the conservative urban craft press. In the end, the conflict succeeded mainly in breeding internal labor bitterness while prompting state lawmakers to begin consideration of right-to-work legislation.[33]

32. Northrup, *Organized Labor and the Negro*, 33–45, 111–13; Marshall, "History of Labor Organization," 373–74; Philip S. Foner, *Organized Labor and the Black Worker, 1619–1973* (New York, 1974), 224; *Louisiana Weekly*, December 2, 1933. For the sentiments of the urban craft press on industrial unionism, see Birmingham *Labor Advocate*, April 23, 1938; Memphis *Labor Review*, September 24, 1937; Atlanta *Journal of Labor*, October 9, 1938; Birmingham *Southern Labor Review*, September 8, 1937; *Federationist* (New Orleans), April 1, 1938.

33. Alabama State Federation of Labor, *Proceedings of the 38th Annual Convention, 1939* (n.p., 1939), 49, 61; and *Proceedings . . . 1940* (n.p., 1940), 60; S. E. Roper to Frank Fenton, September 14, 1939, and Decision and Direction of Election, Case No. R-2523, n.d., both in Alabama Labor Files, Drawer 29, Alabama AFL-CIO Office,

The struggle to organize the Firestone workers in Memphis revealed the labor schism as well as the city's continued stand against industrial unionism. The United Rubber Workers, affiliated with the CIO, failed in the Tennessee plant in 1936, and for three years thereafter, the municipal trades council made no effort to organize Firestone employees. Regional CIO director Lucy Mason charged that the AFL followed the wishes of the Crump machine and left the large factories alone, and the Petrie labor investigations likewise concluded that local craft unions and city officials often worked "hand in glove." Wages in the Memphis plant were lower than national average earnings for rubber workers (50 percent below the scale in Akron, Ohio) and also lower than those paid in other southern rubber firms.[34]

In 1940 the United Rubber Workers entered Memphis again. Organizers were especially active among blacks, who made up nearly half of the local Firestone work force. Industrial union activities prompted city administrators to launch anew their campaign of intimidation against the CIO, while prodding the Memphis Trades Council to move into the Firestone operation to preempt CIO efforts. One municipal official outlined the strategy, pointing out that industrial organizers were alienating whites by telling blacks that "negroes are not living in the South of 20 years ago but in the U.S. of America now under a constitution which protects them and gives them the same privileges and the same race equality as the whites." Local craft leaders successfully exploited the race issue and, with the backing of city hall, narrowly won an NLRB election in December, 1940. The vote divided almost entirely along racial lines and convinced the Crump organization that it had kept its earlier pledge to Firestone management to keep the CIO out. However, when the victorious AFL negotiated its first contract, which kept wages below those paid in other southern firms, workers responded the next year by abandoning the craft union in favor of the United Rubber Workers. The shift gave industrial unionism its first significant foothold in Memphis prior to World War I.[35]

Birmingham; Siegel, "The Growth of Coal and Steel Unions," 36–37; Birmingham *Southern Labor Review*, May 19, October 6, 1937, March 1, May 17, 1939; Birmingham *Labor Advocate*, June 30, 1938, May 29, August 25, 1939; *Hearings on Violations of Free Speech and Rights of Labor* (1938), 75th Cong., 2nd Sess., 6339–40.

34. Tindall, *The Emergence of the New South*, 516; Lucy Mason, *To Win These Rights: A Personal Story of the CIO in the South* (New York, 1942), 104–14; Petrie, "Memphis Makes War," 1273; Harold S. Robert, *The Rubber Workers: Labor Organization and Collective Bargaining in the Rubber Industry* (New York, 1944), 412.

35. A. B. Clapp to Walter Chandler, December 4, 1940, in Mayor's Correspondence File, Drawer 10; Memphis *Commercial Appeal*, August 25, 30, December 24, 1940, March 19, 1941; Memphis *Press Scimitar*, August 30, September 23, December 24, 1940; Marshall, *Labor in the South*, 191.

The labor situation in Atlanta was somewhat less volatile than that in Birmingham, New Orleans, and Memphis. In 1937 the Atlanta Trades Council of the Georgia Federation of Labor expelled all CIO affiliates from its ranks. The split precipitated hard feelings, as the ousted leaders formed a rival organization and refused to surrender federation records in their possession. Industrial union leaders in the city—A. Steve Nance and J. A. Harper, president of the city's central labor committee—were not outsiders, as were many rubber, automobile, maritime, and even UMW and SWOC organizers in the other major municipalities. The standing of these men in the community eased fears that industrial unionists were imported agitators with Communist leanings. The conservative Atlanta *Journal of Labor* remarked that Harper was "one of the best men in the ranks of organized labor."[36]

Nance and Harper helped maintain peace in local organizing drives. In November, 1936, the Atlanta UAW locals called a sitdown strike against the city's General Motors plants, an action predating the nationwide automobile strike by several weeks. Local workers held out for three months and ultimately won recognition, wage increases, paid vacations, and seniority rights. Although Chief T. O. Sturdivant's "red squad" patrolled the factory area during the strike, there was little evidence of force or intimidation. UAW organizers worked with Nance and other local labor leaders, many of whom were still active in the local trades council. Furthermore, when an AFL-endorsed challenger to the UAW moved into the Atlanta area in 1940, although unsuccessfully, organizers from both sides recruited freely, and reports of violence were rare. The same was true in the Atlanta textile mills, where Nance and the Textile Workers Organizing Committee (TWOC) of the CIO encountered few police nightsticks and a minimum of intimidation directed by their AFL rivals.[37]

Although the Wagner Act was important, the NLRB machinery did not guarantee more than a beginning for organizers. Bureaucratic delays and uncertainties of enforcement too often limited enrollment campaigns. At first, many employers challenged or even rejected NLRB decisions, which postponed the implementation of case rulings for years. And even after the Supreme Court in 1937 upheld the federal statute, labor administrators did not always act with confidence and swiftness. A seven-year union effort in the Alden and Lane cotton

36. Atlanta *Journal of Labor*, July 16, 1937. Also see *ibid.*, June 11, July 30, 1937; New York *Times*, April 20, 1937; Atlanta *Constitution*, April 9–25, June 11, 1937.

37. New York *Times*, May 14, 1937; Atlanta *Journal of Labor*, February 5, 12, 1937, February 3, April 12, 1939, April 12, 26, 1940; Marshall, *Labor in the South*, 191–92; Gilman and Sweeney, *Causes of Industrial Peace*, 2.

textile mills in New Orleans exemplified the enforcement dilemma. The Alden operation employed five hundred people, while the Lane firm, owned by ardent anti-unionist Sigmund Odenheimer, had more than two thousand workers under contract. Although the New Orleans economy did not depend on textile manufacturing, the city was the site of scores of related industries whose operations relied on textile output and which might be organized if Alden and especially Lane capitulated.

The UTW, affiliated with the AFL, several years earlier had tried to organize employees at both firms. Leaders called a strike at Lane in September, 1933, which accomplished nothing but a three-week walkout and, ultimately, the release of union activists. Blue Eagle arbitration was never involved, and an agreement between Odenheimer and the New Orleans Trades and Labor Council, in cooperation with the Cotton Textile Code Authority, led to the firm's reopening in late September. The Lane wage scale remained low, ranging from twenty to thirty-five cents per hour for skilled labor, and from three to eight dollars each week under an archaic piece-rate system for the majority of unskilled employees. A similar walkout occurred at Alden in 1934; it too failed when the UTW's national strike committee refused to support it, urging instead that strikers report back to work.[38]

In July, 1937, TWOC organizers opened a new union drive in Odenheimer's plant under Wagner guarantees.[39] The boss immediately announced that he would recognize the industrial union if the majority of employees wanted it, but he demanded a federal hearing before agreeing to an NLRB election. He made it known that he believed that the CIO was trying "to bring about Russian conditions in the country." The organizer in charge was Robert Tisdale, a colleague of Nance.

In late July and early August, both sides argued their cases before labor arbiters. Management charged that workers had joined the TWOC unknowingly when unionists posed as federal agents, while labor leaders reported incidents of company-directed intimidation against organizers and members. In a second hearing in September, 1937, labor reported the existence of the company's new Lane Mills Welfare Association and noted that it could not refute all of Odenheimer's testimony because many wage earners feared for their jobs. Lane had already fired some union sympathizers between the first and second

38. New Orleans *Item-Tribune*, May 30, 1937; New Orleans *Times-Picayune*, September 6–9, 26–27, 1933, September 21, 1934; *Federationist* (New Orleans), July 31, 1936.

39. Information on the labor struggles at Lane, 1937–1942, from New York *Times*, August 26, September 21, 1937; New Orleans *Times-Picayune*, July 2, 7–11, 21–24, August 26, September 8, 17, October 9, 16, 19–27, 1937, April 9, June 15, July 7, 19–27, August 7, November 22, 1938, April 29, October 26, December 13, 1939, May 10, July 10, November 13, 1940, October 20, 1942.

hearings, as it would do again before a third held in February, 1938. Throughout the hearings, the boss and his foremen maintained innocent, low-key profiles, relying on fabricated evidence that labor could not always counter because of conditions in the mills.

Following the first hearing, an NLRB election gave the CIO affiliate bargaining status by a three to one voting margin—a decision that federal officials would not overturn despite testimony in the two later sets of hearings. Ultimately, the labor board declared the company guilty of unfair trade practices and ordered Odenheimer to reinstate more than fifty discharged workers with full back wages while bargaining with TWOC representatives. The sixty-five-page ruling, signed by NLRB chairman J. Warren Madden in June, 1938, was the first of its kind released under Wagner provisions.

The Lane controversy nevertheless remained unsettled for two more years. Odenheimer took the matter to federal court, and while waiting for a decision, he continued to defy the NLRB order. Meanwhile, Department of Labor investigators charged the Lane firm with the use of child labor on government work—a violation of federal law. In May, 1940, a federal court confirmed the earlier order, and the following November, the boss reluctantly signed with the CIO's Textile Workers Union. The contract included an eight-hour day, the organization of shop arbitration machinery, the development of a seniority system, and the promise of future bargaining rights. After a seven-year struggle, the union had prevailed.

Despite the victory in New Orleans, TWOC and UTW southern organizing campaigns in the late 1930s failed in most textile operations. More than 90 percent of the region's textile plants were located in towns with fewer than 50,000 residents, where organized labor's generally radical image, and especially that of the CIO, generated fears that employers skillfully exploited. The many company-owned mill villages facilitated the enforcement of antilabor policies, as did state court rulings against picketing. Sedition laws in Alabama and Tennessee also led to many indiscriminate arrests, particularly in the less-populated areas. The Birmingham *Post* argued that the Alabama statute allowed "any busy body, patrioteer, hired minion of a corporate interest or plain crank to swear out warrants without regard to truth or fact." In the cities, only Lane and the small Atlanta Woolen Company (500 employees) had legitimate contracts with unions as of World War II. There were no reports of union activity in the New Orleans Alden plant or the Avondale operation in the Birmingham area. Labor historian Ray Marshall has concluded that the TWOC effort in the late 1930s, which he calls "the best planned textile organizing campaign ever undertaken," enrolled no more than 5 percent of all southern spindles. In the

1942 Alabama State Industrial Union Convention, the only textile locals present came from three midsize towns, representing a total of 1,500 workers. And even as late as 1952, the largest textile firm in Atlanta remained unorganized.[40]

Yet the unions that appeared in the 1930s in the southern cities, whether they were the result of nationwide settlements or of local efforts or of a combination of both, continued their development in succeeding decades. An independent survey conducted by *Fortune Magazine* in 1943 found that only 30 percent of the southern industrial work force was organized, compared to a national average of 54 percent, but that the southern figure reflected urban union activity almost exclusively. By 1942, Birmingham and Memphis ranked with Cincinnati and Chicago in terms of organization among manufacturing employees, falling into the 50 to 74 percent category. New Orleans and Atlanta fell into a lower percentile and were on a par with several northern and western cities of comparable size. In the early 1960s, AFL-CIO leaders concluded that the major southern cities "can be called strongly unionized" and that "they are comparable to industrial cities in any part of the country."[41] Employer resistance to unionism did not disappear in the post–World War II period, especially in small towns and rural areas throughout the South, so that the hoped-for ripple effect was years in coming, if it ever came at all. Still, the urban base laid in the 1930s kept the pattern of industrial relations in the region from falling farther behind that in the rest of the country.

The willingness of workers to join the labor movement, usually in direct defiance of their employers, was the key to union successes in the 1930s. Without the support of the rank and file, the fortitude shown by organizers would have gained little. Wage earners in the urban industrial areas gradually accepted organization, even setting aside long-standing racial anxieties for the prospect of economic betterment, as long as fundamental employment and social traditions were not seriously challenged. Of course this stipulation automatically set limits. Segregated locals remained in most crafts, and job segregation was not ended in the mills. It even worsened in Birmingham, where

40. Birmingham *Post*, July 3, 1935; Memphis *Labor Review*, May 29, 1935, January 20, 1939; Milton Derber, "Growth and Expansion," in Milton Derber and Edwin Young (eds.), *Labor and the New Deal* (Madison, Wis., 1957), 27–28; Gilman and Sweeney, *Causes of Industrial Peace*, 2; Marshall, *Labor in the South*, 170–71; Hodges, "The New Deal Labor Policy," 398–404; Alabama Industrial Union Council, *Report of Proceedings of the Fourth Constitutional Convention* (n.p., 1942), 185–86; Birmingham *Southern Labor Review*, November 29, 1939; *Federationist* (New Orleans), June 18, 1937.

41. "Labor Statistics," *Business Week*, April 25, 1964. Also see Wyche, "Southern Attitudes Toward Industrial Unions," 67; Stetson Kennedy, *Southern Exposure* (Garden City, 1946), 289–300; Marshall, "History of Labor Organization," 441.

whites apparently succeeded for the next twenty years in keeping unionism within the fixed parameters of Jim Crow. Yet there were individual gains for skilled and unskilled labor, black and white, including better working conditions and wages. As well, community opinion overall, although skeptical of the Wagner Act and the NLRB, and certainly hoping for the continuation of so-called regional advantages, was beginning to accept or at least grudgingly tolerate the general principle of labor organization. The labor movement in general— together with the effects of the depression, the impact of federal relief programs, and the development of new municipal services and commitments—suggests that the southern cities were becoming increasingly aware of the complexities of an urban industrial society and were even willing to accept some changes in the traditional southern way of life. Expansion, tradition, fiscal parsimony, efficiency, and a fixed social and economic order were values still to be perpetuated, but further adjustments and compromises were certain, especially in light of continuing pressures from outside the region and the steady diversification of southern urban society in future years.

 11

A CULTURAL AWAKENING:
FEDERAL ARTS AND THE SOUTHERN CITIES

If the depression brought unemployment to factory workers, teachers, and skilled craftsmen, it also forced thousands of artists into the ranks of the jobless. The result was Federal Project Number 1, the New Deal artist relief network, loosely associated with the WPA's white-collar division. Like federal and community recreational activities, it employed only a few men and women in need but reached many others through the effects of citywide programming.

The project for writers did little more than provide temporary relief for jobless editors and authors in the major southern cities, as well as other regional towns both large and small. Those involved did excellent work, mainly on reference materials. Through the artists' program, only a handful of painters and sculptors found work, yet many art centers were established for instruction and for touring exhibitions. Similarly, the music and theater units employed few, but as regional administrators had hoped, they promoted a cultural awareness in the South, centered in the major urban areas. Where few musicians or actors were locally available, Washington, D.C., often loaned jobless professionals from New York or elsewhere to the Dixie projects. Such efforts were clearly responsible for the advancement of a variety of art forms and an appreciation of their cultural and entertainment value in the South.

Similar to many other relief endeavors in the late 1930s, the Federal Art Project had roots in earlier federal experiments. CWA and FERA painters and sculptors had decorated hundreds of municipal buildings and had worked on park monuments or in city and college museums preparing murals for display in courthouses, libraries, and other public places. So when wage relief expanded in 1935, an artists' program, under national administrator Holger Cahill, was organized to provide continuing emergency employment and to promote the appreciation of art throughout the nation.[1]

The Louisiana branch of the Federal Art Project, with headquarters in New Orleans, was the most active project in the South. It opened in late 1935, and for four years, federal artists in the Delgado Museum of Art and in makeshift studios in City Park completed paintings and sculptures that were donated to tax-supported institutions. The artists also conducted art classes for schoolchildren and for the general public in community centers. Five thousand workshops between 1935 and 1942 enrolled more than 65,000 Louisianians. Finally in 1939, under joint city and federal sponsorship, a WPA art gallery opened in the French Quarter. It became a permanent home for Federal Art Project personnel and an exhibition hall for local and touring shows. The facility, reported federal examiners, was the city's "first modern, well-lighted art gallery" and remained the Federal Art Project headquarters until the project closed in late 1942. Thereafter, it became a municipal museum.[2]

The failure to expand the New Orleans Federal Art Project headquarters into a true regional art center, concludes William McDonald in his study of federal relief and the arts, was the major shortcoming of the southern project. McDonald also argues that national officials could have loaned or resettled unemployed artists where few existed, as they did in the theater program; however, Federal Art Project operations in the Dixie cities other than New Orleans focused mainly on art classes and on the acquisition of loan exhibitions from either New York or the National Gallery of Art in Washington, D.C. Throughout Alabama, for example, only sixteen jobless professionals in seven years secured Federal Art Project positions in the Birmingham, Montgomery, and Mobile museums. The state's largest city had a maximum quota of only four professional artists throughout the project's eight-year history. In Georgia, where federal investigators indicated that "the number of certified artists has been insufficient to warrant a state policy," only one person obtained full-time Federal Art Project employment—a

1. Atlanta *Georgian*, December 17, 1933; Memphis *Press Scimitar*, January 17, 1934; New Orleans *Times-Picayune*, May 24, 1933; McDonald, *Federal Relief Administration*, 80.

2. Gideon T. Stanton to Holger Cahill, December 10, 1935, Stanton to Thomas C. Parker, February 3, 1935, Spofford to Stanton, October 27, 1936 (Box 25), William McHugh to Parker, October 6, 1937, Stanton to Robert Andrews, November 28, 1938, Andrews to Caroline Durieux, June 21, 1939, Hammond to Parker, October 24, 1939 (Box 49), all in Record Group 69, Records of the Works Progress Administration, Federal Project No. 1, Federal Artist Project Records, National Archives, hereinafter cited as FAP.

resident of the small town of Toccoa who suffered from infantile paralysis. Eleanor Roosevelt personally intervened in the case. The state branch of the Federal Art Project in Tennessee, despite its four urban areas of more than 100,000 people each, was almost totally inactive until 1940.[3]

Birmingham's Henley School, also known as the Public School Museum, was a local gallery that sponsored Federal Art Project work. According to field reports, the facility offered only a single exhibition room with "non-descript historic and archaeological material" but represented "the best place in Alabama to start an active gallery." The four Birmingham artists used the school for a variety of purposes — as a workshop, as a place for one-man shows, as a building for free classes for adults and children, and as a meeting place for the revived Birmingham Art Association. National administrators appointed gallery curator Richard Coe as local supervisor and as the first statewide non-relief Federal Art Project chief. When Coe resigned in mid-1937, Mobilian Emma Roche, who worked in the Mobile Federal Art Project museum, took charge of state activities. The only opposition to the popular program came from private art teachers who argued that the free Federal Art Project classes were competing unfairly with private enterprise.[4]

From 1936 until the closing of Federal Project Number 1 in February, 1943, the Birmingham and Mobile centers displayed the works of local artists and brought original pieces from the National Gallery of Art to residents previously unexposed to great art. Furthermore, Federal Art Project productions from the Henley School toured community centers and public schools throughout the state under the sponsorship of the Alabama Board of Education. Federal officials reported that the exhibits "familiarized the public with the work of its native artists . . . encouraged young talent and stimulated public interest in ending a cultural erosion that had been the result of the long years after the Civil War when over sixty-five percent of the South's native talent departed for the large cities in the North." Local art councils appeared in the two cities, and WPA observers concluded that while "the personnel of the program was always small . . . [it] has brought to the State some

3. McDonald, *Federal Relief Administration*, 76–77, 400; Weber to Cahill, February 5, 1936, in FAP, Box 21; [?] Boggs to Parker, June 12, 1937, Parker to Conrad Snell, February 24, 1939 (Georgia Art Project), Report on the Alabama Art Program, n.d. (Final Reports of Women's Projects: Alabama), all in RG 69, Records of the Works Progress Administration, NA, hereinafter cited as WPA.

4. H. M. Holloway to Parker, May 5, 1936, Richard Coe to Parker, November 23, 1936, Dan S. Defenbacher, Report on Birmingham, n.d., all in FAP, Box 21; Cahill to Weber, October 16, 1935, Lawrence Morris to Woodward, October 14, 1937, H. E. Wheller to Cahill, June 1, 1938, Parker to Weber, June 7, 1938, all in WPA, Alabama Art Project.

realization of its true worth, the worth that lies in the creative talents of its own people and the rights of everyone to share that wealth."[5]

Each of the other major southern urban areas had facilities comparable to Henley School. In Atlanta, L. Palmer Skidmore directed Federal Art Project exhibitions and classes at the High Museum of Art, while in Memphis, the Brooks Memorial Gallery and the Memphis Academy of Arts worked with federal authorities. Interested citizens established the last complex in 1936 specifically to attract Federal Art Project and other touring displays. Unfortunately, until the last three years of Federal Project Number 1, the art centers in Nashville, Chattanooga, Knoxville, and Sewanee, as well as Memphis, did little more than acquire exhibitions. After 1940, a handful of artists under the direction of Karl Kershaw produced some pieces of local interest, but because of previous mismanagement in the Tennessee branch of the federal program, regional investigators concluded in 1939 that "the entire project in Tennessee is unquestionably lacking in orientation and direction and from a lack of public knowledge and support."[6]

It is somewhat surprising that the most active Federal Art Project gallery in Memphis was a black project that ranked among the best of its kind in the nation. National director Cahill made a determined effort in Dixie and elsewhere in the country to employ Negro artists and to promote art appreciation within the black communities. So in early 1938, when President Frank Sweeney of LeMoyne College in Memphis proposed the establishment of a Negro extension gallery at his school, Federal Art Project personnel in Washington, D.C., and state supervisor Arnold Bentien quickly approved the plan, naming Vertis Hayes of New York to head the project. Bentien described Hayes as a dependable worker who can "do a good job, who has the correct attitude and who can and does sell the project to the public without getting involved in some fool situation."[7] In 1939, Hayes became a full-time faculty member at the Memphis Negro college.

Until 1943, the LeMoyne-Federal Art Center provided emergency employment for several Negro artists and display rooms for local and touring exhibitions. Staffed entirely with black personnel, the gallery contained three separate chambers, all with modern lighting fixtures

5. Final Report of Federal Art Project in Alabama, n.d., in WPA, Final Reports of Women's Projects: Alabama.

6. Florence McIntyre to Cahill, July 25, 1936, Parker to McIntyre, July 29, 1936 (Box 32), Parker to Morris, June 25, 1937 (Box 44), Arnold Bentien to Parker, February 24, 1936 (Box 21), all in FAP; Andrews to Ralston, July 18, 1939, Karl Kershaw to Betty Luck, December 9, 1939 (Tennessee Art Project), Cahill to L. Palmer Skidmore, November 1, 1935, Van De Vrede to Woodward, December 1, 1936, Kerr to Shepperson, January 12, 1939 (Georgia Art Project), all in WPA.

7. Bentien to Parker, March 16, 1938, in WPA, Tennessee Art Project.

for maximum visual effect. The facility also launched a teaching program for children and adults, promoting the first art classes in the Memphis Negro schools. In addition, Hayes supported the organization of the LeMoyne Art Association, composed of several hundred subscribers who contributed to the gallery's upkeep while promoting its programs within the black community—clearly an example of a self-help program within the segregated urban society. The objective, said Bentien, was to make the project "the center of Negro Art in the country." Although that goal lay beyond reach, the LeMoyne effort culminated in a new college art department that became one of the best in the South and, at least until 1939, remained the most active and visible of all such federal endeavors in the state.[8]

The handful of Federal Art Project artists in the southern cities also directed special art-related relief programs. Two projects in Atlanta were representative. In 1937, Wilbur Kurtz of the Georgia Federal Art Project led a WPA crew in renovating the cyclorama of the battle of Atlanta located in Grant Park. Relief workers retouched faded spots and transformed the piece into a three-dimensional picture by extending the canvas over the floor and adding exploded shells, trees, cross-ties, and simulated grass and dirt. The second special Federal Art Project venture involved New York artist Charles Trumbo Henry, loaned to the Georgia project for assignment in the state prison near Atlanta. The Justice Department funded the operation, contributing funds to the New York City branch of the Federal Art Project, which in turn paid Henry's salary and expenses. The artist resided at the Atlanta correctional institution for seven months, interacting with inmates and advising prison officials in their efforts to establish art-related rehabilitation programs. Although the New Yorker's presence did not trigger massive penal reform in Georgia, the advancement of the idea of rehabilitation was in itself significant in a system wherein chain gangs remained the basic component of prison life.[9]

Like the Federal Art Project, the Federal Music Project was active throughout the urban South, opening under the national direction of Nickolai Sokoloff in late 1935. The project built on FERA foundations of local relief bands and their periodic park concerts, and continued federal sponsorship of community orchestras and music educational

8. Frank Sweeney to WPA, January 13, 1938, Parker to Bentien, January 21, February 11, 1938, Bentien to Parker, September 20, 1938, April 4, June 14, 1939, Andrews to Hayes, July 18, 1939, Hayes to Andrews, July 24, 1939, Parker to Hayes, July 27, 1939, all in WPA, Tennessee Art Project.

9. Alma H. Jamison, "The Cyclorama of the Battle of Atlanta," *Atlanta Historical Society Bulletin*, II (July, 1937), 58–75; Audrey McMahon to Parker, October 6, 1938, Parker to Joseph Sanford, October 19, 1938, Sanford to Parker, n.d., Parker to McMahon, June 23, 1939, all in WPA, Georgia Art Project.

services. Sokoloff's first broad objective was the rehabilitation of jobless instrumentalists, singers, and music teachers, and the establishment of high standards of musicianship. His second, and more important, goal was to promote an appreciation of the art, announcing in 1938 his intention of making at least one hundred American cities "music-minded." He noted that as of the mid-1930s only eleven major municipalities in the entire country were supporting civic orchestras.[10]

Federal administrators recruited and paid musicians, while municipal authorities through parks and recreation departments provided concert halls and orchestral facilities. In Memphis, for example, the federal orchestra often used the Overton Park outdoor amphitheater, constructed as part of a WPA project for that purpose. It later served as a place for the city's own civic symphony. Approximately 75 percent of Federal Music Project personnel, including conductors, administrators, teachers, and performing musicians, came from the relief rolls, earning the WPA white-collar maximum of $75 to $80 for between 75 and 135 hours of work each month. The individual music units throughout the South varied in size, ranging from less than 50 people in Birmingham to as many as 100 in New Orleans.[11]

The New Orleans federal symphony performed under several conductors, but it was the efforts of Rene Salomon that brought success to the Federal Music Project in the Crescent City. In January, 1936, Salomon accepted the position of state music director, leaving his duties as instructor of violin and ensemble at both H. Sophie Newcomb College of Tulane University in New Orleans and Gulf Park Junior College in Mississippi. He had excellent qualifications, including training at the Marseilles Conservatory in Paris. Although technically state project supervisor, Salomon never lost interest in the Crescent City operation, even after his appointment in 1938 as regional music director in charge of eleven states.[12]

During his seven-year tenure as New Orleans music chief, Salomon transformed a small, thirty-five-piece relief band into a modern orches-

10. Atlanta *Constitution*, March 18, 1934; New Orleans *Times-Picayune*, June 23, 1935; Van De Vrede to Woodward, March 25, 1934, in RG 69, Records of the Federal Emergency Relief Administration, Georgia Women's File, NA; Weber to Sandra Munsell, June 3, 1936, in WPA, Alabama Music Project.

11. New Orleans *Times-Picayune*, March 6, 1938; Memphis *Press Scimitar*, March 11, 1936; E. D. Coppedge to Nickolai Sokoloff, February 1, 1938 (Tennessee Music Project), Van De Vrede to William C. Mayfarth, June 4, 1938, Walter Sheets to Sokoloff, November 2, 1938 (Georgia Music Project), J. D. Lockwood to Bruce McClure, December 5, 1935 (Louisiana Music Project), all in WPA.

12. Lockwood to Sokoloff, January 8, 1936, Sokoloff to Salomon, January 22, 1936, Salomon to Sokoloff, October 25, 1937, Mayfarth to Woodward, November 21, 1938, all in WPA, Louisiana Music Project.

tra. The troupe maintained an active concert schedule, with weekly performances in civic and private auditoriums and in City Park. It also participated in special city pageants, such as the "Glamorous New Orleans" festival's musical reenactment of Louisiana history in August, 1937. The group gave frequent performances at the public schools as well; the main orchestra even visited several black schools. These appearances led to the organization of the Junior Philharmonic Society. In addition, Salomon established two military bands, one for whites and one for blacks; a dance group; and a vocal unit and sinfonietta. Between January, 1936, and January, 1939, the New Orleans Federal Music Project offered nearly 4,000 shows, attracting nearly twelve million people; and in 1940 alone, there were 1,200 performances for audiences totaling more than 400,000 individuals. Although Salomon often lamented that "the material I have to work with is far from being comparable to musicians in the East or West," his good management ensured immediate and lasting Federal Music Project benefits in New Orleans.[13]

When not giving concerts, Federal Music Project personnel conducted tuition-free music education classes (from rhythm to choral training) in community centers throughout the city. Salomon reported that in January, 1940, twelve federally funded teachers taught classes for nearly six thousand children. In the same year, using contributions from city hall, he opened a WPA music center on Royal Street. The building contained classrooms, practice rooms, and a small concert hall for lectures and neighborhood band productions, bringing professionals and amateurs together. When national officials approved the complex, they insisted that it remain a "local agency through which all community activities in music will become integrated in the social life of the people." The center allowed Salomon to increase his teaching staff to thirty-five individuals, for whom he organized weekly forums to set class and community lecture schedules.[14]

Federal Project Number 1 provided relief for jobless musicians in Atlanta, Birmingham, and Memphis as well, although neither the size

13. New Orleans *Times-Picayune*, April 17, 1938; Salomon to Sokoloff, October 5, 1936, November 8, 1937, September 13, 1938, all in WPA, Louisiana Music Project; Salomon to Earle V. Moore, January 15, 1941, in WPA, Federal Project No. 1, Records of the Federal Music Project, Louisiana Narrative Reports, hereinafter cited as FMP; New Orleans *Times-Picayune*, March 27, July 12, 1936, June 27, 1937, March 19, 1939.

14. Salomon, History and Development of the Louisiana Music Project, n.d., and Frances Diboll, Louisiana WPA Music Project Activities, n.d., in Salomon to Moore, January 15, 1941, all in FMP, Louisiana Narrative Reports; Louisiana Federal Music Program Monthly Report, November, 1938, Salomon to Mayfarth, June 7, 1939, Sokoloff to Salomon, June 17, 1939, Salomon to Moore, February 13, 1940, all in WPA, Louisiana Music Project.

nor the quality of the federal orchestras in those cities equaled that of the Louisiana unit. The groups were never much larger than twenty-five to forty pieces, and did little more than perform weekly concerts in parks, charitable institutions, and so on, and even from time to time over local radio. The musicians were primarily performers; there was a minimum of educational work accomplished. The Memphis project devoted its maximum forty hours each week to practice and shows only. Some state officials, such as the Georgia director of WPA professional and service programs, argued that their projects had "never been expanded to the extent that other states have permitted," but requests for broader Federal Music Project ventures ran up against repeated administrative conflicts and delays.[15]

Indeed, the Federal Music Project's greatest handicap was administrative conflicts among local, state, and federal personnel. In Atlanta, jealous WPA chief Shepperson opposed a music program outside her charge. Although Shepperson was "enthusiastic about a symphonic orchestra such as North Carolina has had," regional Federal Music Project director Lamar Stringfield reported, "She seems to be skeptical and doubtful that my musical attempts are practical when brought home." Another dilemma involved Governor Talmadge, who likewise cared little for federal musicians. The governor, for example, baited and then deliberately lured Atlanta conductor Harry Glazer into the political arena. The elderly director invested so much time and energy in an anti-Talmadge campaign during the 1936 senatorial primary that his failing health forced him to leave the Federal Music Project soon thereafter. Glazer's political activities and the subsequent change in personnel weakened Atlanta project operations.[16]

In Memphis, a controversy between the director and his assistant over everything from musical arrangements to the appointment of musicians divided the loyalties of orchestral members, undermining the entire program. In Birmingham, the music program triggered hostility between the municipal park and recreation board and state relief officials. As they did elsewhere, local authorities provided concert facilities when the Federal Music Project opened in Birmingham in 1935. However, when Alabama WPA service director Mary Weber

15. Boggs to Sokoloff; December 21, 1936, Van De Vrede to Mayfarth, January 3, February 20, 1939 (Georgia Music Project), R. W. Robinson to Lamar Stringfield, December 24, 1935, Sokoloff to Morris, June 22, 1937, Coppedge to Sokoloff, November 15, 1938, Coppedge to Woodward, December 20, 1938 (Tennessee Music Project), all in WPA; Harry Dillman, Narrative Report, Memphis, WPA Band, November 3, 1938, in FMP, Tennessee Narrative Reports.

16. Stringfield to Sokoloff, December 14, 1935, Harry Glazer to Stringfield, December 24, 1935, Glazer to Sokoloff, July 12, August 30, 1936, all in WPA, Georgia Music Project.

requested the next year that a new supervisor be appointed to improve the program's quality, civic recreation leaders, who had recruited the conductor, mounted open opposition. They opposed Weber's appeal, demanding the right of approval of any future Federal Music Project changes in the city. An investigation by two outside arbiters satisfied neither side, and Weber continued to argue that "funds are being expended for the project, which, to me, has no integrity." Ultimately, Sokoloff closed the Birmingham unit altogether, and from April, 1937, to the music program's reorganization in 1939, the city was without a federal orchestra.[17]

Under fire from both Republican and Democratic conservatives, the Roosevelt administration in 1939 terminated the Federal Music Project as a separate relief endeavor and integrated ongoing work into the WPA's Professional and Service Division. The administrative shuffle did not alter the New Orleans unit, but it did affect the other southern urban projects. WPA officials immediately broadened music activities in Atlanta and Memphis, allowing those programs to reach into adjacent towns and even into rural areas. Meanwhile, Weber revived Birmingham's project with the cooperation of the Birmingham Board of Education, which accepted sponsorship responsibility. The revised program operated through 1942, giving concerts and adding community extension work. A small NYA orchestra in conjunction with the Birmingham conservatory, a square dance band, and two performing ensembles were also organized in the expanded program.[18]

Most important was the Federal Music Project's promotion of music appreciation, not just through concerts, but through the sponsorship of local symphonic organizations. WPA musicians in Atlanta became the professional nucleus of the Atlanta philharmonic society. WPA musicians in Memphis were instrumental in the formation of the Memphis Symphony Orchestra in 1939, and in Birmingham, Federal Music Project personnel worked closely with the struggling municipal symphony established in 1932. The federal music venture's most impressive legacy was in New Orleans, where a number of attempts in the early 1900s to form a permanent music society had failed. Federal

17. Coppedge to Mayfarth, April 29, 1937 (Tennessee Music Project), Weber to Munsell, June 3, 1936, Frank Bentley to McClure, June 12, 1936, Mayfarth to Weber, July 6, 1936, March 10, 1937, Weber to Mayfarth, July 11, 1936, February 3, March 4, 1937 (Alabama Music Project), all in WPA.

18. Narrative Reports for July, 1941, December, 1941, in FMP, Georgia Narrative Reports; Van De Vrede to Kerr, July 5, September 5, 1940, January 30, 1942 (Georgia Music Project), Charles Seeger to Moore, November 7, 1939 (Tennessee Music Project), Weber to Kerr, March 7, 1941, Alabama Music Project Report, November, 1941 (Alabama Music Project), Final Report of Alabama Federal Music Project, n.d. (Final Reports of Women's Projects: Alabama), all in WPA.

Music Project efforts were directly responsible for the organization of the New Orleans Civic Symphony in 1936. Mayor Maestri supported the movement, and in the fall of 1937, he proclaimed "symphony week" as what would later become the New Orleans Philharmonic Society prepared for its inaugural season. Its first director, European-trained Arthur Zack, had at one time worked with the National Symphony in New York and had organized the Cincinnati Civic Orchestra in 1929.[19]

Most of the federal musicians in New Orleans at first worked both with the relief orchestra and part-time with the new city symphony— including Zack, who initially conducted both units. As the local group continued its development, it began employing full-time personnel, which left emergency positions vacant for additional jobless professionals. For a short time in 1939, a group of Zack's opponents, who thought the Russian immigrant a good organizer but not a master conductor, established a second symphony in competition with the Federal Music Project and the New Orleans orchestra. A compromise was quickly reached, which led to Zack's resignation, because both organizations recognized that the Crescent City public could not support two symphonies. The result was the employment of Norwegian Ole Windingstad to lead the merging city companies. During the controversy, Salomon backed Windingstad, reporting soon after that he would "vouchsafe full cooperation of the Music Project to the new organization" because "with a competent leader as at present the orchestra will become a permanent one." The civic symphony shared the remodeled St. Charles Theater with local drama groups and also performed in the city auditorium. In addition, the society prompted local music appreciation groups to bring touring opera companies to the city on a regular basis for the first time.[20]

Of the four New Deal arts programs, the Federal Theater Project was the most visible and the most controversial from its inception in 1935 to its end by congressional order in 1939. Never as elaborate in the South

19. Narrative Report of the Georgia Music Project, December, 1940, in FMP, Georgia Narrative Reports; Glazer to Sokoloff, February 1, 1936, Van De Vrede to C. E. Triggs, May 14, 1940, Boggs to Walter Kiplinger, May 29, 1941 (Georgia Music Project), Coppedge to Woodward, September 17, 1936, Coppedge to Sokoloff, March 5, 1939, Burnet C. Tuthill to Moore, September 16, 1939 (Tennessee Music Project), C. F. Zukoski to Arthur Goldschmidt, August 8, 1935, Stringfield to Harold Stein, November 8, 1935 (Alabama Music Project), all in WPA; Cintra S. Austin, "A History of the New Orleans Philharmonic Symphony to 1944: The Founding of An Orchestra" (M.A. thesis, University of New Orleans, 1973), 24; New Orleans *Times-Picayune*, September 29, 1937.

20. FMP Monthly Reports, September, 1937, September, 1938, and Salomon to Moore, January 26, 1940, all in FMP, Louisiana Correspondence; Salomon to Baker, March 26, 1936, and Salomon to Sokoloff, March 12, 1937, both in WPA, Louisiana Music Project.

as in New York or California, Federal Theater Project residential companies nevertheless brought professional productions to Dixie audiences and support to developing theater groups. National theater project director Hallie Flanagan announced three objectives. First, said the federal administrator, the project sought the "rehabilitation of professional people and the conservation of their skills." This called for relief actors and directors to be used in local companies and to be loaned from New York to municipal projects in need of additional professional talent. Second, according to Flanagan, the Federal Theater Project intended to champion the development of "vital regional plays about life today and of doing these plays in exciting new ways." The establishment of regional play bureaus to encourage local writers and to select topics for federal theater productions met this aim. Third, and the most important aspect of Dixie theater, the program was to be a community service to promote a local appreciation of the art. The national director pointed out that with the exception of "occasional stock companies or third rate road shows," there was no professional theater anywhere in the South. Some amateur units, such as the Birmingham and New Orleans little theaters, were popular and their shows were generally well attended. Yet others, including the subscription-oriented Crescent City Theatre Guild, failed to generate sufficient public support until federal theater productions and publicity stimulated a greater local interest in the art.[21]

By mid-1939, Federal Theater Project units were operating in New Orleans, Atlanta, Jacksonville, Tampa, Miami, and Raleigh; yet it was a one-year experiment in Birmingham that officially launched the southern project. The selection of that city was not altogether surprising, as it boasted a thriving little theater and a nationally acclaimed children's group. Even more importantly, the first southern Federal Theater Project supervisor, John McGee of the Carolina Playmakers of the University of North Carolina, was a former director of the Birmingham little theater. In a detailed report in late 1935, McGee indicated that Alabama was "the best organized in the South from the viewpoint of important projects." He recommended the organization of one theater unit each in Montgomery, Mobile, Tuskegee, and Tuscaloosa, as well as Birmingham.[22]

McGee hoped to have a Birmingham project in full operation by the

21. Hallie Flanagan to Frances Behre, April 8, 1936, in WPA, Louisiana Theatre Project; Hallie Flanagan, *Arena: The History of the Federal Theatre* (New York, 1940), 81–82; New Orleans *Times-Picayune*, July 6, October 7, 15, 1930.

22. John McGee to Flanagan, August 19, 1935 (Box 24), September 17, 1935 (Box 89), Josepf Lentz to Flanagan, July 6, 1939 (Box 546), all in WPA, Federal Project No. 1, Records of the Federal Theater Project, hereinafter cited as FTP.

fall of 1935. But unfortunately for the southern administrator, who according to Flanagan "knew the Southern theatre situation thoroughly," the Birmingham Park and Recreation Board and the state WPA administration delayed the first plans. The city agency demanded a paid Federal Theater Project position for its supervisor, and Alabama relief personnel, jealous of their own authority, opposed all theater activities. The opposition became so strong in early 1936 that McGee threatened to cancel all proposed federal theater work in the state, remarking that he was "tired of having the Alabama Administration lodge protests against a set-up which has been developed after months of careful study." Not until February, 1936, did the Birmingham project open, under the direction of Verner Haldene of the Montgomery little theater, and only then because McGee obtained alternative sponsorship.[23]

Despite McGee's efforts, the Birmingham project survived for only one year. Haldene's troupe, which absorbed the majority of the 118 actors and technicians assigned to the federal project in Alabama, began operations in the Jefferson County Theater, the stage for local road shows. The plan called for a residential company to be on stage six times each week (five evening performances and one Saturday matinee) and for a touring unit to take shows into the smaller towns throughout central Alabama. The top ticket price was only forty cents; nevertheless, shows never drew well. Following the third play, during which the average paid attendance was only one hundred at each performance, the group moved into a smaller building with lower rent. Audiences remained small, and productions were rarely outstanding.[24]

By the fall of 1936, there was increasing sentiment among Federal Theater Project personnel, as well as among state relief officials who never liked the venture anyway, to transfer the company to another city. Flanagan made that decision after attending a regional conference in Birmingham in October. Although 80 percent of the actors were professional talents, she concluded after seeing several shows that performance quality did not justify continuation of the program. So in January, 1937, national officials ordered the transfer of Haldene to the Detroit Federal Theater Project and prepared the Birmingham troupe

23. Mrs. Charles Sharp to Weber, January 9, 1936, in FTP, Box 56; McClure to Holt, September 5, 1935, Flanagan to Sharp, October 3, 1935, Sharp to Flanagan, October 31, 1935, Behre to Stein, December 3, 1935, McGee, Alabama Situation, January 11, 1936, McGee to Lester Lang, February 7, 1936, Baker to Ray Crow, March 9, 1936, all in WPA, Alabama Theatre Project; Birmingham *News*, April 24, 1936.

24. Ira Smoot to McGee, June 20, 1936, in FTP, Box 56; Bentley to Stein, December 3, 1935, Crow to Hopkins, March 6, 1936, Bentley to McClure, June 12, 1936, all in WPA, Alabama Theatre Project.

for a move to Atlanta. The group thereafter became a loan company, resettling in Atlanta in the spring of 1937 to become the foundation of the Georgia theater program.[25]

One important component of the Birmingham theater project, the Southern Regional Play Bureau, which opened in August, 1936, outlived the performance company. Its purpose, according to McGee, was the accumulation of "scripts by Southern writers or [those] concerned with a Southern problem," the analysis of novels and short stories, and the adaptation of such materials for stage productions. The bureau employed fewer than a dozen people, but the small staff under editors Frances N. Greene and Lydia Woodcock functioned until all Federal Theater Project operations ceased in 1939. Its most important work was *Altars of Steel*, perhaps the greatest achievement of the southern federal theater. It was a play about the relationship between a benevolent industrialist and his employees.[26]

The Federal Theater Project in Atlanta, as well as the program in New Orleans, received top administrative priority among the southern city projects. In his preliminary regional report in September, 1935, McGee recommended the organization of an Atlanta company "to serve not only the city, but to act as the basic touring unit to serve the winter resort territory." Clearly local theater organizations desired a federal project, most notably the Atlanta Civic Theatre, formed in 1936 specifically for that purpose. Yet the opposition of Shepperson, jealous of her domain, blocked all efforts until late that fall, when the national theater staff finally approved the transfer of the Birmingham project to Atlanta. A handful of Alabama loan actors arrived in December and, combined with a number of jobless local professionals, officially launched the fifty-member Atlanta company in January, 1937.[27]

25. Flanagan to Ralston, October 17, 1936, in FTP, Box 59; Ralston to M. J. Miller, January 12, 1937, Weber to Flanagan, April 29, 1937, Weber to Woodward, January 26, 1938, John Donovan to Flanagan, September 6, 1938, J. H. Miller to Kerr, May 23, 1939, Weber to Lister Hill, July 29, 1939, Kerr to Malcolm J. Miller, August 14, 1939, all in WPA, Alabama Theatre Project; Flanagan, *Arena*, 89.

26. McGee to Flanagan, May 12, 1936 (Box 89), Lentz to Flanagan, December 11, 1937 (Box 90), Report of Play Bureau for the South, November 18, 1936 (Box 24), Ernest Wooten, Narrative Report of Play Bureau . . . to August 16, 1937 (Box 578), all in FTP; McGee to Verner Haldene, July 29, 1936, Weber to McGee, August 1, 1936, Ralston to M. Miller, October 12, 1936, all in WPA, Alabama Theatre Project.

27. McGee to Flanagan, September 27, 1935 (Box 89), Paula Causey to Boggs, August 21, 1936, McGee to Boggs, September 9, 1936, McGee to Lentz, October 29, 1936 (Box 57), all in FTP; Shepperson to Flanagan, March 26, July 8, 1936, McGee to Boggs, July 31, 1936, August Fisher to Robert Enger, October 10, 1936, McGee to Causey, November 4, 1936, Lentz to Flanagan, December 3, 1936, Woodward to Shepperson, December 28, 1936, all in WPA, Georgia Theatre Project.

The Atlanta Federal Theater Project operated without a permanent stage until January, 1938, when the unit moved into the Erlanger Theater. Relief workers cleaned and renovated the building, which had stood dark for several years, and when federal plays were not in production, the stage was available for touring shows. According to Federal Theater Project reports, the occupation of the Erlanger resulted in a twofold gain in road company business and brought such notables as Tallulah Bankhead to Georgia audiences. And while the theater program required no official sponsor, the Atlanta troupe throughout its two-and-one-half-year history cooperated with local professional and amateur theater guilds. The directors also worked at times with local civic organizations because, as one supervisor said, "a sponsored production and performance is the secret of attracting large numbers of people to the theatre and demonstrating the quality of the work we are doing." By the time the project closed in May, 1939, the company had produced thirty-six plays, drawing more than 100,000 people to over 300 performances. No doubt the New Deal effort in Georgia helped establish Atlanta as a theater town.[28]

The Louisiana unit of the Federal Theater Project opened in mid-1936 with the assistance of the New Orleans little theater, the municipal playground commission, Le Petit Théâtre du Vieux Carré, and the city administration, which pledged $500 per year. The New Orleans unit at first shared buildings with amateur groups, but in May, 1937, the troupe transformed its rehearsal and storage barn into a small playhouse, renamed the Federal Theater. The 150-seat facility remained the group's home until mid-1938, when, in conjunction with federal musicians, it moved permanently into the historic St. Charles Theater.[29]

The New Orleans project employed more relief actors and technicians (ranging from 80 to 150 from month to month) than the Atlanta effort, although supervisors in the two cities selected many of the same shows and performance quality was similar. Most plays, such as Sinclair Lewis' *It Can't Happen Here*, were given small-scale productions. Large performances, of such plays as *Altars of Steel* and the exposé of southern poverty *One Third of A Nation*, were rare. In part because of its smaller playhouse, and in part because of competition

28. Lentz to Flanagan, May 15, 1939, in FTP, Box 90; Arthur Lovejoy to J. Howard Miller, October 29, 1938, Lentz to Flanagan, February 16, May 19, 1939, all in WPA, Georgia Theatre Project.

29. Benjamin Yancey to Baker, December 6, 1935, Behre to Flanagan, January 20, 1936, Crutcher to Flanagan, January 29, 1936, Spofford to Flanagan, November 12, 1936, Spofford to Woodward, May 24, 1937, Irene McMullen to Flanagan, June 15, 1939, all in WPA, Louisiana Theatre Project; Robert Lang to Maestri, April 11, 1938, in Robert Maestri Papers, microfilm roll 420B, New Orleans Public Library.

from a variety of local theater groups, the Crescent City's residential company never drew audiences comparable in size to those in Atlanta. During the fall, 1937, season, for example, 52 shows in New Orleans drew about 5,000 people, while 35 performances in the Georgia city attracted about 20,000. Still, Flanagan selected New Orleans in 1938 as southern Federal Theater Project headquarters under regional director Josepf Lentz. Lentz replaced McGee when the Alabamian moved into the national office that same year.[30]

The management of the major Federal Theater Project units, including those in the South, raised a host of problems that required the full attention of theater and WPA supervisors on all administrative levels. The conflicts prevented the complete realization of a national theater constructed on a regional basis. Allegations of radical influence in the federal arts was the greatest problem nationwide, and a congressional investigation of the issue ultimately killed the entire federal theater program. Following a series of inconclusive hearings chaired by Martin Dies, the House Un-American Activities Committee reported that Communists controlled the national theater office and that the large theater projects, particularly the New York City unit, were using the public stage to spread propaganda to sizeable, unsuspecting audiences. Because of the Dies committee report, and faced with organized opposition in Congress by 1939, New Dealers attempted to save as many programs as possible, concludes William Leuchtenburg, by not resisting the dismantlement of some of the controversial ones, including the Federal Theater Project.[31]

More than the Dies committee undermined Federal Theater Project activities. In the South, for example, problems involving play selection and local censorship troubled the theater program. It was not always easy to find shows that were attractive to an audience not used to the legitimate stage and that could also compete successfully with the twenty-five-cent cinema. Relief officials in Louisiana argued that the New Orleans public "comprised the most difficult audience to be found in any city in the United States." Directors often made poor selections, although shows highly recommended by the regional play bureau also received poor responses at times. The consensus among theater personnel, reported Atlanta director Arthur Lovejoy, was that productions for southern

30. McMullen to Lentz, December 23, 1937 (Box 543), Woodward to Crutcher, July 20, November 7, 22, 1938 (Box 57), Lentz to Flanagan, October 30, November 20, 1937 (Box 90), all in FTP; New Orleans *Times-Picayune*, January 31, October 16, 1936.

31. Leuchtenberg, *Franklin D. Roosevelt and the New Deal*, 273. For an analysis of Federal Theater Project activities nationwide that deals at length with the congressional investigation, see Jane DeHart Mathews, *The Federal Theatre, 1935–1939: Plays, Relief and Politics* (Princeton, 1967).

audiences should be limited mainly to comedies and melodramas and that there should be few political, economic, or social theme shows that "take up so much time and thought of men and women in their everyday business, social and family life." Lovejoy also noted, however, that a high drama, which was "supposed to be the type of play that the Atlanta public doesn't like," often outdrew an acclaimed comedy. The city performance chief concluded that he was "at a loss to gauge the likes and tastes of the legitimate theatre audience in this city." In Louisiana, the WPA service chief out of frustration proposed the creation of a local committee of critics to suggest shows for Federal Theater Project productions. The idea won the support of McGee but was never fully accepted among Crescent City theater personnel.[32]

Some shows, no matter how good, never reached the stage at all, while local censors ruled that others be rewritten for southern theatergoers. Haldene in Birmingham submitted all scripts to a city amusement director who, the Federal Theater Project chief there reported, demanded that he select "decent, wholesome matter" and not "dig into the gutter and garbage" for plays. A local ordinance prohibited nudity and partial nudity, as well as vulgar language and any action that might be interpreted as suggestive. On occasion in Atlanta, local police investigated shows for "damaging and incendiary" material. The Atlanta *Constitution* was surprised when police approved *Altars of Steel*, whose plot, the newspaper said, was "scathing in its arraignment of capital and regularly constituted authority" and "packed full of controversial dynamite." Other dramas, such as *One Third of A Nation*, simply failed inspection. Atlanta City Hall ordered the play revised when municipal housing personnel objected to its realistic depiction of slums and poverty in the South. Even in the arts, it seems, the booster creed reigned supreme.[33]

Censors in New Orleans were equally active, canceling Lewis' *It Can't Happen Here* because its leading character, Buzz Windrip, resembled Huey Long. Another incident involved the road show *Tobacco Road*, dramatized by Jack Kirkland. Local clergymen, working through the mayor's office, delayed the production for two weeks, although it had played to packed houses in Dallas and other southern cities.

32. Lovejoy to Lentz, January 25, 1939 (Box 546), Lovejoy to Flanagan, December 8, 1936, McGee to Spofford, December 8, 1936 (Box 57), all in FTP; Spofford to Flanagan, November 25, 1936, in WPA, Louisiana Theatre Project; New Orleans *Times-Picayune*, November 13, 1936.

33. Haldene to Harriet Adams, October 14, 1936, Adams to McGee, November 3, 1936 (Alabama Theatre Project), Lovejoy to Flanagan, February 16, 1938, Lovejoy to J. H. Miller, November 29, 1938 (Georgia Theatre Project), all in WPA; Lovejoy to Lentz, January 25, 1939, in FTP, Box 546; Holmes, "The New Deal in Georgia," 332–36; Atlanta *Constitution*, April 4, 1937.

Crescent City authorities demanded the revision of its language and all "suggestive blasphemies." Even after the rewrite, the New Orleans *States* would not recommend it. Performance quality was excellent, said the newspaper's theater critic, but "while I grant that there may be moronic, degenerate, sex-obsessed, liquor-obsessed, hapless sharecroppers in Georgia and elsewhere in the South, I am not prepared to admit that they are the rule of the majority."[34]

Serious internal conflicts beset the southern Federal Theater Project units as well. Disputes among actors were especially disruptive, with controversies between local professionals and loan actors from other regions being the most common. Ninety percent of Federal Theater Project personnel were relief certified, but the Dixie jobless rolls contained few out-of-work theater professionals with better than mediocre talents. Thus, national officials moved unemployed actors and technicians, in abundance in New York, to the southern cities in an effort to improve performance quality.

The loan policy generated complaints from both sides. Locals charged that New Yorkers received the major parts and then snubbed their fellow actors, while the outsiders complained of unfair treatment from company directors, most of whom were southern born. The validity of such allegations varied. Clearly, there were loan actors who left their homes at great sacrifice and then worked diligently in their new surroundings. Yet others, such as New Yorker Richard Poe, were apparently unhappy with their relocation. Regional supervisor Lentz reported that Pope was a "deadbeat" who "used his entire salary between liquor, women and possibly enough food to keep body and soul together" during his brief tenure in Atlanta.[35]

The Atlanta company depended the most on imported talent. Its director indicated that of twenty-eight native professionals in the program, only four or five could "by any stretch of the imagination be called actors." He urged that the quality of his unit would "improve in ratio to the number of younger and promising actors we are able to get on loan." New Yorkers and locals, however, never worked well together, as the outsiders continually questioned the Atlanta director's methods and techniques. The two sides refused to cooperate even after the Federal Theater Project regional boss gave, as he said, "the entire

34. Ralston to Flanagan, October 15, 1936, in WPA, Louisiana Theatre Project; New Orleans *States*, November 11, 1937; New Orleans *Item*, November 23, 1937.

35. Lentz to J. H. Miller, January 27, 1939, in WPA, Georgia Theatre Project. Also see McGee to Lentz, October 29, 1936, Flanagan to Will Price, February 11, 1937, Van De Vrede to Kerr, February 14, 1939, Joseph Moss to Lentz, March 23, 1939, Moss to J. H. Miller, March 29, 1939, all *ibid.*; Herbert Aston to Flanagan, March 18, 1939, in FTP, Box 89.

project a serious dressing down about directional interpretation of the plays and their job with the Director." The New Orleans program, too, had problems with imported professionals.[36]

Policy conflicts prevailed among company directors, their Federal Theater Project supervisors, and WPA relief officials. In Georgia, for example, state theater chief Sara Thomas disrupted the efforts of the four directors who headed the Atlanta project during its two-year history. She delayed all supply and personnel requests, which likewise ran into opposition of Shepperson. Shepperson especially disliked the relief theater's policy of importing actors. And when Thomas resigned from the state project in 1938, her replacement, Lovejoy, immediately became entangled in a feud with Lentz. The regional chief demanded shows that would be financially successful, while Lovejoy reserved the right to strive for artistic achievement. The city director's failure to coordinate local and loan actors and technicians, as well as his never-ending pleas for additional imports, further upset regional and national administrators. The result was that the Atlanta company, which Lovejoy maintained had earlier alienated the local theater public "by shortsighted business policies and slip-shod amateurish productions," never became a cohesive unit.[37]

Federal Theater Project administrative conflicts in New Orleans were even more serious. During its three-year history, the municipal unit was headed by six different performance directors under the charge of four different state supervisors. Two of the local artists who were directors resigned when they found private employment. Regional officials released three others either for managerial inefficiency or for refusing to cooperate with the state staff of the Federal Theater Project and local theater groups. The sixth New Orleans director, Edward Dillon, took charge in mid-1938, and during the project's final year, show quality and attendance showed slight improvement. Lentz in 1939 selected the Crescent City as one of two proposed consolidated southern theater sites. The other city chosen was Miami. Lentz hoped to strengthen and thus salvage a couple of the

36. McGee to Lentz, November 24, 1936, McGee to Ralston, December 24, 1936 (Box 56), Lovejoy to McGee, December 13, 1937, January 18, 1938 (Box 609), all in FTP; Woodward to Shepperson, February 26, 1937, Lentz to Flanagan, August 5, 1938, Lovejoy to J. H. Miller, November 29, 1938, all in WPA, Georgia Theatre Project; Mathews, *The Federal Theatre*, 181.

37. Lentz to J. H. Miller, October 13, 1938, Lentz to Flanagan, November 1, December 3, 1938, all in FTP, Box 90; Shepperson to Baker, October 31, 1935, McGee to Flanagan, November 4, 1935, Thomas to J. H. Miller, October 20, 1938, Lentz to Flanagan, November 19, 1938, Lovejoy to Flanagan, May 5, 1939 (Georgia Theatre Project), Fisher to Lindeman, October 28, 1936 (Georgia Recreation Projects), all in WPA.

Dixie projects in the wake of the Dies committee investigations, which seemed to suggest reduced federal theater allocations at the least.[38]

The Walter Armitage case was another of the many problems in New Orleans. The official reason for Armitage's dismissal as city director in May, 1938, was his opposition to a combined federal and community production of *One Third of a Nation*. The director's attitude had alienated several civic theater guilds, which the struggling Federal Theater Project could ill afford, but there were additional factors in the decision. Although the best of the local directors, Armitage was not an American citizen, and his appointment violated the Emergency Relief and Construction Act of 1937. Several jobless artists wanted the head job for themselves and thus publicized the issue loudly and frequently. However, the national theater office, impressed with the quality of Armitage's first productions, allowed a private group initially to circumvent the statute by paying the director's salary. Federal examiners concluded in late 1937 that "the FTP in New Orleans is by far more efficiently directed and managed at this time than at any previous time since its inception." More serious than his lack of American citizenship were headlines that surfaced in late 1938 claiming that Armitage had once been charged with a homosexual offense. According to the state relief office, the news raised suspicions that the director was a "moral pervert who uses the project improperly by taking on young boys for his own purposes." The gossip did not cease, even after an investigation led by Flanagan cleared Armitage of all wrongdoing. The result was his quiet release.[39]

In spite of the problems, the federal theater had value in the urban South, bringing shows to audiences that rarely experienced the legitimate stage. Most productions were light comedies, offering more entertainment than deep meaning, but others were rich with symbolism and with specific messages. *It Can't Happen Here* and the regional theme shows *Altars of Steel* and *One Third of a Nation* were examples of the latter. Occasionally, companies considered original productions,

38. Lois Fletcher to McGee, n.d. (Box 57), Lentz to J. H. Miller, September 7, 1937, Lentz to Flanagan, n.d. (Box 546), Lentz to Flanagan, May 7, November 1, 28, 1938, February 14, 23, 1939 (Box 90), all in FTP; Bernard Cravan to Flanagan, January 13, 1937, Cravan to McGee, January 14, 1937, Richard Parker to Woodward, September 28, 1937, Woodward to Crutcher, December 10, 1937, Lentz to Flanagan, June 28, 1938, Parker to Flanagan, February 3, 1939, all in WPA, Louisiana Theatre Project.

39. McMullen to Ernest Bower, September 18, 1937 (Box 542), Ralston to Flanagan, March 28, 1938 (Box 24), both in FTP; Crutcher to Woodward, July 24, 1937, Crutcher to McGee, August 21, 1937, Spofford to Woodward, December 15, 1937, Flanagan, Report on New Orleans Federal Theatre, March 11, 1938, in Woodward to Ralston, March 18, 1938, J. H. Miller to Gerhardt Lindemulder, April 23, 1938, Lentz to Flanagan, May 2, 1938, all in WPA, Louisiana Theatre Project.

such as a modern comedy version of *Romeo and Juliet*, to be staged in New Orleans against a French, Creole, and Italian background. The writer took broad poetic liberties. He had Shakespeare's couple meet in a dance hall, and Juliet's nurse, he indicated, was to be portrayed as "a typical colored mammy." The show was never produced.[40]

For the most part, the local press received the federal plays objectively, if not favorably. The Birmingham *Post* said that the melodrama *After Dark* left open the question of whether the federal program "shall supply us with sound entertainment or mere dramatic boondoggling," yet most productions in Atlanta, Birmingham, and New Orleans were reported to be, at the least, "enjoyable" or "credible." Of course the expertise of southern critics, many of whom had limited experience with professional theater, was not beyond challenge. One writer for the New Orleans *Times-Picayune*, reviewing the classic *Midsummer Night's Dream*, argued boldly that "Shakespeare wrote plays which are good to read but entirely too long to be endured by modern audiences."[41]

Southern federal theater attendance figures were never outstanding, and they declined over the months as the federal project's novelty wore thin. Yet the shows stimulated an interest in and an appreciation of the art among a variety of urban residents. Because productions were inexpensive and there was a liberal free pass policy, audiences consisted of low- as well as middle- and high-income men and women. In a report of the Atlanta opening of *Altars of Steel*, one observer noted that women in evening gowns and fine jewelry sat next to men dressed in overalls who were asleep when the curtain went up. Once the action began, the reporter continued, everyone in attendance was "absorbed, excited, by a play whose significance for them was as far apart as the quality of their external garments." The same Atlanta theatergoer concluded that the Federal Theater Project created "a valuable consciousness of our city as a community, a valuable consciousness of the possibilities of a community organization of great recreational and educational value."[42]

Each project developed a small following that assisted in the promotion of shows among the general public. Federal Theater Project

40. Bernard Szold to William Farnsworth, July 2, 1936 (Box 86), Calender Report of Birmingham FTP, February 24–August 3, 1936 (Box 76), both in FTP.

41. Birmingham *Post*, May 13, October 28, 1936; Birmingham *News*, May 13, 25, October 8, 1936; Atlanta *Constitution*, November 12, 1936; Atlanta *Journal of Labor*, April 2, May 28, July 23, 1937; New Orleans *Times-Picayune*, April 5, May 15, 1936, October 27, 1937.

42. Lovejoy to Flanagan, January 11, 1939, in FTP, Box 89; Martha Ellis to Richard Job, n.d. (Appraisal Reports: Georgia), Lovejoy to J. H. Miller, October 29, 1938 (Georgia Theatre Project), both in WPA.

supporters in New Orleans were especially vocal. When Congress ordered the project closed in mid-1939, Crescent City theater backers, with the support of Mayor Maestri and the city press, organized a mass rally to protest the termination of WPA arts programs. Newspaper editorials argued that project benefits far outweighed the cost, which was 3 percent of the total relief budget. The Atlanta theater had enthusiastic boosters as well, including the daily newspapers, city authorities, the municipal arts council, and the chamber of commerce.[43]

Despite similar support in Memphis and throughout western Tennessee, the Federal Theater Project was never active there. Theater activities in Memphis, as in the other southern cities before the advent of Federal Project Number 1, were amateur productions presented in community centers and parks under the direction of WPA service personnel. Regional officials did not oppose a professional troupe in Memphis; in late 1935 Flanagan gave southern supervisor McGee a free hand "to approve or disapprove, on the basis of their artistic integrity and social desirability, projects calling for the employment of actors in the state of Tennessee." At the invitation of city newspapers and local theatergoers, McGee visited Memphis in November, 1935, but found the talent insufficient to support the organization of a professional company. He indicated that perhaps unemployed actors and directors in congested areas might someday be relocated in Memphis, but that was never to be. One later effort was led by the Memphis Civic Negro Theater Committee to acquire a black federal theater project, but that request was never seriously considered.[44]

Where programs did exist, federal theater clientele became the basis of a future theatergoing public. Furthermore, beginning in the late 1930s and continuing thereafter, the southern cities began attracting increasing numbers of road productions largely owing to a demand for theater stimulated by federal efforts. According to Lentz, when the federal program moved into Atlanta, the city was "notoriously a bad legitimate show town"; yet the project successfully reestablished the New South capital as an attractive stop for touring companies. At the same time, federal theater activity generated an interest in local professional and amateur productions. In the Georgia city, at least four new theater groups appeared in the 1930s, the most important being the Players' Club and the Theater Guild. In the other Dixie cities, little

43. New Orleans *Times-Picayune*, June 23–28, 1939; Flanagan, *Arena*, 86–87.
44. Will Lawo to Flanagan, September 10, 1935, Lawo to WPA Federal Allotment Board, September 10, 1935, Flanagan to McGee, October 14, 1935, Baker to Berry, January 13, 1936, Virtis Reese to Director of Negro Theatre Project, October 25, 1936, McGee to Reese, November 4, 1936, all in WPA, Tennessee Theatre Project; McGee to Harry Martin, November 9, 1935, in FTP, Box 57.

theaters, university performance units, and other local organizations established longer seasons, and their shows drew larger audiences than ever before. Civic theater organizations also learned new and modern techniques in set design and costuming that were invaluable as the live stage competed with the ever-popular cinema.[45]

The southern projects also supported extension work throughout small towns and rural counties adjacent to the urban areas. Touring groups took legitimate shows on the road, and radio units produced dramas designed especially for individuals without access to a lighted stage. The traveling troupe from Atlanta covered more than six thousand miles in two years—more area than was covered by any other southern company. Furthermore, national theater officials selected Georgia for an experimental drama-consultant project. State theater administrator Herbert Price organized the venture, and in January, 1937, he sent drama specialists to Albany, Augusta, Savannah, Columbus, and Rome, as well as Atlanta. According to Price, the program sponsored plays that would "draw color and background from the life and desires and ambitions of the community itself." Equally important, he argued, was the encouragement of maximum participation so that "audiences and groups will work and grow together—the entire community playing an active role—truly a theatre of, by and for the people." The project lasted only six months as a separate service—administrators ultimately integrated it with the WPA—but many of its neighborhood drama clubs became permanent within municipal recreation programs.[46]

Finally, the residential companies established separate units responsible for performance matinees for young people. The New Orleans marionette troupe, for example, employed a dozen men to make puppets and write and produce shows for the entertainment of area youngsters. The Crescent City unit, as well as the Atlanta project, also contained vaudeville groups that toured small towns, Civilian Conservation Corps (CCC) camps, and places such as Pine Mountain Valley, an experimental self-help community in Georgia. And when relief actors were not in rehearsal, they joined their counterparts in the

45. McGee to Flanagan, March 16, 1937 (Box 24), Thomas to W. L. Ternell, n.d. (Box 609), Lovejoy to Lentz, January 25, 1939 (Box 654), Lentz to Flanagan, May, 1939 (Box 90), all in FTP; Leon Weiss to Crutcher, May 9, 1938, in Robert Maestri Papers, microfilm roll 420B; Flanagan, *Arena*, 84–91; Birmingham *Post*, July 8, 1936; Atlanta *Journal of Labor*, July 2, 1937; New Orleans *Times-Picayune*, May 15, 1939.

46. Price to Eugene Bergman, November 21, December 17, 1936, in FTP, Box 444; Price to Lucy McIntyre, December 28, 1936 (Georgia Theatre Project), Meyer to M. Miller, March 1, 1937, Fisher to Ringe, April 21, 1937 (Georgia Recreation Projects), Report on New Orleans Federal Theatre Project, December 2, 1938 (Louisiana Theatre Project), all in WPA; Holmes, "The New Deal in Georgia," 336.

music project, conducting drama and dance workshops in schools and community centers. Each of these special groups contributed to the overall federal theater effort by demonstrating the versatility of the stage while promoting an appreciation of the legitimate theater.[47]

The New Deal arts programs in the South helped the major cities achieve a sense of cultural maturity. Performance quality varied, and problems from outside as well as from inside the communities often prevented the maximum utilization of available talent. Nevertheless, troupes of relief artists gave more than occasional shows, as they circulated in schools and community centers, and among other civic organizations. As a result, local music, art, and drama guilds of both amateur and professional quality appeared. Equally significant, the new community groups, whether the New Orleans Philharmonic Society or the Atlanta Theater Guild, became permanent urban institutions. Clearly, the federal effort helped generate a greater public demand for the arts, because the new theater societies and municipal orchestras would have never survived in later years without continued community support.

47. Szold to Farnsworth, June 16, 1936 (Box 24), McGee to Flanagan, September, 1936, Fletcher to McGee, December 11, 1936 (Box 56), Lentz to Flanagan, September 24, 1938 (Box 90), all in FTP; Haldene to McGee, July 9, 1936 (Alabama Theatre Project), Lentz to W. T. Bennett, September 17, 1938 (Georgia Theatre Project), both in WPA; Birmingham *News*, August 23, 1936; New Orleans *Times-Picayune*, July 22, 1937.

12

BLACK COMMUNITIES MOBILIZE

Unlike their counterparts in some rural areas throughout the South, urban blacks were not excluded systematically from the New Deal. City residents were sometimes cut from public payrolls and forced into jobs in nearby cotton fields, but vigilante activity directed against Negro relief workers was infrequent. The municipal leadership's quest for stability and continued social order dictated that blacks be offered a share of available federal programs, especially as many whites moved into jobs previously held by blacks. In 1938, Mayor Hartsfield of Atlanta expressed his concern for the order of things while vetoing a council resolution that only whites be eligible for jobs on a WPA-funded sewerage construction project. The mayor noted that if the city neglected black labor, "We would have millions of negroes on our hands, and the political and economic situation arising thereby would set up a demand for national action." He went on to suggest that "surely if there is any place for the negro on our city payroll it would be at the place where sewerage is treated." The council subsequently sustained the veto, but by a single vote.[1]

Clearly, the economic crisis of the 1930s affected blacks in the southern cities more adversely than it did whites. Federal officials in New Orleans in mid-decade boasted that black families represented 65 percent of the total number of relief families while making up only 50 percent of the total number of local jobless. They omitted the fact that blacks accounted for less than 31 percent of the total number of households in the city. The steady increase in the black-to-white ratio

1. Atlanta City Council Minutes, XXXVIII, February 7, 1938, p. 195, City Hall, Atlanta.

on relief suggests that whites went to the front of the reemployment lines. During the 1937-1938 "aftershock" recession, the southern cities reported between 63 and 81 percent of working-age blacks on relief, and in June, 1940, nearly 15 percent of the black work force in New Orleans remained unemployed. Of those in private employment, half earned less than $500 annually.[2]

The color line in the private sector faded throughout the depression period. Sometimes the low-paying, formerly black jobs were lost forever to whites—a trend that would leave many whites economically subordinate to the small black middle class. Changes in traditional employment patterns did not win universal approval. Birmingham labor leaders, for example, reacted angrily when white college students moved into previously all-black jobs during a strike of cafeteria workers in 1934. The "cultured college students as so termed . . . should feel more than proud of their rotten effort," cried union boss William Dalrymple, who objected to strikebreaking activities in general and to efforts to cross racial job barriers. He concluded that "they will live to regret the day they ever took a negro striker's job [which] will haunt [them] to [their] dying days."[3]

Although blacks were included in the New Deal programs, urban whites clearly received preferential treatment in work and direct relief during the FERA and CWA years. When Forrester B. Washington of Atlanta resigned as FERA director of Negro affairs in mid-1934, he was in part referring to home when he concluded that "the way colored people have suffered under the New Deal through the CWA is . . . a disgrace that stinks to heaven." The Atlanta *Daily World* expressed a similar thought in September, 1935: "Under the FERA the Negro was shown the same place assigned to him at the close of the Civil War, which had for seventy years . . . sealed his illiteracy and poverty." Later WPA programs offered greater opportunities, yet blacks rarely gained more than the lowest wages and unskilled positions. The small number of white-collar emergency jobs open to them actually decreased late in the decade, when federal authorities ordered local sponsors to procure public building space to house such projects.[4]

2. Gaston, "A History of the Negro Wage Earner," 379–81, 493; Katharine D. Wood and Gladys L. Palmer (comps.), *Urban Workers on Relief: The Occupational Characteristics of Workers on Relief in 79 Cities, May 1934* (2 vols.; Washington, D.C., 1934), I, 70; Parris and Brooks, *Blacks in the City*, 238; New Orleans Urban League, "A Report of the Community Conference on Employment and Employment Opportunities for Negroes in New Orleans" (Typescript in New Orleans Public Library, 1945), 14.

3. Birmingham *Labor Advocate*, June 2, 1934; Allison Davis and Burleigh B. and Mary R. Gardner, *Deep South: A Social and Anthropological Study of Caste and Class* (Chicago, 1941), 261–62.

4. Atlanta *Daily World*, September 1, 1935; *Louisiana Weekly*, August 18, 1934;

There were no black office and administrative personnel, and few black investigative caseworkers were employed. The New Orleans ERA office would not employ Negro clerks, typists, or stenographers, despite director Henry F. Burt's promise that "there shall be no discrimination toward any race or religion during my administration." Of the 250 caseworkers in the Crescent City in late 1934, only 38 were black; the Atlanta ERA office was operating with 71 caseworkers for 42,000 whites on relief and 57 field investigators for more than 52,000 blacks on relief. Rarely was there more than a handful of black supervisors in any city, even within the NYA, with its active division of Negro affairs. The Memphis area NYA director flatly refused a NAACP request that he hire a black assistant, saying that "so long as there are white people who need work I will not recommend a negro for the place."[5]

Public housing under the New Deal also did not solve fundamental problems for blacks, notwithstanding Gunnar Myrdal's observation in *An American Dilemma* that the New Deal slum clearance effort extended to blacks "a better deal than has any other major federal public welfare agency." The poor were increasingly clustered in inner-city areas; minimum earnings guidelines disqualified those most in need, including relief labor; and units set in black residential areas reinforced existing patterns of segregation. When black units fell too near white neighborhoods, legal action taken to separate residential sites often caused construction to be delayed or halted outright. Such was the case in Birmingham when white opponents secured a court injunction against a proposed $2.3 million black housing project at Brown's Hill, referred to in the legal petition as a "negro nuisance." Whites living in dilapidated homes apparently opposed having black neighbors residing in modern housing. They demanded the adoption of the South's "green belt" plan, as it was called in Atlanta; indeed, Birmingham authorities boasted of setting out shrubbery "so as to cut off the view as well as access between the zones." Naturally, white managers directed most black units, and while black projects equaled the white units in terms of modern conveniences and tenant programs, far more blacks than whites lived on slum properties. Federal studies at the end of the decade showed that between 46 and 60 percent of black

Reginald Johnson to Alfred E. Smith, July 20, 1937, in Record Group 69, Records of the Works Progress Administration, Georgia File, National Archives, hereinafter cited as WPA.

5. James Gayle to Henry F. Burt, February 12, 1935 (Box G-82), Grace Hamilton to Walter White, April 8, 1936 (Box G-199), both in Records of the National Association for the Advancement of Colored People, Box G-82, Library of Congress; *Louisiana Weekly*, June 30, July 7, 1934; Atlanta *Daily World*, February 9, August 3, 1934.

residents in the urban South lived in substandard structures. The range for whites was between 14 and 22 percent.[6]

Even the involvement of black workers in the expanded labor movement, including the CIO, was limited. It seems that the new industrial unions recruited blacks mainly in those manufacturing operations in which they accounted for a substantial percentage of the total work force. In the Atlanta area automobile plants, where blacks were a minority, UAW affiliates achieved bargaining status and then for years thereafter maintained a "whites only" policy. In the Birmingham steel mills, if not in other large industrial operations, substantial wage differentials between skilled and unskilled workers and traditional segregated job assignments, which put blacks in blind-alley positions with no hope of promotion, kept benefits from being equal. Black workers in the early 1940s led two Birmingham steel firms out of the CIO and into the AFL because it was promising the reclassification of jobs and the opening of new, colorblind apprenticeship programs. Of course such AFL counteractivity among blacks, often for the first time ever, did not change the fact that nearly all AFL locals remained segregated. Included were affiliates of the longshoreman's union in New Orleans, whose black leaders openly preferred segregated locals and racial quotas for job assignments. The bosses were protecting their own power, but they also feared that without quotas blacks would have a much harder time getting work on the Gulf Coast waterfronts. Blacks in traditional craft unions fared little better, often depending solely on the availability of PWA and federal slum clearance work, which had established racial guidelines for skilled labor.[7]

Likewise, while black neighborhoods in the cities benefited from WPA service and construction work, in no way did facilities or programs reach levels comparable with those available for whites. Health facilities in Atlanta, perhaps the most progressive of the four cities in question, revealed the inequity. As of 1936, blacks accounted for 35 percent of that city's population but had access to less than 20 percent of available hospital beds — half of what the United States Public Health Service judged adequate. There was only one black physician for each

6. Gunnar Myrdal, *An American Dilemma: The Negro Problem and Modern Democracy* (New York, 1944), 350; Paul Pearson, "Federal Housing Projects for Negroes," *Southern Workman*, LXV (December, 1936), 371–79; Charles R. Palmer, *The Adventures of a Slum Fighter* (Atlanta, 1955), 249–52; Wynn to R. S. Marshall, January 4, 1936, in James M. Jones, Jr., Collection, Drawer 2, Alabama Archives and History, Montgomery; Sterner, *The Negro's Share*, 190–98; Atlanta *Daily World*, March 13, 1937, January 26, 1938, December 6, 1939.

7. Herbert R. Northrup, "The Negro and the United Mine Workers of America," *Southern Economic Journal*, IX (April, 1943), 326, and *Organized Labor and the Negro*, 29–37, 182–83; Tindall, *The Emergence of the New South*, 572–73; Marshall, *Labor in*

group of 3,300 residents—37 in all—and fewer than 10 black dentists and not even 100 registered nurses. Tax-supported Grady Hospital had no black interns or residents on its staff, and not one hospital in the city offered postgraduate training to black doctors.[8]

Conditions were similar in education, despite the many WPA- and PWA-built schools and adult literacy extension programs for both races. Municipal and federal authorities set aside work relief funds for black schools after first considering white applications, and even in late 1936, when PWA benefits for black schools showed an increase, it was found that "as usual this occurred after the spending had reached its apex." By the mid-1940s in Atlanta, blacks composed nearly 40 percent of the city's total number of schoolchildren but had use of only 13 of 65 school buildings—half of a school per 1,000 children in the school age population. Less than 16 percent of the city's yearly expenditures for education went to black schools and programs. Until the opening of Birmingham's Carver High in 1937, the nearly 3,000 students enrolled at Negro Industrial High School, accredited only in 1929, represented half of all black secondary students in Alabama. Some questioned the necessity of a well-rounded school curriculum for blacks. A study of public schools in New Orleans in 1941 concluded that "the preponderance of subjects assigned to teachers such as english, mathematics, social studies and science belies any feeling that the negro secondary education was intended to prepare negro youth for the life they may expect."[9]

the South, 150–51, 188; Robert Weaver, "Racial Employment Trends in National Defense," Phylon, II (Fourth Quarter, 1941), 337–58; Northrup, The Negro in the Automobile Industry, Racial Policies of American Industry Series (Philadelphia, 1968), 17; Ray Marshall, "The Negro in Southern Unions," in Julius Jacobson (ed.), The Negro and the American Labor Movement (Garden City, 1968), 149; Hollis Lynch, The Black Urban Condition: A Documentary History, 1866–1971 (New York, 1973), 215–16; Reports of the Executive Secretary of the Atlanta Urban League, January, September, 1935, January, November, 1937, December, 1939, all in Atlanta Urban League Files, Atlanta Urban League Office.

8. Thomas Deaton, "Atlanta During the Progressive Era" (Ph.D. dissertation, University of Georgia, 1969), 215–16; Atlanta Urban League, "A Report on Hospital Care of the Negro Population of Atlanta, Georgia" (Typescript in Atlanta Urban League Files, Atlanta, 1944), 8–9.

9. Lewis J. Todd, "Development of Public Secondary Education in New Orleans, 1914–1941" (M.A. thesis, Tulane University, 1941), 105; Ambrose Caliver, "The Largest Negro High School," School Life, XVII (December, 1931), 73; Robert Weaver, "The PWA School Building Program and Separate Negro Schools," Journal of Negro Education, VII (July, 1938), 373–74; Atlanta Urban League, "A Report of Public School Facilities for Negroes in Atlanta, Georgia, 1944" (Typescript in Atlanta Urban League Files, 1944), 6–9.

In parks and recreational services, blacks failed to benefit even minimally. The lack of adequate community centers and recreational activities, it seems, did not threaten the overall health and welfare of a municipality as did the lack of medical treatment centers. A few new facilities in Birmingham opened in the late 1930s, such as the Slossfield Youth Center, operated by WPA and NYA workers in conjunction with the Slossfield Health Center. When federal recreation programs ended in the early 1940s, however, planned activities in the Negro centers all but ceased. Municipal funds employed no black recreation personnel. Even in Atlanta, where one-third of the 26 WPA-supervised recreation programs operated for Negroes, only Washington Park (17 acres) out of 60 community parks (1,323 acres) was open for Negro use; and it was not located within two miles of any of the largest black residential areas. Negroes had the use of only 5 of 75 municipal tennis courts and only one 9-hole golf course (11 courses for whites). The value of black park property was $40,000, while that of white property was more than $3 million. Atlanta city councilmen in 1940 adopted the Grant Park law, prohibiting blacks from "frequenting or even appearing at any park . . . designated for whites."[10]

The story of black recreational facilities in New Orleans was even worse. Under early FERA and CWA direction, several Negro playgrounds equal to white areas opened, but that changed after 1935 because the Maestri administration focused mainly on City Park and Audubon Park. Neither was open to blacks. Furthermore, work on the Lake Pontchartrain development project, which resulted in a new housing subdivision and a new beach with picnic grounds, forced the closing of the one-and-one-half-mile Negro beach (Seabrook) on the lake. When blacks protested the closing, WPA and municipal authorities cosponsored a $150,000 alternative lake site, which federal investigators reported was inaccessible to 90 percent of the black population. Known as Little Woods, the new one-mile lakefront park was situated fourteen miles from the corporate limits, with the nearest bus line being five miles from most Negro residential sections. In addition, concluded the same report, "A railroad and an open sewer have to be crossed to gain access to the lake," and "snakes, mosquitos and even alligators infest this section, and even the Negroes with cars are afraid to frequent it."[11]

10. Report on Recreation in Fulton and DeKalb Counties, December 5, 1939, and Report of George W. Willingham, n.d., in Records of the Commission on Interracial Cooperation, Box 17-C-4-a, Trevor Arnett Library, Atlanta University; Atlanta *Constitution*, March 14, 1939; Atlanta *Daily World*, April 22, 1934, January 20, February 14, 1936, June 5, 1939; Birmingham *World*, October 4, 1940; Birmingham *News*, January 5, 1936.

11. S. C. Mays to President Roosevelt, July 5, 1939, and Crutcher to Ernest Marbury,

Even what seemed an exception in recreation-connected programs was not. A handful of experimental arts projects for blacks began in mid-decade, but few survived more than a year and there was a noticeable absence of official municipal support or white patronage. In New Orleans, the Federal Music Project sponsored two small bands for blacks, giving temporary employment to a few musicians who in normal times played in the French Quarter clubs. As well, all of the main Federal Music Project concert units included black schools on their schedules, and blacks obtained several of the federal program's teaching positions bringing music education into schools and Negro community centers. But neither the Memphis nor the Atlanta nor the Birmingham program included jobless blacks—only WPA-sponsored community choirs, which gave periodic concerts. When Atlantan Graham Jackson, a personal friend of President Roosevelt, attempted to obtain a black concert orchestra for his city, he noted that "there is not one single medium of educating the masses to appreciate the finer types of music." Despite Jackson's appeal that he was "just as interested in raising the cultural standard as [in] obtaining financial relief," Washington, D.C., was unmoved.[12]

There were black units of the Federal Theater Project in three of the cities in question, but their success was not great. In Birmingham, the Negro program never found a permanent stage and thus shared facilities with the dramatics department at Negro Industrial High School. The troupe had its own director, a white man, who during the experiment's 9-month tenure produced regional dramas of Negro life all set to work songs and spirituals. A similar program in New Orleans barely lasted a month. The one show produced, a 261-member-cast extravaganza of Paul Green's *Roll Sweet Chariot*, included no unemployed black professionals, although available. According to white Federal Theater Project officials, the entire effort "was mucked up from the beginning by putting it into a house where they had no segregated

August 14, 1939, both in WPA, Louisiana Park Projects; New Orleans *Times-Picayune*, February 15, 1938; *Louisiana Weekly*, February 23, 1935, January 9, 1937, February 19, June 9, 1938, January 14, 1939; New Orleans *Item*, July 9, 1939; *Sepia Socialite* (New Orleans), January 14, 1939; Frank E. Lindahl, Jr., "Functions of New Orleans City Government" (M.A. thesis, Tulane University, 1940), 70.

12. Jackson to Van De Vrede, Jackson to Woodward, March 29, 1937, Jackson to Hopkins, May 9, 1937, J. W. Dobbs to Shepperson, March 8, 1938, Woodward to Shepperson, April 20, 1938 (Georgia Music Project), Alabama Music Project Report, November, 1941 (Alabama Music Project), Report of the Conductor of Birmingham Negro Music Project, March, 1937 (Alabama Service Project), all in WPA; Salomon, Louisiana FMP Report for November, 1938, in WPA; Federal Project No. 1, Records of the Federal Music Project, Louisiana Narrative Reports; McDonald, *Federal Relief Administration*, 614.

section." The sponsor had used "the wrong type of Negro," the report concluded, "very swanky ones, who refused to enter into the spirit of the thing."[13]

Poor attendance and a lack of skilled actors plagued black units throughout the South. National administrators did not hurry to loan professionals to build the black programs as they did in support of the southern white groups. This caused the few legitimate shows, such as the Atlanta unit's production of Eugene O'Neill's *The Emperor Jones*, to be amateurish at best. Still, Atlanta Federal Theater Project personnel continued to seek an expanded Negro project, arguing that "there is so much that is comic, and at the same time, so much that is tragic in [the black's] simple, unpretentious life." Similarly, the Dillard University faculty in New Orleans pleaded on several occasions for a permanent theater troupe sponsored, together with the handful of art classes, through the Federal Art Project. The answer never changed; national personnel even refused to support a proposed Negro theater-teaching program like those operating successfully in Tampa, Jacksonville, Durham, and Raleigh.[14]

The separate and unequal operation of nearly all New Deal programs fostered the self-help and accommodationist tradition within the southern urban black communities. According to Howard Rabinowitz's provocative study, urban blacks in the late nineteenth century came to rely on their own social and economic institutions, which also coordinated the few communitywide programs in black neighborhoods, as an alternative under Jim Crow to outright exclusion. Blacks in the early years of the depression decade also attempted to ease the economic downturn under the self-help banner. A number of separate

13. Haldene, Narrative Report for Birmingham Theatre Project, November 15, 1936 (Box 86), Smoot to McGee, June 20, 1936, McGee to Clyde Limbaugh, August 15, November 5, 1936, McGee to Munsell, November 5, 1936 (Box 56), Behre to McGee, February 27, 1936, Fletcher to McGee, n.d. (Box 57), Semi-Monthly Report of Louisiana FTP, June 15, 1936 (Box 79), all in WPA, Federal Project No. 1, Records of the Federal Theater Project, hereinafter cited as FTP; McGee to Farnsworth, March 26, 1936, Ivan Paul to Farnsworth, April 10, 1938 (Alabama Theatre Project), Limbaugh to Flanagan, December 9, 1936 (Alabama Service Project), Randolph Edmonds to Flanagan, November 4, 1935, Behre to Hiram Motherwell, June 3, 1936, William Nelson to Flanagan, July 6, 1938 (Louisiana Theatre Project), all in WPA; Alan Kifer, "The Negro Under the New Deal, 1933–1941" (Ph.D. dissertation, University of Wisconsin, 1961), 249–50.

14. Extension Division of the Federal Theatre for Negroes, Atlanta, Georgia, n.d., in WPA, Georgia Theatre Project; William Nelson to Thomas Parker, November 17, 1937 (Box 37), Robert Andrews to Caroline Durieux, May 29, 1939 (Box 49), both in WPA, Federal Project No. 1, Federal Art Project Records; Joseph Christmas, Report on the Negro Unit, in J. H. Miller to Flanagan, January 18, 1939, in FTP, Box 546; Ronald Ross, "The Role of Blacks in the Federal Theatre, 1935–1939," *Journal of Negro History*, LIX (January, 1947), 43.

relief committees in Atlanta, for example, joined forces in October, 1931, to form the Atlanta Colored Committee on Unemployment Relief to funnel funds to jobless blacks first from the Family Welfare Service of the community chest and later from a city-sponsored relief agency. Black organizations affiliated with the community chest likewise broadened their activities, although the chest allocated only 10 percent of its budget each year to the black community, arguing that blacks contributed less than 3 percent of its annual pledges. In Memphis, black leaders in 1932 established the Community Welfare League, which later became the city's National Urban League affiliate.[15]

Black store owners and professionals also made efforts to coordinate activities. Memphis blacks in 1931 organized the Negro Business and Civic Association to help retailers through the depressed times and to join forces with white businessmen who were having similar troubles. In Atlanta, the new Colored Merchants' Association, formed in 1932, brought small black grocers together—a tactic adopted in Birmingham as well in conjunction with that city's increasingly active branch of the Negro Business League. In New Orleans and Atlanta, offices of the Negro Business League opened during the 1930s with the goal of making black businesses more efficient and thus more profitable. Apparently, such self-help strategies were effective, at least in part, although Jim Crow's survival throughout the period ensured the continued presence of a "captive" clientele. The number of black-owned businesses in the southern cities and their sales were 33 percent higher in 1939 than they had been twenty years earlier.[16]

Even the New Deal agency considered the least biased toward blacks, the NYA, reinforced traditional socioeconomic patterns. The NYA Negro youth training centers offered few extras, such as gymnasiums and swimming pools, as did their counterparts for white men and women. Some young blacks received instruction in mechanical skills, ranging from automotive repairs to machine-tool work; yet the Birmingham project, according to NYA reports, involved training

15. Howard N. Rabinowitz, *Race Relations in the Urban South, 1865–1890* (1978; rpr. Urbana, 1980), 332; Report on Atlanta, n.d., in National Urban League Records, Box IV-27, Library of Congress; Service Report of the Acting Secretary, December 20, 1930, and memorandum to the Family Section of the Social Welfare Council, November 1, 1932, both in Atlanta Urban League Files; Louis Delphia Davis Shivery, "The History of Organized Social Work Among Atlanta Negroes, 1890–1935" (M.A. thesis, Atlanta University, 1936), 350; Atlanta *Daily World*, March 18, September 16, 1932; Memphis *World*, September 6, 1932.

16. Garrett, *Atlanta and Environs*, III, 900; Atlanta *Daily World*, January 8, May 22, 1932, June 2, 1934; Birmingham *World*, September 27, 1940; Wallace N. Leedell, "The Negro in Louisiana Since 1900: An Economic and Social Study" (Ph.D. dissertation, New York University, 1959), 66.

mainly in landscaping, domestic service, homemaking, laundry work, clerical work, and other traditional "fields open to Negro youth in this locality." NYA and WPA personnel also aided in the operation of locally funded trade schools for blacks, such as the Memphis Practical Trade School, opened in 1938 with the cooperation of local Negro colleges and materials donated from local business firms. Likewise, in Atlanta the combined resources of several agencies and individuals, including a number of white philanthropists who secured financing from the Julius Rosenwald Fund in Chicago, led to the establishment of the Negro Occupational and Trade School in 1937. The Atlanta *Daily World* reported that the program would train young blacks "for a new efficiency and trustworthiness" in gardening, cooking, housekeeping, janitorial work, hotel service, and "those occupations which all along have been open to them as their undisputed fields of service."[17]

Training for black women was almost exclusively in the domestic fields. A maids' school in Memphis, opened in 1936 for WPA and NYA eligibles, put Negro women to work each day under a large banner reminding them that "dishwashing is an ancient art but few are proficient at it." The city press praised the program, which it said offered "everything that goes to make a well-rounded servant." In New Orleans, where WPA officials once reported that "our biggest problem here is the employment of unskilled women, particularly the negroes," the Household Workers Training Program became so popular that the city employment service could not fill all requests for domestic help from the list of "graduates."[18]

Black colleges in the southern cities steadily expanded community services during the depression and New Deal decade, sometimes on their own but often in conjunction with Urban League or NAACP programs. In New Orleans, a unique penny-a-day health insurance plan was made available largely through the efforts of newly established Dillard University. The school opened in 1932, primarily the result of the work of Will Alexander and other white philanthropists, successfully consolidating the resources of Flint-Goodridge Hospital, New Orleans University, and Straight College. Hospital officials administered the insurance program, which was not made entirely free so

17. Atlanta *Daily World*, October 8, 1936, April 12, 1938; National Youth Administration, WPA Application No. 84-1, in James M. Jones, Jr., Collection, Drawer 2; NYA of Georgia, *Report on the NYA of Georgia* (Atlanta, 1939), 4–7; Atlanta *Constitution*, July 4, 1943; *Louisiana Weekly*, December 19, 1936, December 10, 1938; Birmingham *News*, November 21, 1941.

18. Memphis *Press-Scimitar*, March 21, 1935, March 27, 1937; Memphis *Commercial Appeal*, March 11, 1935; Edna Brenan to Woodward, September 10, 1935, April 10, 1936, in WPA, Louisiana Women's Projects; Kifer, "The Negro Under the New Deal," 103-11.

as to promote some sense of responsibility among the clientele. One cent each day qualified the insured for twenty-one days of hospitalization each year. By 1939, the plan reported a surplus, which, when combined with Julius Rosenwald Fund grants, paid for new medical equipment and allowed the hospital to lower its clinic fees from twenty-five to ten cents a visit. Also important was federal funding, which covered the entire cost of training programs. The operation later earned the highest rating granted by the American College of Surgeons. By the end of the decade, the college had expanded the overall facility to include ten separate clinics, all directed by blacks with the cooperation of physicians from Tulane and Louisiana State University.[19]

The Atlanta School of Social Work, which became affiliated with Atlanta University in the 1930s, obtained substantial FERA funding to service black communities throughout the region. Directed by Forrester Washington, president of the city's NAACP branch as well, the school by 1937 was assisting with the Urban League's annual Vocational Opportunity Campaign to direct the "attention of Negro youth to a more positive consideration of the vast problem of vocations." Unlike NYA and WPA training schools, the campaign went well beyond domestic work, promoting the nontraditional fields of engineering, law, journalism, chemical research, social work, and architecture. Throughout Georgia, there was only one black lawyer for every 76,507 blacks, compared to one white lawyer for every 655 whites.[20]

The broadening of the Atlanta Urban League's Vocational Opportunity Campaign was indicative of a new vitality among some organizations and individuals in the 1930s in promoting the interests of the black community. Throughout the country, according to the studies of Robert Brisbane and Nancy Weiss, Urban League branches exerted themselves for the first time both "consistently and effectively," beginning with efforts in 1933 to ensure the Negro's inclusion in New Deal programs. Urban League offices soon expanded their activities, working especially with racially mixed CIO labor affiliates and private employers through more than two hundred emergency councils and workers' councils established throughout the nation. Also through the Emergency Advisory Council (EAC) network, which southern field representative Jesse O. Thomas called "an agency of Negroes for

19. Claire and George S. Perry, "Penny-A-Day Hospital," *Saturday Evening Post,* September 2, 1939, pp. 30, 67–68; Wilma Dykeman and James Stokeley, *Seeds of Southern Change: The Life of Will Alexander* (Chicago, 1962), 171–77; *Crisis* (July, 1933), 151–53; New Orleans *Times-Picayune,* January 31, 1932.

20. Quarterly Report of the Executive Secretary, January, February, March, 1937, March, 1938, in Atlanta Urban League Files, Atlanta *Daily World,* June 19, 1934, March 25, 1937; *Crisis* (September, 1938), 284; Parris and Brooks, *Blacks in the City,* 218.

Negroes," Urban League groups began adopting new mass-pressure strategies, hoping to raise black consciousness and pride, particularly among the young. Forrester Washington concluded in 1943 that recent Urban League efforts had advanced the black community's awareness of employment and job training problems and that it was time to devote energy to areas of social concern, including substandard housing, inadequate recreational facilities, delinquencies, and family and community disorganization.[21] And clearly Urban League branches in the South—the revitalized Atlanta office and new branches in New Orleans, Memphis, and other cities—expanded significantly in the 1940s because of a readiness dating from their depression-era experiences.

One of only two Urban League branches in the major southern cities as of 1930, the Atlanta office early in the decade sponsored an EAC composed of representatives from several civic organizations. Its task was to investigate the various recovery and relief agencies and report inequities directly to federal officials and demand adjustments. A workers' council, one of forty-three in the nation, was also organized to assist blacks seeking to form and, mainly, to join unions under Wagner guarantees. Adding social workers to its field staff for the first time, and in cooperation with the Atlanta University School of Social Work (the only such school of its kind in the country exclusively for blacks), the Atlanta league secured a chapter of the Vocational Guidance Association, launched an annual Negro Health Week that survived the period, and assumed the directorship of the area's longstanding Neighborhood Club Union. The Neighborhood Club Union had coordinated social service endeavors among blacks since 1908 under the leadership of its founder, Mrs. John Hope, who resigned in 1935 because of ill health. Under league guidance, the union added individual neighborhood groups and established a preschool clinic, a kindergarten project, and two orphanages. In addition, it engaged in political education work as part of a broader, citywide movement. By 1939, the executive secretary of the Atlanta branch of the Urban League was writing a weekly column for the Atlanta *Journal*, and the newspaper had agreed as well to capitalize *Negro* and give married black women the title "Mrs.," as was its practice for whites.[22]

21. Nancy J. Weiss, *The National Urban League, 1910–1940* (New York, 1974), 226–29, 262–63, 284–85; Robert H. Brisbane, *The Black Vanguard: Origins of the Negro Social Revolution, 1900–1960* (Valley Forge, 1970), 205–10; Forrester Washington, A Functional Analysis of the National Urban League and Its Affiliates, November, 1943, in National Urban League Records, Box A-68.

22. Reginald Johnson, Twelfth Annual Report of the Atlanta Urban League, 1933, in National Urban League Records, Box A-38; Reports of the Executive Secretary, October 12, 1934, October, 1935, November, 1935, November, 1936, July, 1938, December 7, 1939,

Elsewhere, Urban League branches were never as active as in Atlanta, but then few such offices even existed as of the mid-1930s. The work of southern field director Thomas resulted in the opening of a unit in New Orleans in November, 1938. The two-year campaign for the branch, however, was not without problems. A number of influential white philanthropists, whose financial backing was required, were unhappy because of promises seemingly broken in securing their support for the establishment of Dillard University several years earlier. It seems that Dillard's opening was supposed to decrease the number of blacks frequenting the Canal Street business area and the exclusive St. Charles Street residential neighborhoods by closing New Orleans University and Straight College, but when the institutions were later reopened as secondary schools, more blacks were in attendance than the two colleges had previously enrolled. Another problem in the Urban League campaign was that the Crescent City black community was not a cohesive group. Its history had long been one of mistrust based on residential location (above or below Canal Street), religion (Catholic or Protestant), and cultural background (descendants of slaves or blacks of French ancestry). The organizing drive ran into charges of Communist influence as well; delays also resulted from reports that local Urban League leaders would be imported from outside the community as had occurred when faculty appointments were made at Dillard University.[23]

When the city branch finally opened, it was solidly in the hands of local business leaders and educators, with the state WPA and NYA directors also serving on its executive committee. Its first annual budget was far from substantial—$5,400, raised half by blacks and half by whites. This initially limited field activities to the sponsorship of neighborhood health programs, the establishment of advisory housing, hospital, and educational committees, and the location of private and public jobs for black workers. Still, according to Field Director Thomas, the league gave "to the Negro people throughout the section backbone and a will to fight." Important was the consistent support received

all in Atlanta Urban League Files; Louis Davis Shivery, "The Neighborhood Union: A Survey of the Beginning of Social Welfare Movements Among Negroes in Atlanta," *Phylon*, III (Second Quarter, 1942), 159–60; Atlanta *Daily World*, September 26, 1934, October 11, 1936, October 21, 1938, September 3, 1939.

23. Council of Social Agencies to Thomas, January 22, 1937, Thomas to Wilma Shields, December 10, 1937, Shields to Thomas, December 13, 1937 (Box A-54), Report of the Activities of the Southern Field Director, September 26, 1938 (Box A-55), Clarence Laws to Thomas, October 20, 1938, George Tinker to Thomas, October 19, 1938 (Box A-58), all in National Urban League Records; *Louisiana Weekly*, October 24, 1936, March 12, July 23, November 5, 1938.

from all major city newspapers. The New Orleans *Item* commented that "if we join the Negroes . . . we not only contribute toward improving the living, working, housing conditions of Negroes and stimulating better relationships between the two races, but also contribute toward the sum of social well-being of all the people."[24]

In Memphis, what would become a permanent Urban League branch was formed in the mid-1930s. New offices also opened in Little Rock, Richmond, Louisville, St. Louis, and the three major Florida cities. Only four Deep South cities with populations of 100,000 or more failed to organize Urban League offices, with Birmingham being the largest by far. National officials did not overlook the Alabama city; according to Thomas, "My knowledge of the total picture in Birmingham persuades me that there is not a city in America in greater need of an Urban League." A major organizational endeavor was attempted in 1937, but according to prominent black attorney Arthur Shores, the inability to win sufficient white support for an interracial committee caused the campaign to collapse quickly. Despite having a number of racially mixed industrial unions, Birmingham as late as 1950 was the only major regional municipality without an Urban League office.[25]

Birmingham's failure to support an active branch of the Commission on Interracial Cooperation (CIC) also showed its intransigence on racial matters, an inflexibility more entrenched than in any other Deep South city. No such office operated in the steel center until 1942, even though the city had hosted the first CIC-cosponsored Southern Conference for Human Welfare four years earlier. Following that gathering— the only one that ever submitted to city Jim Crow ordinances—local whites withdrew their support from all interracial activities and called for a Dies committee investigation of local black leaders and their white allies. Among those leaders who consequently resigned was Birmingham-area congressman Luther Patrick.[26]

24. New Orleans *Item*, May 18, 1936; "New Orleans Newspapers Endorse Urban League Project" (Typescript in National Urban League Records, Box A-66, n.d.); Jesse O. Thomas, *My Story in Black and White: The Autobiography of Jesse O. Thomas* (New York, 1967), 108–109; New Orleans *Times-Picayune*, November 7, 1939.

25. Report of Activities of the Memphis Urban League, n.d., (Box A-68), S. M. Jones to Thomas, September 19, 1933 (Box A-40), Thomas to E. K. Jones, October 1, 1937 (Box A-51), Thomas to S. J. Bennett, November 12, 1941 (Box A-66), all in National Urban League Records; National Urban League, *Fortieth Anniversary Yearbook: 1950* (New York, 1951), 20–23.

26. Jessie D. Ames to Dr. H. M. Edwards, January 10, 1941, in Commission on Interracial Cooperation Records, Box 17-C-a; Clark Foreman, "The Decade of Hope," *Phylon*, XII (Second Quarter, 1951), 138–45; Birmingham *Labor Advocate*, December 3, 1938, November 11, 1939; Nelson C. Jackson to Eliot Ness, November 16, 1943, in National Urban League Records, Box C-3.

Founded in 1919, and in 1944 merging with several other groups to form the Southern Regional Council, a CIC regional staff in Atlanta coordinated central state committees that in turn directed the field activities of county chapters. By 1930, the CIC had reached into 604 of the 805 counties in the South, where blacks made up at least 10 percent of the population. Depression-related financial troubles caused most local units to close or substantially reduce activities, and by 1937 only 3 state and 23 municipal groups remained in operation. During those years, CIC activities were mainly confined to educational research, leading to the regional staff's publication of several works focusing on the necessity of improving race relations in the South. Regional personnel were also responsible for channeling foundation grants to various subsidiary committees, most notably the newly organized Association of Southern Women for the Prevention of Lynching. It was during this period that CIC director Will Alexander took charge of the New Deal's Resettlement Administration.[27]

According to one account of the CIC's twenty-four-year history, "The depression accentuated the need for the commission," and after 1937, local field activities reemerged as central to CIC operations. The work in Atlanta was the most visible in the South, probably because of the city's academic community, both black and white, and because of the availability of regional office resources. The Atlanta operation became increasingly assertive; it even withdrew from the community chest late in the decade, despite dwindling national foundation grants, to begin raising funds on its own.[28] The goal was financial and general independence. It seems that the accommodationist tradition was beginning to fade, as blacks and interracial groups gradually took the offensive in their quest for a fair share.

At the top of the CIC's itinerary was the problem of police brutality. Periodic conferences between Atlanta leaders and the city sought, in the words of Mayor Hartsfield, "to raise the level of the Police Department, both in intelligence and in fair and courteous treatment of the public regardless of who they might be." There were a number of grand jury indictments of policemen for the mistreatment of blacks, and there were even instances of individuals being removed from the force,

27. Edward F. Burrows, "The Commission on Interracial Cooperation, 1919–1944: A Case Study in the History of the Interracial Movement in the South" (Ph.D. dissertation, University of Wisconsin, 1954), 92–99, 171–75, 186–201, 225–33, 351–61; Dykeman and Stokely, *Seeds of Southern Change*, 140–49; Henry E. Barber, "The Association of Southern Women for the Prevention of Lynching, 1930–1942," *Phylon*, XXIV (December, 1973), 378–89.

28. Burrows, "The Commission on Interracial Cooperation," 355; Willis King to Arthur Raper, April 15, 1936, in CIC Records, Box 17-C-4-a.

although local trials usually acquitted those so charged. In mid-1940, for example, a city policeman was acquitted of torturing a black youth with a hot iron, despite pictures of the burned youth offered as evidence at the trial. Later in the same year, a couple of six-foot, two-hundred-pound policemen escaped charges in the widely publicized Earl Sands case. Sands was a five-foot, one-hundred-pound black youth, apprehended less than fifty feet from his home and beaten with blackjacks while a chain was wrapped around his neck. Yet that such incidents received publicity at all was important—the public could no longer plead ignorance of brutality in its midst. CIC personnel were also active in a campaign to discourage indiscriminate arrests of blacks, resulting in the repeal of a longstanding city ordinance mandating that 25 percent of all fines be set aside for police pensions.[29]

In addition, black women's groups within the Atlanta area addressed inequities in health and education facilities. The rule of separate but equal facilities was in no way disturbed; yet efforts did result in an increase in salaries for black teachers, the implementation of a school lunch program in black schools, and the establishment and maintenance of day nurseries and neighborhood libraries. The opening of the Dekalb County Medical and Dental Clinic in 1937, funded through a combination of private subscriptions, CIC appropriations, and annual allocations from Decatur authorities, was the greatest single CIC achievement. Aside from a few black wards in Grady Hospital, there was only one small private hospital and a few clinics with a total of twenty beds for blacks. There were fewer than sixty black physicians in the entire city.[30]

The CIC in Memphis, where according to regional sources Boss Crump ruled by "plunder and privilege," was smaller and less active than the branch in Atlanta. CIC personnel even contemplated sending an invitation to the boss to join their restructured unit in late 1941 because they fully realized the machine's steadfast opposition to challenges to the general order. Director Jessie D. Ames of the Association of Southern Women for the Prevention of Lynching indicated that "both the Negroes and white people there would be equally startled by such a suggestion," and the reaction of the Memphis commissioner for

29. Report of Conference with Mayor and Chief of Police, May 31, 1939, Hartsfield to Dr. M. Ashley Jones, May 23, 1940, Mrs. J. M. Boom to Solicitor John Boykin, August 8, 1940, all in CIC Records, Box 17-C-4-a; Atlanta *Daily World*, March 9, June 21, July 13, 1940.

30. Jessie D. Ames and Bertha P. Newell, *Repairers of the Breach: A Story of Interracial Cooperation Between Southern Women, 1935–1940* (Atlanta, 1940), 31–52; Jessie D. Ames, *Democratic Processes at Work in the South* (Atlanta, 1941), 6–13; Washington to Ames, November 7, 1939, in CIC Records, Box 17-C-4-a.

public safety showed why. He informed a group of white ministers that all CIC leaders were troublemakers, responsible for a campaign "calculated to destroy the present friendly relations between the white and negro races in the community." He added that "the white people [here] are making everything possible for the negro."[31]

Similarly in New Orleans, where the Maestri administration was equally hostile to CIC efforts, the police chief announced that any protest against police activities would be treated as "incitement to riot." Further problems there included the residential and cultural divisions among blacks and a serious rift within the CIC office itself. Local sources reported that CIC meetings in the 1930s were "getting ever more sharp in the expression of the Negroes, and with the whites ever more restive." White leaders often refused to call meetings because of the split, preferring to move at a slower pace than many blacks, who were beginning to see a need to direct their own organizations. Some blacks in New Orleans eventually left the CIC for other groups. One longtime official noted that "the whole interracial question has been greatly sharpened and appreciably embittered in the last two or three years by the economic pressure and relief discriminations."[32]

A key development in the 1930s was the advance of blacks in leadership roles as civil rights organizations gradually shifted, according to one account, "from a defensive holding action . . . to a sustained advance." The same study indicates that white liberals were becoming "allies rather than patrons" in the struggle. The participation of blacks in New Deal programs, moreover, prompted black leaders to look increasingly toward the federal government for support, making it easier, argues Shores, to work to influence policy. Neither the alphabet agencies nor even the most enlightened New Deal administrators directly assaulted white racism, the heart of racial problems, and statistics suggest that black workers on the whole were even less a part of the basic American economy at the end of the 1930s than at the beginning. Still, black organizations during the depression decade were beginning to realize the worth of organization and pressure group tactics in their struggle for justice and equal opportunity. Leslie Fishel has suggested that the twenty-year period before the *Brown* v. *Board of Education of Topeka* decision was one of the most active in the history of blacks in America up to that time, concurring with Bernard Stern-

---

31. Memphis *Press Scimitar*, December 5, 1940; S. E. Howie to Ames, March 26, November 7, 1941, n.d., Ames to Dr. S. L. Smith, February 10, 1942, all in CIC Records, Box 17-C-9,10.

32. H. B. Durkee to Richard King, March 2, 1934, in CIC Records, Box 17-C; *Crisis* (May, 1936), 152.

sher's thesis that the 1930s was an indispensable "prelude to revolution."[33]

In particular, the NAACP branches throughout the urban South became increasingly vocal, even if traditional case-by-case investigative methods were not altogether abandoned. Sometimes younger, more activist blacks replaced longtime local leaders of both the white and black races. The resurgent city units took the lead in 1936 in organizing the first of what would become annual southern regional conferences. By 1940, all of the major southern city branches appeared on the NAACP "honor roll," while at the outset of the period only the Baton Rouge office was listed among those units paying their proportional share each year to central coffers. Reorganization occurred in the midst of, if not because of, an economic crisis that drained resources and manpower, and in spite of a division within national headquarters among W. E. B. Du Bois and his "separate economy" movement, young intellectuals proclaiming working class solidarity, and mainstream moderates who remained in control. The last group, led by Roy Wilkins, Walter White, and Thurgood Marshall, believed that money would be more easily raised, especially among whites, by focusing on civil rights and "lynching" through legislative and judicial approaches.[34]

In Atlanta, an unsuccessful membership campaign in 1933 and 1934 prompted a changing of the guard. The drive failed to attract new subscribers, even though an active advertising campaign in the Atlanta *Constitution* attempted to reach whites who might be supportive, while at the same time countering charges of Communist infiltration of the organization. Roy Wilkins in the national office was especially supportive of publicity in communitywide newspapers, as well as in the black press, arguing that "you cannot catch a whale by casting your bait in a trout stream." It seems that the *Constitution*'s support was part of its ongoing financial backing of the struggling, and rather conservative, Southern Negro Newspaper Syndicate, publishers of the various *World* newspapers. Without some kind of arrangement, concluded

33. Charles R. Lawrence, "Negro Organizations in Crisis: Depression, New Deal, World War II" (Ph.D. dissertation, Columbia University, 1953), 69, 383–84; interview with Arthur D. Shores, Birmingham civil rights attorney, May 1, 1975; Leslie Fishel, "The Negro in the New Deal Era," in Sternsher (ed.), *The Negro in Depression and War*, 7–28. For recent analyses of the impact of the depression and the New Deal on blacks, see Sitkoff, *A New Deal for Blacks*, and Weiss, *Farewell to the Party of Lincoln*.

34. *Crisis* (March, 1931), 150, and (September, 1934), 277; Atlanta *Daily World*, April 2, May 3, 1939; *Louisiana Weekly*, May 8, 1937; Wilson Record, "Negro Intellectual Leadership in the National Association for the Advancement of Colored People: 1910–1940," *Phylon*, XVII (Fourth Quarter, 1956), 387–88; Wolters, *Negroes and the Great Depression*, 383–84.

national NAACP personnel, the always supportive Atlanta *World* "would not be able to live two minutes" owing to high overhead costs.[35]

Notwithstanding the exuberance of one NAACP member who claimed that "there has been a great awakening among our people in the attitude toward the association," less than 1,000 active members in Atlanta remained as of 1935, compared to more than 3,300 enrolled in the early 1920s. The result was an open split among branch members, with a group of young men and women, backed by Forrester Washington and the Atlanta *World*, openly challenging the "old guard" for control. Also among the disenchanted was J. W. Dobbs of the Atlanta Civic and Political League, joint sponsor with the NAACP of an active political awareness campaign. The insurgents succeeded in electing Washington branch president in 1936, and within a few months, the expansion of new youth groups and women's committees prompted Walter White to remark that "under Forrester's leadership the Atlanta Branch has become one of our best branches." The new president worked diligently to heal quarrels within the group, finally persuading several former officeholders to join his executive committee. The revived unit apparently was noticed in other quarters, attracting special visits from White Legionnaires and Klansmen, which Washington claimed did not "by one iota [slow] us up in our determination to continue to fight [for] . . . economic, political and social rights." When Washington relinquished the presidency to Clark University's E. Luther Brooks in 1939, the Atlanta unit had launched a campaign to address larger conflicts within the NAACP, and particularly the feeling among southerners of being "put off" by the national staff at national gatherings.[36]

More divisive than the internal schism and reorganization in Atlanta was the discord within the New Orleans unit. Early in the 1930s, factions led by George Labat and black lawyer A. P. Tureaud vied for control. When Tureaud at one point attempted to establish a second and separate Crescent City group, national officials blocked the plan, indicating that they were "distressed over the poor showing of the New Orleans Branch." From 1933 to 1937, under the direction of James Gayle, local membership increased from a few hundred to more than 750. New youth and women's divisions were also organized, although the New Orleans office was neither as large nor as active as national

35. Roy Wilkins to Daisy Lampkin, February 6, 1933, in Records of the NAACP, Box G-44.

36. J. B. Greenwood to Walter White, March 29, 1934, Annual Report of Atlanta Branch of NAACP, January 1, 1935, Washington to White, December 10, 1936, April 27, 1937, Eugene Martin to White, April 24, 1936, White to Marshall Shepard, December 16, 1936 (Box G-44), Washington to White, January 21, 1939 (Box G-45), all in Records of the NAACP.

personnel thought it should be. In seeking the regional staff's assistance for a membership drive in 1938, new president A. W. Brazier indicated a determination to reverse "the lethargy into which . . . [we] have fallen since 1935."[37]

Brazier's enthusiasm was no doubt genuine, but he was closely identified with the "old guard." By 1937 the patience of a number of young members and other dissenters within the New Orleans branch had worn thin. James LaFourche, editor of the Louisiana *Weekly* and former branch secretary, led a movement to open presidential elections to the general membership. The "voting" was then merely the rubber-stamping of the choice of a nominating committee in turn controlled by the president. LaFourche won the sympathy of the national office, as the director of branches concluded that "Dr. Brazier is not a very effective person . . . being a somewhat lightly regarded person in the community"; yet the former branch secretary lost in local showdowns in 1937 and again in 1938. Brazier made an effective counterattack, which he based on earlier administrative decisions LaFourche had made without the authorization of the executive committee. The editor described the 1937 presidential campaign as "an open farce," and following the 1938 elections, just prior to his resignation from the group, he concluded that "the ultra conservatives met with their drafted stooges [and] perpetuated themselves in office with all of twenty-six people voting."[38]

By mid-1939, the New Orleans "old guard" was under attack from two other groups, both led by more activist members. Their anger was touched off when Brazier failed miserably in 1938 to win the right for black groups to use the municipal auditorium. One of the insurgents, Donald Jones of a downtown faction, began soliciting new members without the authorization of local officials—a move that gained the approval of national personnel who had denied Tureaud and also LaFourche in previous years. At the same time, a second challenge was directed by J. E. Wilkins, who led a moderate "progressive" ticket against both the conservatives and Jones's "young turks" in the November, 1939, elections. More than 750 members participated in the voting,

37. A. P. Tureaud to Robert W. Bagnall, November 30, 1931, Bagnall to Mrs. D. L. Guidry, October 13, 1932, William Pickens to James Gayle, December 1, 1933, Gayle to White, March 23, 1935, Oneida Brown to White, March 22, 1935, White to Arthur B. Springarn, April 11, 1935 (Box G-82), A. W. Brazier to Lampkin, March 3, 1938 (Box G-83), all in Records of the NAACP.

38. LaFourche to White, November 27, 1937, Pickens to White, December 12, 1937 (Box G-82), Brazier to White, November 17, 1938, LaFourche to White, November 18, 1938, Pickens to White, November 21, 1938, LaFourche to Pickens, December 5, 1938, Brazier to Pickens, December 16, 1938, January 14, 1939, Marshall to Brazier, February 20, 1939 (Box G-83), all in Records of the NAACP.

which resulted in a narrow victory for Wilkins over the downtown group. The members used an open ballot for the first time, rather than the old nominating committee, and Brazier won only seven votes. Only three of the "old guard" were returned to the seventeen-member executive committee, including the outgoing president, who was chosen, according to one new official, "so as to let him down easily." The same official concluded, and even Brazier concurred, that a new spirit of activism was emerging within the organization, which the official claimed "for some years has been mismanaged."[39]

Reorganization of the Birmingham NAACP occurred in late 1937. The new president's most important appointment was attorney Shores, who took the lead in reviving a long-dormant campaign for political rights. Blacks throughout Alabama had been effectively disenfranchised since the early twentieth century through a combination of constitutional provisions and special voting laws giving total discretion to individual registrars. In 1916, a "lily white" Republican party movement had cast aside the last Alabama black Republicans, and a white primary law eliminated any chance of black involvement in the Democratic party. The last serious voter registration effort had collapsed in 1926, when Birmingham authorities arrested a schoolteacher, Mrs. Indiana Little, and a group of blacks seeking the ballot on charges of vagrancy, misconduct, and boisterousness. But in 1937, things began to change, when Shores and the NAACP launched a series of court challenges against the application of the state's registration law requiring that a registered voter be able to read and write or own property valued at $300 and pay a $1.50 poll tax.[40]

Unlike voter registration drives in other southern cities, which involved political education campaigns, the Birmingham effort included little in the way of grass roots participation. The Jefferson County Negro Democratic Club, chartered by the National Democratic Committee in 1939, cooperated with NAACP lawyers by mobilizing blacks through the racially mixed mine and steel unions, but its initial enthusiasm waned quickly when white Democrats allowed only one black representative for the entire state into the Alabama Federation of Democratic Clubs. In 1940, the NAACP-affiliated National Youth Congress assumed control of the community organization, opening a

39. Donald Jones to White, July 3, 1939, Tureaud to Marshall, July 14, July 21, 1939, Marshall to Jones, July 17, August 31, 1939, Brazier to White, November 4, 28, 1939, Tureaud to White, November 8, 1939, James Lewis to White, November 11, 1939, all in Records of the NAACP, Box G-83; Atlanta *Daily World*, November 20, 1939.

40. Charles A. J. McPherson to NAACP, April 17, 1937, and McPherson to Pickens, November 17, 1937, both in Records of the NAACP, Box G-3; Joseph M. Brittain, "Negro Suffrage and Politics in Alabama Since 1870" (Ph.D. dissertation, Indiana University, 1958), 171–85.

tutorial service designed to prepare blacks for questions asked by registrars administering literacy tests.[41]

Short-term numerical gains were not outstanding. Through the 1930s and 1940s, court battles concentrated on the application of state voting statutes, not their constitutionality. The result was that only a few blacks who could read and write won the vote. By 1951, only about 4,500 Birmingham-area blacks were registered (compared to a few hundred in 1939), but Shores still believed the start to be encouraging. In late 1939 he noted that "we have never had so much interest shown in the matter of the franchise." His challenges later resulted in a grand jury report recommending the dismissal of the entire Jefferson County board of registrars because it was "biased, unfair, of low educational standards, old, and bigoted." The Birmingham lawyer also found time to address municipal authorities in police brutality cases and lead the fight for equal teacher salaries, yet he was far from directing the "militant aggressive band of workers who are courageous and wise enough to attack our problems at the roots," as called for by one local official earlier in the decade.[42]

NAACP attorneys in other southern cities pressed voter registration cases as well—a strategy that continued for years before bringing more than marginal success. General Manager A. M. Trudeau of Safety Insurance Company of New Orleans challenged the constitutionality of the Louisiana "interpretation" clause in the federal courts in 1931—a device that had replaced the state's illegal grandfather clause. The ordeal lasted more than two years, ending when appellate and Supreme Court justices upheld a district court ruling that literacy requirements did not violate the fourteenth and fifteenth amendments. They further concluded that only municipal civil courts by jury trial could overturn the decisions of local registrars, confirming the absolute power of parish clerks over all registration procedures. One prominent black minister sought to register on twelve separate occasions in 1935 and only succeeded after pressuring the registrar, whom he caught filling out forms for illiterate whites while denying blacks who had correctly filed their own applications.[43]

41. Ralph J. Bunche, *The Political Status of the Negro in the Age of FDR*, ed. Dewey W. Grantham (Chicago, 1973), 260, 478–80; Joseph M. Brittain, "The Return of the Negro to Alabama Politics, 1950–1954," *Negro History Bulletin*, XXII (May, 1959), 196–98; John L. Williams, "Struggles in the Thirties in the South," in Sternsher (ed.), *The Negro in Depression and War*, 177.

42. Bunche, *The Political Status of the Negro*, 266; Atlanta *Daily World*, June 17, 20, July 1, 13, 1939; Arthur Shores to Marshall, June 19, July 3, 19, 1939 (Box D-4), McPherson to Pickens, November 17, 1937 (Box G-3), all in Records of the NAACP.

43. Bunche, *The Political Status of the Negro*, 312–14; *Louisiana Weekly*, October 10, 1931, August 12, October 14, 1933.

Although disappointed, black leaders in New Orleans continued the struggle for the ballot mainly in the form of political education campaigns to raise the consciousness of their constituents. A New Orleans Negro Democratic club had launched operations in 1931, hoping to undercut the longstanding pattern of blacks voting Republican simply because it was "the party of Lincoln," and in 1935, the more active League for Civil Rights and Justice opened in conjunction with the NAACP, often working through CIO affiliates. The Southern Negro Youth Congress was active in the Crescent City as well, as it was in nearly all of the major urban areas. The New Orleans congress in 1939 opened citizenship institutes through such agencies as the Young Men's Christian Association (YMCA) to instruct young people on the often complicated registration procedures. Black leaders hoped to prepare a number of blacks for registration when a favorable court ruling finally did come down. The number of registered blacks began to increase steadily after 1944 in the wake of *Smith* v. *Allwright*, climbing from under 2,000 in the mid-1940s to over 30,000 by 1950.[44]

Although quite active, the political education movement in New Orleans paled in comparison to the effort in Atlanta. In 1932, Atlanta University opened its first citizenship school to register blacks for special city elections. In 1933 a similar NAACP program began; it later joined that of the pro–New Deal Atlanta Civic and Political League, organized in 1934. By 1936, the league consisted of more than one thousand members, who volunteered in voter registration seminars, and it had enlisted the support of the several black city colleges and the Urban League. This allowed the push for political education to continue through the rest of the decade and into the war and postwar years. In the 1930s, black activist Ralph Bunche identified five reasons for the lack of political interest in Atlanta among Negroes: first, one-party politics (with city and state white primary laws); second, the poll tax; third, a failure among Negro ministers to attack the status quo; fourth, the failure of black academe to lead the masses; and fifth, the lack of well-organized, continuously functioning mechanisms to promote civic responsibility among blacks. Although the obstacles erected by whites would not disappear until the 1960s, the last two factors, controlled by blacks themselves, did begin to change through depression-era efforts. The hesitancy of Atlanta's black clergy was little shaken in the 1930s; apparently, some ministers worked against change as "hiring

44. *Louisiana Weekly*, July 25, 1931, June 8, October 19, 1935, July 22, August 19, September 2, October 7, December 2, 30, 1939; Daisy Lampkin, "On the NAACP Front," *Crisis* (May, 1935), 153; Atlanta *Daily World*, March 9, 1938; Oliver Evans, *New Orleans* (New York, 1959), 181; David W. Friedrichs, "The Role of the Negro Minister in Politics in New Orleans" (Ph.D. dissertation, Tulane University, 1967), 30–32.

agents" for anti-union employers, urging blacks into church and out of the CIO.[45]

The goal of registering 10,000 blacks by the end of the decade lay beyond reach, but by 1940 a new political interest in Atlanta was in evidence. Black voters had participated in school bond elections in the past, but in the 1932 recall election of Mayor Key, more than 5,000 of 6,000 registered blacks had not turned out, suggesting that political apathy still prevailed. Six years later, however, blacks played important roles in the March vote legalizing the sale of liquor and in the narrow November defeat of a special bond issue referendum. Municipal authorities had worked hard for the funding proposal, which would have brought additional WPA projects to the city. Forrester Washington boasted that "the Negro played no little part in its defeat"; indeed, black leaders had vehemently opposed the issue because so little of the funding was earmarked for black neighborhoods. In addition, blacks were involved in a special county sheriff's election in 1938. During the 1930s as well, the first blacks since Reconstruction ran for municipal office—alderman and board of education positions. Political interest among blacks was not as evident as in some of the emerging Sun Belt cities, especially Dallas, where more than seven thousand registered blacks in 1937 actively backed a victorious ticket in city elections. Yet according to Clarence Bacote's studies of black voting in the South, the political readiness of Atlanta blacks following *Chapman v. King* in 1946, which struck down the Georgia white primary law, was the direct result of "shovel work" accomplished among the young in the late 1930s—which in turn was a result of a feeling of involvement generated by the New Deal.[46]

Noteworthy changes in Memphis politics also unfolded in the 1930s. A number of new and restructured organizations appeared, including a more active NAACP branch. At one time, the Memphis organization had been among the most active in the South, but as of 1932, local sources reported, the Memphis unit existed "in name only"

45. A. T. Walden to White, April 18, 1933, Records of the NAACP, Box G-44; Bunche, *The Political Status of the Negro*, 486; Clarence A. Bacote, "The Negro in Atlanta Politics," *Phylon*, XVI (Fourth Quarter, 1955), 342–43; Atlanta *Daily World*, January 4, February 11, 1934; James Olson, "Race, Class and Progress: Black Leadership and Industrial Unionism, 1936–1945," in Cantor (ed.), *Black Labor in America*, 159–60.

46. Bunche, *The Political Status of the Negro*, 300; Augustus A. Adair, "A Political History of the Negro in Atlanta, 1908–1953" (M.A. thesis, Atlanta University, 1955), 36–50; J. W. Dobbs to A. F. Smith, November 9, 1938, in WPA, Georgia Labor Complaints; Washington to White, February 7, 1939, Records of the NAACP, Box G-45; Atlanta *Daily World*, February 13, 1936, March 6, April 7, 1937, April 1, 3, October 5, 1938, July 17, October 30, 1939; Bacote, "The Negro in Atlanta Politics," 342–43.

and was virtually as "dead as a pharaoh."[47] Under the influence of Robert Church in the years prior to the depression, its fieldwork had all but ceased; in 1932 it sent only eight dollars in support of the national office.

Church and a group of fellow black businessmen, the most important of whom was George Washington Lee, emerged early in the century as "power brokers" between the national Republican party and the Crump machine. Crump provided blacks, according to Bunche, with "poll tax receipts, marked ballots, and hard liquor" and then herded them to the polls in general elections to vote for machine candidates whom he backed. In return, the boss "cared for" the black business community and received a healthy share of federal patronage through Church and various Republican administrations. Church and Lee viewed the deal pragmatically, suggests David Tucker in his studies of Memphis politics—as a necessary step to maintain a viable black middle class to speak for black needs and to promote racial pride as a detour to full equality. It was hoped that southern whites, meanwhile, would develop a colorblind class consciousness, which black leaders argued was the only way that Negro problems would ever be truly solved.[48]

But with the landslide election of a Democratic president in 1932, only to be repeated in 1936, the partnership between Crump and Church crumbled as political conditions changed. Patronage no longer filtered through local "black and tan" Republican leaders, who had amazingly withstood the "lily white" Republican movement of the 1920s. The advent of the many alphabet agencies, which were eager to work through vote-producing Democratic political organizations, also suddenly provided the boss with more jobs at his disposal than ever before.

Clearly because of the depression and the New Deal, new leaders began to take charge of NAACP branch activities in Memphis. The restructured office was more active in pushing for justice and equal treatment for black citizens. In 1938, the first local youth council opened in conjunction with LeMoyne College, and throughout the late 1930s, NAACP personnel assisted CIO organizers among black workers

47. Bagnall to Mrs. Florence C. McCleave, November 14, 1932, Ira H. Latimer to White, April 10, 1932, February 23, 1933, Lampkin to Wilkins, February 23, 1933, Lampkin to White, March 6, 1933, all in Records of the NAACP, Box G-199.

48. W. T. Smith to Wilkins, June 5, 1934, M. S. Stuart to White, December 4, 1934, both in Records of the NAACP, Box G-199; Bunche, *The Political Status of the Negro*, 73; George W. Lee, *Beale Street: Where the Blues Began* (New York, 1934), 246; David M. Tucker, *Lieutenant Lee of Beale Street* (Nashville, 1971), 115–20, and "Black Pride and Negro Business in the 1920's: George Washington Lee of Memphis," *Business History Review*, XLIII (November, 1969), 435–51.

in area automobile and rubber manufacturing plants. Even more important was the work of the black businessman Dr. J. E. Walker, president of the National Negro Business League. Working through the NAACP and the Urban League, Walker sponsored a New Deal Negro Democratic club in late 1935 to woo blacks away from the Church, Lee, and Crump alignment. Walker hoped that Negroes would register as Democrats rather than as Republicans and participate in local campaigns as independent voters. Apparently, the effort ran smoothly at first; in November, 1936, there was a notable decline in black Republican votes.[49]

Crump's reaction—a reign of terror against blacks and their leaders—was altogether predictable. Turning to the stick and eschewing the carrot, he included in his strategy the withholding of municipal and federal funds from public works projects in Negro residential areas. Even the historic Beale Street section, a nationally renowned center for black clubs and the blues, was allowed to fall into shameful disrepair. Physical intimidation was a tactic as well. According to the city's Urban League office, "Those who desire to seek some political allegiance other than Crump's find themselves victims of gang beatings, economic sabotage, and campaigns of slander in the newspapers of Crump's supporters." The report continued: "Negroes have been arrested in wholesale lots and jailed on charges of loitering. Preachers have been warned not to preach against the Crump machine and [black] editors have been advised not to print stories . . . critical of the Memphis political set-up."[50]

It was no coincidence that incidents of police brutality in Memphis increased dramatically in 1937 and 1938. George W. Brooks, a black mailman, was killed by police sergeant A. O. Clark in January, 1938. NAACP officials reported that Brooks was "the third man of color to die at the hands of white people within a week . . . and one of many (some say the sixth, others say the seventh or eighth) said to have been killed by Sargeant Clark." And when Church that year began speaking out against machine tactics, as well as the machine's gubernatorial candi-

49. Bagnall to Norman Jones, April 17, 1931 (Box G-199), Juanita Jackson to C. H. Spears, September 13, 1938 (Box E-5), both in Records of the NAACP; Ralph Picard to Crump, February 12, 1935, in Watkins Overton Papers, Box 2, Memphis State University Library; Atlanta *Daily World*, October 23, November 6, 1936; Tucker, *Lieutenant Lee*, 121–24; Bunche, *The Political Status of the Negro*, 498–500.

50. City and Federal Public Works in Memphis, 1933–1938, n.d., in WPA, Appraisal Reports: Tennessee; Overton to Crump, May 25, 1938, in Watkins Overton Papers, Box 2; Donald E. Williams, "The Beale Street Arena—Memphis, Tennessee: A Case Study of Urban Renewal" (M.S. thesis, Memphis State University, 1970), 19–20; Memorandum on the Memphis Situation, December 13, 1940, in National Urban League Records, Box A-63.

date, he too became a victim of Crump's iron-hand rule. City hall presented the black businessman with a large, overdue tax bill, forcing the sale of all of his real estate to raise nearly $80,000. With the loss of his property, according to Bunche, "Church's last wisp of local political power passed."[51]

A similar fate awaited local druggist J. B. Martin, who attempted to revive Church's Negro Republican organization during the 1940 presidential election. No longer in need of black Republicans, the boss ordered Memphis police to patrol Martin's store, and those of other black retailers, throughout November and December of that year, searching every customer who entered. Police Commissioner Joseph Boyle also sent threatening letters to all involved, including several ministers, condemning them for their "presumptuous ingratitude" concerning "what white people have been doing for the negroes" for years. Boyle warned that "this is white man's country, and always will be, and any negro who doesn't agree to this better move on."[52]

The turmoil in Memphis resulted in a substantial decrease in the number of registered blacks. More important, though, was the anti-Crump sentiment that was steadily emerging among blacks, suggesting in the words of one Urban League official that this time the boss had indeed "overplayed his hand." Even Lee, who managed to survive Church's troubles in 1938, admitted that new strategies would have to be developed to heal the wounds and restructure old political alignments. In a letter to Crump in late 1940, Lee acknowledged that in the past, "Things done by the city for colored people did not trickle down to the masses," and in an obvious effort to recapture his former "broker" status, he outlined what he called a "profitable plan of drawing a picture of Negro progress under the administration in a clear and unmistakable way." Lee's influence, however, was fading. By the turn of the decade, new black leaders were engaged in organizing voter awareness groups throughout their community, preparing for the day when the ballot would truly be theirs. Until then, they made do with a "Mayor of Beale Street" program modeled on the Bronzeville mayor concept operating nationwide, conducting annual elections for officials who became the new "brokers" between municipal authorities and black neighborhoods.[53]

51. Bunche, *The Political Status of the Negro*, 499; Tucker, *Lieutenant Lee*, 126; Memphis NAACP Branch to Wilkins, January 7, 1938, in Records of the NAACP, Box G-199.

52. Memorandum on the Memphis Situation, December 13, 1940 (Box A-63), News Bulletin, Spring, 1941, and n.d. (Box A-68), all in National Urban League Records; Memphis *Press Scimitar*, December 11, 1940; Memphis *Commercial Appeal*, December 5, 1940.

53. George Washington Lee to Crump, November 19, 1940, in Mayor's Correspon-

Developments within the black communities mirrored what transpired in general throughout the major southern cities during the depression period. There were few immediate, fundamental changes; public service facilities and opportunities remained truly separate and unequal. Although many jobless individuals and their families benefited from New Deal programs, the overall status of black life improved very little, if at all. Still, by the end of the decade revived and newly established black organizations were exerting themselves more than in the past, promoting a sense of racial consciousness and pride, particularly among the young. Blacks were beginning to demand more, and many were no longer willing simply to defend their existence to whites, theretofore regarded as "benefactors" of blacks by many of both races. Political education efforts in every city, as well as stepped-up campaigns against the machinery of disenfranchisement, signified that while racial confrontations lay ahead, the challenge of obtaining an equal share, instead of a separate one, was beginning, notwithstanding the continued efforts of the municipal vanguard to preserve a booster environment and as much of the southern way of life as possible. Furthermore, while whites in general were certainly unprepared to make adjustments either quickly or voluntarily in the most entrenched regional tradition, Birmingham was already emerging as the most reactionary of the major Deep South cities—a trend later accelerated by the steel center's lack of postwar population and economic growth and diversification.

---

dence File, Drawer 10, Memphis and Shelby County Archives, Memphis; Atlanta *Daily World*, August 22, 30, October 3, 1939.

BIBLIOGRAPHY

MANUSCRIPT COLLECTIONS

PERSONAL PAPERS

Several collections of manuscripts of southern municipal leaders were useful in this study. In Memphis, the Watkins Overton Papers, located in the Mississippi Valley Collection at Memphis State University, includes personal letters saved by the former mayor and his family; and the Mayor's Correspondence File, 1928–1940, located in the Memphis and Shelby County Archives, contains official reports and other documents on city business transactions made during the 1930s. Also of importance are the papers of Tennessee governors Henry Horton, Hill McAlister, and Gordon Browning, who served from 1928 to 1932, 1932 to 1936, and 1936 to 1938 respectively; the papers are all located in the Tennessee State Library and Archives, Nashville. McAlister was one of Boss Crump's political allies, while Horton and Browning were quite hostile to the Tennessee city machine. Also useful is the Kenneth D. McKellar Papers, in particular the McKellar-Crump subfile, located in the downtown branch of the Memphis public library. All of the above offer insights into the Crump organization. Crump's personal papers have been stored by the family in a Memphis warehouse and are not generally available for scholarly research.

In Atlanta, the Charles R. Palmer Papers, in Special Collections at the Robert Woodruff Library, Emory University, included data on federal slum clearance and public housing throughout the South. The Charles B. Grambling Papers, in the Southern Labor Archives, and the Cater Woolford Collection, in the Atlanta Historical Society Library and

Archives, offer some material on the 1930s by two Atlantans involved in philanthropic activities. The Rhoda Kaufman Papers, at the Georgia State Department of Archives and History, includes data on Kaufman's work as director of several Fulton County community service organizations in the early twentieth century. For Birmingham, the James M. Jones, Jr., Collection, in the Alabama Archives and History, Montgomery, offers the best primary material for the 1930s. In New Orleans, some of the papers of Mayor Robert Maestri have been microfilmed and are available in the New Orleans public library.

FEDERAL RECORDS

The records of the federal agencies established in the 1930s provided the most important material for this study. The collections of the National Archives contain countless reports and correspondence prepared by local and state officials and New Deal administrators on all levels. Unfortunately, few of the record groups are adequately indexed, making their use for municipal research difficult. Especially confusing is the numbering of boxes and folders. Many boxes, for example, have been stamped with three or more numbers; thus throughout this study the names of subfile groups have been used in citations unless box numbers within a specific collection are absolutely clear. The overworked staff at the National Archives, as well as archivists at the regional records centers, are eager to be of assistance.

Among the most valuable collections is Record Group 73, in the National Archives, which contains the records of POUR. The bureau's files are divided by department and subdivided by state. Of the New Deal records, important material is located in Record Group 135, the records of the PWA, and in Record Group 9, the southern regional records of the NRA. The PWA collection in Washington, D.C., is only partially intact but contains a valuable microfilm file on major construction projects financed jointly by federal and local sponsor contributions. The file is organized by project number rather than by state or locality. The NRA material is located in the Regional Records Center in Atlanta, Georgia. Unlike most of the collections in Washington, D.C., this file has been well indexed—reports and correspondence are labeled in boxes and folders for quick, positive identification. There is significant information on code enforcement throughout the South (particularly with reference to urban businesses and manufacturers), cost of living and regional prices and wages, union efforts, and the emergence of new consumer groups that remained in operation in most large cities after the Schechter decision in 1935.

By far the largest and most important federal collection utilized in this study, Record Group 69, is stored in the Natural Resources

Division of the National Archives. It is also the most difficult to use. The collection contains reports and correspondence of local, state, and federal administrators of the FERA, the CWA, and the WPA. Also included is material concerning the NYA, although most of that data is found in Record Group 119 in Washington, D.C. Within Record Group 69, the following files are the most useful: FERA, CWA, and WPA state files (subdivided by category, that is, work projects, theater project, transients, and so on); the FERA Transient Division and Self-Help Cooperative files (each subdivided by state); the WPA Appraisal Report File (subdivided by state); the WPA Professional and Service Project File (subdivided by state); the WPA Federal Project Number 1 File (records of the federal theater, art, music, and writers projects). Materials from the last files, each indexed by state and then by locality, are the easiest to locate, and the majority of documents concern the major cities where the arts projects were by far the most active.

Other federal collections pertinent to the study of the urban South include Record Group 187, the Records of the National Resources Planning Board, and Record Group 33, the Records of the Federal Extension Service. These materials are located in Washington, D.C. Also, the individual project files within the Records of the National Emergency Council and the several housing agencies are sometimes useful in understanding local economic and even political trends. These collections are located in the Regional Records Center, Suitland, Maryland. All of the federal agencies listed above, among others, published statistical and narrative reports, most of which are bound and available in university and college libraries.

STATE AND LOCAL RECORDS

The Alabama State Federation of Labor File (1930–1956) and the Alabama State Industrial Union Council File (1936–1956), both in the Alabama Labor Council office, Birmingham, provide material on union activity and internal labor conflicts in central Alabama. The collections contain numerous reports of local, state, and regional labor meetings in which the Birmingham area miners and steelworkers played important roles. Additional data are scattered throughout the records of the Atlanta Typographical Union, Number 48; the Birmingham Typographical Union, Number 44; and the Atlanta Labor Temple Association, all available in the Georgia State University Labor Archives, Atlanta.

Also of importance on labor matters, but more significant for material on the southern urban black communities, are the Atlanta Urban League Files, at the Atlanta Urban League office; the National Urban League Records and the Records of the National Association for the Advancement of Colored People, both in the Manuscript Division, Library of Congress; and the Records of the Commission on Interracial Cooperation, in the Trevor Arnett Library, Atlanta University. The NAACP and National Urban League materials are divided by category but subdivided by state and municipality for easy access.

The Minutes of the Fulton County Commission (1933–1938) are located in the Fulton County Court House, and the Atlanta City Council Minutes (1930–1939) are in the basement of Atlanta City Hall. There are also numerous reports published by various city agencies, county commissions, labor groups, chambers of commerce, and individual social service and welfare councils. These are stored in the public libraries of the cities in question; some patience is required because many of these reports were filed away long ago, on either top or bottom shelves in corners, and forgotten.

NEWSPAPERS

In this study, all of the dailies published in the southern cities in the thirties were examined, a task facilitated by valuable clipping files assembled and made available by the Atlanta, Birmingham, Memphis, and New Orleans public libraries. Throughout the depression, each of the cities had at least two independent newspapers, which after World War II merged under one publisher. While all of the newspapers in the 1930s expressed probusiness sympathies and were generally supportive of Democratic candidates, the older publishing firms were most consistently reflective of New South, Henry Grady sentiments. The New Orleans *Times-Picayune* and its afternoon *States*, the Memphis *Commercial Appeal*, the Birmingham *Age-Herald* and afternoon *News*, and the Atlanta *Constitution* were long-established Bourbon newspapers in the booster tradition. The New Orleans *Tribune* and afternoon *Item*, the Memphis *Press Scimitar*, the Birmingham *Post*, and the Atlanta *Journal* were all of more recent origin and during the depression era were generally more supportive of federal policies on labor legislation, public welfare, and social service reforms. Several newspapers among the group (the two Memphis papers, the *Journal*, and the *Post*) were controlled by Scripps-Howard, which influenced their editorial policies during national elections. In the machine cities of New Orleans and Memphis, the *Times-Picayune* and the *Commercial Appeal* late in the 1930s took the lead in opposing the Long and Crump organizations.

The labor press contains information on unionism, particularly among the AFL craft locals, and provides insights into the internal labor feud between CIO and AFL affiliates. The Atlanta *Journal of*

Labor and the Birmingham *Southern Labor Review* were the most objective, while the Memphis *Labor Review*, the *Federationist* (New Orleans), and the Birmingham *Labor Advocate* offer mainly hostile accounts of the activities of industrial union organizers.

Also of value were the southern urban black newspapers. The weekly Birmingham *World*, Memphis *World*, and Atlanta *Daily World* (the most widely circulated southern black newspaper) rarely stressed controversial stories challenging the status quo. All were affiliated with the conservative Scott Southern Negro Newspaper Syndicate. The independent *Louisiana Weekly* (New Orleans) was somewhat more vocal on behalf of southern blacks. The New Orleans journal contained stories of local significance, while reports in the Scott newspapers in the thirties were usually more attentive to national race stories.

Also consulted were the New York *Times* (1930–1940), the *CIO News* (1937–1939), the *Blue Eagle* (1934–1935), and the Atlanta *Georgian*, a conservative journal that appeared daily in the thirties until it ceased publication late in the decade. Two multivolume scrapbooks of importance are the "Administration of J. M. Jones, Jr., 1925–1940," cataloged by the Birmingham public library, and the "Administration of Robert Maestri," indexed by the New Orleans public library. Useful as well are numerous articles on the southern cities in a variety of periodicals with nationwide circulations, including *Business Week*, *American Journal of Public Health*, *Time*, *Survey*, *Christian Century*, *American City*, *Nation*, *Monthly Labor Review*, *Southern Economic Journal*, and *Crisis*.

SELECTED SECONDARY MATERIALS

ARTICLES

Bacote, Clarence A. "The Negro in Atlanta Politics." *Phylon*, XVI (Fourth Quarter, 1955), 337–50.

Brittain, Joseph M. "The Return of the Negro to Alabama Politics, 1930–1954." *Negro History Bulletin*, XXII (May, 1959), 196–98. Stresses the idea that southern blacks in the 1930s began to look increasingly to the federal government for assistance.

Brownell, Blaine A. "Birmingham, Alabama: New South City in the 1920's." *Journal of Southern History*, XXXVIII (February, 1972), 21–48. Gives analysis of Birmingham as an emerging modern, industrial city.

———. "The Commercial-Civic Elite and City Planning in Atlanta, Memphis and New Orleans." *Journal of Southern History*, XLI (August, 1975), 336–68. Discusses commercial influence in city hall in the 1920s.

————. "Urbanization in the South: A Unique Experience?" *Mississippi Quarterly*, XXVI (Spring, 1973), 106–20. Suggests that urban development in the South has not been altogether different from that in other sections of the country.

Capers, Gerald M. "The Rural Lag in Southern Cities." *Mississippi Quarterly*, XXI (Fall, 1968), 253–62. Describes how a "rural lag" has made urban development in the South different from that in other regions.

Coode, Thomas H. "The Presidential Election of 1940 as Reflected in the Tennessee Metropolitan Press." *East Tennessee Historical Society Publications*, XL (1968), 83–100. Shows how several urban newspapers in Tennessee opposed Roosevelt's reelection in 1940.

Foreman, Clark. "The Decade of Hope." *Phylon*, XII (Second Quarter, 1951), 137–50.

Guste, William J. "The Orleans Parish-City Board of Public Welfare." *Louisiana Welfare*, IV (April, 1944), 8–19. Examines the organization and early work of this bureau under federal guidelines.

Haas, Edward F. "New Orleans on the Half-Shell: The Maestri Era." *Louisiana History*, XIII (Summer, 1972), 283–310. Examines the administrations of the businessman's mayor from 1936 to the mid-1940s.

Heleniak, Roman. "Local Reaction to the Great Depression in New Orleans, 1929–1933." *Louisiana History*, X (Fall, 1969), 289–306.

Holmes, Michael S. "The Blue Eagle as 'Jim Crow Bird': The NRA and Georgia's Black Workers." *Journal of Negro History*, LVII (July, 1972), 276–83. Discusses how, under NRA codes, blacks often encountered more discrimination than before the legislation.

Ingalls, Robert P. "Antiradical Violence in Birmingham During the 1930s." *Journal of Southern History*, XLVII (November, 1981), 521–44.

Lapping, Mark B. "The Emergence of Federal Public Housing: Atlanta's Techwood Project." *American Journal of Economics and Sociology*, XXXII (October, 1973), 379–85. Gives account of the first public housing development in the South.

Majors, William R. "Gordon Browning and Tennessee Politics, 1937–1938." *Tennessee Historical Quarterly*, XXVIII (Spring, 1969), 57–69. Analyzes the Crump-Browning feud, which involved charges by both sides of the political use of New Deal programs.

Miller, William D. "The Browning-Crump Battle: The Crump Side." *East Tennessee Historical Society Publications*, XXXVII (1965), 77–88. Analyzes the 1938 elections in Tennessee, sympathetic to the Crump organization.

Moore, John Hammond. "The Angelo Herndon Case, 1932–1937." *Phylon*, XXXII (Spring, 1971), 60–71.

————. "Communists and Fascists in a Southern City: Atlanta, 1930." *South Atlantic Quarterly*, LXVII (Summer, 1968), 435–54. Discusses the Atlanta Six, Angelo Herndon, and the Black Shirt movement in Atlanta in the early 1930s.

Norrell, Robert J. "Caste in Steel: Jim Crow Careers in Birmingham, Alabama." *Journal of American History*, LXXIII (December, 1986), 669–94.

Northrup, Herbert R. "The New Orleans Longshoremen." *Political Science Quarterly*, LVII (December, 1942), 526–44. Emphasizes the conflicts between white and black dock workers and unionists.

O'Conner, Stella. "The Charity Hospital of Louisiana at New Orleans: An Administrative and Financial History, 1736–1941." *Louisiana Historical Quarterly*, XXXI (January, 1948), 1–109. Includes an analysis of the construction of a new charity hospital during the depression period.

Ross, Ronald. "The Role of Blacks in the Federal Theatre, 1935–1939." *Journal of Negro History*, LIX (January, 1974), 38–50.

Shivery, Louis Davis. "The Neighborhood Union: A Survey of the Beginning of Social Welfare Movements Among Negroes in Atlanta." *Phylon*, III (Second Quarter, 1942), 149–62. Examines efforts within the black community to organize a community welfare network during the early depression years.

Tindall, George B. "The 'Colonial Economy' and the Growth Psychology: The South in the 1930's." *South Atlantic Quarterly*, LXIV (Autumn, 1965), 465–77.

Toombs, Harry J. "City Planning in Atlanta: Urbanization Without Concentration as an Objective." *Landscape Architecture*, XLIII (April, 1953), 101–104. Describes development and early work of the Atlanta and Fulton County planning organizations that later combined to form the Regional Metropolitan Planning Commission.

Tucker, David M. "Black Pride and Negro Business in the 1920's: George Washington Lee of Memphis." *Business History Review*, XLIII (November, 1969), 435–51. Examines the development of a black-owned insurance company and the relationship between its founder and the Crump organization.

Books

Allen, Robert S., ed. *Our Fair City*. New York, 1947. Includes several articles on twentieth-century Birmingham.

Auerbach, Jerald S. *Labor and Liberty: The LaFollette Committee and the New Deal*. Indianapolis, 1966. Studies the congressional investigation of antilabor activities in the 1930s.

Berglund, Abraham, George T. Starns, and Frank T. DeVyver. *Labor in* the Industrial South: A Survey of Wages and Living Conditions in Three Major Industries of the New Industrial South. Charlottesville, 1930. Provides useful economic survey of the industrial South prior to the depression.

Bernstein, Irving. A History of the American Worker, 1920–1933: The Lean Years. 1960; rpr. Baltimore, 1966.

————. A History of the American Worker, 1933–1941: The Turbulent Years. Boston, 1970.

————. The New Deal and Collective Bargaining Policy. Berkeley, 1950.

Braeman, John, Robert H. Bremner, and Everett Walters, eds. Change and Continuity in Twentieth Century America. Columbus, Ohio, 1964. Includes an especially valuable article by David Brody on industrial unionism in the South in the 1930s and 1940s.

Brisbane, Robert H. The Black Vanguard: Origins of the Negro Social Revolution, 1900–1960. Valley Forge, 1970. Suggests that blacks began to look to Washington, D.C., for assistance in the 1930s.

Brooks, Bessie A. A Half Century of Progress in Family Welfare Work in Jefferson County. Birmingham, 1936.

Brownell, Blaine A. The Urban Ethos in the South, 1920–1930. Baton Rouge, 1975. Analyzes the booster creed of the "commercial-civic" elite in the cities in the 1920s.

Brownell, Blaine A., and David R. Goldfield, eds. The City in Southern History: The Growth of Urban Civilization in the South. Interdisciplinary Urban Series, edited by Raymond A. Mohl. Port Washington, 1977. Offers a series of essays, arranged chronologically, on the development of southern cities.

Bunche, Ralph J. The Political Status of the Negro in the Age of FDR. Edited by Dewey W. Grantham. Chicago, 1973.

Cantor, Milton, ed. Black Labor in America. Westport, 1969.

Cayton, Horace R., and George S. Mitchell. Black Workers and the New Unions. Chapel Hill, 1939.

Chalmers, David M. Hooded Americanism: The First Century of the Ku Klux Klan, 1865 to the Present. Garden City, 1965.

Clark, Thomas D. The Emerging South. New York, 1961.

Cooper, Robert W. Metropolitan County: A Survey of Government in the Birmingham Area. Birmingham, 1949.

Davis, Allison, and Burleigh B. and Mary R. Gardner. Deep South: A Social and Anthropological Study of Caste and Class. Chicago, 1941.

Derber, Milton, and Edwin Young, eds. Labor and the New Deal. Madison, Wis., 1957. Derber's article on labor's growth in the 1930s deals at some length with the depression South.

Dykeman, Wilma, and James Stokeley. Seeds of Southern Change: The

Life of Will Alexander. Chicago, 1962. Provides information on the Atlanta and New Orleans black communities.

Ecke, Melvin W. *From Ivy Street to Kennedy Center: Centennial History of the Atlanta Public School System.* Atlanta, 1972.

Fisher, Robert M. *Twenty Years of Public Housing: Economic Aspects of the Federal Program.* New York, 1959.

Foner, Philip S. *Organized Labor and the Black Worker, 1619–1973.* New York, 1974.

Fulcher, Annie L. *The History, Structure and Program of the Family Counseling Association of Jefferson County, Alabama.* Birmingham, 1957. Provides history of social services that were developed or advanced during the depression era.

Galenson, Walter. *The CIO Challenge to the AFL: A History of the American Labor Movement, 1935–1941.* Cambridge, Mass., 1960.

Gambill, Louise, comp. *Civic Progress, 1940–1944.* Memphis, 1945. Gives a subjective analysis of developments in Memphis during the later New Deal period.

Garrett, Franklin M. *Atlanta and Environs: A Chronicle of Its People and Events.* Vol. III of 3 vols. New York, 1954.

Gelfand, Mark. *A Nation of Cities: The Federal Government and Urban America, 1933–1965.* New York, 1975. Argues that a partnership between the nation's cities and Washington, D.C.—the foundation of later federal policies on urban affairs—emerged from the depression and New Deal experience.

Gilman, Glenn, and James W. Sweeney. *Causes of Industrial Peace Under Collective Bargaining: Atlantic Steel Company and the United Steelworkers of America.* Washington, D.C., 1953. Gives useful discussion of unionism, workers, and management in Atlanta's largest steel operation.

Glaab, Charles, and Theodore A. Brown. *A History of Urban America.* 2nd ed. New York, 1976.

Goldfield, David R. *Cotton Fields and Skyscrapers: Southern City and Region, 1607–1980.* Baton Rouge, 1982. Analyzes southern urban development, stressing the relationship between the cities and the countryside from which they sprang.

Graham, Otis L. *Toward a Planned Society: From Roosevelt to Nixon.* New York, 1976. Gives a provocative analysis of the rise of the "broker state."

Haas, Edward F. *DeLesseps S. Morrison and the Image of Reform: New Orleans Politics, 1946–1961.* Baton Rouge, 1974. Provides useful summary of the Maestri years and machine politics in New Orleans.

Holmes, Michael S. *The New Deal in Georgia.* Westport, 1975. Gives an administrative history of the federal programs in Georgia.

Hon, Ralph C. *Memphis, Its Economic Position*. Memphis, 1935. A prominent southern economist analyzes the city.

Hoover, Calvin B., and Benjamin V. Ratchford. *Economic Resources and Policies of the South*. New York, 1951. Supplies useful cost-of-living and wage information, industrial statistics, and so on.

Howard, Donald S. *The W. P. A. and Federal Relief Policy*. New York, 1943. Provides general account of the WPA's eight years.

Howard, L. Vaughn, and Robert S. Friedman. *Government in Metropolitan New Orleans*. Tulane University Studies in Political Science, VI. New Orleans, 1959. Includes useful discussion of local government during the Maestri years.

Howard, Perry S. *Political Tendencies in Louisiana*. Baton Rouge, 1957. Describes the machine political tradition in Louisiana.

Huberman, Leo. *The Labor Spy Racket*. New York, 1937. Provides useful account of agencies that provided industrial spies during the depression years.

Jackson, Kenneth T. *The Ku Klux Klan in the City, 1915–1930*. New York, 1965.

Kane, Harnett T. *Louisiana Hayride: The American Rehearsal for Dictatorship*. New York, 1941. Analyzes the conservative leadership within the Long organization following the death of the Kingfish.

Key, V. O. *Southern Politics in State and Nation*. New York, 1949.

Kirby, John. *Black Americans in the Roosevelt Era: Liberalism and Race*. Knoxville, 1980. Analyzes the attitudes of liberals in the administration and the reactions of prominent black leaders.

Krueger, Thomas A. *And Promises to Keep: The Southern Conference for Human Welfare, 1938–1948*. Nashville, 1967. Describes first convention, which met in Birmingham in 1938.

La Violette, Forrest, and Joseph Taylor. *Negro Housing in New Orleans*. New Orleans, 1957. Analyzes the inadequacy of public housing in New Orleans.

Leuchtenberg, William E. *Franklin D. Roosevelt and the New Deal*. New American Nation Series. New York, 1963.

Lilienthal, David E. *TVA: Democracy on the March*. 1944; rpr. Chicago, 1966.

Lindley, Betty and Earnest K. *A New Deal for Youth: The Story of the National Youth Administration*. New York, 1958.

Lumpkin, Katherine D. *The South in Progress*. New York, 1940.

McDonald, William F. *Federal Relief Administration and the Arts*. Columbus, Ohio, 1969.

McIlwaine, Shields. *Memphis Down in Dixie*. New York, 1948. Gives general descriptive history of Memphis.

McKelvey, Blake. *The Emergence of Metropolitan America, 1915–1966.* New Brunswick, 1968.

Marshall, Freddie Ray. *Labor in the South.* Cambridge, Mass., 1967. Provides excellent study of CIO and AFL activities and conflicts in the depression South.

———. *The Negro and Organized Labor.* New York, 1965.

Martin, Charles H. *The Angelo Herndon Case and Southern Justice.* Baton Rouge, 1975.

Martin, Thomas. *Dynasty: The Longs of Louisiana.* New York, 1960. Surveys machine politics in Louisiana, including New Deal and New Orleans politics.

Mathews, Jane DeHart. *The Federal Theatre, 1935–1939: Plays, Relief and Politics.* Princeton, 1967.

Miller, William D. *Mr. Crump of Memphis.* Baton Rouge, 1964. A political biography that includes a chapter on the depression period.

Miller, Zane L. *The Urbanization of Modern America: A Brief History.* New York, 1973.

Mitchell, Broadus. *Depression Decade: From New Era Through New Deal, 1929–1941.* New York, 1947.

Mowry, George E. *The Urban Nation, 1920–1960.* New York, 1965.

Myrdal, Gunnar. *An American Dilemma: The Negro Problem and Modern Democracy.* New York, 1944.

Northrup, Herbert R. *Organized Labor and the Negro.* 1944; rpr. New York, 1971.

Parris, Guichard, and Lester Brooks. *Blacks in the City: A History of the National Urban League.* Boston, 1971.

Patterson, James T. *The New Deal and the States: Federalism in Transition.* Princeton, 1969.

Peterson, Lorin D. *The Day of the Mugwhump.* New York, 1961. Contains sketches of several of the New South urban leaders.

Preston, Howard. *The Automobile Age in Atlanta: The Making of a Southern Metropolis, 1900–1935.* Athens, Ga., 1979. Surveys the social, political, and economic impact of the automobile.

Rabinowitz, Howard N. *Race Relations in the Urban South, 1865–1890.* Blacks in the New World Series, edited by August Meier. 1978; rpr. Urbana, 1980.

Reynolds, George M. *Machine Politics in New Orleans, 1877–1926.* 1936; rpr. New York, 1968. Provides useful background on the Old Regulars.

Schlesinger, Arthur M., Jr. *The Age of Roosevelt.* 3 vols. Boston, 1958, 1959, 1960.

Scott, Mel. *American City Planning Since 1890.* Los Angeles, 1969.

Sindler, Allan P. *Huey Long's Louisiana: State Politics, 1920–1952.*

Baltimore, 1956. Gives excellent analysis of machine politics in Louisiana.

Sitkoff, Harvard. *A New Deal for Blacks: The Emergence of Civil Rights as a National Issue*. New York, 1978. Argues that the Roosevelt administration committed the federal government to the cause of civil rights.

Sterner, Richard. *The Negro's Share: A Study of Income, Consumption, Housing and Public Assistance*. New York, 1943.

Sternsher, Bernard, ed. *The Negro in Depression and War: Prelude to Revolution*. Chicago, 1969. Especially valuable is the article on the thirties by John Williams.

Tindall, George B. *The Emergence of the New South*. Baton Rouge, 1967.

Tucker, David M. *Lieutenant Lee of Beale Street*. Nashville, 1971. Examines the relationship between Memphis blacks and the Crump machine.

Vance, Rupert B., and Nicholas J. Demeruth, eds. *The Urban South*. Chapel Hill, 1954. Offers a collection of essays on a variety of topics pertinent to southern cities.

Weiss, Nancy J. *Farewell to the Party of Lincoln: Black Politics in the Age of FDR*. Princeton, 1983. Argues that blacks moved into the Democratic party despite the lack of specific policies designed to advance civil rights.

————. *The National Urban League, 1910–1940*. New York, 1974.

Williams, T. Harry. *Huey Long*. New York, 1969.

Wilson, Donald V. *Public Social Services in Louisiana*. Monroe, La., 1943. Traces the origins of social services in New Orleans and throughout Louisiana.

Wolters, Raymond. *Negroes and the Great Depression: The Problem of Economic Recovery*. Westport, 1970.

SELECTED UNPUBLISHED SOURCES

Adair, Augustus A. "A Political History of the Negro in Atlanta, 1908–1953." M.A. thesis, Atlanta University, 1955.

Arnold, Peter Edward. "Public Housing in Atlanta." M.A. thesis, Georgia State University, 1970. Provides an excellent study of the advent of federal public housing under the leadership of Charles Palmer.

Beall, Young Allen. "The Organization and Administration of the Department of Public Welfare of the State of Georgia." M.A. thesis, Emory University, 1950. Includes material on the New Deal and the coming of public welfare to Georgia.

Bennett, James David, II. "Struggle for Power: The Relationship Between the Tennessee Valley Authority and the Private Power Industry, 1933–1939." Ph.D. dissertation, Vanderbilt University, 1969. Includes a section on the struggles in Memphis.

Brittain, Joseph M. "Negro Suffrage and Politics in Alabama Since 1870." Ph.D. dissertation, Indiana University, 1958. Offers data on the emergence of black voters in Alabama in the late 1930s.

Brownell, Blaine A. "The Urban Mind in the South: The Growth of Urban Consciousness in Southern Cities, 1920–1927." Ph.D. dissertation, University of North Carolina, 1969.

Burrows, Edward F. "The Commission on Interracial Cooperation, 1919–1944: A Case Study in the History of the Interracial Movement in the South." Ph.D. dissertation, University of Wisconsin, 1954. Includes data on the black communities in the depression period.

Carey, Addison C. "Black Political Participation in New Orleans." Ph.D. dissertation, Tulane University, 1972.

Dudley, Julius W. "A Brief Study of Three Subversive Organizations in Atlanta, Georgia, 1915–1946." M.A. thesis, Atlanta University, 1969. Has useful account of the Black Shirt movement.

Evans, Mercer G. "The History of the Organized Labor Movement in Georgia." Ph.D. dissertation, University of Chicago, 1929. Gives background for the labor movement in the depression decade.

Field, Betty M. "The Politics of the New Deal in Louisiana, 1933–1939." Ph.D. dissertation, Tulane University, 1973. Offers detailed analysis of the Long machine and the New Deal.

Fossett, Roy E. "The Impact of the New Deal on Georgia Politics, 1933–1941." Ph.D. dissertation, University of Florida, 1960.

Gaston, Edward A., Jr. "A History of the Negro Wage Earner in Georgia, 1890–1940." Ph.D. dissertation, Emory University, 1957. Supplies facts and figures on the plight of black labor in the South in the early twentieth century.

Hanlon, Edward F. "Urban-Rural Cooperation and Conflict in Congress: The Breakdown of the New Deal Coalition." Ph.D. dissertation, Georgetown University, 1967. Describes how most congressmen from the southern cities stood apart from the southern conservative congressional group.

Hannah, James J. "Urban Reaction to the Great Depression in the United States, 1929–1933." Ph.D. dissertation, University of California at Berkeley, 1956. Shows that local resources were inadequate to meet the crisis.

Henderson, E. M., Sr. "Public Relief in Jefferson County: A Brief Survey." Typescript, Birmingham Public Library, 1934. Analyzes federal and local relief activities. Prepared in cooperation with the Alabama Emergency Relief Administration.

Hodges, James A. "The New Deal Labor Policy and the Southern Cotton Textile Industry, 1933–1941." Ph.D. dissertation, Vanderbilt University, 1963.

Holmes, Michael S. "The New Deal in Georgia: An Administrative History." Ph.D. dissertation, University of Wisconsin, 1969.

Holt, Thad. "Establishment of Unemployment Relief Agencies in the Hoover-Roosevelt Era." Typescript, Alabama Archives and History, Montgomery. Is brief account of relief activities by the director of the Alabama relief administration.

Kuniansky, Harry R. "A Business History of Atlantic Steel Company, 1901–1968." Ph.D. dissertation, Georgia State University, 1970.

Lawrence, Charles R. "Negro Organizations in Crisis: Depression, New Deal, World War II." Ph.D. dissertation, Columbia University, 1953.

Leedell, Wallace N. "The Negro in Louisiana Since 1900: An Economic and Social Study." Ph.D. dissertation, New York University, 1959.

Lindahl, Frank E., Jr. "Functions of New Orleans City Government." M.A. thesis, Tulane University, 1940. Examines changes in city government that occurred during the 1930s.

Marshall, Freddie Ray. "History of Labor Organization in the South." Ph.D. dissertation, University of California at Berkeley, 1955. Offers especially useful description of the labor situation on the New Orleans docks and in the Birmingham steel mills.

Miller, Carroll G. "A Study of the New Orleans Longshoreman's Union from 1850–1962." M.A. thesis, Louisiana State University, 1962.

Minton, John Dean. "The New Deal in Tennessee." Ph.D. dissertation, Vanderbilt University, 1959.

Mitchell [Bigelow], Martha C. "Birmingham: Biography of a City of the New South." Ph.D. dissertation, University of Chicago, 1946.

Moseley, Clement C. "Invisible Empire: A History of the Ku Klux Klan in Twentieth Century Georgia, 1915–1965." Ph.D. dissertation, University of Georgia, 1968. Provides useful information on the Klan's antilabor outburst in the Atlanta area in the 1930s.

Patterson, Charles E., Jr. "The Organization and Administration of the Metropolitan Planning Commission, Atlanta, Georgia." M.A. thesis, Emory University, 1958. Describes how the commission was organized in the late 1940s but born from the municipal and county planning commissions of the previous decade.

Pearce, Arthur R. "The Rise and Decline of Labor in New Orleans." M.A. thesis, Tulane University, 1938. Offers background on the labor situation in the Crescent City.

Runyan, Glenn M. "Economic Trends in New Orleans, 1928–1940."

M.A. thesis, Tulane University, 1967. Supplies facts concerning economic conditions in New Orleans during the depression era.

Scott, Carole E. "The Economic Impact of the New Deal on the South." Ph.D. dissertation, Georgia State University, 1969. Argues that New Deal's economic effects were limited.

Shivers, Lyda Gordon. "The Social Welfare Movement in the South: A Study in Regional Culture and Social Organization." Ph.D. dissertation, University of North Carolina, 1935. Shows how social welfare movement was advancing in the late 1920s and early 1930s, particularly in the major cities.

Shivery, Louis Delphia Davis. "The History of Organized Social Work Among Atlanta Negroes, 1890–1935." M.A. thesis, Atlanta University, 1936. Demonstrates that Atlanta blacks were not excluded from the new social service programs established in the 1930s.

Siegel, Dorothy. "The Growth of Coal and Steel Unions in Two Companies in Birmingham, Ala., 1918–1941." Honor's thesis, Brandeis University, 1969. Copy in possession of Birmingham Public Library.

Thompson, James Robert. "The Forward Atlanta Movement." M.A. thesis, Emory University, 1948. Analyzes the "selling" of Atlanta to outside manufacturing in the 1920s.

Van de Voorf, Anita. "Public Welfare Administration in Jefferson County, Alabama." M.A. thesis, Tulane University, 1933. Surveys welfare work, public and private, in the Birmingham area prior to the depression.

Williams, Bobbie Joe. "Let There Be Light: History of the Development of Public Ownership of Electric Utilities in Memphis." M.A. thesis, Memphis State University, 1972. Discusses TVA and Memphis in the 1930s.

Williams, Donald E. "The Beale Street Arena—Memphis, Tennessee: A Case Study of Urban Renewal." M.S. thesis, Memphis State University, 1970. Includes data on the decay of the Beale Street area during the depression period and on the relationship between Memphis blacks and the Crump machine.

Wyche, Billy Hall. "Southern Attitudes Toward Industrial Unions, 1933–1941." Ph.D. dissertation, University of Georgia, 1969. Emphasizes the obstacles confronted by industrial labor organizers throughout the South.

INDEX